T5-AFO-502

TEXAS RANGER

JOHN B. JONES

AND THE FRONTIER BATTALION, 1874-1881

by

RICK MILLER

Number 9 in the Frances B. Vick Series

University of North Texas Press
Denton, Texas

©2012 Rick Miller
All rights reserved.
Printed in the United States of America.

10 9 8 7 6 5 4 3 2 1

Permissions:
University of North Texas Press
1155 Union Circle #311336
Denton, TX 76203-5017

The paper used in this book meets the minimum requirements of the American
National Standard for Permanence of Paper for Printed Library Materials,
z39.48.1984. Binding materials have been chosen for durability.

Library of Congress Cataloging-in-Publication Data

Miller, Rick, 1941-
Texas Ranger John B. Jones and the Frontier Battalion, 1874–1881 / by
Rick Miller.—1st ed.
      p. cm.— (Number 9 in the Frances B. Vick series)
Includes bibliographical references.
ISBN 978-1-57441-467-7 (cloth : alk. paper)— ISBN 978-1-57441-478-3
(ebook)
1. Jones, John B., 1834-1881. 2. Texas Rangers. Frontier
Battalion--Biography. 3. Texas— History— 1846–1950. 4. Frontier and
pioneer life— Texas. I. Title. II. Series: Frances B. Vick series ; no.
9.
F391.M645 2012
976.4'06092— dc23
[B]

Texas Ranger John B. Jones and the Frontier Battalion, 1874–1881 is Number 9 in the
Frances B. Vick Series

CONTENTS

PREFACE

Texas in the early 1870s was raw and violent. Communities in the eastern part of the state were taking shape, and local governments had come to provide some semblance of competency in the shadow of Reconstruction. However, in the unsettled northern and western areas, in what would be termed the "frontier" portion of Texas, Indian raiding parties posed a serious threat, the red men coming either south from federal protection in the Indian Nation (now Oklahoma), or across the Rio Grande from clandestine sites in Mexico. Settlers in these uncivilized areas risked, at best, loss of livestock, or worse, their lives. It was a take-no-prisoner atmosphere, and the short-term militias or "ranging" squads, created to combat specific Indian threats, fought aggressively to protect their families and their property from harm.

At the same time, the post-Civil War period spawned lawlessness at a level not seen before in the state. Blood feuds broke out, and gunfighters such as John Wesley Hardin and Bill Longley roamed far and wide, leaving the corpses of their victims in their wake. Confederate soldiers returned to Texas to find widespread cattle and horse theft by both Indians and white outlaws. The Reconstruction government of Governor Edmund J. Davis engineered the creation of a state police force, but in spite of some success in restoring law and order, the force's reputation suffered from the excesses of a few villains within its ranks. Worse, from the perspective of a dominant white population smarting from defeat in the war and subsequent military occupation, the practice of enlisting newly-freed ex-slaves into the ranks as peace officers was totally unacceptable. Local law enforcement after the war was often inadequate, largely because many town marshals and sheriffs were incompetents placed into office by political or military appointment. In addition, regardless of competency, these local lawmen lacked the resources to cope effectively with burgeoning lawlessness.

When Richard Coke replaced Davis as governor of Texas in 1874, his priority was to deal with the violence on the western frontier of the state and to protect the settlers. Although statehood was restored, there was still an insufficient response by the United States Army to provide effective protection, even though Coke made repeated pleas for help. Until sufficient troops could man posts along the frontier and act as an effective deterrent to the raiding Indians, the state was forced to look to its own resources to cope with the repeated violence.

In the spring of 1874, the Texas legislature enacted a militia bill for protection at the local level, providing for the raising and arming of local companies of men as needed. Buried in that bill was a provision for a "battalion" of state troops, permanently enlisted, and organized in military fashion. This force was initially intended to confront and fend off marauding Indians, and secondarily to deal with Mexican bandits crossing the Rio Grande. Going after other lawless men was an afterthought. Under the supervision of the state's adjutant general, a slight, frail man was appointed by Coke as commanding officer of the "Frontier Battalion": John B. Jones of Navarro County. As a fellow veteran of the Confederate Army, Coke was familiar with Jones' wartime exploits and administrative ability, and he saw in Jones the sort of man he wanted to oversee this new enterprise. Although Jones had no experience as an Indian fighter, he did have the ability to organize and control a military operation, which was the intent of the legislation creating the Battalion. And that is what Jones did, in the process creating and consolidating the entity that we now term the Texas Rangers.

Jones established a high standard for the Battalion. In terms of the selection of personnel and rules for their conduct, he was a humorless, although not stuffy, man who did not brook any nonsense from his subordinate officers or privates. The Ranger who chose to go on a spree, embarrassing the "service," very seldom got to keep his job and often was "dishonorably discharged." Jones required written documentation of each company's activities, including a record of scouts, arrests, condition of horses and mules, availability of forage and supplies, and a number of other statistics. The historian of today can thank him for being scrupulous about establishing an archive of Ranger documents, given that the ready availability of such information enables an accurate recounting of the events in which the Rangers were involved. Jones' military approach, utilizing a military command structure and a system of general and special orders, was reflected in his tactics, for example in the placing of companies along the frontier at strategic points to best intercept the marauding Indians. His attack on lawlessness in Kimble County, directing a pincer-type sweep, was a classic infantry tactic, proving effective in shutting down the outlaw element in that neighborhood.

The average Ranger was barely a man, and few, if any, had any experience in confronting Indian war parties or quick-on-the-trigger gunslingers. Most had been farmboys or cowboys, at best experienced in horsemanship, hunting, and the use of firearms. The adventure of scouting after bad guys was far more appealing to these young men than pushing a plow or eating trail dust and branding maverick cattle. And they were not hesitant; some readers may be surprised to find that Rangers gloried as much in battle as their Indian counterparts, including scalping those that they killed. It was clearly understood by both sides that no quarter was to be given.

Of necessity, this book concentrates on the chronology of the Frontier Battalion and its administration by Jones. The major activities of the Battalion are chronicled during the 1874-1881 period, but it was not possible to include all of the more mundane daily activities, such as endless scouting, in which each of the Ranger companies were engaged. In addition to the events meriting mention in a report, the companies were constantly on the move, looking for fresh Indian signs, trying to serve arrest warrants on outlaws, in the saddle escorting prisoners, or going to and from various assignments. To attempt to cover these lesser activities would burden the reader and balloon this effort into a multi-volume tome. The reader must keep in mind that, though unmentioned, these more routine activities were constantly occurring, in cold and hot weather, on a daily basis. The February 1878 report of Captain Neal Coldwell's Company A illustrates these often futile activities:

2 to 7. Capt. Coldwell & 6 men attempted arrest of Ben Goodwin, J. Jeffers, Ant. Garcia & arrested L. Ainsworth, murder in Ellis Co.

4th. Sergt. Welch & 2 men in search of Bob Brodenax, an escaped convict—Not found.

10th. Sergt. Horne & 10 men attempted to intercept party of Indians—No trail found.

10th. Corpl. Boggs & 4 men—Same as Sergt. Horne.

20th. Corpl. Wilson & 1 man in search of R. Brodenax, an escaped convict—Not found.

22 to 24. Corpl. Boggs & 1 man searched for Martin Hoag for theft in Randall Co.

22 to 25. Sergt. Walsh & 2 men in search of W. Ridgeway, Thos. Holmes, Ed Grumble, Ed Short & W. Huttleson, Arrested Jno. Rodgers, theft of mule, Live Oak County [notation: "not identified"] & arrested Robt. Dickson, abduction, San Patricio Co.[1]

Although the Frontier Battalion initially began as a force to defend against Indian incursions, it subsequently took on new directions, the stated intent all along to be of service to the local sheriff or marshal. In addition to scouting for Indian trails and wanted men, Rangers were sent to guard jails against lynch mobs, protect courts from interference while in session, deliver prisoners from one county to another, intercede in bloody feuds, and respond to other urgent requests for assistance when local law enforcement was overwhelmed. As time passed and the Battalion became more experienced, it also became more sophisticated and flexible in dealing with new problems. The statewide hunt in 1878 for Sam Bass and his gang of train robbers, which involved coordination by Jones of various agencies and posses, in addition to Ranger companies, was probably one of the biggest manhunts in the history of the state.

John B. Jones, as commander, oversaw all of these activities, many of which have been chronicled in other scholarly studies about the Rangers. What have seldom been dealt with, however, are the critical administrative functions necessarily involved in developing and sustaining the

Frontier Battalion. As with any other organization, there were inevitable personnel problems, supply and logistic issues, and competition for funding resources. These were matters that fell exclusively in Jones' lap, challenging his administrative skills as he labored to keep the Rangers in the field in the face of continual reductions in legislative appropriations.

Many major events in which the Frontier Battalion was involved are not dealt with in as much depth as possible, such as the Mason County War, the Horrell-Higgins feud, the hunt for Sam Bass, and the El Paso Salt War. This was done deliberately. First, each of these events has been studied thoroughly by others, and there are excellent, well-researched books on these events, which are listed in the bibliography. However, such studies tend to concentrate solely on the seminal event, treating it in a vacuum and neglecting the other activities going on in Jones' world. I chose to treat the activities comprising these events in a chronological and global fashion, not only to show where they fit in Jones' concern, but because there was simply not space enough to delve deeper into the nuances of each of these events. The reader is encouraged to consult the other focused works to further understand the development of the Rangers in various lights.

There is no explanation why John B. Jones has not been the subject of a serious biography. Other Ranger leaders, noted for their colorfulness or their bravery and intrepid adventures, have been well documented, but not Jones. Most accounts of his life are drawn directly from so-called "genealogical and biographical" vanity encyclopedias that were popular in the 1880s and 1890s, but these provide only sparse details about Jones' life. While these are a beginning point for detailing his life, considerably more research was necessary to flesh out those anemic entries. The heaviest reliance is made on the Adjutant General, Frontier Battalion, and Governors' Correspondence in the Archives Division of the Texas State Library. It is from these primary sources of information that the unvarnished story of the Frontier Battalion unfolds, free of the inaccuracies that plague the recollections of the few Rangers who penned their memoirs decades after the events they chronicle. Poring through and indexing this correspondence took a number of years and would not have been possible without the guidance and insight of Library archivist Donaly Brice. Donaly, an old friend from other research efforts who shares a mutual interest in frontier Texas, and his lovely wife, Clare, even put me up frequently in their Victorian house in Lockhart whenever I was on a research mission to Austin. For their help and hospitality, I am ever grateful.

Other sources examined include Ranger recollections; contemporary newspapers; official records, such as those in Jones' home, Navarro County; and reliable secondary sources. One source was the collection of Walter Prescott Webb, the author of the first detailed book about the Rangers in 1935, which is housed at the Dolph Briscoe Center for American History of the University of Texas at Austin. For his book, Webb transcribed original Ranger correspondence, but strangely, some of this correspondence is not found in State Library records. In addition, some of his transcriptions are faulty and have to be read very carefully in the context of other more reliable information.

I am also indebted to far too many people to include here, and I hope they will forgive the omission. Dave Johnson of Zionsville, Indiana, my Old West "soul brother" who shares my passion for the Old West and getting it right, nagged me to get this book written, and probably but for that I would still be dithering away at it. In addition to Dave, three good friends and colleagues, all stalwarts in the outlaw-lawman genre, generously reviewed the manuscript and made important suggestions that vastly enhanced my efforts: Chuck Parsons of Luling, Texas, unquestionably one of the most prolific writers on Texas outlaws and lawmen; Bob Alexander of Maypearl, Texas, an ex-lawman who knows whereof he speaks and one of the most energetic of researchers; and the dean of Old West writers, Bob DeArment of Sylvania, Ohio, whose thoughtful observations were an important contribution.

Bobbie Young of the Pioneer Village in Corsicana and her late husband Bill were gracious hosts, kindly allowing me to access information in their collection. Paul Cool of Eldersburg, Maryland, author of an outstanding study of the El Paso Salt War, kindly shared some documents important to this book. Librarians for the Texas Medical Association in Austin were kind enough to dig up some old articles that helped explain a bizarre incident occurring after Jones' death. For those whose names are omitted here, thank you for all of your help.

Of course, the rock in my life is my wife, Paula, who graciously gives me the necessary space to get this stuff out of my system. She understands this peculiar passion of mine to chronicle the Old West, forgiving my vacant stare when she is trying to communicate with me. Dear, it truly was not selective hearing, and I thank you for your indulgence.

Rick Miller
Harker Heights, Texas

1

IRRESISTIBLE ON HORSEBACK

THE YOUNG MEN HUDDLED ALONG the shallow dry ravine as they listened to the pop-pop of gunfire from the Indians facing them on the crest of the ridge ahead. The shots whistled above them, uncomfortably close, occasionally striking one of the horses abandoned to their rear. The hot Texas sun was unmerciful and the men had long run out of water to quench their thirst. One of their force, Billy Glass, badly wounded only yards in front of them, piteously called to his comrades for help.

They had ridden into an ambush, perhaps as a result of the negligence of their commander, Major John B. Jones, in failing to enforce a more disciplined pursuit of the marauding party they had been trailing. Barely organized two months, these were men of Texas' new Frontier Battalion, created to meet the Indian threat, and now here they were pinned down in their first major confrontation with the enemy.

In the face of danger, Major Jones, a man of slight stature and often frail health, stood above the ravine, walking along it in spite of the gunfire, calmly directing the fire of his men. In so doing, he exemplified the standard and set the example for courage that was to become the hallmark of these fledgling lawmen. Although they did not realize it at the

John B. Jones, Frontier Battalion Commander (*Courtesy of Texas State Library & Archives Commission, Austin, Texas*)

time, this was the beginning of the legend known as the Texas Rangers, and their quarry was at hand.

The Frontier Battalion was a relatively new creature in Texas, formed only two months earlier and placed under Jones' command and guidance. Given the general hatred throughout the state of Governor Edmund Davis' Reconstruction state police, it was remarkable that the Battalion would subsequently avoid much controversy and become widely accepted (though not always adequately funded) and would tout very real successes against marauding Indians, Mexican bandits, and other outlaws. Much of this success stemmed from the organizational and leadership skills of John

B. Jones, a most unlikely candidate for the position. He proved himself a capable administrator, at the same time winning the respect and esteem of those who served under him by sharing their danger and privations in the field. Jones also gained the confidence of the politicians in Texas government who established funding and policy priorities that impacted on the Battalion.

John B. Jones came from good stock and a privileged background. His father, Henry Jones, one of six children born to John and Mary "Polly" (Oates) Jones, was born August 22, 1807, in what was then the Fairfield District of South Carolina, near Winnsboro. Henry Jones' great-grandfather had immigrated from Wales to Ireland, and one of his sons, Henry's grandfather, came directly to South Carolina, landing at Charleston before the Revolutionary War.

A marriage between Henry Jones and Nancy Elizabeth Robertson was celebrated on September 16, 1832. Mrs. Jones, born on November 16, 1812, was the daughter of Benoni and Ruth Ann (Mickle) Robertson, also nicknamed "Nancy."[1] Benoni Robertson, a prominent planter and citizen in the Fairfield area, had been a soldier in the War of 1812, leading a battalion of South Carolina troops.[2] The Robertsons could trace their ancestry to Scottish hero Robert Bruce, as the family originally emigrated from Scotland to Pennsylvania, then moved to Prince William County, Virginia, and then on to Winnsboro in the Fairfield District. Nancy Jones' grandfather, William Robertson, who was married four times, took part in the battle of Eutaw Springs in the Revolutionary War, and her father, Benoni, was one of eight children. She herself was one of thirteen children.[3]

Both the Jones and Robertson families were slaveholders, certainly not unusual in South Carolina during the antebellum period. Slaves were considered personal property, and last wills of various family members reflected bequests of slaves in their possession at the time the documents were drawn. For example, after Nancy Jones' death in 1848, her father, Benoni Robertson, drafted a will bequeathing the slaves "Lizay," "Leah," "Aaron," "Darry," and "Brister" to young John B. Jones and his sisters, the slaves already being in the possession of Henry Jones under a loan to Benoni Robertson from Benoni's deceased daughter. Robertson also bequeathed to his grandchildren "a negro [*sic*] woman named Henrietta, to be equally divided among them, share and share alike."[4] In 1830 there were a total of 21,546 persons living in Fairfield County, 9,705 of them white and 11,841 black.[5]

Prior to moving to Texas, Henry and Nancy Jones had three children. Polly N., also identified as Mary, was born August 30, 1833. The second child, John B. Jones, was born on December 22, 1834, followed by Caroline Robertson "Carrie" Jones on February 1, 1837.[6] Despite diligent research, John Jones' middle name has proven elusive, but a reasonable guess is that the "B" stood for Benoni. A later brother, who only lived a short time, was given the biblical name of Benoni.[7]

Henry Jones and his family migrated to the Republic of Texas some time in 1838, settling first in Travis County, near Gilleland Creek twelve miles below Austin. His brother-in-law, Dr. Joseph William Robertson, had moved to Texas two years earlier, settling first at Bastrop, then moving to Austin in 1839 where he served briefly as a Ranger and as a representative to the Republic's congress. The Jones family lived here about four years.[8] There is no explanation why the Jones family made the dramatic move from a settled environment in South Carolina to the raw frontier of Texas. Several reasons have been postulated, ranging from possible losses during the Panic of 1837, to the desire of Henry Jones' wife to be near her brother, or even as a result of Jones' vision and desire to "blaze the pioneer trails."[9]

During this time, Henry Jones was a participant in the battle with the Comanche Indians in their daring 1840 raid that culminated in Comanche defeat at the hands of militia companies at Brushy and Plum Creeks in Caldwell County. He was elected as colonel by the members of his particular regiment, an appellation that he would attach to his name for the rest of his life.[10] A daughter, Frances E., called Fannie, was born on April 17, 1839, in Travis County, followed by Ann P. on December 5, 1840.[11] On May 8, 1839, Henry Jones was issued a conditional certificate for 640 acres of land in Matagorda County on the Texas coast; the certificate specified that the sale of the land could not be finalized until certain conditions were met, such as three years of continuous residency in Texas.[12] In 1840 the Travis County tax rolls reflected that Jones owned 1,143 acres and that he was surveying another 1,260 acres. He worked that land and maintained his homestead with twenty-four slaves.[13]

In March of 1842, only six years after the defeat of Santa Anna at San Jacinto, General Rafael Vasquez and troops of the Mexican Army marched back into Texas and occupied San Antonio. Texas President Sam Houston, who was at Galveston when he heard about the raid, was concerned that the Mexicans would move north and attack Austin. He decided to hold an emergency legislative session at Houston. However, the story quickly took hold throughout Austin that President Houston wanted to designate the city named after him as the new state capitol, and a vigilance committee in Austin warned that any attempt to remove state papers would be met with armed violence. The legislature met at Washington-on-the-Brazos and Houston sent a Ranger company to Austin to remove the archives for safekeeping. On December 30, 1842, the Rangers secretly loaded the archives in wagons and attempted to leave Austin, but not before the vigilantes directed some cannon fire in their direction. The Rangers camped about fifteen miles from Austin but were surrounded by the vigilantes with their cannon, led by a Captain Mark Lewis. A parley was held and the papers were promptly transported back to Austin with no further violence.[14] Colonel Henry Jones was later credited with being in command in Austin during the so-called "Archives War," the vigilantes being led by him, his brother-in-law Dr. Robertson, and others, although no mention of them is made in general histories of the event.[15] In 1861, without explaining his role, Henry Jones promised to write a "true history" of the "Archives War,"[16] although he apparently never did so.

Colonel Jones' involvement in the Archives War can be questioned, since, in 1842, the Jones family had already moved once again, this time to Matagorda County where Colonel Jones established a farm and grew sugar and cotton.[17] Nancy Jones gave birth there to another son, Benoni Robertson Jones, on December 10, 1842, but the infant lived only until the following July. Another son, Mickle C. Jones, was born on December 20, 1844, but also died at an early age on August 5, 1849.[18] At the same

time, Colonel Jones gained in political prominence, serving as a representative from Matagorda County in the first state legislature held after Texas
became a state and attending the regular session in Austin from February
16 to March 13, 1846.[19] On February 19, the Republic of Texas formally
entered into the American Union as a new state. Colonel Jones took his
seat on February 24 and was named to the committees on county bound-
aries, state affairs and finance, and the militia, as well as the committee
overseeing the Land Office.[20]

Nancy Jones died in Matagorda County on February 5, 1848, at the
age of thirty-six, along with an infant daughter, and the 1850 county census recorded Henry with only his five surviving children.[21] Colonel Jones
continued to prosper, the citizens of the county appointing him to a committee of five citizens to draw up resolutions protesting the "interference"
of the federal government in organizing a "Santa Fe County" out of territory claimed by the state of Texas.[22] He was remembered as one of the
first settlers of the county and was a shareholder in the county's "Social
Library Tax for 1847."[23]

Young John B. Jones, called "Bud" by his family, began his education,
although the record is incomplete. According to a niece, Mrs. Helen
H. Groce, that education began in Matagorda County, then continued
at schools in the Texas communities of Independence and Rutersville,
although when and for how long he attended those schools is unknown.[24]
The institution at Independence in Washington County was a prominent Baptist school called "Old Baylor." The school opened in 1846,
initially directed by Professor Henry F. Gillette, then, in 1847, by its first
president, Henry Lee Graves. The school subsequently became a part of
Baylor University.

Rutersville was located seven miles northeast of LaGrange in Fayette
County, and it was there in 1840 that Rutersville College was chartered,
supported by the Methodist Church. The original faculty was composed
of the president, the Rev. Chauncy Richardson, his wife, Charles W.
Thomas, and Thomas S. Bell. There were men's and women's divisions,
the facilities sitting on fifty-two acres donated by the town. By 1844-
1845, enrollment reached a high of 194 students. Advanced students were

exposed to a curriculum that included various foreign languages, calculus, logic, philosophy, surveying, geology, and botany. Most students, however, confined themselves to more elementary subjects.[25] The college was described as presenting "educational advantages of a superior character" with "pure atmosphere."[26]

Early on, the school was located in an area frequently visited by marauding Indians. As one incident involving the college soon after it opened was described,

> Two young boys in the neighborhood, while hunting horses were attacked by Indians, and one of them, Henry Earthman, was killed; his brother Fields escaped and brought the news to the school. The excited boys joined in the search for the body, which lay a mile away in a dreadfully mutilated state. The scalp had been taken, the hands cut off and thrown into the grass, and the heart, with ligaments unsevered, laid on one side of the body; it was found to have a bullet in the centre [sic], and was, no doubt, exposed in a spirit of bravado to show how unerring was the aim of the red man. Nearly all the boys in the school, ranging in age from fourteen to sixteen, joined in the pursuit of the Indians, which lasted about three weeks. In fact, one of them still living says they did little but hunt Indians while at school at Rutersville prior to 1842.[27]

However, in addition to the threat of periodic Indian attacks, the emergence of the Mexican War and the establishment of the competing Baylor College in 1845 led to a decline of students at Rutersville. By 1848, Fayette County had withdrawn its support for the college, and faculty members were accused of misconduct. In 1856 the college merged with a military institute, then was later purchased by a German conference of the Methodist Church, before it finally closed for good in 1894.[28] Again, when John B. Jones attended this school is unknown.

Colonel Jones apparently decided that his son should go back to South Carolina for his higher education, where he could stay with one of the Colonel's sisters at Winnsboro. The Mount Zion Society had initially incorporated a school in Charleston, South Carolina in 1777, primarily for the education of orphans. However, the school became a college in 1787 and subsequently moved to Winnsboro.[29] In January 1853, the president of the Mount Zion Collegiate Institute was J. W. Hudson, who was also professor of Roman literature and English. Tuition for a session, which ran from January 1 to October 31, was ninety dollars and included board. Extra tuition might be required for certain courses, such as chemistry or French.[30]

Mount Zion's philosophy was "to improve and confirm the moral character, through the imparting of knowledge, and to see that learning morals, and religion go hand in hand." There was a rigorous curriculum that leaned toward the classical, Latin grammar, philosophy, and Hebrew taught to advanced students, and a more common curriculum used for other students. In addition there were strict rules of conduct:

> Duelling, challenging, fighting, quarreling, tricking, kicking, pushing; all stealing, pilfering, secreting, detaining, abusing; all intoxication, all unlicensed visits to the taverns, street and houses in town or country; all betting, horse racing, gaming or cards or dice; all breaking of doors, corridors, chests, trunks, and boxes, the property of others; keeping in any part of the college any species of war armor or ammunition, any loaded whip or stiletto, crossbows, or arrows, darts, clubs, knives, or any kind of weapon forbidden by the teachers; practicing any kind of diversion or relaxation on the Sabbath except Psalmody in the rooms, or decent walking in the background—all these misdemeanors are punishable with penalties such as reproof, degradation and suspension.[31]

Young Jones apparently was not happy with his stay and studies in South Carolina, perhaps even homesick. In 1851 the sixteen-year-old sent a flurry of letters home to his father, pleading to be allowed to return to Texas. Henry Jones finally relented and agreed to permit him to withdraw from Mount Zion and to return home, asking him to make a side trip to Macon, Georgia, where his four sisters were attending the Wesleyan Female Academy, a school for young ladies. However, upon his arrival at the school, the young man learned that his sister, Polly, had died of typhoid fever. Unnerved by the news, he reportedly fainted.[32] Recovering, he continued his trek back to the homestead in Texas.

Although the Jones family was headquartered in Matagorda County, Henry Jones was also purchasing land as early as 1841 in Navarro County, east of Waco and McLennan County. In April of that year he purchased acreage from the widow of John A. Barkley, as well as additional properties in 1846.[33] In May of 1846, he leased 790 acres in Navarro County to Samuel Bowman, provided Bowman cultivated at least five acres, built a "comfortable cabin," and prosecuted all trespassers. Colonel Jones also required Bowman to surrender the premises, except for 200 acres, on May 20, 1851.[34] In 1856, Jones moved his family and slaves to western Navarro County, purchasing one tract of 4,609 acres several miles west of Corsicana, the county seat, and another tract of 4,000 acres near the Hill County line.[35]

Colonel Jones engaged once more in cotton planting and stock raising, assisted by his son John. They also operated a saw mill. Young John had a "special passion" for beautiful horses, and was an excellent horseman, riding very erect in the saddle. His niece Helen Halbert Groce observed,

> He was simply irresistible on horseback and such lovely high spirited horses, as he always rode, usually a rich deep bay or shining mahogany . . . How well I remember those magnificent stallions. I always remember them with gold rosettes and fluttering blue ribbons at their ears, Gold Eye, Delinger, Lion and the equally splendid brood mares.[36]

John B. Jones was not a big man. When fully adult he stood about five feet seven or eight inches tall and weighed only about 125 pounds. People who met him were struck by his dark black hair and thick black moustache that contrasted with a fair face. He was a careful dresser, usually clad in a dark, well-kept suit. His dark soulful eyes were penetrating, seeming to "see through your very soul, and seeing sympathized as he understood."[37] Contrary to the loquacious, outspoken Henry Jones, his son was gifted with a great sense of tact and was recognized as the only member of the family who could calm their excitable father and convince him to take a more measured course of action.[38] It was this ability to work through issues in a low profile manner that enabled John to face some

J. L. and Fannie Halbert *(Courtesy of Corsicana, Texas, Public Library)*

of the most serious, sometimes violent problems that he confronted during his Ranger administration. A temperate man who also did not use tobacco in any form, Jones was fond of sponge cake and fresh buttermilk, and later was addicted to strong coffee.[39]

Jones was also very religious, refusing to curse, and completely devoid of a sense of humor, although he was never perceived as stuffy.[40] More importantly, he was plagued from childhood with a fragile physical constitution and suffered periodic health problems throughout his life. This contrasted sharply with his public image as a hardy frontiersman, and he was willing to push himself despite the nagging maladies that struck him.

In 1857, Henry Jones once again threw his hat into the ring as a Democratic candidate for the state legislature from Navarro County. He spoke at a series of barbecues and vigorously opposed the election of Sam Houston as governor, but was unsuccessful at the polls.[41] It was at this same time that John B. Jones entered into the Masonic Order, a personal dedication that became a prominent obligation throughout his life. He was initiated into Dresden Lodge Number 218 on October 3, 1857, holding the elected office of Worshipful Master in 1859 and 1860.[42] In 1860 he attended a meeting of the Masonic Grand Lodge at LaGrange where he was elected Grand Lecturer for the middle part of Texas during 1860-1861 and placed on several important Masonic committees.[43]

John B. Jones first began to appear in Navarro County records when he and his brother-in-law Roger Q. Mills, who married Jones' sister Carrie in 1855, witnessed the sale on August 7, 1858, to Henry Jones of a forty-four-and-a-half-acre tract on Richland Creek from Elijah Beauchamp, a minor in Lavaca County.[44] On February 7 the next year, John B. Jones bought at public auction for twelve dollars a lot in Corsicana that had been foreclosed on by his own father.[45] On September 6 of the same year, he purchased another lot in Corsicana for $150.[46] Now a prominent member of Navarro County, Jones regularly brought Austin newspapers for the local Corsicana newspaper and took his place in community affairs.[47] In January of 1860 he served as secretary of the county's Agricultural and Mechanical Association.[48]

Jones' sister Fannie married Joshua L. Halbert on February 29, 1860. Halbert, a twenty-seven-year-old native of Alabama, was an attorney and would serve alongside Jones in the Civil War.[49] Thirteen days later, 1,000 acres were conveyed by Henry and John B. Jones, Fannie Halbert, and Roger Q. Mills to Thomas J. Hunter for over $8,000.[50] Clearly these were prosperous times for the Jones clan.

Yet dark clouds promulgated by the oncoming Civil War now hovered over Texas. The question of secession by Texas from the Union was the focal point of public discussion, the possibility of Republican Abraham Lincoln's election to the presidency and the question of slavery being the key divisive factors. One group gaining political strength nationally called itself the Knights of the Golden Circle. Founded in 1854 by George W. L. Bickley, a Virginia-born doctor, the group promoted the scheme of gaining control of the American south, Mexico, Central America, Cuba, as well as Washington D.C., as a means of expanding the institution of slavery. Chapters of the KGC, known as "castles," were forming throughout the south, largely in reaction to Republican efforts to limit the spread of slavery into Kansas after passage of the Kansas-Nebraska Act. Opponents of the KGC claimed that the organization's sole purpose was to bring about secession of states from the Union in order to create a large slave empire. The first KGC "castles" in Texas began to appear in 1858, and twenty-one were in existence statewide by the spring of 1860.[51]

Corsicana saw the first vestige of the KGC in March of 1860 when twenty-five or thirty men rode through town carrying a banner with "KGC" prominently displayed.[52] Corsicana's newspaper, the *Navarro Express*, carried a story from Centerville that an Upshur County man was trying to develop a force to invade Mexico for KGC purposes. Bickley was organizing a national convention of the KGC at Raleigh, North Carolina, but the *Express*, perhaps misreading local sentiment, termed him a "humbug."[53] Navarro County citizens did not share that viewpoint. In May of 1860, thirty-seven county citizens, including Henry Jones, John B. Jones, and Roger Q. Mills, attached their names to a resolution calling for a public meeting to protest Congress' interference with states' rights when it came to the issue of slavery, terming such interference as "Black Republicanism" and "squatter sovereignty."[54] On June 2, the meeting was conducted at the county courthouse in Corsicana; Joshua Halbert was appointed secretary and Mills was called on to explain the object of the meeting. The assembly unanimously adopted resolutions holding that "African slavery" was "morally, politically and socially a right," protected as property under the United States Constitution, and calling for the defeat of the "Black Republicans" in the upcoming presidential race. The group boldly announced that anyone in the county who supported the Republicans should probably leave, "for we will not be responsible for their continued health and prosperity."[55]

Violence sprang from the boiling issue of states rights and the advent of the KGC. Across North Texas, a number of unexplained fires broke out during the hot summer of 1860. Abolitionists were blamed by partisan newspapers, and a number of slaves were beaten until they confessed to arson and poisoning. Some fifty-six black and white men were reportedly executed by vigilantes. Such violence only served to increase the ranks of the KGC and underscore the push for secession.[56]

While the political turmoil continued to roil, however, the daily routine of community life continued in Navarro County. John B. Jones served as secretary of the first county Agricultural and Mechanical Association Fair, which largely promoted livestock, but also sponsored exhibits of sewing, cooking, and "other fields of domestic accomplishment."[57] In June of 1860, Henry Jones organized a "Stray Horse Association" composed of horse raisers from Freestone, Limestone, Falls, McLennan, Hill, and Navarro Counties, and those in attendance clarified their personal stock brands, Jones' being an "O" on each shoulder of a horse.[58]

Roger Q. Mills (*L. E. Daniell*, Personnel of the Texas State Government, Austin, Texas: Smith, Hines & Jones, State Printers, 1889.)

John B. Jones was named as a "traveling agent" for the *Navarro Express* and was authorized to "receive and receipt" for the office.[59] The 1860 census recorded 4,133 whites and 1,920 blacks in Navarro County, and Henry Jones' family consisted of son John, daughter Ann, and two laborers, Robert Mabry and John Loftin. Henry also operated a grist mill, available for the grinding of corn every Tuesday "for the usual toll."[60]

The election of Abraham Lincoln, however, brought about a new urgency in Navarro County. The *Navarro Express* was apoplectic: "The North has gone overwhelmingly for NEGRO EQUALITY and SOUTHERN VASSALAGE! Southern man will you SUBMIT to this DEGRADATION?[61] On November 23, 1860, Henry and John Jones joined 207 other men calling for a citizens' meeting the next day, declaring themselves unwilling to submit to the "infamy and degradation" of "Negro equality."[62] A large number turned out for the meeting, refusing to be "intimidated by Northern fanaticism," and calling on Governor Sam Houston to convene the state legislature to determine what course Texas would take in the face of "Black Republicanism."[63]

As 1861 got underway, some land transactions were made inside the Jones family, perhaps in contemplation of the coming strife. On January 1, Henry Jones transferred to John a 773-acre tract on Richland Creek in return for any interest John might have as an heir to his mother's estate.[64] In another deed, John and Ann Jones, along with Roger Q. Mills and the Halberts, transferred to Henry any interest they had in the estate of the deceased Nancy Jones.[65]

The question of Texas' secession now grew frantically more pressing, and a KGC "castle" was organized in Navarro County by Roger Q. Mills and his brother-in-law, John B. Jones.[66] In a special session of the state legislature in February 1861, likely called with the connivance of the KGC against the opposition of Governor Houston, an ordinance of secession was adopted, and county elections were quickly called to ratify that decision.[67] Just as quickly, 46,151 voters across Texas approved secession, opposed by only 13,020.[68] Also in February, the KGC held a state convention in San Antonio, with forty "castles" representing a membership of 8,000, likely including Navarro County.[69] In March it was announced that W. T. Patton of Fairfield, Texas, was organizing KGC castles in Navarro, Freestone, Henderson, Limestone, Leon, and Grimes Counties, but there was no mention of either Roger Mills or John B. Jones.[70] Henry Jones, caught up in the emotion of the moment, exclaimed,

> I see that our State Convention has taken the necessary steps to annex Texas to the Confederate States. Thank God! We are now free from the reign of negro [*sic*] equality, and have the ablest of men, Jeff Davis, for our leader. If we will only be true to ourselves and families, we have nothing to fear, notwithstanding I see the Abolition party at Austin is making a death struggle to defeat us.[71]

The excitable colonel vowed to make himself again available to protect official papers should there be another "Archive War" as in 1842.[72]

The decision was made. Texas seceded from the Union on March 2, 1861, and subsequently joined the Confederacy. Thousands of young men across the state put aside their tools of trade and their everyday pursuits and readied themselves to take up arms. John B Jones was one of them.

2

DARING GALLANTRY

PREPARATIONS FOR THE COMING conflict began quickly in Navarro County. On Monday, May 6, 1861, Colonel Henry Jones organized a company of Home Guards, scheduled to meet and drill regularly at Corsicana.[1] On June 4, Brigadier General L. T. Wheeler of the Nineteenth Brigade of the Texas Militia, which consisted of regiments furnished from Navarro, Limestone, Freestone, and Ellis Counties, issued General Order Number One creating the brigade. The intent of the unit was to enroll men for the "protection of our homes" who were unable to leave for permanent military service. Henry Jones was appointed a brigade major of cavalry.[2]

Rather than wait for the organization of Confederate units in Texas that would join other units, John B. Jones traveled to Virginia, perhaps intending to enlist there, apparently going by way of Galveston and New Orleans by ship. In June he was thanked by the Corsicana newspaper for sending recent newspapers from those two cities.[3] Three months later, in September, Jones' presence as a visitor to the Navarro Rifles at Camp Davis, a short distance from Richmond, Virginia, was acknowledged in a letter to Corsicana, and Jones sent Virginia newspapers back to the local newspaper in Corsicana.[4]

It was later asserted that Jones first went to Virginia, then joined Terry's Texas Rangers as a private at Bowling Green, Kentucky, but only for about a month; he then allegedly was appointed as adjutant of the Fifteenth Texas Infantry.[5] There is no official record of such a scenario, but it is recorded that Jones returned to Texas from Virginia and was mustered on January 4, 1862, as a private in Captain M. D. Herring's company, which was a part of the Texas infantry battalion of Waco planter Colonel Joseph W. Speight. In April, Herring's company became Company B of the Fifteenth Texas Infantry Regiment. Jones joined the company for duty and formally enrolled for twelve months' service at Galveston on February 18, 1862.[6]

The regiment was assigned to the Confederate Trans-Mississippi Department in May. By that time, Jones had already been elevated from the rank of private to lieutenant and was serving as the adjutant of Speight's battalion.[7] The Fifteenth Texas Infantry remained encamped at Millican, near Houston, additions of new recruits to the company being made in anticipation of the unit's march that summer through East Texas to Arkansas.[8] One of the original company commanders in the regiment was Richard Coke, a future Texas governor.

On June 29, after a delay of some three months because of a shortage of transportation in the quartermaster department, the regiment began its march from Camp Crockett at Millican through Navarro and Smith Counties, finally arriving at and establishing Camp Nelson east of Austin, Arkansas. Almost immediately the unit experienced an outbreak of dysentery and other such camp diseases.[9] In September and October, Jones was reported as present for duty at Camp Nelson. For the three-month period from July through September, First Lieutenant Jones was paid ninety dollars per month, as well as an additional ten dollars for serving as adjutant.[10] On October 6, Fannie Halbert wrote her husband, who commanded Company E in Speight's regiment, that she had ordered two pairs of "blue-jeans" for "Bud."[11]

In October the regiment was reorganized into the Fifteenth Texas Infantry Division, and on November 23 marched to the Arkansas River Valley for a new encampment at Camp Bayou Metre.[12] The following month the division began a march to Vicksburg, Mississippi, the town under threat by Union troops advancing from Tennessee, but the move was called off. The division instead moved west to reinforce troops retreating from Prairie Grove, and the two units assumed a defensive position in a cold rain near Clarksville, Arkansas, but no Union troops appeared. Soldiers became demoralized by the constant movement, leading to a high rate of desertions. The Texas regiments were ordered to report to Brigadier General William Steele, who had just taken command of the Indian Territory at Fort Smith.[13] Steele was another person who, as adjutant general of Texas, would have a significant influence on Jones. The men of the unit trudged through eight to ten inches of snow, braving cold rains. One hundred mules used for supply wagons and artillery caissons froze to death, forcing the troops to use cattle and oxen to pull supplies. The division finally established its camp near Fort Smith on January 15, 1863, reduced in numbers by desertion, sickness, and casualties from occasional skirmishes, but then was ordered to Doaksville for winter quarters.[14]

However, before Speight's brigade could march to Doaksville under Steele's orders, the commander of the Trans-Mississippi Department, Lieutenant General Edmund Kirby Smith, diverted the brigade to Western Louisiana to reinforce an effort to thwart the advance north from New Orleans of Union troops under the command of Major General Nathaniel P. Banks.[15] Meanwhile, in April of 1863, Jones' rank of first lieutenant was confirmed, and in May and June he was shown on detached service,[16] perhaps to return to Texas on a search for deserters.

In May the brigade moved again, this time to Shreveport where Kirby Smith reviewed the troops, becoming alarmed at their condition, but deeming the Fifteenth Texas as acceptable. On May 16, the Fifteenth and other units of Speight's command went down the Red River to Alexandria, recently evacuated by federal troops, then camped for two weeks at Simmesport, where Speght's men had a skirmish with a Union gunboat. Driven off by three federal warships, the brigade crossed the Atchafalaya River in hopes of reinforcing Port Hudson, then under siege, but that post subsequently fell along with Vicksburg early in July.[17]

In May of 1863, a Second Texas Brigade was formed and placed under the command of Brigadier General Camille Armand Jules Marie, Prince de Polignac, a Frenchman who had served in the French Army during the Crimean War, and who had offered his services to the Confederacy. The following October, Speight's brigade, including the Fifteenth Texas Infantry, was merged with Polignac's brigade in the Second Infantry Division of Brigadier General Alfred Mouton. This infuriated the "hard-drinking" Speight, and the Frenchman became an object of mockery among the soldiers, who sarcastically dubbed him as "Prince Polecat."[18]

Speight's brigade encountered only very minor skirmishing as it changed positions along the Atchafalaya River. On September 27, orders came down for an attack against a federal post on Stirling's Plantation on Bayou Fordoche. The Fifteenth Texas was a part of the advance through the sugar plantation, and infantrymen occupied a ditch to the front of the enemy line, which was hidden from view by the high cane. Lieutenant Colonel James E. Harrison, who was in charge of the Fifteenth in Speight's absence, ordered a charge on the Union position, and Texas soldiers rushed forward shouting the "Texas yell" and "up and at them." After about an hour of close, sometimes hand-to-hand fighting, the federal troops were dislodged and surrendered in mass. The Fifteenth Texas suffered a loss of fifteen killed, fifty-two wounded, and one missing, out of total Confederate casualties of 121.[19] However, the fight resulted in 475 federal prisoners and seizure of a large quantity of arms and supplies. Especially singled out in the report of Confederate Brigadier General Thomas Green, although not elaborated on, was "the gallant bearing and activity of Lieutenant Jones, assistant adjutant-general of Speight's brigade."[20]

On October 18 the Fifteenth Texas and other units were placed under the consolidated command of General "Polecat." Five days later, Jones' commander, Lieutenant Colonel Harrison who was temporarily in charge of Speight's brigade, highly praised the actions of his subordinate at Stirling's Plantation and recommended his promotion to captain:

I wish to call attention of Lt. Genl. Smith through you [Col. S. S. Anderson, Adjutant General] to Lt. Jno. B. Jones, Adjutant of the Regt.

Lt. Jones has been Adjutant of this Regt. From its organization until Speight's Brigade was organized, about ten (10) months since. He has since that time acted as Brigade Adjutant and aid to Col. Speight. Lt. Jones is a young man of high moral and intellectual worth. A good disciplinarian & drill officer, I know of no young man of superior merit. In our recent engagement on the Fordoche, being in command of the Brigade, he was most efficient, rendering me invaluable services, and bore himself with daring gallantry throughout, worthy of all praise, and after the enemy had fled, he mounted Maj. Boone's horse (who had been severely wounded) and led a cavalry charge upon the routed enemy, capturing two field officers and from one hundred & fifty (150) to two hundred (200) others. There was no other officer present, and the surrender was made to Lt. Jones. He had with him in this charge not exceeding twenty privates of Maj. Boone's command, whom I induced to follow him.[21]

The recommendation was strongly endorsed by General Tom Green: "Lt. Jones is one of the most gallant young officers in our army and is well worthy of the promotion asked for. He comes from the best of stock, his father having been one of the most distinguished men and gallant soldiers of Texas."[22]

Harrison was named to command Speight's regiment, Speight having departed in a huff when Polignac was placed in charge of the brigade. On November 3, 1863, Harrison's regiment was joined at Opelousas by that of Col. Wilburn H. King, who would succeed Jones as Texas adjutant general, and Oran M. Roberts, who would later serve as a Texas governor, to make an attack on a federal brigade at Bayou Bourbeau. Two companies of the Fifteenth Texas were to act as skirmishers. In the face of enemy cannon fire, Harrison's men engaged the Union troops, driving them from their positions, the Union dead lying "in heaps." Jones warned Harrison that the Confederates had been flanked by Union cavalry, which was about to attack them from the rear. Harrison quickly organized a counterattack to the rear, routing the cavalry with "men tumbling from horses, screaming . . . others throwing up their hands for mercy . . . horses running wildly over the field without riders." However, the Union forces were bolstered by additional units, ultimately forcing the Southern forces to finally fall back. Richard Coke, the future governor, was wounded in this battle, but for a brief period, the Confederates had held strong against the enemy.[23]

For the remainder of the year, although General Banks held his federal troops in winter quarters, Polignac roamed the Red, Atchafalaya, and Mississippi Rivers, hoping to sink a federal gunboat, but unable to do so.[24] The winter of 1863-1864 proved a cold and miserable one, the abysmal weather, food shortages, and the constant movement seriously affecting morale. Polignac's brigade was kept along the waterways, then ordered to Harrisonburg, largely to maintain defensive positions and to protect engineers rebuilding Fort Beauregard.[25] Adjutant John B. Jones, stationed near Trinity, Louisiana, was reported as "absent" in the January and February 1864 muster, and there is no information about his location.[26] On February 6, Polignac led a raid on the small village of Vidalia, across the Mississippi from Natchez, earning the renewed respect of his men when he raised himself in his stirrups, waving a sword, and shouted, "Follow me! Follow me! You call me 'Polecat;' I will show you whether I am 'Polecat' or Polignac."[27] In March, Polignac's brigade was reorganized with another brigade into an infantry division commanded by Brigadier General Alfred Mouton.[28]

On March 2, 1864, federal gunboats engaged Polignac's troops for almost two hours at Harrisonburg, and the town was almost destroyed by fire. The attack was renewed the next day with an insufficient number of Confederate troops in place trying to defend the town.[29] The strength of the federal forces moving northward necessitated that the Confederate forces reluctantly yield and move back, which led Union commanders to mistakenly believe that Southern troops would not stand and fight. To the contrary, on April 8, north of Mansfield on the road to Shreveport, Polignac's Texas forces marched eagerly toward battle on the road to Pleasant Hill. The Union troops walked on, unaware they were within range of the hidden Confederate forces, and the opening fire quickly panicked the advancing federal cavalry. A major battle ensued in which

General Mouton was killed. A stalemate between the opposing enemies was reached by the next day, and on the tenth, federal forces finally retreated.

Polignac's overall losses were high, although the Fifteenth Texas lost only two killed and fourteen wounded.[30] Polignac was appointed to replace Mouton as division commander, and James Harrison was temporarily elevated to brigade commander, although he was then replaced by Wilburn King, disappointing the Texas troops who respected Harrison.[31]

Neither Harrison nor Jones was present for this conflict, as they were visiting the Jones home back in Navarro County. Fannie Halbert wrote her husband on April 2, 1864, that "Colonel Harrison and Bud will leave for the regiment Monday." She explained that while the men discussed military affairs at supper, all female family members were excluded. In a letter dated April 10, she expressed concern about her brother's health, wishing that he could stay at home to be cared for.[32]

Polignac concentrated his artillery on Union gunboats below Alexandria and proved successful in capturing or sinking a number of the vessels.[33] On May 16, 1864, Harrison's troops engaged Banks' retreating federals at Mansura, at the edge of a long prairie, but were forced to retreat after a four-hour artillery duel. Two days later, on Yellow Bayou, the battle was renewed, and this time the Confederates proved the better force. The Fifteenth Texas lost twelve killed, thirty-seven wounded, and twenty-four missing.[34] The successful routing of the federals and their retreat marked the end of Banks' Red River campaign, and his dismal performance during that campaign, measured by casualties suffered and loss of equipment and materials at the hands of Southern forces, led to his dismissal by the Union command.[35]

Now ensued a series of movements across northern Louisiana without any apparent plan. The rumored threat that Polignac's Texas troops were being ordered to cross the Mississippi and go east to fight in support of other Confederate troops generated major morale problems, and desertions skyrocketed. It was one thing to defend Texas by battle in Louisiana, but to go further east was not acceptable. As a result of this smoldering issue, Polignac's division was instead ordered north into

Arkansas, a district under the authority of Major General John B. "Prince John" Magruder.[36]

At this time, on August 8, Jones again managed to visit home on leave, much to the surprise of his family, as Fannie wrote her husband:

> Bud reached here day before yesterday evening. Took us all completely by surprise, for we were not looking for him . . . He is looking very badly. The trip nearly finished him. I am glad that he has come for I have been so lonely since you and Pa left. He spent the day here yesterday and came up and took breakfast with us this morning . . . [37]

On September 18, the Fifteenth Texas and the rest of the division set up camp at Monticello, Arkansas, near Magruder's headquarters, where a parade was held for the general's review.[38] From there the division was ordered to Camden by way of Warren, Arkansas, a trek involving a difficult march through dense woods and swamps in torrential rains. Camp Bragg was established near Washington, Arkansas. However, desertions, sickness, and shortages again severely affected morale, leading a desperate Polignac to ride to Shreveport looking for any supplies he could muster for his "poor naked soldiers."[39]

In November the division set up a new camp near Minden, Louisiana. Desertions continued, forcing Polignac to order the execution by firing squad of three men who had been captured after deserting. The troops worked on improving the road from Minden to Shreveport, and during this time a religious revival took hold in the camp, to which Jones certainly would have had no objection.[40] In January of 1865, the Texas division again moved, this time to winter camp at Grand Ecore on the Red River in present-day Nachitoches Parish, where the men occupied their time building fortifications. It was now obvious that the war was not going well for the Confederacy, and Texas troops in Louisiana gradually commenced a westward movement back to their home state. By March 15, most were encamped in Texas a few miles east of Hempstead in Waller County in southeast Texas, including Jones.[41] Convinced that there was no need to remain as an army, units began to dissolve as, one by one, soldiers left for their homes and families. On May 24, Jones made his last official entry as acting adjutant-general of newly-promoted Brigadier General Harrison's brigade, issuing General Order Number Thirteen, directing discharges from the Confederate Army.[42] Lieutenant General Kirby Smith formally surrendered the Trans-Mississippi Department on June 2, 1865.[43]

Although there is no official record that Jones was promoted to captain as urged, the promotion did occur. It was subsequently reported that his various commanding officers—Harrison, Green, and Polignac—later urged his promotion to major, some of the more senior line officers waiving their opportunities for promotion in his favor. The appointment to major was supposed to have been made, but "owing to irregularities of the mail," the promotion did not reach him until after the war.[44] Regardless, the carnage and violence of war ended and, with the onset of Reconstruction in Texas, Jones faced the task of resuming his life in an uncertain future.

With Republicans still in political control of the nation even after Lincoln's death, the fears of radicalism that were felt before the war were even more intense. In June, President Andrew Johnson appointed Andrew J. Hamilton as provisional governor of Texas, his charter being to establish a loyal and Republican government. This appointment was followed on June 19, 1865, with a general order from General Gordon Granger emancipating Texas slaves. The plantation economy of Texas was now a thing of the past, leaving in doubt the economic and social future of the state.[45] Because Texas had been physically untouched by the war, there was a general feeling that the state had never been subdued,[46] but now rumors abounded of dire punishments to be inflicted on prominent Texas rebels and about confiscation of property, generating a panic.

There were those who declared the rule of Reconstruction could not be tolerated, and thoughts turned to emigration outside the state.[47] Even before the war ended, efforts had been made by Southern-sympathizing officials to establish a Confederate colony in Mexico, and by the early summer months of 1865 it was estimated that as many as 1,000 Confederates had crossed the border. Confederate officers such as Generals Kirby Smith, Sterling Price, and Jo Shelby led soldiers into Mexico with a view to joining Emperor Maximilian.[48]

Jones was reportedly in bad health when he returned to Navarro County, and a period of recuperation was called for. On June 26, 1865, his father gave him full power of attorney to handle the Colonel's affairs.[49] However, friends and acquaintances, concerned about their treatment under the imposition of reconstruction, approached Jones about scouting out a location in Mexico for a colony. When this occurred is unknown, although it could not have been long after his return home, likely at the beginning of 1866. He later testified that he spent "nearly a year" in Mexico.[50] While he was gone, his father deeded over to him 511 acres in Navarro County.[51] Jones reportedly returned to Texas from Mexico in December 1866, declaring that, after extensive traveling through that country, he found no suitable place for an American colony.[52] With the withdrawal of French troops from Mexico after the death of Maximilian, the political climate changed; most of those who had settled in Mexico quickly returned to Texas, despite Reconstruction, and colonial endeavors in that country ceased.[53]

Jones was no sooner home than another group from Navarro County, along with a commission of citizens of Claiborne Parish, Louisiana, asked him to act as their agent to explore Brazil as a potential site for an expatriate colony of 300 families.[54] Henry Jones was in favor of the expedition, thinking that horse raising in South America could be profitable.[55] John Jones left for Brazil in January 1867, accompanied by engineers, interpreters, and guides, and was welcomed in that country as an honored guest.[56]

Some eight to ten thousand expatriates made an exodus to South America in the years following the Civil War, 3,000 to 4,000 of whom settled in Brazil. The Brazilian government encouraged the immigration, promising the construction of roads to isolated colonies, free board and lodging on arrival in the country, and exemption from military service upon taking an oath of citizenship.[57] Jones reportedly spent some eighteen months in the country, exploring some twelve provinces, observing climate, resources, and available facilities.[58] He concluded that there was not a "congenial" location for a suitable colony and returned to Texas to make his report. His niece, Helen Groce, recalled:

> I shall never forget the night of his return. He brought to us children
> a large wooden box of delicious candy . . . This he opened with a
> little hammer and leaving it on the dining room table, told us to help
> ourselves, while the grown ups discussed their affairs in the adjoining
> sitting room. At the first chance I slipped into the sitting room and lis-
> tened in. I heard him say, "No, Pa, we could never be happy there; that
> is a priest-ridden (I had never heard the word before) country."[59]

Jones then described for his family all of the conditions to which he
objected, but his eavesdropping niece sneezed, was discovered, and, as she
expressed it, "shunted from a conversation that was not meant for childish
ears."[60] Another niece, Mrs. James K. Parr, also remembering her uncle's
lovely gifts, believed that Jones was not willing to have Americans settle
in Brazil because of an overwhelming love of Texas, and perhaps a tinge of
homesickness.[61] Jones' international jaunts were at an end, and it was time
to return to the business of stock raising and farming with his father.

Jones resumed his work with the Masonic Order in 1868 as a representative from Navarro County.[62] However, it was also in this year that an
event was attributed to Jones that cannot be verified. Biographical entries
published about Jones while he was alive asserted that he was elected in
1868 to the Twelfth State Legislature as a representative from a district
composed of Navarro, Hill, Ellis, and Kaufman Counties. One account
stated that he was "counted out" by the legislature because the Kaufman
County vote was thrown out.[63] Two other accounts merely stated that he
was "counted out by the Republican Returning Board and did not take
his seat."[64] A listing of the representatives who took a seat in the Twelfth
Session does not mention Jones, nor does it include any mention that
he did not qualify, although such situation is mentioned for others who
did not take a seat in that session, which commenced in February 1870.
H. W. Young of Hill County was the elected representative from Jones'
district.[65] Diligent search for election records has failed to turn up any
mention of an 1868 election, much less of Jones' candidacy.

In 1869, Colonel Jones moved within Navarro County to just outside
the small community of Cross Roads where he owned about 2,500 acres

and raised about the same number of horses.[66] His plantation home was described as sitting on a hill surrounded by trees, under which Roger Q. Mills had taken Carrie Jones as his bride. A slave graveyard was located in the nearby woods.[67] In June of that year, Henry Jones deeded to his son over 500 acres lying seven miles west of the town of Dresden, known as "Jones Rancho," as well as one-half interest in all of his horse stock, which included a black stallion recently purchased from Pennsylvania.[68] The 1870 census saw John Jones living with Henry, along with seven Hispanic laborers named Lacerino.[69]

Jones was soon again involved in business pursuits and community affairs. He opened a private bank in 1870, joined by future brother-in-law and fellow Masonic lodge member, A. F. Robbins, and others.[70] In March of 1871, he was chosen as a member of a group of delegates from Navarro County to attend the State Democratic Party convention in Houston in early June in order to nominate a candidate for the Third Congressional District.[71] But about this same time he absented himself from the county, apparently for health reasons, arriving back home in early April, his health having "considerably improved."[72] In May he was elected director of the county's Agricultural and Mechanical Association.[73] At the county's Democratic Convention on September 2, 1871, he was nominated for state representative from that district, as well as chosen as delegate to a taxpayers' convention to be held in Austin on September 22.[74] While election records for that period have not survived, he was not elected as a state representative.

At the county's Central Texas Agricultural and Mechanical Association Fair in November, Jones and his father displayed stallions that they had bought in Pennsylvania shortly after the war. A draft horse, Harry, stood seventeen hands high. Two harness horses, Brampton and Dellinger, were eighteen and seventeen hands high respectively, and were jet black in color.[75] Jones was always a fancier of fine horse flesh, even when commanding the Frontier Battalion.

In April of 1872, Jones purchased a lot on Beaton Street in Corsicana for $2,800, buying out the store of the Cerf brothers, along with all of the "goods, wares, merchandise, groceries, and furniture" on the premises.[76] His sister, Annie, married his partner, A. F. Robbins, on January 16, 1873.[77]

Jones served as a delegate from Navarro County to the State Democratic Convention in Austin in September of 1873, which met to find a successor to Reconstruction Governor Edmund J. Davis[78] and nominated Richard Coke. In the meantime, merchant John B. Jones, doing business as John B. Jones & Company from the former location of the Cerf brothers, purchased cotton and corn crops for resale, and sold such items as horse-drawn wagons.[79] On September 26, 1873, he executed a deed of trust to H. A. Halbert to secure a ninety-day note to Roger Q. Mills, signed by Jones and Robbins in the amount of $8,180.80 and secured by 1,000 acres of the Jones ranch twenty miles west of Corsicana.[80]

In December, Y. W. H. McKissack sued Jones' company on behalf of a widow, Mrs. John C. Wells, because the company refused to pay over $2,200 to her without a proper probate of her late husband's estate. After a hearing, the court ordered Jones' company to pay the amount.[81]

As 1874 began, Jones' world was that of horses, mercantilism, and Masonic affairs. That was about to change dramatically.

3

_{୧ᳩᳩᳩᳩᳩᳩᳩᳩᳩᳩᳩᳩᳩᳩ}

THE RIGHT MAN

JOHN B. JONES & COMPANY, partnered by Jones and A. F. Robbins, described itself as a business of "bankers and exchange dealers," "general commission merchants," and "wholesale and retail grocers," maintaining a "full stock of groceries constantly on hand."[1] To complement the prominence of their retail enterprise, Robbins also served as a Corsicana alderman in the early 1870s. Classified legally as "second class merchants," Jones and Robbins also sold liquor in quantities of one quart or more, which brought about a legal hassle. Navarro County Sheriff S. J. T. Johnson contended that Jones and Robbins owed a seventy-five-dollar occupation tax in addition to an occupation tax in the same amount already paid by the business. Johnson claimed that the right to sell such liquor was a second occupation in that second class merchants were not authorized to sell liquor. The company sued for a temporary injunction against the sheriff on December 23, 1873, and later prevailed when a permanent injunction was granted the following July.[2] At the same time, Texas politics were playing out in Austin, and the outcome would affect Jones greatly. In his inaugural address on January 13, 1874, newly-elected Governor Richard Coke pledged that

I will add a system which will supplement the efforts of the Federal government for the protection of our suffering frontier, and give that protection to the inhabitants of that portion of the State to which they are clearly and justly entitled, thereby opening up an area of magnificent territory to settlement and productiveness, while discharging a high obligation to the frontier people.[3]

News stories published statewide of depredations by Indians, Mexican raiders, and outlaws fomented concerns about safety. For example, the *Brownsville Sentinel* voiced serious concern over the frequency of stock raids being made by armed Mexicans from the other side of the Rio Grande. "Bad blood is brewing," warned the newspaper as it reported that ranchers were meeting in large numbers to discuss Indian

Governor Richard Coke (*L. E. Daniell,* Personnel of the Texas State Government, Austin, *Texas: Smith, Hines & Jones, State Printers, 1889.*)

and Mexican raids.[4] Another report out of North Texas warned that the Comanches were taking livestock in large amounts.[5] When some responded to the attacks by taking the law into their own hands, such as in the hanging of Mexican stock thieves in Nueces County, protests from the Mexican government about the lack of due process complicated the state's political picture.[6]

One of the first appointments made by the new governor was that of William H. Steele to the post of adjutant general, Governor Coke expressing full confidence in Steele's "integrity, ability, and patriotism."[7] Born in New York in 1820, Steele graduated from West Point in 1840, subsequently fighting in the 1841-1842 war with the Seminole Indians in Florida, and serving at posts on the frontier. He led troops in the Mexican War and served as an army quartermaster in Austin during the 1850s. Steele was credited with fighting Apaches, the Sioux, and Comanches prior to the Civil War, during which he was a Confederate brigadier general. After the war and until his appointment to adjutant general, he conducted a mercantile business in San Antonio.[8]

Steele's first task as adjutant general was to inventory the condition of his state office, which he found in abysmal shape. Various accounts, such as one for frontier defense, were overdrawn from Governor Edmund J. Davis' administration, leading Steele to ask for additional staffing and conditional funding to tide him over through the end of August.[9]

Governor Coke addressed the state legislature on January 26, acknowledging the violence being committed on Texans along the state's western frontier, as well as the failure of the federal government, up to that date, to do more than they previously had in regard to providing adequate troops for protection. In order that the "tomahawk and scalping knife must be stayed in their bloody work," the governor urged the legislature to come to some consensus for "repelling the incursions of the Indians and protecting our people from their predatory raids" without onerous taxation, suggesting a scheme similar to one enacted in 1863.[10] Since the Civil War, the state government had tried various ill-fated military schemes to stem Indian incursions, their failure usually resulting from inadequate financing.[11]

The 1863 statute authorized militia companies composed of residents of frontier counties, divided into three districts, each organized and commanded by an appointed major of cavalry. The companies were required to keep at least one-fourth of their number in the field at all times and were subject to any regulations or orders promulgated by the governor.[12]

In response to the governor's suggestion, Senator Thomas Ball of Jack County promptly submitted a bill for frontier protection, authorizing the raising of twenty companies of seventy-five men each,[13] but much political struggle lay ahead before a decision would be made as to an acceptable format for frontier defense. For example, the Committee on Indian Affairs proposed raising a company of salaried men in every frontier county, with four to twelve-month enlistments.[14] Senator Will Russell of Brownsville introduced his own scheme, proposing twelve companies, with each man furnishing his own horse and clothing.[15] Coke mustered out of service most of the existing Ranger companies that had previously been called to action by former Governor Davis in 1873.[16] At the federal level, Jones' brother-in-law, Roger Q. Mills, now a congressman, introduced an ill-fated bill to remove all United States troops from Southern states and send them to the frontier of Texas.[17]

In anticipation of a frontier force being created, the governor's office began receiving petitions recommending various individuals for positions within that force. For example, citizens of Blanco County urged the appointment of Cicero Rufus "Rufe" Perry, "an old frontiersman," "one that thoroughly understands the traits of Indian character," to fill some new vacancy.[18] As debate over frontier protection heated up, there was growing impatience in frontier counties affected by Indian raiders. The previous method of dealing with the problem—the raising and arming of temporary militia companies—was seen as ineffective, and calls were made for a cavalry-type unit based on the federal military model, with men enlisted from interior counties for up to four years.[19] The debate began to focus on the number of men to authorize as well as the anticipated expense involved.

In March the legislature began to close ranks behind a bill. General discussion seemed to agree that up to 750 men would be authorized for frontier protection. The men would be subject to the rules and regulations governing federal army troops. A paymaster would be responsible for wages being paid. Steele voiced some concerns with the proposal, specifically a suggestion that troops be recruited from the area in which they would serve, as they conceivably could be compelled to leave their unit in order to protect their families in times of peril. He wrote Governor Coke to point out the ineffectuality of the twenty-eight minute companies created under Governor Davis. No Indians had been killed by these companies, but nevertheless they acted as a drain on the state treasury, and Steele urged a scheme other than companies organized from the counties in which they were to serve.[20]

While all of this was playing out in Austin, Jones remained in Navarro County engaged in ongoing land transactions and commercial business. However, not all was business. On March 12, 1874, he was out for an evening buggy ride with Miss Lula Martin. The high-spirited horse pulling the buggy became spooked and ran away with the pair. The buggy turned over at some point, throwing its occupants several feet to each side of the road. They both suffered unstated injuries from which they ultimately recovered.[21] On the business scene, Jones and Robbins now offered the service of scales to weigh produce without having to unload it from a wagon.[22] On March 28, Jones organized a Grange, or Patrons of Husbandry, at Dunn's School House, the tenth such organized in Navarro County.[23] The Grange, first organized the previous year in nearby Bell County, was a nonpartisan, agrarian order intended to benefit farm families. At the same time, Jones & Company improved the appearance of its building on Beaton Street in Corsicana by filling up and grading the sidewalk with sand and gravel.[24]

The state legislature finally decided on authorizing a "battalion" of men to be raised for frontier defense, in addition to organizing militia companies in the various counties.[25] On April 10, the Texas House and Senate agreed on "An Act to provide for the protection of the Frontier of the State of Texas against the invasion of hostile Indians, or other marauding or thieving parties." The act authorized the governor to create a militia company in each county affected by Indian or other violent raids, up to a statewide total of 750 men, the companies to be mustered for no more than a three to twelve-month period. Beginning with Section Nineteen of the statute, the legislature additionally authorized the governor to organize a battalion of men, consisting of six companies of seventy-five men each. A major would be appointed to command the battalion, and a captain and two lieutenants would command each company. In addition the governor would appoint a battalion quartermaster.[26]

Privates in the battalion were to earn forty dollars per month, to be paid quarterly, while the major would receive $125, captains $100, lieutenants seventy-five dollars, and sergeants fifty dollars. The battalion was not designated as a "standing force," but would always be subject to the orders of the governor. Each "soldier and officer" was to furnish his own horse and be reimbursed only if the horse was killed in battle.[27] To insure that the state was not cheated in such event, each Ranger's horse was to be appraised by three neutral civilians.[28]

Enlistments in the "service" would be for up to four years. In addition, minutemen could also be called out by the governor if the battalion proved insufficient, and the state was to provide battalion members with ammunition, as well as an "improved breech-loading cavalry gun" at cost. "Each officer of the battalion" was to have all the authority of a peace officer, and it would be his duty to "execute all criminal process directed to him, and make arrests under a warrant properly issued, of any and all parties charged with offenses" against the laws of Texas. Use of the term "officer" in the statute would come back to haunt the Frontier Battalion at the turn of the century.

Governor Coke was authorized to disband all existing troops now engaged in frontier protection, and previous acts establishing militia and ranging companies were repealed. In addition, both the governor and the adjutant general were authorized to "make all additional regulations not contrary to the laws" of Texas that were necessary to carry out the statute. The legislature appropriated $300,000 to fund the act.[29] For the first time in the state's history, the "Texas Rangers," a term not used in the statute, were institutionalized as a permanent force, rather than as periodic, short-term ranging companies.[30] It was clear that the primary focus of the Frontier Battalion was confronting the Indian menace, and only secondarily dealing with Mexican raiders or other outlaws.

The legislature also promulgated a joint resolution authorizing General Steele to apply to the United States Army for additional troops on the Texas frontier.[31] Steele promptly wrote to the general commanding the Department of Texas, Christopher C. Augur, concluding that the present number of federal troops on the Texas frontier was "totally inadequate" and that "nothing but a cordon of sentinels can prevent entirely the forays of both our Mexican neighbors or the tribes domiciled with them, and the tribes fed and protected by the United States at Ft. Sill."[32] However, the only response was that there was no regiment of cavalry available to reinforce those already in Texas.[33]

An unstated concern that had to have filtered through the legislature in developing the Frontier Battalion was the Reconstruction Texas experience with the state police under Edmund J. Davis. The force, which operated from July 1870 to April 1873, had been the brainchild of the radical Republicans in power, which was enough by itself to earn general hatred statewide. However, that disaffection was compounded by the inclusion in police ranks of Hispanics and blacks, not to mention criminals and others in the ranks who willfully abused their authority. In the public mind, the force was a tool of the arbitrary will of Governor Davis, "the very emblem of despotic authority." Several studies have since concluded that the state police force, in spite of some flagrant abuses, nevertheless served rather effectively its purpose of confronting widespread lawlessness at a time when local law enforcement was unable to cope, and accomplished much for which it should be praised. Regardless of the need for such a force and the benefits it produced, however, on the departure of the Davis administration, the legislature was quick to repeal the organization's authorization.[34] With the creation of the Frontier Battalion, the members of the state legislature had to be patently concerned about a police force that might overly dominate civilian life beyond guarding the frontier,[35] and probably more than anything focused on the integrity of the men chosen to lead it. As Governor Coke observed: "A body of state police under the command of the Governor, attached as they always would be to his interests, knowing no law but his will, and ready at all times to obey, is an engine of power which under a free government should be entrusted to no man."[36] The popular disdain for Davis' state police would negate inclusion of blacks and Hispanics in the new Frontier Battalion except for positions as cooks and teamsters rather than as full-fledged Rangers.

With the Frontier Battalion now confirmed, applications for appointments poured in to the governor's and adjutant general's offices. Even legislators in session got into the act, for example recommending Cicero "Rufe" Perry for a command.[37] Six representatives urged the appointment of John R. Waller of Erath County for the major's position.[38] Multiple petitions arrived asking that William J. Maltby be named as commander of the Battalion. Governor Coke even met with Maltby, but he was looking for an individual who possessed administrative skills that went beyond a record of Indian fighting.[39] On May 6, the initial organization of the command of the Frontier Battalion was announced by Steele. A relative unknown by the name of John B. Jones would command the six companies.

Named to command Company A was Waller, an experienced Indian fighter who had once been accused of being involved in the 1859 murder of Indian women and children.[40] George W. Stevens of Wise County was named to head Company B. Born in Alabama in 1830, he, too, had experience confronting marauding Indians. He had served as sheriff of Wise County and ridden with several minute companies.[41] Company C was to be commanded by Elisha Floyd Ikard, another experienced Indian fighter,[42] while Rufe Perry headed Company D. Perry was fifty-two and had fought Indians since the 1830s, suffering a number of wounds, and had also served in the Mexican War.[43] William Jeff Maltby, referred to as "Captain Jeff," was named to Company E. Born in 1829 in Illinois, Maltby served as a company commander in the Seventeenth Texas Infantry during the Civil War and also functioned as a Ranger in Burnet County to protect against raiding Indians. He was a cattleman prior to enlisting with the Frontier Battalion.[44] He was described as "a most impartial man, one who never flattered nor spoke other than his honest sentiments on any subject."[45] Finally, elected to command

Company F was Neal Coldwell. Thirty years old, Coldwell had served in the Thirty-second Texas Cavalry during the Civil War and engaged in farming and stockraising in Kerr County.[46]

Maltby recalled, with just a touch of sour grapes, that he had been recommended for the Battalion commander position by prominent state Democrats and legislators, but that Governor Coke

> gave the majorship to John B. Jones, a man that had no experience whatever in Indian warfare; a man that never lived on the frontier and was not identified with the frontier in any way. His only apology was that he knew John B. Jones and did not know our Captain Jeff, and that he intended to give the appointment to Jones from the start, regardless of fitness, for he was his personal friend and that he had seen his bravery tested many a time on the battle field in the Confederate war.[47]

Maltby related that a letter from his wife about Indian threats at home convinced him to accept the commission as a company commander. On the way to the governor's office in Austin, he encountered James G. Connell and convinced him to accept a commission as one of his lieutenants.[48] John M. Elkins of Coleman County was appointed his second lieutenant, but declined the appointment, which then went to B. F. Best, a former Coleman County minuteman.[49] According to Elkins, he declined the appointment and recommended Best because Maltby "had no real experience as an Indian scout . . . I did not wish to hamper myself under a command that was no way competent."[50] Maltby enlisted thirty men from Lampasas and Burnet Counties on May 30, issued them arms and ammunition sent by the state, and then set up camp near Brownwood.[51]

Upon Perry receiving his commission, and George Freeman having declined appointment as second lieutenant, the new captain wrote to Dan W. Roberts, a personal friend who had shared an Indian fight or two in the past, and, without explaining, urged him to meet him in Austin. Roberts, who would be awarded a Winchester rifle by the state legislature in 1875 for an Indian fight with others in Blanco County in August of 1872,[52] did as he was requested and immediately upon his arrival was handed a commission as second lieutenant in Company D. Somewhat

Adjutant General William Steele *(Courtesy of Chuck Parsons, Luling, Texas)*

taken aback, Roberts responded, "I guess you've got me," and decided to accept the commission.[53] William Henry Ledbetter was named first lieutenant of Company D. Perry's company mustered in on May 25 at the Blanco County courthouse, was sworn in by a justice of the peace, and then camped two miles outside of town until weapons arrived.[54]

Exactly how much input Jones had in the selection of his company commanders is unknown, but he apparently had very little influence. His own selection as commander of the Battalion probably had more to do with his military experience than anything else, and Maltby was likely not very far off in assessing the reasoning behind Coke's selection of him. Both Adjutant General Steele and Governor Coke were familiar with Jones because of his admirable service during the war. As it turned out, his administrative skills and reputation as a disciplinarian in the Confederate Army were important influences in the success of the Battalion. No doubt also, considering the petitions that flooded the Governor's office, the selection of the other officers in the Battalion was to some degree politically influenced, but not without regard to experience in dealing with Indian incursions. However, as one of his officers later said of him, Jones "was the moving spirit of the field work . . . the right man in the right place."[55] Nevertheless, public reception of Jones as commander was varied. His hometown, of course, felt the appointment was an "eminently worthy one."[56] On the other hand, a San Antonio newspaper sarcastically asserted that Jones was appointed only because of his Confederate service, whether or not he had ever seen an Indian.[57] In Dallas, some disappointment was expressed, but only because there may have been worthier candidates with considerably more experience with Indians. However, after noting the frontier experience of Henry Jones, the newspaper concluded,

> Since the [Confederate] flag went down at Appomattox, we have seen him in the wilds of the tropics, after which he made the tour of Brazil, and finally settled down as a man of business at Corsicana. Feeble in health, he is lithe, energetic and capable of great endurance, and we hope our frontier fellow citizens will uphold his hands and give him a fair showing.[58]

An acquaintance, Clinton M. Winkler, defended the appointment based on the experience of Henry Jones as "an old time Indian fighter," as well as on the friendship between Jones and Governor Coke, forged during the combat of the late war. "[E]re many moons pass, Maj. Jones will command and enjoy the confidence and respect of the best and bravest of them," he said, urging that Jones be given a fair trial to earn respect and trust. "Energy, conscientious devotion to duty, and *pluck*, will win."[59]

Ultimately Jones was accepted by the statewide press: "He is known to be a brave, energetic and dashing officer, and takes command of his battalion determined to hunt down and chastise the murdering, thieving bands of savages, who for so long have been laying waste the beautiful region of country on our extreme border."[60]

Steele immediately laid out the order of business for the Frontier Battalion: the captains and lieutenants would commence recruiting and organizing their companies. Only "sound young men without families and with good horses" were to be enlisted, and those under indictment, of known bad character, or who were habitual drunkards would be rejected.[61]

Jones went to Austin and took command. His first order was to the Battalion Quartermaster, A. P. Blocker, to begin purchasing the mules, saddles, tents, and other materials necessary for setting up the company camps, as well as related subsistence.[62] His General Order Number One to the company commanders set the tone for how he would administer the Battalion: they were to take an oath to honestly and faithfully serve the state for twelve months, and to administer the same oath to the men they recruited. Jones' bureaucratic leanings were reflected in the requirement of monthly muster rolls from each company. In addition, captains were to "keep an accurate count of all depredations, numbers of settlers killed or carried off, amount of property stolen, amount of property recaptured, number of Indians killed, distance traveled in pursuit, etc."[63] The intent was to run the Battalion on a business-like basis, contrary to the informalities observed in past ranging procedures.

As soon as the captains received arms and ammunition, they were to assume their duties at their assigned posts, resulting in a north-south line of coverage along the outlying frontier counties on the western side of the settled state through which Indian raiding parties were most likely to ride on stock-stealing expeditions. Jones saw no need to assemble the Battalion for a meeting, deeming it a waste of time and money, and ordered the companies to duty at once on the frontier.[64] Waller's Company A was to post itself near the western corner of Erath County, patrolling north to Stephens County and southwest into Brown County. Both Stevens' Company B and Ikard's Company C were to patrol from Wise County. Perry's Company D was to report to Mason County, while Maltby was to scout in Coleman and Brown Counties. Coldwell would keep his company in Bandera County and patrol north to Kimble County and southwest to the Nueces River, although Coldwell suggested that the head of the Guadalupe River would be a better point because of the difficulty of the terrain in the assigned area.[65]

Although Blocker was commissioned as quartermaster and paymaster and gave bond for $50,000,[66] he just as quickly resigned and was replaced by Martin M. Kenney of Brenham, who at the same time declined a lieu-tenancy offered by Jones.[67]

In mid-May Jones returned to Corsicana, likely to clear up some loose ends in his business with A. F. Robbins and other private matters. But with the aid of the telegraph, he was able to stay in touch and continue with the formation of the Battalion. On May 20, he sent word to Ken-ney, suggesting San Antonio as the place where mules could be purchased cheaply. He also advised him that he had enlisted six men in Navarro County for Company A, who would be assigned to his personal escort, although they would report to Kenney on detached duty.[68] Jones took six men from each company to serve in his personal escort.[69] On Tuesday, May 26, Jones took the train back to Austin.[70] The Navarro County men he had enlisted arrived in Austin on May 28 and set up tents a short dis-tance from the state capitol. They were issued single-shot Sharps breech-loading carbines, which "kick worse than a little Spanish jack," and Colt six-shooters, with which they practiced until Jones sent them to their assignment with Kenney.[71]

Arms and ammunition were purchased and sent to the companies. Steele sent seventy-five Sharps rifles to Captain Waller's Company A, along with slings and swivels, cartridge boxes and belts, and 5,000 rounds. Approximately the same amount went to the other companies.[72] The Battalion would later switch from the single-shot Sharps rifle to Winchester carbines.

Jones' strategy in the placement of the companies from the head of the Nueces River to the Red River during the first six months was to keep the men "moving constantly," "whether they knew anything to hunt or not." He wanted no more than half the strength of a company in camp at any one time.

> My orders were to do all the work that the horses could stand, and they can stand enough to keep half of them out all the time—one party in camp and the other half in the saddle. At first some of the older men thought it a newfangled thing to make them ride all the time. They had been in the habit of lying around in camp, playing

cards and racing horses, until somebody would come and tell them that horses had been stolen.[73]

It didn't take long for some of the companies to swing into action. An apparent log of battalion activities from May to November of 1874 shows that as early as May 10, Maltby and his men had caught up with some thieves and recovered two horses and returned them to their owners. One of his Rangers, Hiram "Curley" Hatcher, later claimed that he killed the first Indian of those killed by the Frontier Battalion. Maltby gave him fifty dollars for the Indian's scalp and took it to Austin.[74] On the same date Ikard and his Company C chased and fought a band of Indians, wounding one and capturing two horses and 200 head of cattle.[75] It is not clear if it was the same action, but Ikard and six men of his company fought ten Indians in Clay County in May, killing one and capturing another and recovering 150 head of stock.[76] Ikard apparently got caught up in the excitement; on May 29, he wrote Jones suggesting a better campsite in Archer County: "Think that to be a much better place to find Indians & scalp them after finding them, as that is a prairie country from that point west."[77] All of the companies were scouting for Indian trails and handing over to local officials any wanted criminals they ran across.

Adjutant General Steele wrote to officials in all organized Texas counties that if a known criminal from their county was believed to be in a frontier county, they should send the warrants to his office so that they could be executed by the Battalion.[78] At the same time, concerned about justifying future Battalion budgets to the state legislature, Steele instructed Jones to have his commanders submit reports on all scouts after Indians.[79] Jones was also instructed that Rangers making arrests were to turn their prisoners over to the nearest sheriff, regardless of in which county the prisoner was wanted. The local sheriffs could arrange among themselves for the appropriate delivery of the prisoners.[80]

Almost as soon as the Battalion was organized, there began a constant stream of petitions from various points on the frontier urging that detachments of Rangers be sent to those locations for protection. Such requests continued throughout the life of the Battalion. For example,

on May 28, 1874, citizens of Comanche County asked Governor Coke
to send a portion of Waller's Company A to that county to assist in the
capture of noted gunman John Wesley Hardin. Just three days earlier,
Hardin and several others had gunned down a Brown County deputy
sheriff in the neighboring county at Comanche.[81] Dispatched there by
Jones, Waller and his men searched the area thoroughly, some of them
riding with a citizen's posse that caught up with and killed two of Hardin's associates, although Hardin escaped the area.[82] Waller and his men
subsequently arrested seven men believed to be part of Hardin's gang
and delivered them to Austin.[83] The egocentric Hardin later wrote of the
incident, describing Waller as a leader of a mob rather than a bona fide
lawman trying to restore order.[84] Maltby and some of his men were also
involved in the pursuit; at the same time, he asked Jones to send him two
nickel-plated six-shooters for his own use, along with other arms for his
men.[85] Between May 28 and June 12, Waller's company was credited with
over twenty-two arrests of cattle thieves and "desperadoes."[86]

The offenses committed by Hardin and others underscored the
increasing violence and lawlessness being experienced in Texas, sometimes leading to vigilante actions. For example, the murder of a lawman
by Hardin and others triggered the lynching of his brother and two others in Comanche.[87] Governor Coke, confronted with reports of crimes
from the frontier counties, issued a proclamation on June 13, calling on
local magistrates and peace officers "to observe increased vigilance in the
prevention of crime, the arrest and punishment of all offenders, and the
general execution of the penal laws of the state." He called upon all citizens to obey the law and charged the Frontier Battalion with the execution of warrants in arresting fugitives that they may run across, noting
that the Rangers were "generally required to second the efforts of the civil
authorities for the suppression of crime and maintenance of the law."[88]
On July 3, the governor proclaimed a hefty $1,800 reward for Hardin's
arrest, an amount that would subsequently grow to $4,000.[89]

At the same time that the Frontier Battalion was getting underway,
other ranging companies were temporarily created, although not as a part
of the Battalion. Governor Coke authorized the raising of a company

of men in El Paso County because of the Indian threat. On May 27, the company was mustered in under Lieutenant Telesforo Montes, ready to begin operations as soon as arms were received.[90] Another company of fifty men, under the command of Warren Wallace, was organized at Corpus Christi in June for the "protection of all the counties below the lower Nueces and the Rio Grande."[91] Steele ordered Wallace to station half of his men about twenty miles from the Rio Grande, and the other half near the Cameron-Hidalgo County lines.[92] Wallace chose the town of Concepcion as his headquarters.[93] Assuming authority he did not have, Wallace almost immediately ordered ranchers in the area to register themselves and their employees in order to detect wanted persons.[94]

In Laredo in South Texas, Refugio Benevides of Webb County, an experienced Indian and Mexican bandit fighter, mustered in a company of men on June 13 to thwart the crimes of bandits marauding from Mexico. Steele instructed him that "when in close pursuit of robbers you will not hesitate to cross the Rio Grande if by so doing you have a good prospect for the recovery of property belonging to citizens of this State."[95] This order to a "military force" to invade Mexico prompted a warning to Steele from the United States Department of Justice that he was subjecting himself to prosecution under federal law.[96] This in turn led to a lengthy, detailed response by Governor Coke contending that conditions necessitated such an order, including failure of the Mexican government to take any steps on its side of the border and the inadequate protection afforded by the few American troops then stationed along the Rio Grande, but he pledged that the order would be revoked if in contravention of federal law. However, he argued, it would be "unjust to Texas" not to allow the state to defend itself unless the federal government took adequate steps to protect the border.[97]

As an example of the violence in South Texas necessitating the special companies, Mexican sheepherders were suspected of having slaughtered Thadeus Swift and his wife near Refugio on June 7. Swift was stabbed eighteen times and his throat was cut. His wife was stabbed twenty-four times and her throat cut, as well as a bullet wound to her face. A posse arrested three men who were believed to have harbored the murderers,

Cicero "Rufe" Perry *(Courtesy of Texas Ranger Hall of Fame and Museum, Waco, Texas)*

but a group of vigilantes took them from the posse and killed them. Two other men escaped into Mexico. This led to some citizens forming their own company and organizing a meeting with citizens in adjacent counties to explore means for mutual protection.[98]

On June 19, after Jones had left Austin on his first inspection tour of the new companies, Steele appointed a Frontier Battalion surgeon in the person of Dr. E. G. Nicholson, who had sought the appointment. The good doctor became a close companion of Jones, more colorful than most of Jones' friends.

The doctor was a quaint old bachelor who loved his toddy. The boys would sometimes get him as full as a goose, and the major would give the doctor some vicious looks at such times. Dr. Nicholson was a great favorite with all the men, and it is said he knew every good place for buttermilk, milk, and eggs from Rio Grande City to Red River, a trifling distance of eight hundred miles. The doctor always messed [ate] with Major Jones, and, mounted on a fine horse, traveled by his side. I don't think Dr. Nicholson ever issued a handful of pills to the boys during the year--he was just with us in case he was needed.[99]

On July 2, Nicholson, who was in Comanche, wrote General Steele that he accepted the appointment and immediately left to join Jones on his inspection tour.[100]

Committed to evaluating his men and their operations in the field rather than from behind a desk in Austin, Jones almost immediately initiated the first of many inspection tours "up and down the line," as he termed it, visiting each of the Battalion's companies. He established an escort for his tours, initially composed of five or six men from each company, but later utilizing just a single company from his command. This group of men was large enough to defend against any Indians that might surprise them, as well as to reinforce the companies if the need should arise. According to one source, Jones, who rode in a light wagon with a saddle horse drawn behind, did not stick to the roads so as not to allow Indians any hint as to his location or direction on return.[101]

> Two four-mule wagons hauled the camp equipage, rations for the men and grain for the horses. One light wagon drawn by two mules and driven by George, the negro [sic] cook, carried the mess outfit, bedding, tent, etc., of Major Jones and Dr. Nicholson . . . On the march Major Jones and Dr. Nicolson rode in front, followed by the captain of the company, the orderly sergeant and the men in double file. Following these came the wagons. An advance guard of two men preceded the column about one-half mile. Four men, known as flankers, two on each side of the company, paralleled the column at a distance of one-half to one mile, depending on the nature of the country . . . The noncommissioned officer with the remaining guard covered the rear and

brought up the pack mules. Thus protected it was almost impossible for the command to be surprised by Indians.[102]

One of the early members of Jones' escort was George F. Steinbeck of Coldwell's company. He described Jones as

> One of the toughest little men I ever met, I mean, by tough, was his endurance. He could sit up perfectly straight on horseback, and ride all day, and never drink a drop of water or eat a bite . . . but Major Jones held himself aloof somewhat; I presume holding his command he had to.[103]

James B. "Jim" Gillett, another member of Jones' escort, recalled that after a day's march, a quartet of musicians—guitar, banjo, and violin—would play around the campfire. Jones would frequently leave his tent to listen to the music. The escort also had a seine net with which to catch fish in any nearby creek.[104]

Jones' first inspection after leaving Austin on June 6 was the Kerrville camp of Captain Neal Coldwell's Company F, which formally organized on June 11 and was readying to move to its camp in Edwards County on the head of the Guadalupe River, as Coldwell had earlier suggested. The company was delayed in organizing because newly-commissioned Lieutenant Pat Dolan was late in arriving at camp. Arriving at the camp on June 13, Jones' only critique was that the company was short of small arms and asked Steele to have twenty pistols and 2,000 cartridges sent. At the same time, Jones expressed to Steele a preference for Colt ammunition, rather than the "unreliable" Smith & Wesson cartridges. On the same day, Jones left to visit Rufe Perry's Company D in Mason County, striking out over rocky, mountainous country with twenty men, three pack mules, and a small wagon for the four-day trek.[105] A dubious honor, the first Ranger to be officially discharged from the Battalion at this time was Fred Newman of Company A, who failed to provide himself with a good horse. Jones enlisted William Callicott in his place.[106]

Captain Jeff Maltby had his own answer for a company surgeon. Dr. W. H. King was enlisted to fill a private's vacancy in Company E. Each member of the company was to pay eighty cents out of each month's salary in addition to the regular salary that King was paid.[107] Unfortunately, the adjutant general, even at this early time, was becoming quite perturbed with Maltby because of the captain's failure to submit the required monthly muster rolls. He found that Maltby's "disposition to make excuses," i.e., that he was too busy chasing Indians and bad guys, was "not creditable in a commander." On June 26, Steele wrote Maltby and called for the reports and an explanation of the delay.[108] When the roll was submitted, Steele found it woefully lacking and returned it for correction, chastising Maltby for his actions, such as mustering in only part of a company, hiring and discharging members of his command without going through Jones or Steele, and arresting men without a warrant.[109] Maltby subsequently defended himself, stating that he acted with local authorities who had "papers properly issued," and that he had understood that he had some discretion in raising a company of men.[110]

Jones reported from Perry's camp on June 22, Company D having moved from Mason County and now camped on Celery Springs, six miles northwest of Menard. He had no criticisms of the company's operations and felt that it would do "good service" given the number of Indian trails in the area.[111] However, the governor received a complaint from Mason County's presiding judge, Wilson Hey, that the company's move from there was unfortunate, stating that a man named Roberts in neighboring Llano County was responsible for wholesale cattle thefts in Mason County.[112] This complaint was a forerunner of significant troubles that Jones would face in Mason County. Traveling on to Maltby's camp without road or guide, Jones moved Company E to Coleman County, as well as Waller's Company A to the northeast corner of Eastland County.[113]

At the end of June, Jones continued to move up the line of companies, expecting to turn around and return to Austin after reaching Jacksboro. He was not aware that his leadership was about to face its first test under fire.

4

NO CARPET-KNIGHT

MAJOR JONES CONTINUED his tour of inspection, arriving next at Maltby's Company E, fifteen miles west of Brownwood, on June 28, 1874. After reviewing the company's activities, Jones determined that all was quiet locally and that the company could do better service elsewhere. He ordered Maltby to move his men to Post Oak Springs, some fifteen miles west of the Santa Anna Mountains in Coleman County. John Waller of Company A was at Maltby's camp at the time, and Jones praised Waller and his men for having "done good service in breaking up bands of outlaws which have been scourging the frontier for several years past, having arrested quite a number of them and driven others to parts unknown," his reference likely being to John Wesley Hardin and his associates in Comanche County. Jones assigned Company A to the southwest corner of Stephens County once Waller could be equipped with some pack mules.

In reporting to Steele from the camp on July 1, Jones made this observation:

> There is a disposition on some portions of the frontier to make use of this command for police purposes which I do not like and which

I give the officers special instructions not to do except in case where the authorities are openly defied by organized bands of outlaws and the civil officers unable to enforce the law, or to arrest such parties for whose arrest they have legal process as may be found in their vicinity.[1]

Jones also appointed J. T. "Tom" Wilson, "recommended by the best citizens" of Palo Pinto, as one of Waller's two lieutenants, although Jones temporarily retained Wilson with his escort.[2]

At the same time that Jones was making his inspection tour, Adjutant General Steele, at Governor Coke's behest, went to DeWitt County to investigate firsthand the ongoing bloodletting in that vicinity, subsequently referred to as the Sutton-Taylor Feud. Steele's investigation determined that when a company of the State Police was in operation in that county several years before, captained by a nefarious villain named Jack Helm, two young men, William and Henry Kelly, were arrested in August of 1870 and started off to Lavaca County where they were wanted for shooting up a circus. However, the guard accompanying the prisoners killed them en route. According to Steele, William Sutton and other members of the guard were subsequently tried for the murder but acquitted, a verdict that did not sit well with the Taylor clan, into which one of the Kellys had married. Steele concluded that the killing of the Kellys triggered the onslaught of violence and assassination in DeWitt County.[3] In actuality, the violence involving Sutton, the Taylors, and others could be traced back to the late 1860s. Steele even noted the presence of John Wesley Hardin in the growing violence.

On March 11, 1874, William Sutton and Gabriel Slaughter were gunned down on a steamer at Indianola by Bill Taylor and a cousin, Jim Taylor, an act that violated an informal peace treaty previously arrived at by both sides. Returning to Austin from DeWitt County on July 10, Steele immediately reported to Coke, envisioning more gunmen joining both sides and the bloodshed escalating.

The conclusion I arrived at is that nothing short of an armed force from some other locality & having no interest in the feuds or quarrels of that county, and of sufficient strength (not less than 50) to ensure the safety

of prisoners against mob violence and to aid in making arrests, will put
a stop to the existing state of violence in DeWitt County. At present
the courts are powerless as against these armed & organized parties.
Indeed, so great is the fear of assassination that was stated to me, that
no information on which to base an indictment could be found in the
case of a murder to which there was not less than forty witnesses.[4]

Governor Coke's response was to authorize the formation of a new
militia company of fifty men from Washington County, appointing a
respected former State Police captain, Leander H. McNelly, to its command. Termed Company A of the Volunteer Militia of Washington
County, the men recruited were to serve for six months and to proceed
without delay to DeWitt County to aid the sheriff there "in the enforcement of the law and to act in all cases in strict subordination to the civil
authorities."[5] Although not a part of the Frontier Battalion, these "Special
Troops," as they came to be termed, subsequently proved most effective in
cleaning up the feud, as well as later gaining prominence and notoriety in
dealing with bandits coming across the Rio Grande from Mexico.[6] Unfortunately, McNelly's force was funded, as were other special units, from the
same appropriation for frontier defense as Jones and his Battalion.

Far removed from the feud in DeWitt County, Jones continued his
inspection tour, arriving on July 10 at the campsite of Captain Stevens'
Company B on the east side of the Brazos River in what subsequently
became Young County. The next day Jones ordered Stevens to move
his camp ten miles east to the Salt Creek where grass and water were
better for the stock. At sunrise the next morning, July 12, during breakfast, two Rangers who had been out looking for some horses that had
strayed off rode into camp and reported the discovery of a fresh Indian
trail.[7] Jones had already posted two small parties on nearby high points
to watch for Indian movement. He now sent Lieutenant Tom Wilson
and a small scouting party of six men to investigate. They rode east and,
about four miles away, ran across a fresh Indian trail headed southeast
from Salt Creek toward Jack County. Wilson sent a man back to the
Ranger camp summoning assistance.[8] Only a week earlier, fifty Indians

had trapped some of Stevens' men in a thicket, the fight going on for close to four hours, and the only casualty being one of the Rangers' horses was slightly wounded.[9]

Jones was aware that the day before, on July 11, a raiding party of Comanches had struck the ranch of J. C. Loving in Jack County, shooting to death a cowhand, John Heath, and stealing several horses.[10] When Wilson's courier relayed the news of the trail, Jones quickly organized a party of men, including Captain Stevens, and set off to catch up with Wilson, who had already begun to follow the trail. Finally joining Wilson, the Ranger party now totaled thirty-five men. Jones examined the Indian tracks and estimated there were about fifty Indians ahead of them. The trail could be clearly seen as they rode quickly over some fifteen miles of open prairie, and they noted places where the Indians had stopped at water holes. The Rangers also spotted chunks of charred beef strewn along the trail that were dropped by their quarry. The lawmen passed the site of a monument commemorating a wagon train massacre three years earlier.[11] The trail then led into mountains located about halfway between old Fort Belknap and the town of Jacksboro, in northwestern Jack County.

As the Rangers began climbing the rocky, rough terrain, the Indians looked back from their position of height and were able to see the oncoming men. The Indians descended the mountains on the east side, then doubled back in order to set up an ambush.[12]

The party of Indians that Jones was following were Kiowas led by Lone Wolf, a chief, and a medicine man, Maman-ti, not the party of Comanches that had killed Heath at Loving's ranch. Lone Wolf was determined to have his braves make a raid somewhere in Texas as a means of avenging the death of his son and his brother, who had been killed by soldiers the previous December while returning to Fort Sill from a raid into Mexico. Maman-ti agreed to help him get that revenge.[13] Why not this group of white men riding pell mell toward them? Some sources relate that the Indian force facing Jones was a combined one of Comanche and Kiowa. Jones himself was of the opinion that the Indians that raided Loving's ranch and the Indians that attacked him had come together, composing a force of at least one hundred, but he failed to designate which tribes were involved.[14] Other sources believe it was solely a Kiowa war party,[15.] and that was likely the case.

The Indians descended into Lost Valley, a hardscrabble habitat of dry washes and ravines below the rocky hills, the slopes of which were dotted with post oak and scrub.[16] Jones and his men, who had been at a gallop, lost the trail in a rough rocky place as they entered the valley at about 11:30 a.m. Searching for the trail, Jones allowed his men to ride on both sides of the ravine. Beyond Jones' experience in the war and Captain Stevens' early experiences with Indians in Wise County, the young men making up the Ranger party were inexperienced and raw, and they were facing experienced warriors hellbent on revenge for their chief's personal loss.

Lone Wolf and Maman-ti quickly devised a plan for the ambush. Hiding his braves on the hillside overlooking the valley floor, Maman-ti and another warrior determined to expose themselves to the oncoming Rangers by dismounting and leading their horses in view of their pursuers as if worn out.[17] But the Rangers apparently never saw the decoy. Still looking for the trail, Jones men were split, part of his force on one side of the ravine running through the valley, and the rest of them about a half mile back in the open prairie. One member of the group described it as "scattered over the prairie looking for the trail."[18] Another Ranger confirmed that "our men became much scattered, every one trying to find the trail himself," when the Indians attacked.[19] Jones' official report too succinctly described what happened:

> We fell back two or three hundred yards where we were joined by the rest of our men, charged them, repulsed them, and drove them about two miles, where they took refuge among the rocks and caves of a mountain ridge. Several of our men having been dismounted in the charge, having only twenty-eight present, all told, we were unable to dislodge them from their position, but formed in a ravine and continued firing at them until they ceased firing and abandoned their position.[20]

The fight lasted close to three or four hours, and, Jones' terse description notwithstanding, much more was involved than a mere trading of shots. As the Rangers entered the valley, Jones split his party into a number of groups to follow different trails left by the Indians. He directed them to remain in touch with each other and be ready to reunite in the event of an attack, although the fact that the men were so scattered spoke loudly to a lack of discipline. Jones led one small party of men into the vicinity of the hidden Kiowas. The Indians opened fire on them with breech-loading rifles, wounding some of the Rangers' horses, and then charged. But the small party temporarily stood its ground, returning the fire, then backed up toward the head of Cameron Creek. The other Ranger parties rejoined their commander and the battle was joined, the war whoops of the charging Kiowas almost as loud as the gunfire.[21] Ranger Ed Carnal recalled riding up to Jones' group and seeing the major calmly astride his horse and directing the placement of his men.[22] Slowly, the Rangers were able to push back the Kiowas, the Indians taking cover at the crest of a rock-capped hill.

Early in the fight, Ranger Lee Corn was hit, his right arm broken near the shoulder, and his horse was killed. Another Ranger, George Moore from Maltby's company, suffered a severe flesh wound in his right leg.[23] When Corn was wounded, he was cut off by the Indians from the rest of his companions and forced to hide in the water, mud, and bushes of a water hole adjacent to the dry creek. A fellow Ranger named Wheeler came to his aid, plunging into the water hole with him,[24] and the two remained concealed there for the rest of the battle.

With the Indians entrenched on the hillside and directing a fierce fire at the Rangers, Captain Stevens urged Jones that the men needed to find cover. Jones ordered his men to fall back and take cover in the dry ravine that ran through Lost Valley. As the Rangers retreated, Walter Robertson's horse was killed, hit by five bullets, and Ranger William A. "Billy" Glass, of Stevens' company, was shot down. Glass' companions thought he was dead and left him where he fell as they scrambled for the cover of the ravine about 300 yards from the Indian force. The ravine was only about four or five feet deep, and they were forced to hunker down to avoid being hit. Their horses weren't afforded any protection and a number suffered gunshot wounds. The Rangers now returned fire with their pistols, there not being enough time to stop and reload their single-shot Sharps rifles.[25]

As the two sides began potshotting at each other, Billy Glass, who had been shot five times, began to laboriously crawl toward his comrades, calling out to them piteously for help and to not let him fall into the hands of the Kiowas. Two Indians could be seen stealthily trying to sneak up to him between the trees that dotted the hillside.[26] Zack Wattles, who had been recruited in Corsicana by Major Jones, tossed his weapon aside and ran to his wounded friend. The 130-pound Wattles straddled the groaning Glass, who, with what little strength he had left, locked his arms around his rescuer's waist. Slowly, laboriously, with his comrades providing strong covering fire, and with the Indians continuing to blanket them with gunfire, Wattles dragged the wounded man toward the ravine, stopping twice to catch his breath.[27] The wounded man said nothing more and died a short time after he was brought to the ravine, earning the dubious distinction of being the first Ranger of the young Frontier Battalion to die in the line of duty.

A siege set in, the Indians no longer charging the Rangers, and desultory gunfire was traded between the two parties for several hours. Jones posted Rangers William Lewis and Walter Robertson on a ridge, behind some trees vacated by the Indians, in order to watch the Rangers' flanks and rear positions. During a lull in the fighting, Lieutenant Wilson, who had been cut off by the Indians from the main party, approached the two men. As he fanned himself with his hat in the July heat, Indian fire cut through a dead limb in the tree under which he sought cover, the limb falling on Wilson's head, cutting him. Looking at the blood, Wilson exclaimed, "God, boys, I'm shot, sure as hell." He hastily went down the hill where Dr. Nicholson assured him that he had not been shot.[28]

Major Jones did not join his men crouched down in the ravine; he walked along the ravine in full view of the Indians 300 yards away, encouraging his men: "steady boys," "fire low," "tend strictly to business and all the Indians there can't pull us out of this ravine," and urging them to conserve their ammunition. Ed Carnal, seeing his commander leaning casually against a post oak tree above him while Indian fire was

George W. Stevens (*Author's Photo*)

cutting limbs off above his head, suggested to Jones that he was expos-
ing himself unnecessarily. Jones responded that he didn't think so; that
someone had to be out of the ravine to observe the enemy's actions.[29]
At one point, an Indian bullet struck the tree near Jones' head, flinging
bark and splinters into his face, causing him to fall over backward to
the ground, but without any injury.[30] If he saw an Indian stick his head
up from behind a rock, he would point him out to a Ranger and direct
him to aim steady and shoot to hit.[31] Foolhardy or not, Jones demonstrated that brand of leadership and personal courage that had stood
him in good stead during the war and would continue to do so while he
commanded the Frontier Battalion. Jones' esteem among his men was
forged that day.

The strong July heat began to impact the Rangers huddled in the ravine, and lack of water became as much a prevalent concern as their diminishing ammunition. As the afternoon wore on, Jones assumed that the Indians were in no hurry to leave, given their commanding position, and were prepared to stay there all night. Driven by thirst, at least one Ranger allegedly used his Bowie knife to dig up moist dirt in the river bed, which he crammed into his mouth, alternately cursing and praying for relief. Not having had any water since that morning, tongues began to swell. Wounded men begged for water. Because of the immediate Indian threat, Jones was reluctant to allow any of his men to take canteens and risk going for water. His men persisted, however. D. W. H. "Dave" Bailey and Mel Porter insisted that they were going for water, even if they got killed. They gathered empty canteens from among the men, then mounted horses and raced to a water hole several hundred yards off.

While Porter filled the canteens, Bailey remained mounted, keeping a vigilant eye for Indians. The firing had subsided somewhat and the Rangers watching from the ravine began to feel more confident about their mission. Suddenly, some twenty-five Kiowas appeared from the west, headed directly toward the water hole. The men at the ravine began firing, hoping to alert the two men. Porter leaped up and jumped into the creek, racing away on foot as fast as he could. Bailey attempted to race back to the ravine, but he was quickly surrounded by the Indians and his confused horse stopped. The men at the ravine, helpless to do anything, knew that their companion was a dead man.

Porter continued running along the creek, finally plunging into a water hole to hide from two Indians in pursuit. It was the same hole in which Corn and Wheeler had taken refuge. Porter's sudden appearance alarmed the wounded Corn, who, thinking the interloper was an Indian, took a shot at him, cradling his rifle between his knees, but fortunately missing. The three men drove off the two Indians chasing Porter.[32] Bailey, captured by the Indians, was not so lucky. Depending on whose account is most accurate, the Kiowas exacted Lone Wolf's revenge in a most blood-thirsty manner. According to William Callicott:

After killing Ed [*sic*] Bailey they scalped him, carving him up like a beef steak and then taking the butt end of their guns and stamping his skull and brains in the ground in sight of the Major and the boys in the creek. After they had satisfied themselves with Bailey's dead body, they then took his horse, a fine one, gun and pistols, all the canteens of water and also the Major's spy glass.[33]

Another version by Ranger Jim McIntire was more exaggerated and gruesome:

After shooting seventeen arrows into Bailey's back, they rode up and pulled him from his horse. Then we were compelled to witness the most revolting sight of our lives. They held Bailey up in full view, and cut him up, and ate him alive. They started by cutting off his nose and ears; then hands and arms. As fast as a piece was cut off, they would grab it, and eat it as ravenously as the most voracious wild beast . . . We could see the blood running from their mouths as they munched the still quivering flesh. They would bat their eyes and lick their mouths after every mouthful.[34]

An account ascribed to the Indians gave their version of what happened to the unfortunate Ranger:

When I got to the place where they had killed the other ranger, I learned that Dohausen had thrust him off his horse with a spear, but that Mama-day-te had made first coup by touching him with his hand. Lone Wolf and Maman-ti and everybody was there. Lone Wolf got off his horse and chopped the man's head to pieces with his brass hatchet-pipe. Then he took out his butcher knife and cut open the man's bowels. Everyone who wanted to shot arrows into it or poked at it with their lances.[35]

The Indians had divided into three parties, one directly in front of Jones and his men, the other two to either flank. The Rangers expected a charge, but shots directed at the flanks drove them off.[36]

With a yell from their chief at about 4 o'clock, the Indians melted away. Once he was convinced that the fight was ended, Jones surveyed the damage, finding that two men—Glass and Bailey—were dead, and two were wounded—Corn and Moore. Thirteen horses had been killed or seriously wounded, and two more only slightly wounded. Jones determined that at least three Indians had been killed and three more wounded, although the Kiowas could very well have carried off or buried additional dead and taken other wounded with them.[37] The most immediate need for the Rangers was to move to a place with better protection, since they could not be sure whether or not the Indians were still lurking in the vicinity. The few horses remaining were rounded up, as well as a few stray Indian ponies. Glass' body was wrapped in a blanket and strapped to a horse, and the wounded mounted on others. Jones sent a courier, John P. Holmes, on a wounded horse to Jacksboro, his instructions to contact the commander of United States troops quartered there at Fort Richardson to come to their assistance. The message sent by Jones indicates that at the time he sent Holmes, he was not fully aware of the status of his force:

> I was attacked today four miles South of Lovings ranch by about one hundred well armed Indians. Had only thirty-five men and lost one man killed, one wounded and five missing. Fought them three hours and drove them off, but have not force enough to attack them. Can you send me assistance to Lovings. The Indians are still in the valley. Lost twelve horses.[38]

Although he was pursued a short distance by Indians, Holmes made it to Jacksboro where he contacted a cavalry captain named Baldwin.[39] Within an hour, Captain Baldwin and 100 black troopers of the Tenth Cavalry Regiment were en route to Lost Valley, arriving there at about one the next morning.[40]

With many of his men on foot, and leaving behind Bailey's mutilated body, Jones led his force to Loving's ranch some twelve miles from the scene of the fight. Along the way, as they came to pools of stagnant, scum-covered water, young Rangers broke from the slow-moving column and drank the brackish contents. They reached the ranch at about midnight and food was obtained. Using boards from a smokehouse to construct a coffin, Billy Glass was buried there, after which everyone got a few hours of some badly needed sleep. Before sunrise, at about 3 a.m., Jones returned with his men to Lost Valley to meet Holmes and the cavalry troop, who arrived at daylight.[41]

Once at the scene of the fight, the force quickly secured the mutilated body of Dave Bailey.

> Poor fellow! There was little of him left. His clothing was all gone and his body was terribly mutilated. He had been lanced and cut with Bowie knives until it was with difficulty one could recognize the remains as being those of a human. Even his head had been taken entirely away. It was a sandy location where he lay, and we dug a grave with our Bowie knives and drinking cups and wrapping the body in a blanket we laid it away in the shallow grave.[42]

Jones' men and the army troops rode around the better part of the day looking to find the trail of the Indians, but located only scattered trails, making it nearly impossible to determine the right direction. Finally, at the end of the day, the army troops returned to Jacksboro, and Jones rounded up the men who had been on the scout with him and headed back to Captain Stevens' camp on Flat Top Mountain. Jones subsequently went to Jacksboro to leave his two wounded men at the Fort Richardson post hospital and to find replacement horses. After that, he resumed his inspection tour, going to the camp of Captain Ikard's Company C at Wichita.[43]

Jones' first conflict as commander of the Frontier Battalion can probably be rightfully criticized. A lack of military-type discipline in approaching the Lost Valley led to his men being ambushed and placed in a difficult defensive posture. Men and horses were lost, perhaps needlessly, because of a lack of proper caution. It was a fresh Indian trail indicating a party larger than the Ranger force. Nevertheless, Jones himself came out of the fight with an unblemished reputation for coolness and courage. One newspaper stated: "He is highly commended for his daring bravery on the occasion, and for his skill as a commander. We have no doubt but he will teach the Indians before long that they can not murder Texans with impunity."[44] Indeed, Jones had rallied his inexperienced troops and ultimately achieved a stalemate with the superior force of Kiowas. One of his own men, Zack Wattles, in writing home to the *Corsicana Observer* just after the fight, observed:

> In conclusion, I must say a word or two concerning our Major's management of the affair. His cool conduct, and at the same time his unmistakable, determined courage elicited, though not uncalled for, many remarks from both experienced and inexperienced frontiersmen, as to his capacity as an officer, and carried conviction to the hearts of many not knowing him personally, that we in truth had an officer in whom we could put the utmost confidence in all cases of emergency.[45]

An Austin newspaper recognized Jones' "marked military ability."

> Major Jones is no carpet-knight, no stay at home officer who commands troops from a secure distance, but goes to the front himself and shares the danger and the fighting with his men . . . We firmly believe that Major Jones, by his forethought and by his judicious action in connection with the United States troops, will so thoroughly chastise the Indians during this campaign that there will be peace for a long period thereafter.[46]

Having experienced battle with the Kiowas at Lost Valley, Jones was now of the opinion that large parties of Indians would be regularly coming into Texas from Fort Sill. It would be necessary to combine the operations of Companies B and C in order to have sufficiently strong scouting parties in the area that could stand up to an attack.[47] Jones ordered Ikard to move his company to the southwest corner of Clay County, near Stevens' camp in the northwest corner of Young County,[48] from where the two could work in tandem to thwart the Indian incursions. Fortunately for the state's concern about providing adequate frontier defense, the federal government at this point got serious about the Indian problem. On June 10, a group of buffalo hunters had stood off a combined attack by Comanche and Cheyenne warriors at Adobe Walls in the Texas Panhandle. One result of that battle was that the United States Army launched a major campaign to protect the Panhandle, ultimately referred to as the

Red River War. Large numbers of soldiers were introduced into North Texas—an effort that ultimately played the most important role in stemming Indian raids into Texas, even though Jones and the Frontier Battalion were given significant credit.[49]

While in Jacksboro on July 15, Jones issued his second general order directing his company commanders to arrest eighty-six named persons for which warrants had been issued in various counties. Included on the list was a warrant for John Wesley Hardin, charged with carrying a pistol, as well as for a cowboy with which the Frontier Battalion would have considerable trouble, Richard "Dick" Dublin, wanted for a murder in Coryell County.[50] In Jacksburo, Jones likely learned that his brother-in-law, Joshua Halbert, died in Navarro County on July 19.[51]

The major reached Ikard's Company C, located on the Big Wichita River in Archer County, on July 22. Determining, while at Jacksboro, that the company was too far out to do any good, he had ordered it moved some twenty miles southeast near the southwest corner of Clay County, closer to Stevens' camp.[52] While at Ikard's camp, Jones issued his first personnel discharges, H. Davies for "having been involved in a difficulty that renders it necessary for him to be absent from his company," and D. C. Kyle, for whom Dr. Nicholson had issued a "certificate of disability."[53]

Captain Maltby's Company E had the next encounter with Indians. On July 24, Maltby ordered Lieutenant B. F. Best with twenty-one men to scout the Table Mountains in northeast Runnels County. Not finding a fresh trail, Best allowed Sergeant M. T. Israel to go on with ten men. They rode all night, finally stopping for a brief rest, and at daylight discovered six Indians not very far from them. A hasty pursuit began, and after about five miles, the Rangers drew close to the fleeing Indians. Gunfire was exchanged and Corporal H. Sackett's horse was killed, throwing him to the ground. Sackett grabbed his rifle and shot the nose off an Indian who was aiming at him and who was later captured and died the next day of his wounds. Two other Indians were killed outright and the other three, one of whom was believed to be a woman, escaped. It was confirmed that these Indians had also come from the reservation at Fort Sill.[54] One Ranger, L. R. Davis, received a minor wound in a hand,

and two other horses were slightly injured. As a trophy, Maltby proudly displayed the scalp of the wounded Indian who died, as well as beaded ornaments, quivers, and a shield.[55]

One member of Maltby's company, William Lowrance, wrote many years later that an Indian named Jape surrendered to the Rangers during this fight and was taken back to Company E's camp in Coleman County. According to Lowrance, the Indian was kept there for five or six days, even sharing a drink of whiskey with Maltby. Then the Indian was taken to a point west of the camp, released on an "old poor horse," and told to "run for his dear life." After giving him a good start, four Rangers were then dispatched to go after him and kill him, which they did. Official records do not mention such an episode, but another Ranger, C. M. Grady, repeated the same tale.[56]

Starting back "down the line," Jones stopped off again at Company B's camp, in Young County, where he discharged four privates. He allowed one man to leave the service when another substituted in his place. Another was married and should not have been enlisted, while another's family needed their son's assistance at home. The fourth had a physical disability from an "old wound."[57]

Because some confusion had developed regarding how different ranks were to be allocated in each company, Adjutant General Steele sent out a clarification. Henceforth, each company would have one captain, one first lieutenant, one second lieutenant, six sergeants, six corporals, and sixty-three privates.[58] However, such strength would never be achieved in any company, a problem that would persistently plague Jones in directing the operations of the Battalion.

5

A HEAVY TASK

AS JONES MADE HIS WAY BACK DOWN the line to his headquarters in Austin, the companies continued their hunt for raiding Indians and wayward outlaws. On August 3, General Steele commissioned J. T. Nelson of Stephenville as a second lieutenant in Waller's Company A, apparently without consulting Jones.[1] Along the way, as he revisited each company, Jones stopped off at Fort Griffin where he discussed the Indian problem with Army General Don Carlos Buell, who promised his cooperation with the Battalion. Captains Stevens and Waller were instructed to keep the general apprised of Indian activity in their jurisdictions, and Buell made available to them two Tonkawa Indians as scouts and trailers.[2]

Although there is no record of it in Frontier Battalion files, Private Thurlow Weed wrote his brother that on August 3 a lieutenant in Maltby's Company E, leading ten men, came upon a party of thirty-seven Indians attacking a stagecoach that had an escort of twenty United States soldiers. While the soldiers apparently failed to help fend off the attack, the Rangers were reported to have routed the attackers, killing at least two with four others carried off by the Indians, and recovering some forty horses.[3]

Another personnel problem reared up in August when Captain Neal Coldwell in Frio County received written notice from his second lieutenant, F. H. Nelson, complaining that Private Jasper Corn willfully disobeyed his order to take water to other men of Company F who were tending a campfire. He said that Corn had refused to submit to arrest, and asked for his discharge. Vociferously complaining about "such damn officers, giving such damn shitten' orders," Corn had come to Nelson's tent mounted and armed, daring the lieutenant to arrest him.[4] Coldwell forwarded to Jones the letter from Nelson, regretting that the lieutenant "does not get along very well with the company," and knew nothing of frontier service or "wood craft." Corn had made a good Ranger, he said, and Coldwell regretted having to discharge him.[5] Jones ultimately discharged Corn on September 8 for "mutinous conduct."[6]

Patently aware of the animosity of the men of Company F toward him, Nelson applied to be transferred to Jones' personal staff, "not wishing to remain longer in a company where we do not have strict military discipline as the law provides." Nelson stayed away from the company, in Boerne in Kendall County, "as I do not think my life is safe with a portion of our company."[7] Jones' response was that no such appointment could be made, and, since there was no other company to which he could be assigned, the only option was to either return to his company or resign.[8]

Jones had already reduced to the ranks a first sergeant assigned to Coldwell because of similar insubordinate conduct toward Nelson, even though Coldwell had reported that the sergeant was also a good man. The men in Coldwell's company had even generated a petition calling for Nelson's resignation. Jones concluded that Nelson was "not a suitable man for the position . . . It seems that he has never had command of any of the men but what he has had some personal difficulty with them."[9] Nelson finally got the hint and resigned from the Battalion on September 12, 1874.[10]

Arriving at Maltby's camp on August 9, 1874, Jones was dismayed to find the men of Company E idle in camp, all of the officers being absent. Maltby had been gone for about ten days and it was anticipated he would not return for another two weeks, having left camp partly to visit his home and also to go to Austin for pistols that he had ordered. Lieutenant Connell was supposedly sick at home, and had been for a month. Jones was unaware of any of this. The other company lieutenant, B. F. Best, was in Brownwood to settle a problem with a contractor who had provided the company with bad flour. The company was spread out over some ten to twelve acres, and the horses were "scattered promiscuously in and around camp, foot loose with only one man guarding them during the day and only two on guard at night." In addition, Maltby had left instructions giving furloughs for a number of men simultaneously to go home to their respective counties for visits, which Jones immediately countermanded. He wrote General Steele:

> I find it the most difficult thing to make the men of this command and some of the officers understand that they are not at liberty to go home when they please or get substitutes or have their brother or friend take their place for a while. I have established the rule however and am determined to maintain it, hoping that I will be sustained by the Governor and yourself, otherwise I can have no system or discipline in the command.[11]

Chagrined at the sloppy manner in which Maltby was leading his company, Jones instructed Best, upon his return, to get the company actively engaged in scouting. He then proceeded on to Perry's Company D on the San Saba River.[12] Writing Maltby, Jones issued a lengthy admonishment: "This is no holiday service in which we are engaged, but real and earnest work for the proper, faithful, and constant performance of which we will be held to a strict accountability by the Governor and the people of the State." He directed Maltby to "require and enforce strict obedience to orders, a rigid observance of guard duty, and instruct your company in the simple and ordinary movements of the company drill so as to be able to handle it with facility on the field."[13]

Maltby attempted to excuse his absence by claiming that he had to go to Austin to attend court and decided to wait there a little longer to pick up the shipment of pistols. Finding no urgency justifying Maltby's absence from his company, General Steele supported Jones: "I will say that if you wish any officer discharged for not attending to his duties, a statement to that effect will cause his immediate removal."[14] Lieutenant J. G. Connell, who reported on his extensive illness that had commenced on July 7, submitted his resignation from the Battalion on August 25, "being incapacitated for duty on frontier service."[15]

Arriving at Mason, Jones issued orders to Captain Rufe Perry to move Company D to twelve miles below Menard. He casually mentioned that the people of Mason were "a good deal excited in regard to the cow thieves

W. J. "Captain Jeff" Maltby (*W. J. Maltby*, Captain Jeff or Frontier Life in Texas With the Texas Rangers, *Colorado, Texas: Whipkey Printing, 1906.*)

and numerous coming in now of more depredations of the same kind." He stated that he would "look into it and go after them if I find there is anything in it."[16] This was prophetic, as the bloodletting that would occur in that neighborhood would draw the Frontier Battalion into a controversy that threatened to mar its growing reputation for effectiveness.

In June, Mason County's county judge, Wilson Hey, petitioned Governor Coke for Rangers to be stationed there, complaining of men from other counties, such as A. G. Roberts of adjacent Llano County, stealing cattle from Mason County citizens.[17] According to an account published in the *Fredericksburg Sentinel*, alleged to have been a letter submitted by Mason merchant David Doole, Mason County Sheriff John Clark, with a posse of eighteen men, rode into Llano County on August 9 and arrested eleven cowboys working for Roberts who were in possession of 200 head of cattle, supposedly taken from Mason County. The cattle were reportedly penned, but some of Roberts' men, angered by the arrests, were said to have shot at and stampeded the herd in an effort to get rid of the evidence. Two of the jailed cowboys were tried in Mason County on August 13, but acquitted for lack of evidence.

As the court adjourned on the 13th, some forty armed men led by John Baird confronted Judge Hey, telling him to set bond for Roberts' men or they would take them out of jail anyway. Hey agreed to set bonds, but quickly notified Sheriff Clark, who rushed some fifty well-armed men to guard the jail. Hey then refused to set any bonds. The next morning, additional citizens joined the jail guard to fend off any attempt to free the prisoners. Baird and his men reportedly left Mason, in their anger shooting at cows and at a schoolhouse as they passed by. Charges against three of the men were dropped so that they could testify as witnesses, and the remaining six were convicted of cattle theft and assessed a fine of $2,500. The prisoners posted an appeal bond and were released, but threatening letters were soon directed by Roberts at important Mason citizens.[18]

It was also reported that Jones, with forty Rangers and a posse of Mason County citizens, started after a party of Roberts' men, supposedly again busy stealing cattle.[19] A purported log of Frontier Battalion activity for the May-November 1874 period makes this notation for August 20, although it does not state who is involved: "Went into Mason County at request of citizens to investigate troubles there; succeeded in quieting the disturbance."[20] Although there is no official record that Jones led such a mission, he did write his father that upon receipt of a petition from Mason County officers and citizens, he took his escort and joined Sheriff Clark and his posse in a hunt for the alleged thieves. No such band could be located, and Jones believed that the number of thieves and "the mischief done by them" had been greatly exaggerated. Satisfied that the thieves, if any, had departed the area, he "succeeded in quieting the fears of the citizens, most of whom were Germans, and restored peace to the troubled neighborhood."[21]

Another Ranger of Perry's company, S. P. Elkins, wrote years later that he was part of Jones' escort as they started from Mason to Fredericksburg. As the party reached Fort Mason, however,

> We found a big crowd of men gathered there. The sheriff came to Major Jones and told him that Roberts, an outlaw, was camped two miles from Fort Mason and was stealing all the cattle that he and his gang could find and they had sent the sheriff a challenge to come to a certain place. The sheriff and his large party fell in front of our little bunch and we went about six miles out on the Fredericksburg road, when they sidetracked. Major Jones called for thirty volunteers and they promptly stepped out. Twelve men were left with the pack mules and we went on for two or three miles when the sheriff made the proposition that the rangers, when they came up to the outlaws, demand their surrender, and if they refused, we were to open the fight and the citizens would reinforce us. We were about three hundred yards from the outlaws' camp, and Major Jones sent a man to demand their surrender. When the man reached the camp he found it had been vacated, and no outlaws were there. So the citizens returned to Mason.[22]

The problems in Mason County would reemerge shortly, but for now Jones was satisfied that Ranger involvement was no longer required, and he resumed his trek to Fredericksburg. Nevertheless, Mason merchant David Doole published another letter in the *San Antonio Herald*, the wording of which was interpreted by Jones that the men of Company D were "depredating extensively in the settlements" and that Jones would "bring them to time." Taking exception to the insinuation, Jones wrote to Doole, demanding that he make a corrected statement. Doole apologized to Jones and said that he would write a clarification to the *Herald*, but such correction apparently never occurred.[23]

Jones now having completed his first tour of inspection, which took nearly three months, the men of the Frontier Battalion had all seen and met their commander, and had been introduced to the high standards he was setting for them. It was understood that the Battalion "was a military organization and not a holiday excursion at state expense."[24] In a rare moment of introspection, Jones optimistically reflected at this point in time on the significance of his position:

> I find that I have a heavy task before me. To protect five hundred miles of frontier from Indian depredations for twelve months with four hundred and fifty men, and only three hundred thousand dollars, is an undertaking that a much stouter heart than mine might very reasonably hesitate to engage in, especially when the appropriation is also to pay any minute companies that may be called out during the year, four of which are now in the field. But I have undertaken it and will go through with it, doing the best I can with the limited means at my command . . . My health has been good all the time, and was never better than it is now. I believe that I can stand as much hardship, fatigue, hunger and thirst as any man in my command; have never been very much worn out with fatigue, very hungry or suffering from thirst; though I have had many of my men to complain terribly from all these causes . . . I believe the Battalion has so far given entire satisfaction to the people of the frontier and to the officials here [Austin]. I have been very heartily congratulated by many of the leading men here, and believe that we have rendered valuable service to the frontier . . . [25]

Jones wanted to deploy his men for an extended campaign in the fall against the Indians, starting at Jacksboro, where supplies would be stored. It was his idea to take five companies and make a scout of some six or seven hundred miles over a three-month period to the headwaters of the Pease, Wichita, Brazos, and Colorado Rivers. However, the plan was immediately in some jeopardy because the United States Army was now beginning to concentrate federal troops in the Texas Panhandle, likely rendering his expedition an unnecessary one. In addition, Governor Coke was of the opinion that it was more important for the Battalion to remain as it was on the frontier to thwart any raid the Indians might make in the interior of the state, especially once the Indians discovered army troops were missing from other posts in Texas when those troops were transferred to the Panhandle.[26]

Indian raids had not subsided yet. On August 24, 1874, a raiding party struck at Decatur in Wise County, stealing some 100 horses. On the next night, some thirty-five warriors brought 250 horses back up through Wise County from Denton County, killing and scalping the wife and two children of a man named Huff, who was himself missing. A party of men recaptured the horses, but the Indians escaped. General Steele was asked by citizens to move Stevens' company closer to them, and Steele suggested to Jones that several of the companies might be concentrated at the upper end of the line.[27] Jones pointed out that to move two companies would leave Jack and Young Counties unprotected, as well as portions of Parker and Palo Pinto Counties, concluding that the current placement of companies was appropriate to the threat.[28] Maltby reported to Jones that twelve of the men from Company E, who were in Jones' escort on August 12 when the major went to Captain Perry's camp, were attacked by Indians upon their return to the company camp. Eleven horses were lost, and the Rangers were only able to wound several of the Indians, who got away.[29]

Jones did not linger long in Austin before commencing another inspection tour. By September 5, he was in Menard County with Coldwell's Company F. He found the company in good shape, but Coldwell's horses were worn out after a long pursuit of Indians a few days earlier.[30] While at Coldwell's camp, Jones issued a general order directing a procedure for couriers along the line between companies and requiring semimonthly activity reports from commanders in addition to the regular

Neal Coldwell (*James B. Gillett*, Six Years With the Texas Rangers,
Austin, Texas: Von Boeckmann-Jones, 1921.)

end-of-month reports. With Maltby's experience in mind, Jones directed the commanders to provide for strict and prompt obedience to orders and to provide instruction in the "ordinary and simple maneuvers of the company drill." Furloughs could be granted by commanders, but for no more than four men at any one time, and sufficient to allow for no more than a two-day visit at home, given thirty miles per day travel time. Preference was to be given to "the most necessitous or deserving."[31]

Among some other personnel actions brought to his attention, in this case on the recommendation of Captain Perry, Jones terminated the employment of Private Martin Sublette of Company D for being asleep while on guard duty.[32] However, members of Perry's command, including Perry himself, petitioned the major to reinstate the private. "He was drinking at the time and not able for duty . . . He pledges himself to remain a sober man & not touch intoxicating liquors while in the service." Jones revoked his order, although it was to no avail; Sublette deserted in mid-November.[33] Also while at Coldwell's camp, Jones sent out directives to Companies A, B, C, and E moving them to new campsites.[34] Jones also took notice of deserters from the Rangers, even posting notice in the newspapers.[35] Some rumblings of discontent were being heard in the companies because of the delay in pay getting to the troops in a timely fashion.

The first of Jones' captains to leave the Battalion was Company A's John R. Waller. Jones granted him leave of absence on September 20, 1874, until such time as his resignation was received.[36] Jones wrote Steele: "I regret this resignation, particularly at this time when there is so much disaffection in the command on account of getting no pay, but he has reasons sufficient for himself and which induce me to approve it . . . I am at a loss how to replace him."[37]

Maltby suffered another embarrassing lapse about this time, a disaster that involved the death of a third Ranger. In the early morning hours of September 23, 1874, Company E was camped on Home Creek, about eight miles south of Coleman. There having been no rain for about three months, the creek was practically dry. Maltby's camp was on the west bank. At about one o'clock in the morning, rain began to fall in torrents. It was not long before a Ranger guarding the horses came to make sure the men were awakened, as the creek was quickly rising. Hiram "Curley" Hatcher was sharing a tent with Rangers Jim Paulk and W. H. Cliff when the alarm was given. Within five minutes of the alarm, the men in the camp, after trying to reach their horses on the picket line, had to take to any available tree surrounding the camp. Hatcher and two men tried to ride their unsaddled horses to high ground, but a wall of water, estimated from four to ten feet high, struck them and washed them off their mounts. Carried some distance in the strong current, accompanied by lightning and thunder, Hatcher and Paulk were finally able to latch onto a pecan tree, where they stayed in the branches for about an hour, shivering in the cold temperature. Using flint and steel, a fire was started on land above the rushing water and men began clambering out of trees in the area. Those who could not get out of the trees fired their sidearms to alert the others to their whereabouts. Ranger Cliff was swept away by the flood and drowned.

With daylight and the subsidence of the water, what surviving horses could be located were rounded up and returned to the camp. Hatcher volunteered to ride to Brownwood where Maltby was located at the time. Maltby immediately ordered that bread be secured from the nearest ranch and a search begun for additional subsistence for men and horses. In addition to the loss of Cliff, who was from western Kentucky, seven horses and one pack mule were drowned, and four horses were badly disabled. Much camp equipage was lost, but by September 30, Maltby was able to report that the company was "properly and militarily encamped, capable, and ready to do the State good service."[38] Hatcher would be dishonorably discharged from the Battalion the following November for "mutinous and insubordinate conduct."[39]

Jones remained concerned about the failure to get his men paid on time quarterly. He complained to General Steele,

I find much dissatisfaction and disposition to "quit and go home" among the men on the whole line, on account of not being paid at the expiration of the first quarter. Many of them had contracted debts to be paid at that time. Others have mothers, sisters, and brothers dependent upon them to whom they expected to send money, and all of them are warned by the cool nights that it is time to provide their necessary supply of winter clothing, which they are not able to do without their pay. I have succeeded, almost beyond my expectations, so far, in meeting them, but you are aware that the government only furnishes them rations, and they must have clothing before a great while. If we can get as much as fifty thousand dollars, pay funds, by the last of this month, or the middle of next, all will be well; otherwise, I fear serious trouble with many of the men. I have made them no promises, but assure them that the Governor and other officials are doing all in their power to get the money, and that they will be paid as soon as a sufficient amount of bonds can be sold, or the money comes in from taxes. I hope, moreover, that no attempt will be made to pay them with warrants; this would be scarcely more satisfactory than no pay at all, as they would have to submit to such a serious discount to get money for them.[40]

The burden was on Quartermaster Martin Kenney to make the financial arrangements in Austin and get the funds disbursed as quickly as he could. Jones sent him Sergeant J. P. Holmes with twelve men to act as escorts.[41]

On October 3, Jones arrived at Stevens' Company B near Jacksboro, having encountered considerable delay because of excessive rain and high water encountered en route. Finding that prairie grasses had been burnt off, he pondered the difficulty the company would have in locating appropriate campsites where horses could graze. He could report with some satisfaction that there appeared to be no immediate Indian threat at the time.[42]

An Austin newspaper reported that a Ranger from Company A, Corporal G. B. Morphis, had been killed after Indians had charged into the company's camp on October 15.[43] However, no such incident occurred. Morphis was reported by his commander as "quite low" on October 3,[44] and the Ranger was sent to Stephenville for treatment of "typo malarial fever."[45] While he may then have died, Ranger records show only that Morphis was discharged on October 15.[46]

Taking 100 men with him, Jones left Jacksboro on October 8 to scout to the Pease River and the upper waters of the Wichita for Indians as he had earlier planned. The scheme was to intercept any raiding parties, or find a trail and follow it to where the Indians were making camp. However, recent rains had removed any sign of Indian passage, and Jones and his party found no Indians after riding for 350 miles. Returning to Jacksboro on October 24, he was able to tell Steele:

I am happy to report that the whole Battalion is now in good working order, the officers and men in fine spirits and doing their duty in protecting the frontier of the State from the depredations of the Indians as well as it can be done by so small a number of men . . . Having passed over the entire line of frontier from the head of the Nueces to Red River three times recently, I am satisfied that the Battalion is so disposed as to render all the service possible to the frontier, in proportion to the necessities of the different localities.[47]

Pleased as he was, Jones cautioned company commanders not to share government-provided rations with "such camp-followers and loafers as may choose to congregate at and lie around camps of the several companies under pretence [sic] of wanting to join the Rangers."

Anticipating that the Frontier Battalion's appropriation may be reduced, Jones ordered that no more recruits be hired "in view of the fact that it may be necessary to disband a portion of the command before a great while." Urging the command on to greater effort, he directed the captains to "require of the men all the service that can be performed with justice to their horses, in scouting up and down the line, or on such longer scouts or expeditions against the Indians as it may be expedient for them to make."[48]

But personnel problems continued to plague Jones and the Frontier Battalion. On October 27, Captain Stevens complained about multiple lapses of behavior on the part of his first lieutenant, Seborn Graham Sneed McGarrah. Stevens alleged that McGarrah gambled off a captured Indian pony, that he became intoxicated on two occasions while on duty, that he disobeyed an order to keep scouts out while Stevens was absent, and that "on various other occasions he has visited Jacksboro and acted in a very unbecoming manner and in his visits to that place, he has invariably overstayed his time."[49] McGarrah tendered his resignation and the charges were not pursued.[50] However, that was not the end of it. In November, McGarrah preferred charges against Stevens, claiming that the captain improperly enlisted married men, as well as hired three men suffering from ruptures, thereby being disabled, all in violation of Governor Coke's orders.[51]

Jones sent a copy of the charges to Stevens asking for his response.[52] Stevens responded that he had, indeed, enlisted married men, but he defended his actions by proclaiming them as neighbors of his who were well experienced as Indian fighters prior to their enlistment and who had promised that "the incumbrance [*sic*] of a family" would not be an excuse in failing to meet their duties or in obtaining a leave of absence. "I recognized the spirit and intention of said order, but as I anticipated by the enlistment of these men none of the evils intended to be avoided by it have arisen." As to the ruptured men, a physician certified that such medical condition did not render them physically disabled for duty.[53] The two men involved (the third was deceased), David Manning and A. B. Cartwright, both swore that they had concealed the fact of their ruptures, and Company B's noncommissioned officers swore that both men had performed their duties "cheerfully" and had never complained of any disability.[54] There is no record that any action was taken on McGarrah's complaint.

Company D experienced a party of five Indians charging its horse guard on October 19 as horses were being unhobbled before sunset to go into camp. Gunfire was exchanged, but no one was hit. A pursuit was quickly organized, but the Indians scattered and no trail could be found. On the next day, the trail was found, and the Rangers finally encountered the Indians on the Little Saline Creek, the Indians firing at their pursuers and then scattering once more without any reported injuries. Company D also reported that on October 13, County Judge Hey of Mason County came to the camp asking for assistance in anticipation of a vigilance committee being formed at Mason in a few days. Sergeant N. O. Reynolds and five men were dispatched to the town on the 14th to "quell the intended riot," and they returned to camp on the 22nd reporting all quiet.[55]

Leaving Stevens' camp in Lost Valley on October 29, Jones started down the line back toward Kerrville and Coldwell's company, anticipating arrival there in mid-November. He could report happily that the quartermaster was now traveling from company to company paying the men.[56] However, the legislature would be convening in January and Governor Coke asked Jones to meet with him in Austin after visiting Coldwell's camp in order that the Governor could include in his message to the legislature information regarding the impact of the Frontier Battalion.[57] In addition, the governor was looking for some means of reducing expenditures by downsizing the Battalion.[58]

On his own initiative, without consulting Jones until after the fact, Adjutant General Steele ordered Coldwell, on November 17, to take his company to Duval County in response to reports of attacks from across the Rio Grande there and in adjoining counties.[59] The authorities in Nueces County had applied to Steele for aid, their desperate concern stemming from incursions by up to 150 Mexican bandits.[60] Steele instructed Coldwell to exercise discretion, in that there was a large Hispanic population in the area who were not robbers and thieves. Coldwell was to confine his operations to the state limits and not enter Mexico.[61]

Indians continued to make life busy for the Rangers in the latter part of 1874. On November 18, a fresh Indian trail was discovered by a Ranger within 400 yards of Company E's camp in Coleman County. Lieutenant B. F. Best of Maltby's company was notified, Maltby being again in Brownwood on business. At about 3 p.m., Best and eight men left camp in pursuit, making their way through rain, snow, and sleet. Following the trail at a gallop, they came upon some twenty to twenty-five Comanches about six miles from Brownwood. Without slackening their pace, the Rangers charged and fierce fighting commenced, at times hand-to-hand, and the Indians slowly gave ground until fleeing when it grew dark. The Rangers scalped two dead Indians that they could find, then reported to Maltby in Brownwood. The next morning Maltby and his company struck another fresh trail, which went back toward Coleman County, but the weather dissolved the tracks and they returned to camp. A Ranger named Scott had been creased in the head, but there were no other Ranger injuries although one horse was wounded.[62] Sergeant Ed Mather of Company E, who was part of the fight, gained some notoriety during this time by sneaking up on a group of twelve Indians in Callahan County and single-handedly firing at them from a distance of twenty or thirty yards. No one was hurt and the Indians vanished immediately.[63] It was reported by one man that the bodies of the two Indians were "suspended by the neck" for public display in Brownwood.[64]

Hiram "Curley" Hatcher (*Curley Hatcher, "Got Fifty Dollars for an Indian's Scalp,"* Frontier Times *1, no. 10* (July 1924), 7.)

Jones and his escort were with Rufe Perry's Company D in Menard County, on Elm Creek, and preparing to mount and leave. On Saturday, November 21, Rangers William Scott Cooley and William B. "Billy" Traweek of Perry's company rode out to kill a beef for the company, when they spotted a party of nine Indians riding in the distance. Thinking to lure the Indians to the company, the two charged toward the Indians firing their rifles, then turned and raced for the Ranger camp. The Indians refused to accept the bait and continued on their way. Jones' camp was about 200 yards from that of Company D, and Captain Perry was with Jones when the two Rangers raced in. Since Lieutenant Larkin Pinkney Beavert of Jones' escort was already saddled, the major directed him to take some men and start in pursuit. Lieutenant Dan Roberts of Company

D didn't wait for Perry to return to camp. He sent Traweek to the horse guard to get the horses to camp as quickly as possible. Roberts then detailed a squad of nine men to go with him, also inviting an armed civilian, John Staggs from Menard County, to join them. Jones' party had a half-hour lead on Roberts, who was following at a gallop. After about eight miles, Roberts came up with Beavert and some of his men. Thinking that Beavert was tracking too slowly, Roberts diplomatically asked the lieutenant if he could assist in "trailing," and on receiving an assent, Roberts and his men resumed the pursuit at a faster pace, leaving Beavert and his men behind. The nine Indians they were trailing had picked up their pace, no doubt aware that they would be pursued, and after about twenty miles Roberts and his men came up with them.

Because of the difficult run, all but eight of the Rangers' horses had given out or dropped behind. The Rangers charged and a running battle took place over a two-mile distance. Rather than run, the Indians faced about with military precision and returned the fire. The Rangers halted and all except Roberts dismounted, holding their fire. The Indian in command and Roberts rode toward each other, the Indian shooting Roberts' horse in the shoulder. Roberts jumped clear, although the horse did not fall, and the Indian also dismounted. The Ranger fired once and missed, then fired again, killing his adversary. Corporal Thurlow Weed shot and killed another Indian who was shooting at Roberts. Seeing this, the other Indians gave up the fight and fled the field, firing at the Rangers over their shoulders. The Rangers mounted, including Roberts on his wounded horse, and the chase resumed.

With Ranger George Bryant keeping pace with him, Roberts drew close to the two rearmost Indians. Bryant killed one of them with a shot to the head, and the other Indian, realizing that his horse was flagging, stopped and jumped off, throwing his hands up in surrender. Roberts held the Indian as prisoner, rather than killing him, and turned him over to Weed, instructing the Ranger not to let anyone hurt him. The lieutenant resumed the pursuit with his men, and two more Indians were killed before the Rangers' exhausted horses ran themselves out. By this time, Beavert and two of his men had caught up and continued the pursuit.

After a run of some three or four more miles and some more exchange of gunfire, the Indians fled into a cave. The two sides traded shots until dark, one Indian being killed and one wounded. Beavert tried to guard the four entrances to the cave until daylight, but the remaining Indians tied blankets around their horses' hooves and made their escape, leaving only pools of blood behind. The dead Indian was scalped and hung up in front of the cave.

A total of six Indians were killed, one wounded, and one captured in the hours-long fight. Three of Roberts' horses were wounded, and all of his horses were broken down from the chase.[65] Reportedly, most of the dead Indians were scalped. Ranger Scott Cooley was said to have taken a strip of skin out of the back of one warrior, the intent to make a quirt out of it, but when he hung it on a bush to dry in the sun, "it nearly all went to grease and dripped away."[66] Captain Rufe Perry apparently had some sour grapes about the fight, feeling that Jones' escort received more credit for the fight than his own men. "My report was never publish the escort got all the glory alto I doo not think that airey one of them fiord a gun." [*sic*][67]

The Indian prisoner was taken under guard to Fort Mason, then Austin and paraded through the streets while strapped to a mule. Hundreds of people surrounded and gawked at the Indian at the capitol grounds where he had been taken to meet Governor Coke before being jailed. The Comanche, named Little Bull, told his captors that he had come with his fellow braves from Fort Sill.[68] He was taken out of jail on Sunday, November 29, and displayed at Austin's opera house, much to General Steele's displeasure, who immediately prohibited any further exhibitions.[69]

Indians continued to present a problem for the Frontier Battalion, but now the state administration would prove an even bigger one.

6

THE ABOMINABLE LEGISLATURE

ON NOVEMBER 24, 1874, THE BAD news came for the six-month-old Frontier Battalion. At Governor Coke's direction, because the current appropriation for frontier defense was insufficient to sustain the battalion until the next legislative session in January when a new budget would be adopted, Steele ordered a reduction of the Battalion's manpower. Companies A through E would now be commanded by a lieutenant instead of a captain, and each company would be composed of two sergeants, three corporals, and twenty-five privates. The one exception, Company F commanded by Neal Coldwell, would continue to be commanded by a captain, with one lieutenant, three sergeants, three corporals, and thirty-seven privates. Jones was directed to discharge all Rangers over this number.[1] From a force numbering 471, the Battalion would now encompass only 200 men.

In compliance with his orders, Jones directed that First Lieutenant George W. Campbell of Company C, First Lieutenant W. H. Ledbetter of Company D, First Lieutenant B. F. Best of Company E, and First Lieutenant Pat Dolan of Company F be "disbanded." Company commanders were to immediately reduce the strength of their units in obeyance of Steele's order, with discharges to go first to married men, to those having dependents that needed their presence at home, and to any others that are "disqualified on any account whatever for active, faithful, and efficient service" or who wanted to quit the service. After that, any further reductions would be done by lot. In addition, no furloughs would be granted except in extraordinary circumstances or on account of protracted illness.[2]

No immediate public outcry arose from the reduction in force, even though the Rangers had already attained fairly widespread esteem for their efforts, as reflected in at least one newspaper editorial:

> We publish in today's issue General Order No. 8 of the Adjutant General, reducing the force of the Frontier Battalion. This is made necessary by the decrease in the appropriation. Major Jones has made a very efficient officer, and has done the State great good on the frontier. His officers have been brave, active and vigilant, while he has been constantly at his post, overlooking the operations of his subordinates and joining personally the companies in their rapid movements and fights with the red skins, who, like wolves, come down upon the citizens of that exposed region and commit deeds of murder and rapine which make the blood almost curdle.
>
> But not the officers alone deserve the praise. The privates have shown a chivalric bravery worthy of all praise. Whenever the enemy was announced, they were in the saddle ready for the fray; and when the word to move "forward" was heard, those brave riders proved, by their deeds, that they realized the situation and the responsibilities which rested upon them. It is not, then, surprising that in their contests with the Indians they were irresistible. The frontier has been almost cleared of the brutal Indians . . . [3]

Camping with Coldwell in Kerr County as preparations were being made to move the company to Duval County, Jones gave General Steele a six-month report reprising the activities of the Battalion since its organization. He calculated that the companies had scouted some 22,500 miles in thirty-six counties. In addition, he and his escort had personally traveled an additional 2,500 miles during four inspection tours, taking a different route each time. Jones proudly pointed to fourteen engagements with Indians by the Battalion, resulting in fifteen Indians killed, ten wounded, and one captured. The Rangers had recovered 200 stolen cattle and seventy-three horses. In addition, two outlaws had been killed and some forty-four "desperadoes and fugitives" turned over to local authorities.

Jones also pointed out that, while merchants had initially over-priced supplies sought for the Battalion, such as an exorbitant seventy-five cents per pound of coffee and fifteen dollars for 100 pounds of flour, Quartermaster Martin Kenney had managed to find reasonable rates and paid with cash on hand, rather than resorting to warrants. The major concluded,

> Although the force is too small, and the appropriation insufficient to give anything like adequate protection to so large a territory, the people seem to think we have rendered valuable service to them; and there is a degree of security felt in the frontier counties that has not been experienced for years before. Many on the extreme border are moving further out, while others from the interior are taking their place, and many more coming with them.[4]

The reduction of the force was a significant point of regret for Jones. Although he recognized that there were only enough funds remaining in the appropriation to keep a smaller force in the field until the end of the year, he suggested, "I have reason to believe the entire force will be needed here during the winter." He could only hope that the legislature would see fit to restore the Battalion to its original strength.[5] As the legislature prepared to convene early in January 1875, one newspaper called on it to increase the force to 1,500 men.[6]

Following up on the activities to reduce the force, Jones issued an order on December 9 from Menard County disbanding five more of his commanding officers: Lieutenant J. W. Millican of Company A, Captain George W. Stevens of Company B, Captain E. F. Ikard of Company C, Captain C. R. Perry of Company D, and Captain W. J. Maltby of Company E.[7] First Lieutenant Ira Long, who could not read or write, but could "figure in his head faster than any man in the country," now commanded Company B.[8]

In the meantime, Governor Coke and Adjutant General Steele had discovered problems with Quartermaster Kenney's supply purchases. Drafts were being presented from around the state to the bank in Austin without funds available to honor them.[9]

Another significant Indian fight occurred with Company D on the Little Saline. On the morning of December 17, a report came to Lieutenant Dan W. Roberts, the company commander replacing Perry, that Indians had stolen horses at a nearby ranch. Roberts, who was unwell, placed Sergeant N. O. Reynolds in charge of twenty-three men to begin pursuit. The Indians left a very plain trail, which was located about eight miles from the Ranger camp, and some ten miles later, the Rangers found themselves within a mile of their quarry, who were breakfasting. Spotting the Rangers, the party of nine Indians took to their horses and raced off, leaving the stolen horses to wander. The Rangers took up the chase, and after about fifteen miles only three Rangers were able to continue the pursuit—James B. Hawkins, William H. Springer, and John D. Cupp. Hawkins gave a vivid description of what happened:

> I rode in the center. Cupps [*sic*] on the right, and Bill [Springer] on left. I had got one and slacked up to see that he was sure dead, and when I caught up again, they [had] both of their horses about 100 yards apart shooting at the Indians who were 200 yards away. As I rode between them I turned my head towards Cupps and yelled, "Give 'em H, Cupps." Then I heard him say, "Look out, Jack." I was wearing a wide brim black hat. A big bullet cut the brim within an inch of my face. The wind of the bullet knocked my head back, so I had to catch the front of my saddle to keep from going over backwards. There was one short Indian quite a ways behind the others. I yelled all the Spanish words I had ever heard to him to stop, but he wouldn't stop. He was running down a gentle slope. When he started up the other side, I rode down and jumped off my horse. Cupps and Springer were back about 200 yards of their horses shooting. I was in 30 or 40 yards

of the short Indian. The others were strung out. I hadn't more than struck the ground before 8 of the devils spread out and came running back, 3 on each side, 2 in the center. The boys yelled for me to come back, but I was off my horse. There [were] three little live oaks about 10 steps to one side. I turned my horse loose. I thought he would run back to the boys, but Old Button would not leave me. When I got to the trees he got right behind me with his head against me. The boys shooting at the Indians on the ride gave me time to mount and the second my leg was over the saddle, Button was sure showing that old boy had more sense than I did. The only Indian that was mounted on a big gray horse stolen from Alf Beard of Mason took after me, yelling "Ky yi." I was so darn scared I was mad. Before I got back to the boys, I turned Old Button with my six-shooter in my hand. He turned at the same time. He had one of them old dragoon cap and ball six-shooters. I sure sent him back in a hurry. He rode his horse about a mile and left him.[10]

Hawkins killed one Indian and scalped him, Springer killed another, and a third Indian was wounded by Cupp. The Rangers recovered sixteen horses, along with Indian weapons and equipment.[11] Given continuing raids such as this, it was not remarkable that Governor Coke eagerly congratulated Lieutenant General Phil Sheridan of the United States Army for the decision of the federal government to finally establish a strong military presence in the Texas Panhandle.[12]

Jones continued his latest inspection tour, slowed by rain, high water, sleet, and up to ten inches of snow, accompanied by severely cold temperatures. He arrived at Company E's camp just before Christmas. The discharged Maltby had already left for his home, but was credited with some $500 in state funds for which no accounting had yet been made. Since the orders for disbandment had not yet reached the company, Jones took the matter in his own hands and completed the task of reducing the company.[13] Surgeon Nicholson, who traveled with Jones, reported an outbreak of scurvy in both Companies B and E, and ordered extra rations for the men of potatoes, onions, and fruit.[14]

Moving on, Jones arrived at the Ranger camp at Jacksboro on December 31. He finished his inspection tour, completing the reduction in force of the Battalion, and prepared to return to headquarters in Austin as soon as Quartermaster Kenney completed paying the troops.[15] On January 4, 1875, Jones first went to Dallas where he arranged for supplies for Companies A, B, C, and E to carry them through the first of April, while Kenney went directly to Austin.[16] Jones arrived in Austin on January 11, checking in at the Avenue Hotel.[17] The next day Governor Coke delivered his annual message to the state legislature praising Jones and the accomplishments of the Frontier Battalion.

> The labor of the officers and men have been severe and unremitting and well performed, the length of the line over which they have kept guard and watch, being so great for the number of men, that they have been constantly in the saddle, and while they have had but few opportunities of displaying their prowess in battle, they have shown themselves on those occasions fully equal to the task of maintaining the historic fame of the Texas Ranger.[18]

His praise notwithstanding, though, Coke proposed that the Battalion, in its reduced state, could be maintained at an annual cost of $150,000. It was his belief that the state would still be adequately protected, especially considering that the federal government finally appeared to be increasing the number of its troops and strengthening Indian policies to more effectively protect Texas citizens. There was a diminished role for the Rangers.

> It is believed that so long as the "peace policy" heretofore adopted by the general government, in management of the Indians, is pursued, that no force that the State can place on the frontier will prevent the incursions of raiding bands of Indians on the frontier of Texas. The line is so great in extent, and the country so well known to the Indians, and so favorable to their predatory operations that the utmost vigilance of four times the number of men that Texas could afford to station on it, will not prevent their coming in occasionally and harassing the settlements.

The value of the state troops consists more in the confidence given the people, which induces settlement and civilization of the country, than in the actual protection given.[19]

The *Dallas Daily Herald* disagreed with Coke, insisting that the force should be 1,500 strong: "The protection of the wives and children of our citizens from the barbarous cruelties and captivity of the thieving, murderous red wretches should be the state's particular pride."[20] However, in hopes that a more peaceful era would prevail, General Steele issued an order to state troops to allow parties of Indians residing in Mexico to pass unmolested on their return to reservations in the Indian Territory and other such designated spots.[21] It can only be assumed that Jones had the opportunity to voice his thoughts on the pending entrenchment at the appropriate time, then, like a good soldier, steeled himself to carry out whatever orders ensued. Reduction notwithstanding, Jones could look back on 1874 with satisfaction. The Battalion had proven effective in helping to stem the Indian threat, at least gaining the respect of Indians making forays into the state. No Ranger had acted lawlessly or arbitrarily, and the Battalion had distanced itself in the public mind from the perceived excesses of the former state police under the Davis administration.[22]

Cold weather continued to dominate in the beginning months of 1875, and company operations slowed, primary concerns centering on acquiring adequate subsistence and forage to see the Rangers through the winter. In Duval County, Coldwell's Company F continued to scout the Rio Grande and adjoining counties, everything being quiet for the most part. Coldwell suggested to Jones that he might be more effective if the company was headquartered in Hidalgo County, although the grass in that area might not be suitable for his stock.[23] Steele, however, preferred that the company be stationed nearer to the Rio Grande,[24] and Jones directed Coldwell to move his company some fifty or sixty miles closer to the river, near the Starr-Hidalgo County lines.[25] Coldwell still found no action for his men, and he opined that "the necessities of this part of the frontier have been greatly exaggerated," especially since, in his opinion,

Dan W. Roberts (*James B. Gillett,* Six Years With the Texas Rangers, *Austin,*
Texas: Von Boeckmann-Jones, 1921.)

there were abundant federal troops at key points in the area. With the
frequent federal patrols along the Rio Grande, "there is little left for this
company to do."[26]

One company commander following Jones' instruction to maintain
discipline and order was Second Lieutenant J. T. "Tom" Wilson of Company A. Even before the force reduction, Wilson regularly drilled the
men of his company.[27] Now in command, he established his own directive
system. On February 1, he ordered his company to turn in all cartridges
upon return from a scout and to hobble horses during the daytime as well
as at night.[28] This was followed by orders that no one could leave camp

for any purpose without his permission, nor trade a horse either within or outside the company without his permission.[29] Any Ranger caught on guard without his rifle and pistol and horse saddled would be placed on extra duty for the first offense and discharged for the second.[30]

As might be expected, some bad feelings toward the lieutenant began to smolder among the men of the company, his authority to issue such directives being challenged. This led Wilson to recommend to Jones, if appropriations were found for a new Battalion, that Company A should be disbanded and men in a new company should come from the interior of the state, being "invariably better soldiers" than those from the frontier.[31] And he wasn't deterred from imposing his command policies. In February, he directed that no member of the company could shoot a weapon within one mile of camp without permission,[32] and the following month he prohibited the blowing of a horn in camp while the horses were out, as it would signal an alarm to herders to bring the horses into camp.[33]

State finances remained in a precarious condition, and it was finally necessary to allow men of the Frontier Battalion to opt to receive their pay in state warrants, rather than waiting interminable months to receive cash. Availability of cash depended on the sale of state bonds to banks on the east coast, which was not occurring at the rate desired. State warrants could be held for future redemption by the state or sold off to third parties at a discount, such as ninety cents on the dollar. General Steele suggested that the men give a power of attorney to someone in Austin to receive their warrants to properly dispose of them.[34] While Jones returned to Corsicana for a much-needed vacation with family in February, Martin Kenney resigned as Battalion quartermaster.[35]

Continuing from the previous year, the problems in Mason County were still festering. Severe animosity existed between the German settlers on the eastern side of the county and ranchers on the opposite side. The causes were several, such as ethnic discrimination and fallout from disparate Civil War allegiances.[36] Jones and the Rangers had already been involved in a minor way, given the occasional complaints they received and to which they responded. Mason County Sheriff John Clark, who himself was wanted by Llano County for his actions against A. G. Roberts' cowboys [see Chapter Five], arrested nine stockmen and a boy on February 12, 1875, in McCulloch County, north of Mason County, supposedly in possession of cattle that did not belong to them. This was the second time that he had made such arrests outside his jurisdiction. The sheriff left the herd unattended and took his prisoners back to Mason. About this same time, the body of seventeen-year-old Allen Bolt was found lying on a road in Mason County, a card affixed to him declaring, "Here lies a noted cow thief."[37]

On the evening of February 18, a mob broke into the home of Mason County Deputy Sheriff John Wohrle, partially strangling him in order to get the keys to the jail. The mob's aim was to lynch the prisoners arrested in McCulloch County as a message not to depredate in Mason County. Lieutenant Dan Roberts, now commanding Company D, was in Mason to buy grain for his company and staying at Hunter's Hotel. Gaining the jail keys from the deputy, the mob marched on the jail. Sheriff Clark burst into Roberts' room yelling for him to get up. Accompanied by local cattleman James Trainer, who himself had been recently wounded, Roberts and Clark hastened to the jail. The mob of about forty men was assembled at the door of the building and ordered the approaching lawmen to halt.

Leaving his two companions, the sheriff backed off and went inside the adjacent county courthouse to an upstairs room where he aimed a rifle out a window at the mob and threatened to kill the "first damned man" who touched the jail door. Roberts, exercising discretion over valor, prudently stepped aside as ten men from the mob brushed by Trainer and him without a word and went up to talk to the sheriff. They made it clear that they intended to get the prisoners, even if it meant hurting the sheriff. Clark saw that his resistance was futile and came downstairs, instructing Trainer and Roberts to back off and watch the mob while he tried to find some help. Clark left and the mob, apparently finding the jail keys useless, brought battering rams to bear on the jail door, and as Roberts and Trainer watched, the mob entered, grabbed five of the prisoners, and took them south from the jail.

Sheriff Clark returned to the scene with five or six men and, along with Roberts, they started after the mob, all trotting down the road on foot except Clark. After about half a mile, they heard shots, and, thinking that the mob was shooting at them, the posse fired back but with no response from the mob. The lawmen pressed on to find the mob had fled, leaving three men hanging from a tree and one man shot and mortally wounded, but the fifth man, Charley Johnson, had managed to escape. Clark cut down the three men and Roberts was able to revive one of them. The Mason County violence had ratcheted up and a full-scale war was now in the making.[38]

The escaped Johnson turned up at Lieutenant Roberts' camp and was taken back to Mason. The district judge sent word to Roberts to hold on to Johnson rather than turn him over to the sheriff. Johnson was then taken before the grand jury, but he professed not to know anyone in the mob; Roberts also testified, but kept whatever he knew close to his vest.[39]

Historians have been critical of Roberts for his apparent inaction after the lynching. There is no indication that he made any sort of investigation into the incident, and there were no official reports regarding any of the events leading up to the lynching. He has been accused of a "severe error in judgment bordering on dereliction of duty," his "lackluster leadership" termed "inexcusable."[40] In his memoirs, Roberts stated only that he was glad that Johnson did not reveal anything to the grand jury "as it might frustrate our plans of catching them,"[41] but those plans, if any, were never revealed. In one report to Jones on March 1, Roberts obliquely referred to the death of a man named Wages at the hands of a mob, opining, "As yet they've harmed no good men."[42] That observation certainly hints, at a minimum, that Roberts was making some value judgments about which side was right, and his dearth of investigative effort would seem to be a direct result of such a bias.

Steele telegraphed Roberts to furnish District Judge Everett whatever aid may be required to protect his court at Mason and enforce the law.[43] When Roberts had to absent himself in order to go to Austin, Sergeant N. H. "Plunk" Murray, acting as company commander, responded to a request for assistance by sending nine men to aid the sheriff. The detachment returned to camp on March 13 and reported everything "all quiet."[44] Nevertheless, the violence in Mason County did not abate and the Rangers would continue to be called on to intercede. Jones, however, was apparently not overly concerned about the bloodshed at this point; he even ordered Roberts to send a scouting party from his company as far south as Kerrville to look for any outlaws that may be infesting that area.[45] On April 1, Roberts reported "everything quiet in regard to the Mason trouble," at the same time dispatching the requested scout to Kerrville.[46] Two weeks later he proclaimed: "The excitement among the stock men of Mason County seems to have subsided. All gone to work & quit quarreling."[47]

In Corsicana, Jones followed legislative activities closely, the legislature having convened in January. His commanders were making their reports to him there, so he was aware that Indian incursions and stealing continued. The reduced Battalion, of course, was his greatest concern, and he knew it would be insufficient against the greater number of Indians that would come south in the spring. The small appropriation had even forced him to order short rations for the horses of the command, especially given the higher price for corn during the winter, and thus perhaps not allowing the horses sufficient diet to sustain hard scouts.[48] Jones received letters of support from well-known citizens throughout the state, which he forwarded to Steele: "Would it not be well to give this information to some of our legislators who are weak-kneed in regard to appropriation for frontier defense?"[49] From Corsicana, he made arrangements for provisions for the various companies, as well as taking care of personal business, such as a March 12 default judgment on a contract for $210.75 in a Navarro County court.[50]

Coldwell's sense that there was nothing to do in Hidalgo County and other border areas dissipated in March. On the 4th, Hidalgo County Sheriff Alexander Lea wrote Governor Coke that a gang of six Mexicans came across the Rio Grande and murdered a justice of the peace and a deputy inspector of hides.[51] At the same time, Coldwell notified Jones that the army had discontinued its patrols along the river, and that he was aware of the organization of two to three hundred Mexicans on the other side of the river, "with what intention no one knows," but what was thought to be a revolutionary movement. The army offered Coldwell as many as two companies of cavalry if the force crossed into Texas, and Coldwell reiterated to Jones the occurrence of the two Hidalgo deaths.[52]

Preparing for yet another tour of inspection, Jones asked Lieutenant Wilson of Company A to send H. F. Damon, Zack Wattles, and Napoleon "Nep" DeJarnette, all originally recruited in Navarro County by Jones, to him at Corsicana, to arrive no later than April 5. He also invited F. A. McIver if he wanted to come along. Leaving right then for Dallas but planning to be back by the first of April, Jones wanted them to accompany him on the tour.[53] Wilson did not want to send McIver, and Wattles was not in good condition for the trip, so DeJarnette and four other men were sent in their place.[54]

The state legislature adjourned on March 15 after having approved an appropriation of $150,000 for the Battalion, as recommended by the governor. However, by mistake or otherwise, the budget statute did not make the appropriation effective until September 1, 1875. "We will be able to keep only a small force on the frontier and may have to disband a portion of the force now in the field," lamented Jones.[55] Only two days later, following orders, Jones instructed Lieutenant L. P. Beavert to disband his Company C because of the pending exhaustion of the current frontier defense appropriation.[56]

As another budget move, Governor Coke decided to have Jones do double duty and fill the quartermaster slot vacated by Martin Kenney.[57] It was understood that Jones would not be required to disburse any funds, just to purchase supplies for the Battalion, and that any vouchers for supplies purchased by him would be sent to Adjutant General Steele for payment. Jones was also to draw up to an additional $125 per month for traveling and other contingent expenses.[58] In addition to disbanding Company C, Jones was directed to also discharge a sergeant and nine privates from each of the remaining companies.[59] Leander McNelly's Special Troops were also ordered to be disbanded.[60] Jones met in Austin on March 17 with the governor, General Steele, and the state comptroller and treasurer.[61]

Coldwell took his company to Brownsville in Cameron County because of a threat to burn the town, but he also took time to apply to

Jones to be retained in the service as the sole Ranger captain, "if the organization is kept up."[62] In a friendly letter from Corsicana to F. A. McIver,
another Navarro County native, Jones commiserated that "business of
every kind exceedingly dull here, scarcely anything doing though the
town is still improving some." But he had not had much time to relax at
home given the funding crisis of the Battalion.

> I have spent about two weeks here in all since I left the frontier, having
> been in Austin most of the time worrying with the abominable Legisla-
> ture, trying to prevail on them to make something like a fair appropria-
> tion for our service, and at last they gave only half as much as the last
> appropriation, and by an awkward blunder or rather an unpardonable
> oversight, it is not available and cannot be drawn until the first of Sept.
> So that at this time I can see nothing for us to do but disband on the
> last of May and re-assemble on the first of September, leaving the fron-
> tier entirely unprotected during the months of June, July & August. But
> there is no help for us unless we continue in the service during those
> months and wait for our pay until the next Legislature meets, which
> will be next January. The appropriation can be use[d] for any service
> rendered after the first of Sept., but not for services rendered before
> that time.[63]

Jones left Corsicana for Dallas as planned, arriving there on Monday,
March 30, 1875.[64]

The border problems plaguing Texas led General Steele to suggest to
Governor Coke that a state of war existed in the Nueces Strip, that portion
of land lying between the Rio Grande and the Nueces River. The bound-
ary between the United States and Mexico had been formally established
by treaty in 1848 as the Rio Grande. Nevertheless, the area remained the
steady target of Mexican stock thieves that repeatedly crossed the river to
replenish their herds at home with little or no interference by the Mexican government. American army posts in that strip, largely composed of
infantry rather than cavalry, had little effect in discouraging the banditry
attacking small towns and ranches in that area. In addition, the thick
chaparral growing in the Strip hindered small patrols from effectively

scouting. Steele recommended the establishment of six mounted companies to be kept "in constant motion" outside of the thicket,[65] although he made no mention of how to pay for it. Coke wired President Ulysses Grant on March 30, appealing for protection of Texas citizens from Mexican outlaws who were attacking with impunity. The Secretary of War, William Belknap, responded that he would order military authorities "to take immediate steps toward the protection of the people of Texas on the Mexican frontier."[66] Coldwell, in Hidalgo County, was scouting regularly but not turning up much activity. Even though violence was occurring, he contended that reports coming to him of crimes being committed usually turned out to be false. He suggested to Jones that a company of local citizens, who knew the area and the inhabitants, would be more effective than his Rangers. "It is impossible for a stranger to distinguish the thieves from the citizens, as nearly all of them are Mexicans."[67]

Steele, concerned that Coldwell was confining his scouting only to the Brownsville area, urged him to make contact with Captain McNelly in the Corpus Christi area for the purpose of "concerted action" against larger parties of bandits. Calling for Coldwell to "act as harmoniously as possible" with army troops, he urged him to quickly see to the security of people there so that he could return his company to frontier duty.[68] Although funding had initially been denied to McNelly and his Special Troops operating in DeWitt County, the legislature decided to continue the company, but shifted its area of operations to the Rio Grande.[69] Steele instructed McNelly to gather what intelligence he could concerning robbers, then "destroy any and every such band of freebooters," being careful not to disturb innocent people who spoke Spanish. He also urged him to get in contact with Coldwell where the combined strength of both companies may be needed. McNelly and his men started for the Rio Grande on April 10.[70] Steele responded to Secretary Belknap that more companies of Rangers had been required to watch the border, asking him to authorize issuance of army supplies from military posts in the area to Rangers.[71] This request was refused for want of legal authority.[72]

Jones arrived back in Austin on Wednesday, April 7.[73] He wrote Coldwell that his application to be retained in the service had been forwarded to Governor Coke with his approval. "If any Captain is to be retained in the service, I know of no one that I would prefer to yourself." This comment, a little more personal than Jones usually expressed, indicates a friendship and respect between these two men that rose above the regular commander-subordinate relationship. Jones also cautioned him, as he did the other company commanders, that the present appropriation would terminate at the end of May, leaving June through August unfunded until the next appropriation took effect. If any of the Rangers were going to re-enlist under the new quota, they would have to do so with the understanding that there would be no pay for those months until the next legislature met, if at all.[74]

Almost immediately after McNelly arrived in the Rio Grande area, a plea for McNelly and his men was made by the Nueces County sheriff, five ranches in the area having been burned.[75] From his headquarters in South Texas, McNelly issued a special order warning in no uncertain terms that there would be no shirking of duty in arresting any band of outlaws his men might encounter.[76]

Jones launched his next inspection tour, leaving Austin for Fort Mason, although he requested from Steele that he have a leave of absence around the first of June to attend to some business in Houston, probably to do with the Masons.[77] Two weeks of leave was approved "when his services can be dispensed with on the frontier."[78] Jones visited Roberts and Company D, finding everything in good order. Roberts had intended on quitting the service on May 25 when the funded service time was to expire, but Jones convinced him to continue until the first of September when the authorization would take effect. About half of Roberts' men were willing to re-enlist with the understanding there would be no pay in the summer months, and the same was true in the other companies. Most of the men preferred Steele's suggestion that they be paid by checks on the Austin bank, which would be deposited in their banks, really having no need for the money in camp. Jones made no mention in his report to Steele of the Mason County troubles.[79]

Desperation was growing along the Mexican border. On April 19, ten bandits rode into Carrizo, in Zapata County, during the early morning hours and assassinated the county judge in his store in the course of a robbery. The sheriff contacted authorities in Guerrero, Mexico, about the murder, soliciting cooperation, but the communication "was replied to in a derogatory manner."[80] Governor Coke wrote Army General E. O. C. Ord, urging that the federal government should bear the major responsibility for protecting the border. The expense on the state of protecting against both Mexican bandits and Indians was onerous.[81] The army's sole response was that the local citizens ought to organize into armed bodies to assist army troops already there.[82]

Finally, by the end of April, some tranquility could be reported in the border area. McNelly was given credit for restoring order, at least temporarily.[83] Jones continued his inspection tour, going from Mason County to Stephens County, reporting that all remained quiet. However, on April 30, he disbanded Company A, commanded by Lieutenant J. T. Wilson, except for one sergeant, one corporal, and three privates who would be terminated on May 31.

> My principle [*sic*], and I think sufficient, reason for disbanding the company now is that if the entire force is kept in the field until the first of June, the balance of the appropriation unexpended at that time will be insufficient to maintain the force that will be required during the months of June, July and August, for which we have no appropriation. By disbanding one company now, I save some sixteen hundred dollars which with the balance that will be unexpended on the first of June will be sufficient to subsist four companies of forty men each for three months. This part of the frontier having been subject to fewer incursions than any other portion, I can better spare this company and have therefore disbanded it.[84]

From Hidalgo County, despite the pleas for help and the operations of McNelly's men, Coldwell reported that because of an epizootic disease, his horses had not been in sufficient shape for him to be doing much scouting. All he could do was pass on reports of crimes that had reached him, but he still argued that far too many of them were false.[85] On May 5, General Steele ordered Coldwell to return his command to

Duval County from Hidalgo.[86] At the same time, inquiry was made of ten counties on the Mexican border asking for a list of persons liable to militia service in the event "that it may become necessary at any moment to call upon the militia of the State to resist invasion or repress disorder," and that organization of such units should commence at once. The companies would be required to arm themselves "as best they can," since the state had no arms or authority for paying any expenses unless called into active service by the governor.[87]

Arriving at the camp of Lieutenant Ira Long's Company B in Lost Valley on May 5, Jones found seven or eight men recovering from the measles, with new cases breaking out, rendering the company currently unfit for service. He kept the eleven men of his escort in a separate camp so as not to expose them, temporarily canceling plans to make a scout on the Brazos and Wichita Rivers for Indians reported to be in the area. However, on May 8, word reached Long's camp that some horses had been stolen the previous evening from Jim Loving's ranch, about four miles off. Jones, Doctor Nicholson, Lieutenant Long and his company, along with four men from Company D rode to the ranch. From the ranch they searched, finally locating an Indian trail five or six miles to the south of the ranch. Entering the same valley as his fight the previous July, Jones followed the trail at a brisk gallop in a northeasterly direction. Looking ahead, Long spotted a man standing under a tree and pointed him out to Jones.

Through his field glasses, Jones watched as the man ran into some nearby woods. Long rode up to the tree, and while he was intently examining the footprints on the ground, seven Indians were spotted fleeing on horseback. The Rangers raced in pursuit, a running fight lasting some five or six miles through woods and over rocky hills. Long outpaced the lawmen, firing as he went. Seeing one Indian take aim and draw a bead on him, he fired, hitting the Indian between the eyes. The remaining six Indians changed course, making almost a complete circle, and the Rangers moved in response. As one of Long's rounds felled an Indian's pony, the warrior leaped to the ground and took cover in the brush, taking potshots at his pursuers. One of his shots hit Long's horse in the forehead, dropping it. Before the horse could pin him, Long loosed himself from his stirrups and landed on his feet. The Indian rushed at Long from his cover, both men emptying their pistols at one another without effect. Smashing into each other, a hand-to-hand duel commenced, Long later exclaiming "I had never then, nor have I since, seen such strength and agility as that Indian possessed."

The record is not clear as to what happened next. Long said that one of his men risked hitting him when he shot to break up the fight, the shot striking the Indian in the knee. Jim McIntire said that he and others came up, put a pistol to the Indian's head, and told him to surrender. The Indian supposedly said, "No, you heap Tahomes (Texas) son of a bitch." With that, the Rangers fired, leaving only a small piece of his skull stuck to the back of his neck. Just as he did in his account of the first Lost Valley fight, McIntire again leaned to the bizarre.

Another Indian encountered was a woman, who emptied two six-shooters at the oncoming Rangers while astride her pony. Again according to McIntire, she jumped to the ground, exposed her breasts, and shouted, "Me squaw, me squaw!" That didn't have much impact, and one of the Rangers shot her in the stomach. She staggered over and sat down by a tree, holding her wound. Jones later reported her to General Steele as "a squaw, but handled her six-shooter quite as dextrously [sic] as did the bucks."[88]

Three other Indians were killed, still bravely fighting after they went down, while two escaped through the woods and into the mountains. On the Rangers' return to the scene, they found the Indian woman still alive, and, according to McIntire, finished her off. McIntire claimed that he skinned her, later making a purse "out of the squaw's belly," and the other Rangers allegedly made quirts from the skin of the other Indians.[89] Private L. C. Garvey of Company B received a very slight wound, and two horses were wounded. Jones praised his men for not scalping any of the dead Indians until after the fight was over. The Indian killed by Long was scalped, as were the other bodies, although, contrary to McIntire's likely exaggerated account, Long later recollected that he did not let his men mutilate the bodies in a manner such as Indians would do to their victims.

After the Rangers departed the scene, the post surgeon at Fort Richardson at Jacksboro ordered the beheading of the Indian bodies, likely to be kept in some medical display. Jones credited his men for acting with "great courage, coolness, and discipline," with special recognition of Long's bravery.[90] Long was subsequently reimbursed 150 dollars for the loss of his horse.[91] The official report claimed the killing of five Indians, but the recollection of Long years later embellished the score by one.

Regardless of Long's actions, however, he resigned from the Battalion, effective June 10. Jones said, "I regret to lose the services of so good an officer; circumstances which he cannot control compel him to resign." He asked Steele to reappoint George W. Stevens as commander of Company B, Stevens having been "disbanded" the previous December, and Steele subsequently did so. On May 11, Jones left the company and headed back to Mason, continuing his tour.[92] Countering the bravery of Long's Rangers, Lieutenant B. S. Foster of Company E, in Coleman County, sheepishly reported that two of his men, George H. Gerrish and J. R. Daniels, slept too soundly by their horses, which were stolen by Indians.[93]

7

❧◦♥◦❧

KILL ALL THE DUTCH

THE ACTIVITY ON THE RIO GRANDE reached such a level
of international tension that Adjutant General Steele felt compelled to
make a tour of the area in May of 1875.[1] Leander McNelly and his men
were encamped at Edinburg, fending off horse, cattle, and oxen thieves.[2]
Governor Coke again made an appeal directly to President Grant for the
state to be relieved of the burden of defending a national border.[3] Steele
met with Neal Coldwell, hopefully to reenlist the men of Company F who
had not been paid, and who, "being very ragged and without the means
of procuring the real necessities of life,"[4] were opting to go home. Coldwell went to San Antonio with a mind to reorganize his company there,
but was directed to return to Kerr County to complete the mustering out
of his company.[5] Jones directed him to raise a new company restricted to
two sergeants, three corporals, and thirty privates, with Coldwell as the
only commissioned officer, to serve until August 31. It was understood
that they would receive no pay until an appropriation for that purpose
was made by the legislature.

On his way back to Austin from the inspection tour, Jones left his
wagon and two horses at Mason under the care of Lieutenant Roberts
and Company D until his return there about the middle of June.[6] He

and five of his escort then arrived in Austin on the evening of Thursday, May 27, proudly displaying their "trophies" from the Lost Valley fight, including the scalps of the Indians killed, one of which was plaited with what was believed the hair of a white woman. Along with buffalo hide shields, bows, quivers and arrows, and charms of beads, the men displayed blankets clearly marked with the initials of the United States Indian Department.[7] First checking in with the adjutant general's office, Jones then went home to Navarro County for a short vacation.

An event at this time in Kerr County created a mystery that may have involved the Frontier Battalion. On June 14, 1875, a report of Indians driving off horses in that county resulted in a citizens' posse going in pursuit. About twenty miles from Kerrville, the posse engaged the thieves in an hour-long fire fight, finally prevailing and discovering that the Indians were actually five white renegades dressed as Indians. One of the thieves was mortally wounded and died the next day; the other four made their escape on foot into a dense thicket. The one dying prisoner told his captors before expiring that he was Norman Cole from Delaware County, New York, and that he had belonged to Major Jones' escort.[8] No official records discuss this, and a review of Ranger personnel records turns up no Norman Cole, although there was an N. V. Cole, a member of Maltby's Company E, who enlisted on June 6, 1874, and was discharged on December 9, 1874, some six months before the incident. There was no additional information, either in official records or the news media, and no official comment was made in response to the news report, although the two were likely the same man.

Prior to starting a new tour of inspection, Jones, in his role as quartermaster, made arrangements for provisions for the various companies. As an example of what a typical list of supplies would involve, he contracted with a Dallas merchant to order 2,300 pounds of flour, 650 pounds of bacon, 280 pounds of beans, 165 pounds of rice, 370 pounds of coffee, 370 pounds of sugar, twenty candles, twenty-four pounds of soap, seventy-two pounds of salt, twenty pounds of baking soda, four pounds of pepper, and twelve gallons of vinegar for Company B at Jacksboro. Jones advised Lieutenant Stevens that this was only a half-ration of bacon and that it would be up to the company to supplement it with beef. Also, Jones sent him a draft for $150 to purchase beef and potatoes, up to 360 pounds per month. In addition, four boxes of carbine cartridges were sent, and pistols and pistol ammunition were ordered for twelve of Stevens' men.[9] Similar arrangements were made for Lieutenant B. S. Foster's Company E and Dan Roberts' Company D.[10]

Coldwell reported to Jones on June 28 that he had organized a new company and was establishing camp about twenty miles northwest of Kerrville.[11] Jones arrived at his camp, reporting to General Steele that, given recent white and Indian raids in the area over the past two months, there was a "great necessity" for this company. He casually mentioned the recent capture and confession of the renegade Cole, but did not indicate any former affiliation of the dead man with the Battalion. Illustrative of his grit and tenacity, Jones took out after the renegades on a scout on the second of July, his Rangers accompanied by Kerr County merchant Henry Schwethelm and a company of Germans from Comfort, Texas.

> I found no organized bands of robbers, as has been reported, and am satisfied that the active robbers have all left the country. I found some very suspicious people living in the mountains of the Llano who beyond a doubt are confederates of the robbers and harbor them and conceal their plunder . . . I called upon these suspected persons and informed them that they would be visited occasionally by detachments of this command and would be dealt with if found harboring them or with stolen property in their possession. I think the good people of those sections will not be molested by white robbers again soon.[12]

On July 1, General Steele made a lengthy report to Governor Coke concerning his tour of the Rio Grande area. Reciting the violence that had occurred in Nueces County and the history of the state's attempts to deal with such incidents, such as Wallace's now disbanded company, he concluded that forces were being organized in Mexico to plunder property on the Texas side of the river with the knowledge of Mexican officials; that American bands organized to defend their property had themselves committed murder and arson; that an active trade in the buying of stolen hides was going on in Corpus Christi; and that there was a total lack of security in the area. Failing earnest cooperation between American and Mexican officials, he suggested there would then have to be a large force on the Rio Grande with orders to pursue felons into Mexico if necessary.[13]

Jones rode on to Roberts' Company D, on Los Moras Creek near Menard, finding it in good shape. "They are having or anticipating more trouble in Mason, and at the request of the court which meets there next week."[14] Jones also wrote Coldwell about company matters, but included this curious statement about Mason County without explanation: "I learned as I returned to camp that the men who were [illegible] those cattle took a [illegible] and turned the cattle loose and were seen coming in a day or two after we were there, which pleased our German allies greatly."[15] Perhaps this suggests, as was later rumored, that Jones had a partisan interest in the outcome of the county's troubles.

Before leaving Menard County on July 10 for Foster's camp in Coleman, with retrenchment of the Battalion still on his mind, Jones proposed to Steele increasing the Battalion to five companies on the first of September, then reducing it again on December 1. He suggested at the same time that Steele could furnish the companies, before the Rangers' present term of service expired, with blank discharges and certificates of indebtedness that stated they would be paid out of a special appropriation to be made by the state legislature at some point in the future. Jones also remarked that, in the future, Springfield carbines were better suited to the service than the Sharps, they "being less liable to get out of order and having longer range and greater accuracy."[16] A requisition was subsequently issued for 225 such carbines.[17] Reflecting the standards he had imposed on the Battalion, Jones also discharged Private J. A. Dunn of Company D for "being drunk, attempting to discharge a pistol in a private residence, and for using obscene and insulting language in the presence of ladies."[18]

Since the lynching of the jail prisoners at Mason in February, the violence in the county had gained momentum. In March both sides had begun organizing their forces and parading their strength before the other.[19] On May 13, 1875, Mason County Deputy Sheriff John Wohrle arrested Tim Williamson in Llano County and, accompanied by cattleman Karl

Camp Scene of Company D (*Courtesy of Texas Hall of Fame and Museum, Waco, Texas*)

Lehmberg, began to escort the prisoner back toward Mason. The three men were intercepted and surrounded on the road by masked men, the German "Hoo Doos," and Wohrle, who obviously sympathized with the Germans, shot Williamson's horse to prevent an escape, then stood by as the masked men shot Williamson dead.[20] This act of killing translated into a major escalation in the feud. In the aftermath, Wohrle resigned as deputy sheriff.[21]

According to Ranger Jim Gillett, a good friend of Tim Williamson was former Ranger Corporal Scott Cooley, who had left the Battalion the previous December. Perhaps reflecting a hair-trigger temperament, one Ranger recalled that no one in Company D would share a tent with Cooley because "he was one of these nervous fellows that would jump up in his sleep and grab his six-shooter."[22] Generally considered a dangerous man not to be trifled with, Cooley was visiting in Roberts' camp when news of Williamson's death was received.[23] Cooley had worked for Williamson and made several cattle drives with him, even being nursed by Mrs. Williamson through a typhoid attack.[24] Shaken, the ex-Ranger reportedly cried on hearing the news, then determined a plan of vengeance, blaming Sheriff Clark and ex-Deputy Wohrle.[25]

However, the problems in Mason County had yet to insinuate themselves in any significant way in Battalion operations. Reporting to Steele on July 27 from Lost Valley in Jack County, Jones announced the completion of his latest tour and his preparations for an almost month-long scout for Indians along the rivers and creeks there, anticipating returning to Austin about the first of September.[26] The Indian problem in Texas had diminished considerably, leading one observer to comment: "It is strange, yet nevertheless true, that less than two hundred undisciplined men have accomplished in a few months what ten times that number of well disciplined United States troops failed to do in as many years—stopped Indian depredations upon nearly four hundred miles of border."[27]

Jones issued an order on August 5 announcing that all Rangers would be discharged on August 31, immediately followed by the reorganization of five companies on September 1. Each company would be composed of three sergeants, three corporals, and thirty-four privates for a term of twelve months. "None but well mounted men will be received, and no man will be allowed to keep more than one horse in the service."[28] Coldwell was reduced from captain to first lieutenant on Steele's insistence that Company F be placed on the same footing as the other companies.[29] At the same time, Steele ordered company commanders to return to him each month a detailed report indicating personnel changes, property and equipment disposition, and the status of arms and ammunition.[30]

The violence continued in Mason County. On July 21, cattleman Heinrich "Henry" Doell was mortally wounded, and another man, August Keller, was wounded while sleeping at a cow camp when they were fired upon by unknown persons.[31] While initially there was an idea that Indians might have done the shooting, it was quickly concluded that the attack was "probably committed by white villains who have banded together for the purpose of murder and robbery."[32] Dispatched by Jones, Dan Roberts took six men to Mason on July 12, then returned to his camp in Menard County after providing security for the court. When Roberts heard the report of Doell's shooting, he was still of the opinion that the shooters were Indians, and he led a scout of ten men. The Rangers found a trail that indicated a party of fifteen, but rain obliterated the tracks and after three days, the Rangers returned to camp. It was never fully determined who or what left the trail.[33]

On August 7, Second Sergeant Daniel M. Gibson of Ira Long's Company B arrived at Decatur, in Wise County, carrying a dispatch from Jones to Long. He had been in town but a few minutes when the town marshal, Napoleon Cargill, a man known locally to have "a very overbearing disposition," approached him in a store and demanded that he give up his arms. Gibson refused, citing his duty as a member of the Frontier Battalion and as a Texas peace officer. Cargill began cursing Gibson and drew his pistol on the Ranger. Gibson likewise drew his pistol and warned the marshal to stand back and leave him alone. Cargill vainly snapped his pistol twice in Gibson's face, forcing the Ranger to fire. The marshal was struck in the right breast and the pistol ball lodged under his left shoulder blade. The wound was considered a "dangerous one," but Cargill survived.

Gibson mounted a friend's horse and quickly rode out of town directly to Lieutenant Long's camp. Long was moved by the incident to suggest to Jones that the law be clarified as to the right of Rangers to bear arms like other peace officers.[34] In response, however, General Steele promulgated a general order reminding members of the state service that they were to consider themselves subordinate to the law, under threat of termination. Rangers were strictly prohibited from going to Decatur or any other town wearing arms.[35] Gibson was never charged with the shooting and continued his duties as a Ranger.[36]

On August 10, 1875, ex-Mason County Deputy Sheriff John Wohrle, now working as a handyman and carpenter, was helping Charles "Doc" Harcourt clean out a well. Harcourt was in the well bucket being pulled up by Wohrle and another man when Scott Cooley rode up and shot Wohrle to death. Harcourt plunged to the bottom of the well, temporarily dazing him. Cooley, in separate accounts, shot Wohrle seven times, cut off his ears or scalped him, then fled.[37] Nine days later, Carl Bader, another German, was killed, some placing that deed also at the hands of Scott Cooley.[38] Tensions in the county continued to climb.

Dan Roberts and Company D were still in Menard County, however. In mid-August a party of Apache Indians rode into Kimble, Mason, and Menard Counties, bringing with them two captured youths, one a Mexican boy, thirteen or fourteen years old, who had been captured from a ranch west of San Antonio. The other was a white boy with long, bright red hair, named Herman Lehmann, who had been captured five years earlier in Gillespie County and who had adopted Indian customs. The two boys were left on top of a small mountain to watch the Kimble-Mason road for pursuers while the rest of the Indians raided a nearby pasture for horses. When two cattlemen rode by the mountain, unmindful of the presence of danger, Lehmann proposed to his Mexican companion that they ride down and kill them, but the Mexican boy refused.

When Roberts was informed of the raid on August 20, Company D was about fifty miles north of where the raid occurred. With eight men, the lieutenant pressed to find the Indians' trail. It was not difficult to find, as the Apaches had stopped to remove the shoes from the stolen horses, and for several days the Rangers followed their tracks. At one point Roberts' horse was bitten by a rattlesnake, and he was forced to continue on riding a mule. On the morning of August 24, Roberts spotted the Indians about 150 miles northwest of the Menard County camp, between the Pecos and Devils Rivers, and he had his men ride in single file so as to diminish their visibility as they gained on the Indians. When the Rangers were within 200 yards of the Indians and their stolen herd, two braves in the rear spotted them and alerted their companions. Yelling, the Rangers charged the warriors. The Apaches made one brief stand, exchanging gunfire with the charging Rangers, then rode off, making another stand about a half mile away. The Rangers wounded several of the Indians' horses and some Indians. The leader of the Apaches rode off with six of his men, including Lehmann and the Mexican boy, closely pursued by Roberts and three men, the remainder of the Rangers chasing the other Indians who were scattering.

As Roberts and his men closed in, the Mexican boy reined up, turned toward the oncoming Rangers, and, waving his arms, shouted in Spanish that he was a friend. One Ranger was left to guard him while the chase continued. Some two miles later, as the Rangers' mounts began to weaken, the Indians disappeared into some brush, then appeared again, much too far ahead for the Rangers to catch them. The Rangers returned to where they had left their companions and where the Mexican prisoner was being held. The red-haired Lehmann had been pinned by his horse when it was shot, but he was able to free himself and escape into the nearby brush. The other Rangers had killed one Indian and wounded another. Hungry, as their pack mule had been killed during the race and the men were not willing to eat horse meat, the Rangers managed to capture twenty-three horses and to return to the camp of a man named DeLong, where they had beef and milk.[39] On the 28th, Roberts and his men returned to Menard with an Indian scalp, their Mexican prisoner, and numerous Indian "trinkets."[40]

In Austin, as part of the reconstitution of the Frontier Battalion, Major Jones authorized Ira Long to raise Company A on September 1, then telegraphed him to enlist only fifteen men as he wanted to recruit men "from different parts of the country for this company." He selected the non-commissioned officers for Long, leaving Long to enlist only his first sergeant. As soon as the company was organized, by the middle of September, Long was to meet Jones on the head of the Pedernales River, thirty-five miles south of Mason. It was Jones' plan to combine Company A, Coldwell's Company F, and part of Roberts' Company D "on a big scout" from there. Jones would supply Springfield carbines for the men.[41] The major wrote Roberts asking him to send Sergeant N. O. Reynolds and twenty men to join the scout. Jones wished that Roberts would go with him, "but presume you will be at home at that time."[42] The reference was to Roberts' pending marriage on September 13, 1875, to Luvenia "Lou" Conway in Colorado County,[43] who would share her husband's quarters in the Ranger camp. According to Roberts, Jones fully agreed to this arrangement, apparently to head off Roberts' resignation.[44] While enlisted men were not permitted to be married, the same did not apply to company commanders.

Jones also directed Coldwell to bring thirty men, his plan being to go to the Rio Grande near the mouth of the Devils River, then go up the

Pecos River to the El Paso-Concho road. He urged secrecy, even from the privates, so that the public would not learn of the plan.[45] When Long was held up in reaching Coldwell's camp, Jones delayed the planned start of the scout one week. He directed Roberts to send his Mexican captive to Company C to be interrogated.[46]

After the murder of Wohrle in Mason County, Governor Coke issued a $300 reward on September 6 for the arrest of Scott Cooley. He described the ex-Ranger as claiming to be half-Indian, five feet six inches high, and having a dark complexion, dark hair, small eyes, legs rather short in proportion to his body, and a "mincing walk."[47] On the same day, Moses Baird and George Gladden were riding from Loyal Valley in

James B. Gillett *(James B. Gillett, Six Years With the Texas Rangers, Austin, Texas: Von Boeckmann-Jones, 1921.)*

Mason County to the county seat. When they stopped at a store on the way, Sheriff John Clark and a "large number of Germans" attacked them and chased them down, finally killing Baird and wounding Gladden, although the German contingent in Mason County later claimed that the two men opened fire on them first. Henry M. Holmes of Mason wrote Governor Coke two days later urging that troops be sent to Mason County.[48] On September 24, James Chaney, who identified with the German population, was shot to death by John Ringo and another man named Williams while having breakfast with his family. Immediately afterwards, Gladden, Cooley, Ringo, and others rode into Mason and ate breakfast at the hotel, boasting of Chaney's killing, claiming that they had "made beef of Chaney, and if somebody did not bury him he would stink." A warrant was subsequently sworn out against them for this murder.[49]

Still showing no apparent concern about the violence in Mason County, for which he would be justly criticized by historians,[50] Jones continued to prepare for the planned major scout. On September 18, he left Austin for Coldwell's camp near the head of the Guadalupe River, intending to lead Companies A, D, and F to the Rio Grande and other rivers. "We must, if possible, have some scalps to show for our work this Fall or the next Legislature may stop our pay."[51] However, the events in Mason County now made it imperative that something be done. Governor Coke ordered Jones on September 23 to "at once place a Lieutenant and at least thirty men in Mason County to preserve the peace," to remain there until further notice, but to be "subordinate to the civil law, of course."[52] Jones was directed to "arrest all parties in or near Mason for whom rewards have been issued or against whom capias has issued."[53] Since Jones was already in the field and unavailable by telegraph, Steele dispatched Corporal W. T. Griffin of Company D to overtake him and deliver the orders.[54] "The Governor thinks it of more importance to preserve the peace than anything else. He says whilst you may find Indians on Devils River, you will be sure to find devils in Mason."[55]

Griffin reached Jones on the evening of September 27 and, after formally abandoning the plans for the scout, the major left immediately on a forced march for Mason County with a detachment of twenty men from Long's Company A and eight men from Company D as his escort. Two days later, before the Rangers' arrival, another German, Daniel Hoerster, was shot from ambush while riding down the street in Mason. The assailants were believed to be Scott Cooley, George Gladden, and John Baird.[56]

On September 28, while passing Keller's store at Hedwig Hill, on his way to Mason, Jones and his escort were confronted by fifteen or twenty armed men headed up by Sheriff John Clark, who rose up from behind a stone fence ready to do battle. Venturing forward to negotiate, Jones was told that some thirty men, led by Gladden and Baird, were believed to be planning to come into Mason and "burn out the Dutch." Clark and the men had assembled out of a sense of self-preservation, assuming that the incoming Rangers were the Baird-Gladden bunch. Jones turned his party around and rode to nearby Cold Springs, arriving there at sundown and finding an overwhelming sense of dread throughout the small community. He spent the night there concocting a plan to have a "friendly interview" with the Baird and Gladden party and induce them to disperse. "If I fail in this, then, of course, I shall resort to other means to quash the disturbance."[57]

The next evening, September 29, Jones arrived in Mason, as did Lieutenant Long and his detachment, and found the town still in a grip of pandemonium stemming from the murder of Hoerster. Almost immediately Sheriff Clark handed Jones warrants for Baird, Gladden, and Cooley. The major sent out three groups of Rangers to look for the suspected killers, but had "very little hope of catching them at present as they are well mounted, know the country well, and have many friends in this and the adjoining counties." The biases of the feuding parties made themselves very apparent to Jones, and few of the "Americans" were willing to cooperate in nabbing the killers. Jones, however, entertained some hope of restoring quiet in a few days.[58] At the same time, County Judge Wilson Hey gave Jones warrants for the arrest of Clark and seven or eight of the German faction, who were all subsequently arrested; however, all charges were then dismissed except those against Sheriff Clark.[59]

Roberts led one of the Ranger squads, instructed to locate William Coke, a witness to the Hoerster killing, but the man disappeared, and it was suspected that he had been killed by a German group.[60] On October 4, nineteen men from Loyal Valley petitioned Major Jones, complaining that the day before a group of thirty to forty armed men under the leadership of Sheriff Clark had entered the community and searched nearly every house. The posse returned the next day and repeated the search, followed by a threat from the Gladden-Cooley party that they were coming to make everyone take sides and to "kill all the Dutch." Mortally afraid, the citizens asked for Rangers to be stationed there. Jones rode there with a detachment of his men, calming most fears by leaving a squad there for a few days.[61]

From Austin, Steele acknowledged receipt of Jones' reports from Mason County and passed on the wishes of Governor Coke that Jones would "be able to secure obedience to the law, and peace in the county."[62] While he wrestled with finding the right plan of action, Jones posted Corporal J. D. Nelson of Company A and seven men at Cold Springs to preserve peace and quiet with the assistance of citizens.[63]

According to Gillett, Jones maintained scouts in almost all directions, the primary focus being the capture of Cooley. But Cooley had been a member of Company D and had a considerable number of friends among the Rangers in that command. Gillett said that they were in sympathy with their vengeance-driven comrade and were "making no serious attempt to locate or imperil him." It was even rumored that some of Company D's men were meeting Cooley secretly outside Mason, telling him that "they did not care if he killed every damned Dutchman in Mason County" that had anything to do with Tim Williamson's death. One account stated that Cooley had even sent the scalp of John Wohrle to the Ranger camp.[64] It was painfully obvious to Jones that the sympathies of some of Roberts' men were with Cooley, and perhaps tinged with a violent prejudice against Sheriff Clark and the Germans in the area.[65] Because of this, Jones took the drastic step of calling together Roberts' men and the men from Long's Company A.

He said he had a special pride in the Frontier Battalion and was making it his life's study and that he personally had a kindly feeling for every man in the service. He then reminded the men in the most feeling manner of the oath they had taken to protect the State of Texas against all her enemies whatever—an oath every true man was bound to honor. He declared he knew many of the command had a friendly feeling for Scott Cooley, especially those boys who had shared the life of a ranger with him, and that he, himself, felt keenly the position in which they were placed. While Tim Williamson had met a horrible death at the hands of a relentless mob, that did not justify Cooley in killing people in a private war of vengeance in defiance of the law and the rangers.[66]

Jones then offered an honorable discharge to those Rangers who did not want to pursue Cooley "to the bitter end," expecting those who did not take this opportunity to use all due diligence in apprehending the fugitive. Gillett says that about fifteen men stepped forward.[67] However the record reflects a lesser impact. On October 7, Jones honorably discharged Second Sergeant N. O. Reynolds and Private James P. Day, both of Company D, "for the reason that they say they cannot conscientiously discharge the duty to which they have been assigned."[68] Four days later, another Ranger, Paul Durham, requested a discharge on the same basis as Reynolds and Day, which was granted by Jones.[69] Apparently there may have also been some men who deserted as Jones directed Roberts to recruit men to replace those "recently discharged and deserted."[70] One applicant for the company was Charley Johnson, who had escaped the lynch mob, but Jones felt that he was disqualified because "he was in the ranks with Gladden, Beard [sic] and Cooley last week."[71]

Jones also requested General Steele to look in his desk at Austin and retrieve petitions that he had received from County Judge Wilson Hey regarding the A. G. Roberts "gang of cow thieves," as well as a similar petition received by Captain Rufe Perry. "Some parties here have 'changed sides' since that time and I want to show up their former record."[72] The alleged partisan bias on the part of the Rangers reached the ears of Governor Coke, leading Steele to caution the major "that you do nothing

N. O. Reynolds (*James B. Gillett*, Six Years With the Texas Rangers,
Austin, Texas: Von Boeckmann-Jones, 1921.)

outside of the law and that you give no cause to think you favor one or the other party to the feud that exists in Mason County."[73]

Jones wrote to Dan Roberts, who was keeping his company in Menard County, that it was rumored that Gladden and Cooley had been in Menard, the two making threats "of what they were going to do with certain parties" at Mason.[74] Roberts responded that the rumors were not true.[75] Likely sensing the need for more manpower in the face of ongoing violence, Jones ordered Roberts to bring his company to Mason by October 25, and sent a wagon to assist in moving the company.[76] Three days later, however, he changed his mind, still acutely aware of the support given Cooley by Roberts' men, and directed Roberts to stay where he was because of the prospect of new Indian incursions, but to send ten well-mounted men and two pack mules to Mason for about a month's service.[77]

On October 20, in response to the allegations of partisan leanings on his part in the feud, Jones wrote Steele that he had been "as careful as possible from the first to act in such a manner as to give no cause for such a suspicion ever." However, within ten days of Jones' arrival, both sides had accused him of being partisan.

> My object at first was to quiet the immediate trouble and stop further bloodshed, and then in due time take the proper course to vindicate the law by arresting all parties who had offended against it. I have been so far successful that there has been no bloodshed since I came here. I have arrested some fifteen persons, some of them have been tried and acquitted, and others bound over to answer charges before the District Court of this and Llano Counties and the community is more quiet, I am told, than it has been for several months.

Given that he felt the disorder was under better control, Jones decided to leave Lieutenant Ira Long in charge with twenty-six men while he began another tour "up the line." Long's men had been recruited from other counties and had no personal acquaintance with the citizens of Mason County, better insuring no prejudice for or against either party in the feud.[78] Jones wrote to Coldwell that if Long needed any assistance, he was to come to his relief "with all possible dispatch."[79] A local partisan, extolling in a lengthy editorial the patience of the German faction in Mason County that had been "compelled to assume the aggressive or be all assassinated," praised Jones and his Rangers for accomplishing "much good."

> But for the timely arrival of the Major with his men, there would have been a large addition of fearful and bloody tragedies in this county. The commendations of the whole State are due Governor Coke for the timely and efficient protection he has given us in sending so just and capable commander here as Major Jones, whom, a perfect stranger to the people, and to their troubles when he came, set about at once to understand the situation; which, having accomplished, he proceeded with unequalled courage to discharge the grave duties of his most

delicate mission. Mason county was most fortunate when this able soldier was sent to remedy calamities which have befallen us; for had one of less judgment and impartiality been sent, the disorders would have been increased rather than removed. We do trust the Governor will permit him to remain here with his company until all trouble is ended and peace reigns.[80]

By October 28, with his plans for another inspection tour on hold, Jones was able to report success to Steele:

The entire county is now perfectly quiet and there has been no serious trouble of any kind since the day I arrived. The good citizens attribute the peace of the last four weeks to the presence of my force here, say they are satisfied other murders would have occurred if I had not come just when I did, and though some of each party have accused me of act-ing harshly and partially against them, I am conscious of having done all that I could and in the manner best calculated, from a moral as well as legal standpoint, to restore peace and quiet and enforce the law in this community, and now that I am about to leave, they beg me to remain, fearing that as soon as I am gone the trouble will be renewed. I have some fears on the subject myself, but hope that Lt. Long, who is a very discreet officer, will be able to keep things quiet until I return.[81]

The financial problems of the Battalion had not gone away, the appropriation of $150,000 not being sufficient. From Mason on October 25, Jones requested that Steele again send each company a sufficient num-ber of blank discharges and final statements for another contemplated reduction of the Battalion at the end of November. He anticipated that it was likely that there would be funds available at that time to pay the men. Accordingly, he issued an order directing his company command-ers to discharge all on November 30 except two sergeants, one corporal, and seventeen privates.[82] Having for the time being seen to the peace of the Mason County area, Jones departed on October 28 for B. S. Foster's Company E.

8

GALLANT AND UNTIRING

LEAVING THE MASON COUNTY VIOLENCE behind him for the time being in November 1875, Jones began another inspection tour, arriving first at Foster's Company E, which he found "in good condition and doing good service." The people in the area credited the presence and vigilance of Lieutenant Best and his men for stopping Indian depredations against them.[1] He next rode to Jack County and Lieutenant G. W. Stevens' Company B.[2] Here, as part of the retrenchment, Jones issued a special order accepting Stevens' resignation, effective November 30, as Stevens cited a need to be home during the winter. Jones turned the temporary reins of the company over to First Sergeant C. H. Hamilton.[3] Given that the company would remain small, Jones decided that it was not immediately essential to have a commissioned officer in command until the next spring. "In the meantime [I] wish to test the fitness of Sergt. Hamilton for the position." On November 13, Jones and his escort started back down the line toward Mason.[4]

While Jones was en route, Dan Roberts received information that Scott Cooley had recently been in Menard, where he quickly had his horse shod and then immediately left town. Roberts was able to track him in the direction of Llano, but could not overtake him.[5] However, the attention of the state was taken temporarily away from Mason County by the actions of Captain Leander McNelly and his Special Troops on the Rio Grande border. A party of Mexican cattle thieves had crossed the river, and then returned to Mexico with a stolen herd. In the early morning hours of November 19, 1875, with federal troops standing by on the Texas side, McNelly and thirty-one of his men crossed the river in pursuit, violating international law. His force attacked the wrong ranch, killing over a dozen men in the resulting battle. They then rode on to the town of Las Cuevas, but finding themselves outnumbered, retreated back to the river. The Mexicans attacked them but were driven back by fire from both the Rangers and American troops across the river. That afternoon, under a flag of truce, the Mexicans offered to return some of the stolen cattle, and McNelly finally crossed back to the Texas side of the river.[6] Needless to say, this event kicked off an international squabble, subsequently leading Congress to call for hearings in Washington that necessitated the presence of McNelly and others.[7]

Jones briefly visited Mason, where on November 30 he sent out orders to all company commanders to do as much scouting during the winter as possible, having due regard for the health of the men and the condition of the horses.[8] By December 4, he was in Fredericksburg purchasing corn and arranging its delivery to Lieutenant Long at Mason.[9] At the same time, Coldwell with Company F in Gillespie County reported an unusual situation. In October, Lieutenant Pat Dolan of Coldwell's company had been sent with a warrant to arrest one E. S. Gillcrease for horse theft. Dolan made the arrest, but the evidence was determined to be insufficient to bind the man over to court and he was released. Gillcrease promptly filed a lawsuit against Coldwell for $5,000, alleging false imprisonment. Coldwell insisted on a trial in the matter, but Gillcrease withdrew the lawsuit, leaving Coldwell with a personal expenditure of forty dollars for a lawyer and board for witnesses. Steele agreed to reimburse Coldwell for that amount.[10]

In mid-December, Company F was ordered to Oakville in Live Oak County to help the civil authorities cope with an outbreak of lawlessness there.[11] In response, Coldwell was concerned about how long the company would be away from his home turf near Kerr County. "If we are to remain there until Spring, I will be forced to tender my resignation as I do not feel justified in leaving my family for a lengthened period without a protector, as they will be left and I am not able to take them with me."[12]

On November 30, perhaps as part of the retrenchment, Jones' good friend, Doctor E. G. Nicholson, was mustered out of the service of the Frontier Battalion.[13] But the retrenchment also led to Jones ordering Ira Long to make a further reduction in Company A by discharging all but two sergeants, one corporal, and seventeen men on December 31.[14] Jones had decided to leave Long and his men at Mason for some time, until perhaps as late as April of 1876.[15] The violence there had been threatening to break out again. Cooley and others were reported to be in the vicinity in mid-December, and Jones was still receiving requests for Long's men to be augmented with additional Rangers.[16]

Jones made a quick trip home to Navarro County to spend Christmas with his father.[17] At the same time it was decided to keep the strength of Long's company at Mason to thirty men.[18] Long expressed a need to have all the men he could. "All is quiet here now, although I do not like the prospect very well. Not quite so flattering as has been for some time. Cooley, Gladden and Beard [sic] are still in this country."[19] On December 27, Cooley and Ringo were arrested in Burnet County after becoming involved in an altercation with the sheriff there. Some twenty men raised a disturbance around the jail, threatening to liberate the two men, who were then transferred on January 2 to the Travis County jail for safekeeping.[20] General Steele reprimanded Lieutenant Long on a report that the company commander had sent a squad of Rangers to take charge of Cooley after his arrest in Burnet. "It is not expected that the frontier troops will act as a police force for any town or county . . . It will probably [be] better for you to select a camp not in the town of Mason."[21] This was a charge that Long angrily disputed, his men having been sent solely to hand over warrants from Mason County in case the men were released.[22]

At the dawn of a new year, it was a time to reflect on what had been accomplished by the Battalion to date. In his annual message to the state legislature, Governor Coke was full of praise for Jones and his men for the protection that had been afforded on the frontier.

> This improved condition is due very greatly to the services of the frontier battalion, under the admirable and energetic management of Maj. John B. Jones. The incursions of Indians have constantly become less frequent since this battalion has been scouting the frontier line . . . These facts speak volumes in praise of the efficiency of this gallant and untiring body of men, and of the energy and ability of their commander, when it is remembered, that since December, 1874, the battalion has not averaged over 175 men and officers, all told, and that the field of their operations extends from the head of the Nueces to the mouth of Pease river, on Red river, a distance of 400 miles, and an average width on that line of fifty miles. In addition to this arduous labor, valuable service has been performed by this force in breaking up the bands of thieves and law breakers, and arresting fugitive criminals congregated on the frontier, and in preserving the peace by preventing collision with armed parties, when the civil authorities were unable to maintain the law unaided.[23]

On January 5, 1876, Neal Coldwell, holding true to his promise, telegraphed from San Antonio his resignation as commander of Company F.[24] Citing a lack of response from Steele regarding how long his company would have to stay in Live Oak County, Coldwell stated that he had to go ahead and resign "in justice to myself and my family."[25] That same day, Steele immediately wired him that he was expected to carry out his duties as ordered until a successor was appointed, and Coldwell dutifully led his twenty Rangers to Oakville.[26] Jones was in Galveston at the time,[27] probably on Masonic business, and was at a loss as to whom to recommend to replace Coldwell, leaving it to Steele to come up with a suitable candidate. In the alternative, Jones suggested that Ira Long might be considered for temporary command, and recommended that, in that event, Second Sergeant K. Aycock of Company A could command the Rangers in Mason during Long's absence, although Aycock himself had already asked to resign.[28]

Steele sent Coldwell a reassuring message that Company F might return to the Kerr County area in four or five weeks once service was rendered to the local authorities in Live Oak County. He urged the lieutenant to keep his movements secret so as not to alert the outlaw element while the Rangers went about executing warrants. Coldwell was to work in the county for two weeks, then move up the Nueces River from "point to point," turning over prisoners arrested to local sheriffs, until he reached his Gillespie County station.[29] And Coldwell was not the only one unhappy about the move. The *Kerr County Frontiersman* also lamented the move, contending that the area would be exposed to the "sudden inroads of thieving Indians and the more-to-be-dreaded visitations of roving bands of desperadoes." The editorial protested the order to Coldwell and his men "in the name of an ill-used and indignant people."[30]

Once in Oakville, Coldwell reported that any difficulty there was not all that bad, the parties in dispute having worked out their differences.[31] By January 15, he was able to report seven arrests and that he would be leaving in a few days to work his way back to Gillespie County by the end of February.[32] Coldwell apparently rescinded his resignation, although there is no correspondence on file regarding such decision. In February it was reported in the media that two "state rangers" engaged in some horseplay in camp in Live Oak County, during which a James E. Drury accidentally shot and mortally wounded a John Odem.[33] No such names are listed in Frontier Battalion records, and there was no official correspondence concerning such an incident.

In Navarro County, although not personally present, Jones was named to be a delegate to the Democratic Party's national convention to be held at St. Louis on June 27, an event that he did not attend.[34] In Mason County, despite Ira Long's report that all was quiet, violence flared anew. On January 13, Peter Bader was gunned down in Llano County by John Baird and George Gladden, although newspaper reports asserted that the murder occurred in Mason County. This led to a meeting of indignant Mason County citizens who resolved that such media slur against the county was not called for. The citizens also expressed their appreciation to Long and his men for their "uniformly excellent conduct."[35]

Steele directed Long on January 28 to move his company temporarily to Burnet and report to District Judge E. B. Turner for duty while court was in session there, then to return to Mason when his presence in Burnet was no longer required.[36] On his return to Mason on February 28, Long wrote Jones that, because "there seems to be perfect peace in this county now," it was not necessary to station his company there any longer once newly-elected officials took office.[37] Besides small episodes afterward, such as the mysterious shooting in the hand of a new sheriff and the burning of a store, the Mason County War was over, although it may have spilled over into adjacent counties.[38]

Jones was in Galveston on February 18 and 19, and back in Austin by the 22nd, when he wrote a lengthy letter to Alfred M. Hobby, a prominent Galveston merchant, detailing the operations of the Battalion. In addition to discussing the various reductions in the strength of the Battalion because of insufficient funding, he gave a statistical report on Indian engagements and assistance to local authorities in dealing with outlaws. As to Mason County,

> I went there in September with a detachment of my command, ascertained that fifteen men had been killed since the feud began, within four or five months past, found two parties of thirty men each in arms, one of which was fortified expecting an attack from the other. I put a stop to the hostilities and in ten days made about twenty arrests and restored peace and quiet to the community. Remained there two months and no breach of the peace occurred during the time.[39]

Jones also described how, as quartermaster, he had shifted from engaging local contractors for the furnishing of supplies to the individual companies, opting instead to purchase only from "first class merchants" in major cities, finding that it was more cost effective. He estimated that subsistence and forage for a company each month now averaged $1,300 to $1,500, when before some $2,500 to $2,700 had been incurred by companies appointed under Governor Davis in 1873. He gave credit to the Battalion for providing the protection that made it possible for the formal organization of nine new counties on Texas' frontier.[40] In writing all of this to Hobby, Jones utilized verbatim excerpts from his formal report to General Steele on March 8.[41]

On March 1, after assessing available state funds, Jones ordered an increase in the strength of the Battalion, effective April 1. Each commander was to recruit his company to three sergeants, three corporals, and twenty-six privates, Jones also ordering that forage for horses during April would be seven pounds of corn per day, then, beginning in May, six pounds.[42] Jones, however, had apparently failed to consult with higher authority. Governor Coke admonished Steele that the Battalion had exceeded its appropriation by $20,000 for the fiscal year ending August 31, 1875.[43] Steele hastily wired Jones at Corsicana that he should consult with him at Austin before arranging to increase the Battalion,[44] and the plans were apparently scrapped for the time being.

From Corsicana on March 10, Jones requested Steele to reappoint Dr. E. G. Nicholson as Battalion surgeon, as well as to promote Sergeant C. H. Hamilton of Company B to second lieutenant, which Steele did.[45] On Thursday, March 23, Jones left Navarro County for Austin.[46] He didn't stay there long, leaving on April 1 for another tour "up the line," going first to Coldwell's camp, then on to Long's company, still at Mason.[47] Long's camp had been struck by an outbreak of measles, and Jones directed that four of the ailing Rangers be left at a private house in Mason while Long and his company accompanied Jones on his tour, which was resumed on April 14.[48] After going to Coleman County then to Jacksboro, where there were hints of the violence to come in that area, Jones returned to Austin once again by the first of May.[49]

Another quick trip to Corsicana by Jones delayed his plans to renew his inspection tour. Word had already reached the state press that the banking house of John B. Jones and Company was failing and that a number of depositors had suffered losses.[50] His brother-in-law, A. F. Robbins, had been running the company in Jones' absence. On May 10 the company sold off some land that it owned in Corsicana, no doubt to obtain some capital to head off the failure.[51] Even though Jones was busy dealing with this matter, he was still ordering supplies for the various companies of the Battalion, anticipating being at their camps by the end of the month.[52]

While there is no record as to what happened to his business at this point in time, Jones was soon back on the frontier by the middle of the month. He reached Menard, then left there on May 27 for Austin.[53]

Jones' and Robbins' business was indeed failing. Liabilities totaled almost $40,000, with assets amounting to only half that amount. Among the creditors with the greatest loss were Jones' sister, Fannie Halbert, to the tune of $9,000, and Jones' brother-in-law, Roger Q. Mills, $14,000.[54] Nevertheless, Jones was commuting between Corsicana and Austin, balancing his personal problems with his professional duties.

A major scout was organized by Jones in June, drafting about twenty men from Company D. Combined with his escort composed of thirty men of Company A, Jones and the party rode to Coldwell's camp, where another twenty men were added to the force. In addition, there were three wagons carrying tents and supplies, along with some twenty pack mules. The plan was to scout the Pecos River and see if they could rout any Lipans or Kickapoos they might run across.[55] On June 18, Dan Roberts sent Jones a communication abjectly apologizing for not personally accompanying the men from his company. His wife was sick and Roberts had been under the impression that the scout had been canceled. If a sufficient appropriation was not made by September 1, Roberts intended to submit his resignation.[56] The records do not reflect any response from Jones, but the scout departed on June 23, and by the 28th, he was well underway and able to telegraph General Steele that he had scouted the "heads of Nueces," and was en route for the Devils and Pecos Rivers.[57]

Jones called this twenty-five-day expedition the "roughest scout" he had ever made, and for good reason. Much of the country over which the scout traveled was unknown to the Rangers. Abandoned Indian camps were discovered. Some ten days into the scout, riding over dry tableland between the Pecos and South Concho Rivers, no water could be found, and both men and stock suffered for about five days. When they reached the South Concho, fresh water was finally available and two straggling buffalos provided fresh meat. After camping there for two days, the companies dispersed and Jones continued on with his inspection tour without having discovered any Indians or fresh trails.[58] The nagging concern on Jones' mind throughout the scout, however, was the amount of any appropriation approved for the Battalion by the state legislature, which was slated to adjourn in August.[59] Reaching Fort McKavett by July 15, he decided to remain there until the amount of the appropriation was determined.[60]

Although Jones had no luck locating Indians, a scout by Company E was more successful. Starting out from his camp on July 5, Lieutenant B. S. Foster and ten men located a trail along the Colorado River. Following it for some thirty-five miles, the Rangers found a party of about fifty Indians just after 4:00 in the morning on July 11. Charging the Indian camp, the Rangers routed the warriors and recovered about forty horses. However, the Indians reorganized and attacked the badly outnumbered Rangers, managing to recapture and escape with the horses.[61]

Still at McKavett, Jones decided that he could wait no longer to hear news of the new appropriation, so he continued his tour on July 19.[62] Hearing of Foster's encounter, he decided to take fifty men and twenty days' rations and go to the head of the Colorado River on July 25 to see if the Indians could be relocated.[63] The Indians were not found, they having hastily abandoned the country without leaving a trail. Reorganization of the Battalion was still uppermost on Jones' mind.[64] All Steele could tell him, though, was that the appropriation was yet to be passed and for him to stand by the telegraph for a week at Fort Griffin in Shackelford County.[65]

With yet no word about the legislature's actions, Jones and his escort went into Throckmorton County to check with Company B. From this point he forwarded to Steele on August 12 the resignation of Lieutenant Ira Long. Jones planned to discharge fifteen men of Company A in his escort since their terms of enlistment were about up and the men lived in the northern part of the state.[66] On August 16, Dan Roberts of Company D also resigned, effective at the end of the month.[67] William Maltby, "Captain Jeff," who had been disbanded as captain of Company E back in December 1874, wrote Major Jones asking for appointment to another command.[68] There is no record of any response.

The state legislature finally acted on August 21, appropriating in its biennial budget a total of $150,000 for frontier defense for each of the next two fiscal years, through August 31, 1878, then added an additional $50,000 to carry the Battalion through December 31, 1878.[69] On the same day, Steele wired Jones that he could reorganize the Battalion on a basis of one lieutenant and twenty men per company.[70] Following up with a letter, Steele passed on Governor Coke's wishes for a new emphasis by the Battalion:

> The matter of lawlessness is more prominent now than anything else & it is the Governor's desire that your companies should do all they can to aid civil authorities and to arrest known criminals. To enable this to be done, I am preparing a list of fugitives from justice, a copy of which will be sent to each company. I have over 3000 names & lists are still coming by every mail.[71]

Coke's decision triggered a major change in the mission of the Frontier Battalion. The governor sent a letter to the counties asking for submission of the names and descriptions of indicted fugitives from those counties, which were to be collated and published to each Ranger company.[72] While still worrisome, the threat of Indian raids had greatly diminished, both through the efforts of the Battalion and the renewed efforts of the United States Army. From Menard, Jones issued a general order on August 25, dealing with yet another reorganization of the Battalion. On September 1, each company was to have one lieutenant, two sergeants, two corporals, and sixteen privates. "The men enlisted for this service must be sound, able-bodied unmarried men of good moral character, and no drunkard and no one against whom an indictment is pending . . . shall be received." Company A was to continue as Jones' escort. Jones' last paragraph signaled the Battalion's new thrust:

> Commanders of the companies will give particular attention to the maintenance of law and order, and to the arresting of criminals and fugitives from justice, large lists of whom, with orders for their arrest, will be forwarded in a few days.[73]

Pat Dolan *(Courtesy of Texas State Library & Archives Commission, Austin, Texas)*

With the appropriation and reorganization of the Battalion now determined, Jones was faced with the need to find some new company commanders: Long and Roberts had resigned, and Coldwell had resubmitted his resignation. Lieutenant C. H. Hamilton of Company B was in poor health and also wished to leave the service. Jones got in touch with several possible candidates. "I much fear, however, that I shall not be able to get as competent and experienced officers to succeed them."[74] However, he finally made his selections.[75]

Jones' concern with the command vacancies had to have been shared equally with his concern over the complete failure of his business in Navarro County. On August 28, Corsicana City Marshal F. J. Barrett held a public sale of property belonging to the "late firm" to satisfy city taxes owing in the amount of $260. The property offered for sale included a sewing machine, desks, stoves, a safe, and scales.[76] Certainly this was an embarrassing distraction for Jones, who nevertheless continued with the reorganization.

The companies were mustered out at the end of August and immediately rechartered on September 1. Sergeant Francis M. "Frank" Moore was promoted to lieutenant to take Roberts' place as commander of Company D. Moore, a Civil War veteran and former member of Company F, was a forty-three-year-old confirmed bachelor.[77] Pat Dolan, who had been a lieutenant under Coldwell in Company F, was selected to replace his commander as a first lieutenant.[78] To replace Ira Long over Company A, Jones selected Joe M. Denton of Kerr County, who was not in good health but stated, "I think I am fully able to discharge the duties of the position."[79]

At the end of the fiscal year on August 31, Jones was able to point to the Battalion's accomplishments. He had made eight inspection tours, traveling some 3,200 miles, as well as two major scouts totaling an additional 1,160 miles. In Mason County, about twenty-five men had been arrested, with two parties making fight. About fifty fugitives from justice on the frontier had been turned over to local authorities.[80] At the same time, General Steele gave a detailed report of Battalion operations to the governor, rendering his own conclusion as to the result:

> During the past year, the Indian raids have been by small parties, who depended upon their adroitness in concealment, rather than in their strength, for safety. The bloody reception which has been given to war parties during the past two years has evidently had its effect in diminishing the number and proportions of the forays upon our frontier.
>
> The troops, however, have not been idle, for, in addition to the scouting parties constantly employed in pursuit of Indians and outlaws, both detachments and companies have frequently been sent to aid the civil authorities of the frontier counties whose calls for assistance, in executing the laws, have been more numerous than could be complied with by so limited a force.

The lawless element collected on the frontier, and many of them engaged in cattle stealing, have learned that it is so easy to escape justice through forms of law, that an arrest has but little terror to them, when they know that the arrest will not be followed by lynch law; in consequence, they have rarely resisted arrest by Rangers, and have applied to be guarded by them instead of a Sheriff's posse.

Steele did criticize company commanders for not reporting all arrests, but he was even more critical of counties for failure to act and for allowing felons to get away. In Mason County, he asserted, murder committed "in open day, in presence of numerous witnesses, was ignored by the grand jury, saying, 'they had not time to examine into the many cases,'" and therefore they found no indictments. As a result, prisoners held there by the Rangers had to be released.[81]

Reorganized, and the emphasis now on seeking out and arresting wanted outlaws rather than the day-in and day-out scouting for Indian trails, Jones and his Rangers were re-energized, the slight appropriation notwithstanding.

9

TERRIBLY TONGUE-LASHED

RANGERS CAME UNDER CRITICISM in San Antonio when, on September 13, 1876, several men from Company A were confronted by city policemen for "parading the streets . . . armed to the teeth." The company, as Jones' escort, was camped on the Leon River eight miles west of the city. The Rangers were finally induced to disarm while in public, but the local newspaper accused them "of a mind to break rather than preserve the law."[1] One of the men was arrested for carrying a pistol, but was acquitted by a jury upon hearing from Lieutenant Denton that the commander had reported to the sheriff the presence of his men in Bexar County, as well as a willingness to provide any assistance the lawman might need while the Rangers were there. A second charge against the Ranger for "intimidating an officer" was dismissed after a jury failed to agree on a verdict.[2]

The citizens of San Antonio felt they had good reason to exonerate the Rangers. On September 21, a group of citizens met and petitioned Governor Coke to station some Rangers closer, "either at Paint Rock water-hole, or about the head of the Llano." Otherwise, they claimed, with all due deference to Jones' opinion as to where troops should be stationed, the area risked being overrun by the "dreaded influx of thieving and lawless bands."[3] At the same time, Neal Coldwell, recently resigned from the Battalion, was elected in Kerr County as captain of a newly-organized militia force established to protect against the "inroads of Indians and white outlaws." In similar language to the San Antonio petition, Coke was asked to also provide better protection to the Kerr County area by a closer stationing of Rangers from the Battalion, again with all "due deference" to Jones' opinion.[4] In response, Jones exclaimed rather testily that no Indians had been seen in Kerr County since the previous June, and explained that the Battalion now consisted of only five small companies, each consisting of one lieutenant and twenty men, hardly a sufficient force to cover the Texas frontier from the Rio Grande to the Red River, some four hundred miles.

> I have been studying the frontier country for two and a half years; have traversed it from one end to the other about twenty times, each time by a different route as far as practicable; I know all the passes and "divides;" know where all the Indian raids have been made within the last four years, and have stationed the companies where I think there is the greatest necessity for them, and where I think they can do the most good, without reference to the opinions or desires of the citizens of any particular locality. There are about twenty towns on the frontier, each one of which would like to have a company of rangers stationed near it, and each one of which thinks its situation most exposed and most in need of protection (the citizens of most of them have so expressed themselves to me), but, as that is impossible, I make such disposition of my small force as my knowledge of the whole situation and my desire to render the most service to the frontier induce me to think is the best.[5]

Adjutant General Steele received word of a "disturbed state of affairs" in Llano County, and ordered a scout by the Rangers through that area. Jones' role in this is unknown, and he was likely on an inspection tour when the order was received.[6] The major clearly was not in Austin, as Steele also ordered Lieutenant Hamilton of Company B to aid the sheriff in Denton County to run down wanted fugitives in that area.[7] One account had Jones in Houston for a Masonic meeting.[8] Steele also ordered

the scout, once the Rangers were finished in Llano County, to go to Burnet to aid the local authorities there.[9]

On September 19, after arriving by stagecoach back in Austin,[10] Jones
issued a special order naming Lieutenant George W. Campbell as commander of Company B to replace the resigned Hamilton. He also directed
Campbell to move his company to a suitable place for a winter camp and
to do as much scouting as possible with his small force.[11] By September
23, Jones was home for a short stay in Navarro County;[12] then, he was
back in Austin two days later, ready to address reports of lawlessness in
Burnet, Llano, and Lampasas Counties.[13]

Jones issued a special order naming John C. Sparks as commander of a
new Company C, directing him to recruit fourteen men for the company.
Sparks, who was also from Navarro County, was "six feet odd inches high,
spare built, and has a face that betokens a quiet determination and a spirit
that knows no fear."[14] And as time passed, it would reflect that he liked a
good drink. Once organized, this company was to proceed immediately
to Burnet County, from where Sparks was to also scout Llano, Lampasas,
Hamilton, Bell, and Williamson Counties. Jones cautioned Sparks not
to recruit any drunkard or professional gamblers and to enlist only able-
bodied, young unmarried men of good moral character. The recruits had
to be mounted on "good serviceable horses, about fifteen hands high."
Jones also instructed Lieutenant Joe Denton to move Company A to
Uvalde County for the time being, to work closely with Pat Dolan and
Company F.[15]

Beginning another inspection tour in October, Jones joined up with
Foster's Company E at Lampasas. Sparks also reported there to Jones with
his new company. Finding everything peaceful in the area, the major and
Sparks rode on to Burnet, and Foster returned to his former camp.[16] Jones
and Company C camped at Miller Spring, some four miles west of Burnet,
ready to assist Sheriff John J. Strickland.[17] Satisfied that everything was in
good hands, Jones returned to Austin where, on October 21, he directed
Lieutenant Frank Moore of Company D to take or send eight to ten good
men to Junction City in Kimble County. The district judge there had
expressed alarm that outlaws might try to prevent the court from being

held. Jones left Austin the next day for the Nueces River country as part of his next inspection tour, staying at the Menger Hotel in San Antonio on October 24.[18]

The Frontier Battalion was now more involved in chasing down and arresting outlaws, as reflected in increased reports of such action. Two prisoners arrested in Burnet and Mason were jailed by Company A in San Antonio. Four men were jailed by Rangers in Austin for cattle theft in Burleson County, after leading the lawmen on a fifty-mile chase. Two other outlaws, one wanted for murder in Burnet County, were jailed at Georgetown in Williamson County. Other Rangers guarded the Burnet jail, at one point having to repel a mob intent on freeing prisoners, and Captain Sparks in Llano County pursued wanted fugitives.[19] As one early author put it, Texas had come to be home for a large number of bad men who had fled there from other regions. "These in time required the attention of the law; and the armed bodies of hard-riding Texas rangers, a remedy born of necessity, appeared as the executives of the law."[20]

One of those bad men was Billy Thompson, brother to noted Travis County pistoleer Ben Thompson. Billy and Eb Stewart were arrested by Rangers about thirteen miles from Austin on October 25, with eighty cattle suspected as stolen from several counties, but Thompson was released three days later for lack of evidence. He was then promptly rearrested by Sparks as wanted in the 1873 murder of a sheriff at Ellsworth, Kansas, with a reward pending. Thompson was initially held temporarily in General Steele's office, Travis County Sheriff Dennis Corwin refusing to jail him on the authority of only a telegram from Kansas, until Sparks was able to swear out a local warrant for the prisoner. There was great concern that Thompson's friends might try to free him, either legally or illegally.[21] Steele even contacted Galveston authorities to confirm that Thompson was wanted there for the murder of a man named Burke in 1867, and determined that he was also wanted for murder in Runnels County.[22] Awaiting a decision as to the disposition of the prisoner, Sparks and his men dined on oysters at Salge's Austin restaurant.[23] However, before Thompson could be arraigned on Sparks' warrant, a murder warrant from Aransas County arrived, and he remained in jail awaiting further court determination as to which jurisdiction had priority.[24]

While all of this was going on, on October 31 a detachment of McNelly's men, headed up by Sergeant A. W. Robinson and working in conjunction with the Battalion, arrested John Ringo, George Gladden, both veterans of the Mason County War, and Neal Cain, an associate of Billy Thompson.[25] These men were brought to Travis County and jailed there.

Jones was involved about this time with an unusual legal action in Navarro County when he was sued by his sister in a "friendly lawsuit." Fanny Halbert filed the cause on October 2, 1876, alleging that when her husband died in July of 1874, her brother had told her that Halbert had given him $1,000 to be deposited with Jones' company as "an open account or deposit." She had asked for the money, but Jones declined, asserting that the money was tied up in 300 acres for which a deed was filed on behalf of Halbert's heirs. Jones admitted that the money was due to his sister and the court awarded Fanny $1,180, secured by a mortgage on 300 of 600 acres purchased by Jones on Chambers Creek. The lien was foreclosed and the property sold to satisfy the judgment.[26]

Jones did not appear in the Corsicana court, as he was engaged at that time with his men at Fort McKavett and in Menard County, where he advised citizens that he was unable to station Lieutenant Moore and his company in that area.[27] From there he hastened to Montague County, where Lieutenant George Campbell and Company B were trying to keep the lid on violence swirling around the scheduled executions of two murderers, and where a deputy sheriff had recently been shot down.[28] At Montague, Jones took exception to any plan to keep Campbell's company there for an indefinite amount of time while the court of appeals considered the case of the condemned men. He suggested that the prisoners be transferred to another, more secure jail and that Campbell remain only long enough to clean up the rest of the lawbreakers in the county. This solution was satisfactory to local officials, and Jones left Montague on November 21 to return down the line.[29]

On Saturday, November 4, 1876, a requisition for Billy Thompson was received in Austin from the governor of Kansas. Governor Coke issued orders to local authorities to turn Thompson over to Sparks and his men for delivery back to Ellsworth, but Sheriff Corwin refused, basing his stance on the Aransas County murder warrant.[30] It was finally determined that the Kansas warrant would prevail, and on Thursday morning, November 16, Sparks bundled Thompson aboard a northbound train, quite concerned that an attempt might be made to liberate their prisoner.[31] As the train approached Dallas, Sparks became concerned, "from the manner of a number of men who boarded the train," that a rescue attempt was imminent, and on Saturday morning, November 18, he had Thompson placed in the Dallas County jail. A legal attempt was made by friends of Thompson to charge Sparks with kidnapping and to apply for a writ of habeas corpus, but that was denied and Dallas Sheriff Marion Moon placed a guard around the jail, along with the local militia, to discourage Thompson's cohorts.[32]

Sparks' journey to Kansas continued, and the prisoner was safely delivered to Ellsworth. The Rangers left Kansas for Texas on Sunday morning, November 26, with hopes of claiming the outstanding reward.[33] Almost immediately upon arriving home in Navarro County, Sparks became seriously ill with pneumonia, but recovered and took a break during the Christmas holidays with his family.[34]

Lieutenant Joe Denton submitted his resignation as commander of Company A on November 18, citing his health as being "entirely unequal to the labor and expenses attendant upon the position."[35] Jones accepted the resignation, pointing out to General Steele that Denton "is in fact not able to do duty now and is growing worse every day," and reappointing Neal Coldwell to the Battalion as Company A commander with the rank of captain. As justification for the rank of captain, Jones advised Steele that "his fitness for the command is well known to yourself and for the good of the service desire that he shall rank the lieutenants now in the Battalion." Steele went along with the decision.[36] Coldwell had apparently changed his mind about being away from his family. In addition, Jones' good friend, Dr. E. G. Nicholson, the Battalion surgeon, once again resigned, citing personal business that he had to take care of at home in Hamilton County during the winter.[37]

Governor Richard Hubbard succeeded Richard Coke on December 1, when Coke resigned his office, having been elected as a United States Senator from Texas. Almost immediately upon taking office, Hubbard received a petition from Coleman County complaining of Lieutenant B. S. Foster of Company E and alleging that "instead of devoting his time and energy to the protection of the country, he spends it hunting, fishing, etc., while the citizens of this and adjoining counties are exposed to the invasion of Indians & marauders." The petition labeled him as "slothful, negligent of his duties & wholly insufficient as a commanding officer."[38] However, in January 1877, likely in response, a petition was forwarded from Coleman and surrounding counties asking to keep the company there.[39] One citizen of Coleman County credited Foster with doing a good job, and blamed the discontent on the fact that the Rangers may have performed their duties too well and arrested some friends of the first group of petitioners.[40] It was not until March 1877, however, that General Steele directed Jones to make a full investigation and a written report.[41] Jones did not submit a report until the following May, unable to locate any evidence to sustain the charges made against Foster.[42] Perhaps partially because of the dispute, in March of 1877, Jones ordered Company E from Coleman County to Kickapoo Springs to combat lawlessness in Tom Green, Concho, and Menard Counties.[43] Of course, another petition was sent to the governor from Coleman County asking the company's return.[44]

As he returned down the line in December, Jones brought with him Coldwell's Company A and posted it in Frio County, there having been some Indian activity reported there. With Dolan's Company F nearby on the Nueces River, Jones thought that it would be easier to detect and deal with Indians passing through the area.[45] Jim Gillett wrote years later that Jones turned this into a forced march without stops for dinner; he claimed that Jones' urgency was strong so that he could then go what was still a considerable distance to Houston for a Masonic meeting.[46] Although five men had been killed by Indians near Frio City in

October, Dolan reported that there had not been any Indians seen in his area since November.[47] However, on December 30, a band of Indians stole twenty-five horses in the vicinity. Coldwell went in pursuit but was unable to overtake them, although some local citizens recovered forty horses.[48]

On his way back to Austin, Jones passed through San Antonio and stayed at the Menger Hotel on December 19, arriving at his office the next day.[49] He promptly went to Navarro County to spend the Christmas holidays with his family.[50] On the last day of 1876, he wired Steele that he was leaving for Alexandria, Louisiana, the next day, and he requested his mail be forwarded there to J. C. Paul.[51] The purpose of this trip is unknown, and Jones did not reappear in any official records until February 8, 1877.[52]

The year 1877 unfurled as a significant period for the Texas Rangers, a year that would test the Battalion on a number of fronts.

Symbolic of the violence that would overwhelm the area and significantly involve the Battalion, on January 17, in Donnelly and Carroll's Variety Theater at Fort Griffin in Shackelford County, two drunken cowboys shot and killed two men and wounded a deputy sheriff and the county attorney. One of the cowboys was shot and killed at the scene and the other escaped.[53] Lieutenant Campbell and six men went to Fort Griffin but, finding everything quiet, returned to camp on January 29.[54]

Captain Leander McNelly's company of Special Troops was disbanded on January 25, 1877, and Lieutenant J. Lee Hall was authorized to "reconstruct" a new company of twenty-five men to serve for the next three months. General Steele expressed his regret over the ill health of the tubercular McNelly, who was weakening daily, but stressed that circumstances called for a smaller force commanded by a lieutenant.[55] Nothing was uttered about Steele's irritation with McNelly for late or abbreviated reports of operations. In the meantime, the Frontier Battalion was held to twenty men per company during the winter for the purpose of reducing the demand on the appropriation, with the idea that, with more activity in the spring, sufficient funds might still exist to fund an increase in manpower to meet the need.[56]

In Lampasas County another Texas-style feud was breaking wide open. On January 22, Merritt Horrell was gunned down in a Lampasas saloon by rancher Pink Higgins, who blamed Horrell for tampering with his cattle. Horrell and his four brothers were notorious for their involvement in a wild shootout in Lampasas in 1873 that killed four state policemen, after which the Horrells had taken their families and fled to Lincoln County, New Mexico Territory. Their antics there quickly wore out their welcome, and they had only recently returned to Lampasas.[57] Merritt Horrell's death sparked a bloody confrontation that, like the events to unfold in Shackelford County, would call for Ranger intervention, which was requested by Lampasas County authorities.[58] A posse arrested Higgins and others, but Higgins managed to escape.[59] Sparks dispatched Corporal Robinson and five men on January 26 to try to arrest Higgins and Bob Mitchell, which they were unable to do.[60] Although there is no official record, it was reported that Jones and Sparks, along with Company C, camped at the Lampasas fairgrounds in mid or late February to investigate the difficulty.[61] The company did move to Lampasas on February 21, but without any mention of Jones.[62]

At the same time, the mixture of alcohol and two Rangers in Uvalde proved embarrassing to Lieutenant Pat Dolan of Company F. Two of his men, Sergeant Richard Jones and Private H. S. Joines, got into a drunken argument on the evening of January 15 while gambling with two other men. Joines accused the men of stealing his pocket book, and both he and Jones pulled their pistols and forced the men to look for the item with candles. However, the pocket book was where it had been all along, in Joines' pocket. When the two men made a break for it and ran, Jones and Joines both fired after them. As a result, the Rangers were arrested by local authorities and charged with assault with intent to murder and jailed for three days until they could make bond.

Dolan reported that Sergeant Jones was a good man who had expressed great regret at the incident. Joines, on the other hand, "has manifested every impudence that he is master of and he is master of a goodly stock of impudence." He recommended Joines' dismissal from the service, but put in a good word for the sergeant. In addition, the men of Company F sent Dolan

J. Lee Hall (*Dudley G. Wooten, ed.,* A Comprehensive History of Texas, *1685 to 1897, Dallas, Texas: William G. Scarff, 1898.*)

a petition urging him to be lenient with Sergeant Jones.[63] Having apparently returned from Louisiana (and perhaps from Lampasas), on February 8, John B. Jones dishonorably discharged Joines, who promptly "ran off," but in light of the pleas on Richard Jones' behalf, he only temporarily suspended him as a sergeant for two weeks, to serve as a private.[64] And almost immediately, Major Jones was off on another tour of inspection.[65]

But another lapse would add to Dolan's embarrassment. During February he and his men had been successful in arresting a number of men in possession of stolen hides, including a man named Jim Goodman, who was arrested with two others on February 7. When the authorities at Uvalde would not accept some of the prisoners because they were wanted in different counties (and the sheriff did not want the expense of feeding them), Dolan decided to return to camp with his prisoners, then take them on February 10 to Kerr County where they were wanted. Goodman complained that he was sick, and Dolan left him with a wagon under the guard of Rangers S. C. Bowman and R. Chute while he proceeded on. Dolan had gotten no more than a mile and a half away when he received word that Goodman had stabbed Bowman, not seriously hurting him, and then taken the Ranger's horse and gun and escaped. A heavy pursuit followed, and finally, on the same day, Sergeant J. J. O'Reilley and five men ran the fugitive into a frozen river where he was forced to surrender. Dolan was understandably perturbed at the negligence of the two Rangers in allowing their prisoner to escape, but both kept their jobs.[66]

The lapses weren't confined to Company F, however. Three men from Campbell's Company B—H. P. Stevens, Thomas Pickett, and Joe Callis—became drunk and unruly in mid-February, firing some 200 pistol shots into a local business at Fort Belknap.[67] Callis subsequently deserted.[68] Upon learning of the incident, Jones wrote the victims of the shooting asking for their account of what happened and urging them, if the story was true, to swear out warrants against the Rangers.[69] He also wrote to Campbell to find out what defense, if any, the men had.[70] The first sergeant for Company B, George Kisinger, sought to downplay the actions by the three Rangers, asserting that there had been a rowdy crowd of buffalo hunters and cowboys also "shooting simply for fun."[71] Stevens was subsequently discharged from the Battalion at the request of his father as the young man was a minor.[72] Pickett pleaded guilty and paid a $4.75 fine and costs, but the county attorney complained to Jones that the Ranger refused to pay the remainder of twenty dollars due, and Jones asked Campbell to investigate. Campbell reported that the money being demanded was not owing.[73]

This episode sparked new allegations. Concerning an alleged lack of discipline in Campbell's Company B, G. W. Stevens, the former company commander, wrote Jones from Decatur that Campbell "takes no control over the men at all and consequently the men has [sic] been going into Graham and Belknap and cutting some very big swells."[74] Jones was somewhat taken aback and cautioned Campbell,

> I can scarcely believe the report is true but mention it to call your atten-
> tion to the necessity of keeping your men at all times well in hand and
> enforcing strict obedience to orders & attention to duty. A body of
> men without discipline and proper control and management is a mere
> mob, unfit for any kind of service that is valuable to the State and if I
> should have good reason to believe that one of my companies was in
> such a condition, I would disband it at once and enlist new officers &
> new men. I will never allow an officer to remain in my command who
> does not control his men, if I knew it.[75]

Jones also instructed Campbell to make an extended scout in Montague County because of continuing violence there, and curiously added:
"If you get in close pursuit of them and they cross Red River, you may
follow them, provided you think you can catch them and get back to this
side of the river without attracting the attention of the authorities in the
[Indian] Nation, and without molesting any citizen of the Nation . . . If
they resist & you will have to kill them, so much the better, provided you
have to do it in self-defense."[76]

Campbell was defensive as to Stevens' allegation: "I may not have
done as some others might have done, tho a outsider man does not know
what I have to contend with the men in this company . . . I could not
help it no more than you could at Austin as I was not at camp."[77]

One Ranger who was glad that he was armed was William Rascoe of
Sparks' Company C. In late February or early March of 1877, he was in
Coleman attempting to arrest a cowboy named Dave Lehpart. Lehpart
was accompanied by Charles Elston, and both men, who had consumed
copious amounts of alcohol, drew their sixshooters and opened fire. In
the exchange of gunshots that ensued, Rascoe winged Elston in the shoulder, and Lehpart and Elston ran to their horses and rode off. Assisted by
a deputy sheriff, the Ranger was able to overtake Elston, whose horse had
fallen. The deputy went on alone but had to back down when Lehpart

got the drop on him and escaped. Rascoe was praised for exhibiting "great coolness and discretion."[78]

The lawlessness in Kimble County was coming more and more to the attention of the Frontier Battalion. Repeated requests to the state for help emphasized how overrun the county was with thieves and outlaws. As one citizen put it, "our horses, cattle & hogs are being stolen almost daily, cattle from other counties by tens, thirtys and fiftys are stolen and drove to this [county]."[79] Not to be outdone, citizens in Tom Green County asserted that there had been six murders there in three months and that only the Rangers could deal with the organized bands of stock thieves prominent in the county.[80] A recently enlisted private in Sparks' Company C, H. D. Waddill, sent Jones a detailed account of affairs in Kimble County, accusing the county judge and other officials there, including the sheriff, of harboring stock thieves, and he was able to identify some of the fugitives who had flocked there, including Dick and Dell Dublin.[81]

On March 21, under orders from Major Jones to report to him at Fort Mason, Waddill left the Company C camp, reaching Fort Mason on the 23rd. Receiving his instructions from Jones, Waddill made his way to Kimble County to determine the state of affairs in an undercover capacity, subsequently declaring the county to be a "thiafs' [sic] stronghold."[82] At the same time, Jones sent his commanders an order cutting the amount of forage for horses from seven to six pounds daily, the renewed austerity likely resulting from diminished appropriations. He also reminded them that the men should understand that discharges from the service were not available merely for the asking. None were to be given except for bad conduct or for "good and sufficient reasons," of which he would make the final determination.[83]

Jones and Sparks both enjoyed a brief vacation in Navarro County during early March, and while there Jones took applications for new troops.[84] Back in Austin, where Sparks was celebrated for knocking a man down with his revolver,[85] Jones issued a general order on March 10 curtailing extensive scouts to the west in search of Indians.

The operations of the companies will be directed, more than has here-tofore been the case, to the suppression of lawlessness and crime, will be confined mostly to the sparsely settled frontier counties and to the particular localities and route through which cattle will be driven dur-ing the Spring & Summer.[86]

In early March Steele placed a notice in the *Rockport Journal*:

Persons desirous of hunting their stolen stock can have the aid of the Frontier Troops by reporting to Major Jones at Frio City on or before the 15th of April. They should go prepared with all necessary legal authority to receive stolen stock and arrest thieves.[87]

It had been reported to Steele that Frio County citizens had been meet-ing, resolving to stop the ongoing cattle thefts. Local authorities worried that open warfare between the good citizens and bandits would break out, and pleas were made for intervention by the Frontier Battalion.[88] Citizens from Frio County subsequently sent a petition to the governor protesting the removal of Coldwell and Company A to Kimble Coun-ty.[89] It was reported by the media that, on April 9, before leaving, some of Coldwell's men raided a camp in Frio County occupied by cattle thieves, arresting three. The next day they were confronted by another cattle thief, James Quigley, who made the mistake of drawing his pistol, for which he was immediately riddled with bullets.[90] With respect to the plea not to remove Coldwell's men, Jones pointed out that this was the thirteenth call he had received within the last month from a locality not to disturb the presence of Ranger companies in those areas.

We are doing all we can in the interest of law and order. The men do all the work their horses can possibly stand, and are making many arrests of lawless characters, but with the small force now in the ser-vice (and it as large as the appropriation will allow) it is impossible to respond promptly to all calls upon it, consequently, to those places first which from my knowledge of the whole frontier I believe to be in the greatest need.[91]

Taking note of this response, the *San Antonio Daily Express* praised Jones as a "brave, vigilant, and judicious officer, who is well qualified for the responsible and delicate duties of his position." The paper criticized the state legislature for its "penny-wise and pound-foolish" slicing of the Battalion appropriation.[92]

The lawlessness in Kimble had not slackened. Lieutenant Frank Moore's Company D sent out continuous scouts to try and track down the multitude of stock thieves pestering the area. Late in the evening of March 14, First Sergeant M. F. Moore with nine men, along with some local citizens, scouted the South Llano River. They arrested Charles D. Edwin for cattle theft, then went to the house of a man named Tom

Gov. Richard B. Hubbard (*Clarence R. Wharton,* Texas Under Many Flags, *Chicago: American Historica Society, 1930.*)

Doran looking for Cale Hall. The arrival of the Rangers set dogs to barking, and Hall ran out the back into the brush. Moore heard him running, but thought it was only hogs making noise and didn't pursue any further. Moving on up the river, the detachment arrested Tom Potter, then went to the Dublin residence, arriving there just before daylight. An attempt was made to arrest Dick Dublin, but he ran and escaped, four shots from the Ranger whizzing harmlessly past him. Sergeant Moore praised the local citizens helping him: "The good citizens of the county have organized themselves to assist us in getting out the bad ones. The thieves of the county have taken up arms against those that assisted me the night & have been making strong threats."[93] Jones was greatly interested in establishing if any of the county's officials, including the sheriff, were involved with the stock thieves,[94] and he privately laid plans to bring in three companies in April to make a vast sweep of the county.[95]

The feud that had been festering in Lampasas County between Pink Higgins' faction and the Horrell brothers flared anew on March 26 when an assassination attempt was made against Mart and Tom Horrell, both of whom were wounded. Sparks and his men, getting no cooperation from Sheriff Albertus Sweet, scouted for the assailants, obviously suspected as being from the Higgins faction, and arrested a man named Tinker.[96] District Judge W. A. Blackburn wrote Jones about the hazardous conditions existing in Lampasas County, praising Sparks and his men for holding the bloodshed down, and expressing concern that the violence would continue.[97] Jones ordered Sparks to remain in the county to prevent any further trouble.[98] Ultimately, Pink Higgins and a companion, Bob Mitchell, accused of killing Merritt Horrell, surrendered to Sparks the next month and were admitted to bail.[99]

Judge Blackburn, concerned that he would be prevented by force from holding court at Junction in Kimble County because of the pervasive lawlessness, requested Jones' assistance in traveling to and holding court there.[100] As Jones continued to plan for a sweep of Kimble County, Company D worked tirelessly. Sergeant L. P. "Lam" Sieker and seven men went to Junction and arrested the sheriff, J. M. Reynolds, on April 2, and he was escorted to jail in Menard County.[101] On April 11, Jones readied to make his sweep of the county with Coldwell's and Dolan's companies, and, from Frio City, he directed Frank Moore to have three men from his company meet him at Paint Rock on the South Llano on the 18th, as well as to be ready to move Company D to Junction to participate in the sweep.[102] From General Steele, Jones requested that thirty Winchester carbines be sent to him at Fort McKavett, as it was reported that the outlaws in Kimble County were well armed.[103] While he was in Frio County, Jones also refused yet another citizens' petition asking that ten or twelve men from Coldwell's command remain there.[104]

In the midst of planning for the raid, Jones received another petition directed to him from the Nueces Canyon, apparently in response to an earlier petition complaining about Pat Dolan and asking for the removal of Company F from that area. The new petition defended Dolan, declaring him "speedy and willing to bring offenders of the law to justice." Jones, who was not aware of the first petition, responded that, while sheriff of Uvalde County, Dolan had made enemies because of the "avidity and zeal" with which he did his job. "I regard that of itself as evidence of his qualification for much of the duty which is required of the Frontier Battalion now."[105] Even three former prisoners held by Dolan wrote in his defense, swearing that they had received "the greatest kindness and attention" from him and his men.[106] Dolan himself denied all of the charges made against him.[107]

On April 16, Jones was in Edwards County, three days away from launching the raid into Kimble County. He was concerned that "the desperadoes are in strong force, laying in [a] large supply of ammunition and occupying a threatening attitude."[108] On the 19th he divided his force into four detachments, and that evening rendezvoused at Junction with Moore's company. Jones telegraphed Steele that his force had moved into Kimble County, initially taking two prisoners.[109] Sadly, Steele's wife died two days later in San Antonio.[110] Enjoying the role of conquering warrior, Jones was later quoted in the newspapers:

> My advent was a complete surprise to the entire community. Only three persons in the county knew of my coming. I had notified them

only two days before. In three days I made twenty-three arrests. Many of the best citizens of the county—in fact nearly all of them—came to my camp as soon as they heard of my arrival, greeted me with much cordiality and kindness, and offered to assist me in any matter and at any time I would call on them.[111]

The arrests throughout the county began to multiply as the Rangers examined all of the nooks and crannies where bad guys could hide. Jones' pincer movement was much akin to the manner in which cowboys rounded up a herd of cattle: driving men to a central point where they could be sorted out.[112] On April 23, Jones wrote Judge Blackburn:

I have been in this country three days, have had out from three to five scouting parties all the time; have four out now. Am scouting every hollow, hill and dale of this section of [the] county and will have all the active law breakers captured or driven off in a few days. We had captured twenty up to last night . . . The violators of the law and their sympathizers are mightily scared up and are "hiding out," while the honest law-abiding citizens are much gratified by the turn events have taken in the last few days, and are doing all in their power to assist us in ridding the country of the lawless characters with which it [has] been infested for some time past.

Jones added a postscript that three more prisoners had just been brought in by a scouting party.[113]

The next day, Jones boasted of twenty-six prisoners in custody, a number of whom were wanted in other jurisdictions, but he lamented that stock thieves Dick and Dell Dublin, along with their cohorts, Mack Potter and Lew Cathey, had eluded the Rangers, although Roll Dublin, a brother, had been arrested.[114] Steele telegraphed Sparks at Lampasas to see if he could perhaps arrest the Dublins in that vicinity.[115] The impact of Jones' operation was reflected in a petition he received from seventeen "ladies of Kimble County" asking that he station Frank Moore and his company there.[116] Jones and some men escorted eight prisoners to Fredericksburg on April 28, one of whom was Al Roberts from the Mason County feud, and Jones reveled in the arrest of thirty men in five days.

Jones declared that the "backbone of the rebellion against law and order in Kimble" was broken, and on the 29th escorted Judge Blackburn and other attorneys into Junction to hold court.[117] He was ultimately able to tally a total of forty-one arrests, thirty-seven of them in Kimble County, including the county judge and sheriff, and a grand jury quickly returned twenty-five indictments. However, no trials could be scheduled because the jury commissioners could only find "nine good honest citizens" who were qualified to serve as jurors. Several indictments were found against Sheriff Reynolds, and both he and the county judge resigned. There being no courthouse, Judge Blackburn held forth at Jones' camp in a post oak grove. Blackburn sat on a log, the lawyers on exposed tree roots, and the grand jury on grass some fifty yards away so they couldn't be overheard. The prisoners, heavily guarded by Rangers, stood nearby.[118]

Jones decided to leave Moore's company in the area for a few months to prevent any reassembling of the outlaws.

> I must commend the men of my command for their conduct in this arduous and unpleasant service. The work was very fatiguing, much of it having to be done at night. Several parties were caught by surrounding their houses, or finding their camp fires in the woods at night. Some-time we came in contact with their women, and were terribly tongue-lashed by them for searching their houses and arresting the men.[119]

The raid on Kimble County was an outstanding success, a model of "careful planning, sound intelligence, organization, secrecy, rapid movement, and decisive action,"[120] for which the Frontier Battalion received statewide praise. However, once law and order was restored, Jones was again off "up the line" to visit his other commands.

10

A BEDOUIN IN THE SADDLE

MAJOR JONES LEFT KIMBLE COUNTY and by May 6, 1877, was at Fort McKavett, where he requested of General Steele that Dr. E. G. Nicholson be once again reinstated as Battalion Surgeon, the appointment to date from April 19.[1] Jones then moved on to Coleman County. A brief report, without details, stated that Jones and Sergeant N. O. Reynolds pursued and captured at Coleman City wanted murderer J. H. Curtis and jailbreaker Edward Vontress "Pete" Casner on May 9.[2] All the while desperate crimes were being reported from around the state. Jails were being broken into and prisoners removed, either to liberate or lynch them, leading Governor Hubbard to offer a standing $500 reward for arrests of such mobs.[3] One such break occurred on May 11 in Brown County when twelve men forcibly released six prisoners.[4] In Mason County, Rube Boyce, a known mankiller, shot and killed Bob Anderson at a ranch when the two got into an argument.[5] Outside of Comanche, a deputy United States marshal, M. R. Greene, was shot to death while trying to arrest two suspected counterfeiters, the brothers Dee and James Bailey.[6] Clearly, the demands on the Battalion were growing.

On May 16, 1877, Jones dispatched Sparks and his Company C from Lampasas to Coleman. In Jones' opinion there was more of a need there now for a Ranger presence than in bullet-riddled Lampasas. "There are more desperate characters in this and adjoining counties than any section of country I know of now."[7] Citizens of Lampasas quite rightly asked that at least a small detachment of Rangers be left behind, reminding Sparks that the Horrell-Higgins dispute was still ongoing and that other law-breakers might use their absence as an excuse to seek refuge in the county. Sparks agreed, thanking the citizens for their kindness and hospitality and leaving Sergeant T. M. Sparks and Privates Dave Ligon and H. B. Waddill behind.[8]

After briefly searching for the Brown County jailbreakers, Jones moved on to Fort Griffin and Shackelford County. In April, Judge J. R. Fleming had requested that four or five Rangers from Campbell's Company B be stationed there.[9] By May 25, Jones had arrived at Fort Griffin.[10] On that date, Jones and Sergeant George W. Arrington arrested John Golden for an 1877 assault in Travis County, but released him for want of sufficient identification.[11]

While all of this was going on, Lee Hall's Special Troops, operating independently of the Frontier Battalion, had been doing good work round-ing up criminals in southern counties. In May, General Steele notified the governor that the appropriation for Hall's unit would be exhausted by June 15.[12] Once word got out, alarmed cattlemen in South Texas, who looked to Hall and his men for protection, cast about for a way to keep the unit in service. In Goliad County, stockmen scheduled a meeting for June 11, 1877, to raise money to keep the command going until the legislature met and could find a new appropriation.[13] Governor Hubbard hoped that the cattlemen would accept certificates of debt from the state, promising that he would do everything in his power to keep the command in service, fail-ing which he promised to assign a portion of Jones' command to fill the breach.[14] Citizens of Refugio County and others petitioned the governor to keep Hall's command in operation.[15] At the meeting in June, an initial total of $7,705 was pledged, and more was sought from the ten counties represented.[16] Citizens of Victoria County later raised some $3,000 in sup-port of Hall and his men, and over $2,000 was raised in Gonzales County.[17] The company was continued for the time being.

No sooner had Sparks departed Lampasas County in May with most of his company than new violence broke out related to the Horrell-Higgins feud. On June 7, Pink Higgins, Bob Mitchell, and two others rode into Lampasas. The Horrells opened fire on them and a gunfight commenced, all parties running for cover. Both Frank Mitchell of Higgins' group and Buck Waldrop, a member of the Horrell party, were killed, and Bill Wren of Higgins' group was seriously wounded. When the shooting broke out, Higgins quickly left town to retrieve some help, then returned. After about three hours of combat, some local citizens got both parties to agree to withdraw, and a semblance of peace briefly settled over the town. Several of the combatants were reported arrested.[18] One witness, who could hear one of the shooting victims vomiting blood, stated that all was quiet about one o'clock in the afternoon with the "arrival of reinforcements getting to their several forts."[19]

On this same date, Company E's Lieutenant B. S. Foster, claiming he desired to "change my occupation," tendered his resignation after almost three years' service, although it was actually done at Jones' urging for unspecified reasons. "I think it is necessary to make some changes in the battalion." Jones urged Steele's acceptance and temporarily attached the company to Coldwell's Company A.[20] Jones left Coleman to return to Austin via Brown, San Saba, Hamilton, Lampasas, and Burnet Counties.[21]

He arrived in Lampasas a week after the June 7 shooting incident, on June 14,[22] finding the town still greatly excited over the violence. The major had been suffering from a fever for about a week and had to be hauled while lying down in a wagon for part of the journey. He consulted with Lampasas County Sheriff Sweet, who on the 7th had summoned thirty-one men for a posse, only three of whom responded. Commiserated Jones, "I fear . . . that I will not be able to accomplish the desired object as from what I can learn, each party has many friends and supporters and it is difficult to find any one in the county who is not in open or secret sympathy with one or the other of the contending parties."[23] But ever the administrator, Jones managed to find time to remonstrate with Sparks, who was at Coleman, that the company payrolls had not been filled out, which was "quite a disappointment" to him.[24]

At the same time, complaint had been made that Captain Sparks had engaged in disorderly conduct at Mason and discharged his pistol. Jones made inquiry and determined that Sparks was not personally involved in the incident.[25] Also, Joe Leverett, one of Sparks' sergeants, was reported to have shot in the stomach a member of the grand jury at Mason; although no details were given, it may have been the same episode for which Sparks had been accused.[26] Leaving a detachment at Lampasas under Sergeant N. O. Reynolds, who had rejoined the Battalion, on June 21, Jones and his escort took prisoners to Austin from Reynolds' operations.[27]

In Erath County, near Stephenville, County Sheriff James Martin was shot to death on June 25 by Napoleon "Bone" Wilson while the lawman was attempting to arrest him for horse theft. Wilson traded shots with a deputy and escaped on foot.[28] Wilson then became the subject of a Ranger manhunt, Sheriff Martin having been a well-respected peace officer.

On July 7, 1877, near San Antonio, a man named Robert Trimble was shot and stabbed to death, his body dragged by a rope into some brush in order to conceal it, and his wagon taken. An alarm for the culprits was spread and Pat Dolan of Company F received information of suspects driving what was believed to be Trimble's wagon and headed for Mexico. Dolan assigned G. K. Chinn and four men to investigate and to bring any suspects in to Uvalde. Chinn and his men quickly overtook a suspected wagon east of Uvalde, which was occupied by five men and accompanied by two men on horseback. Because the seven men were Hispanic rather than the expected Anglos, Chinn believed that they were not the responsible parties, although the wagon fit the description of the one taken from Trimble. Without searching the men on the wagon, he directed Privates B. L. Temple and R. Chute to accompany the wagon to Uvalde for further investigation, while he and the remaining Rangers went to look for any other wagon on the road.

Temple and Chute escorted the wagon to within a quarter of a mile of Uvalde, when the horses pulling the wagon faltered. While Chute rode to the rear of the wagon, Temple took a whip from one of the prisoners and applied it liberally to the horses, urging them to continue the journey. As Temple focused his attention on the wagon team, one of the Hispanic prisoners produced a rifle and shot him in the back, seriously wounding him. The man then jumped to the ground and fired at Chute three times, killing the Ranger's horse but not hitting the Ranger, who returned the fire and believed that he hit the man. The Hispanics fled. In nearby Uvalde, John McNelly, a member of Hall's command, heard the shooting and rode out to investigate. A frightened Chute shot at the approaching McNelly, believing him to be one of the escaped prisoners, fortunately missing him.[29] Temple subsequently recovered from his wound.[30] Dolan blamed the "shameful business" on Chinn for failing to follow his orders to the letter.[31]

An intensive search was made for the culprits, now believed to be a band of Mexican horse thieves led by Jose Cordoba and his family. A party of Rangers led by F. A. Zorn of Hall's Special Troops, including Chute, received permission from Mexican authorities to pursue the gang on Mexican soil. On the evening of July 16, they crossed the Rio Grande and, after beating off fierce watchdogs with their pistols, surrounded a ranch house. As Zorn felt in the dark for a door and started to enter, young Joe Cordoba rushed out and fired a wild shot at the Rangers. Chute's weapon discharged into the bandit's shoulder, and, with his shirt on fire from the blast, the bandit attempted to flee over a nearby fence. Chute shot him in the side, killing him. An old man at the house was slightly wounded, and four men managed to escape. Zorn and the men decided that it would be prudent to return to the Texas side of the river before reinforcements showed up. The dead man was identified as a half-brother of old man Jose Cordoba.[32] On July 24, Uvalde Sheriff George Johnson lodged the elder Cordoba and his wife in the San Antonio jail. On July 7, 1879, Cordoba was hanged in the Bexar County jail for the murder of Trimble.[33]

Major Jones returned to Lampasas from Austin, determined to find some answer to the ongoing violence between the Horrell and Higgins factions.

> This trouble is one of the most perplexing to me that I have ever had
> to contend with. Putting the parties under bonds for their appearance
> at court will not prevent them from fighting if they meet. That has
> already been tried and failed. So I am taking the responsibility in the

interest of peace and quiet, rather than in accordance with the dictates of law, to intercede and endeavor to reconcile the difficulty and thus terminate this long continued feud. I am on good terms with both parties and hope to effect something towards the declared object in a few days. In the mean time, it is believed that the presence of my force here exercises such a restraining influence upon both parties as will prevent any collision between the parties while I remain here.[34]

While wrestling with the problem, Jones dispatched Corporal Henry W. McGhee and twelve men to Williams Rancho in Brown County for only a week or two to resolve yet another feud, this time between alleged cattle thieves and local citizens.[35] But Jones, seeing no prospect of ending the Lampasas feud, wrote on July 22 that he had decided to return to Austin.[36] However, on July 24 a man named Grayhorn, believed to be aligned with the Higgins faction, was shot from ambush in the northern part of Lampasas County, and Jones remained to investigate,[37] leading seven men in search of the killer.[38]

On the evening of July 27, Jones was camped with Sergeant N. O. Reynolds and his men on the Sulphur Fork, about a mile from the town of Lampasas. Bob Mitchell of the Higgins faction rode in and informed him that the Horrells were grouped together on School Creek, about ten miles from town. Jones ordered Reynolds to take six men and check it out, to be guided by Mitchell, his brother, and another Higgins follower, William Wren. Reynolds subsequently redirected the party to the home of Mart Horrell on Mesquite Creek. At about five the next morning, in a heavy rain, Reynolds and his men quietly surrounded, then cautiously entered the house, finding all of the inmates, a total of eleven, sound asleep. Suddenly aroused, the Horrells reached for their weapons, and Sam Horrell wrestled Reynolds for the Ranger's Winchester, the rifle inadvertently discharging harmlessly when Reynolds wrenched it from Horrell's grasp. As soon as the Horrells realized that they were in the custody of the Rangers, they readily surrendered.

Releasing the others, Reynolds returned to camp with Sam, Tom, and Mart Horrell as prisoners, all of whom were later released on bond.[39]

Jones reported the capture to General Steele, concerned that he and only ten Rangers were holding six other prisoners in his camp, which he had moved to the courthouse square, but he expressed a general belief that both factions would abide the decisions of the court.[40]

Jones nevertheless was not hopeful that the strife would end. He ordered Corporal McGhee to return with his detachment to Brown County. In the meantime, he continued to communicate with both factions in an effort to bring a halt to the bloodshed. On July 31, he expressed his frustration:

> Much more bitterness has been manifested in the investigation than I had been led to expect and as I can see no prospect of an immediate settlement of the trouble, and think it will probably be necessary to keep a force here for some time to come, and as I cannot longer defer arranging for the reorganization of the Battalion on the first of September . . . I shall come to Austin in a day or two.[41]

But, in spite of the negative tone of his correspondence with Steele, Jones had apparently already realized the Horrell faction's willingness to stop the fighting. After vigorous encouragement by the major, on July 30, the Horrells were the first to acknowledge the suffering that the confrontation had caused and, in a statement to the Higgins faction witnessed (and probably dictated) by Jones, agreed "to lay down our arms and to end the strife in which we have been engaged against you and exert our utmost efforts to entirely eradicate all enmity from the minds of our friends who have taken sides with us."[42] Jones' misgiving about the prospects of peace notwithstanding, he took the statement to the Higgins side. On August 2, Higgins, Mitchell, and Wren reciprocated, promising to "commence at once and instantly the task of repairing the injuries resulting from the difficulty."[43] With the stacking of arms by both sides,[44] the Horrell-Higgins feud was at an end and the local newspaper was pleased to report that "very little acrimony and hostility" was being exhibited, and "a disposition towards reconciliation" was beginning to be demonstrated.[45] Jones was given credit for his "unwearied patience and persistent efforts to appease the wrath and to unfold to each party the wrongs and injuries they were inflicting upon society, each other and themselves by a continuation of so foolish a warfare."[46]

On August 6, with the shaky peace in Lampasas County restored, Jones and an escort of six men left to return to Austin, bringing with them three prisoners. At Jollyville the party was hailed by a man complaining that five men had stolen his corn. Jones sent four men in pursuit, continuing on with the three prisoners. The four Rangers arrested three men and delivered them to Round Rock in Williamson County, north of Austin.[47]

The Frontier Battalion was now acknowledged statewide as having confronted both the Indian threat and lawlessness and coming out victoriously. In an overblown statement of praise, the *Galveston Daily News* noted the diminishment of the violence of the past along the frontier borders of the state:

> The companies are scattered from the Red River to the Rio Grande, and so fine is the discipline that this body of men is moved in squads of from five to ten men, crossing and connecting their lines, and entangling in the meshes men who for years have been at large—defying the law and reveling in spoils of their victims, and holding carnivals in their maddening glee over some poor unfortunate being's grave, who may have happened to differ in opinion with them, and most probably for nothing more.[48]

Jones himself received just as grandiose a compliment in another letter printed statewide:

> Impervious to the extremes of cold or heat, able to endure the tortures of hunger and thirst, a Bedouin in the saddle, he leads his wild Rangers through the gloom of midnight, along the forest trails, and the wolf and the owl fly from his path, but the red fingered murderer he drags into light to toil in chains or dangle at a rope's end, as justice decrees . . . [He is], in short, a commander, a detective, a quartermaster, a clerk, a scholar, and a gentleman.[49]

Back in Austin, Jones again turned his attention to reorganization of the Battalion at the end of the fiscal year. Company commanders were ordered to once more discharge their men on August 31, then reorganize the next day. Each company was to consist of two sergeants, two corporals, and twenty privates.[50]

On August 12, a group of fifteen bandits from Mexico stormed the jail at Rio Grande City, shot two jailers and the county attorney, and freed two prisoners held for murder and horse theft. The United States Army was called on for help, as was Lieutenant Lee Hall and his men of the Special Troops. Demand was made on Mexico for the arrest of the bandits.[51] To supplement their efforts, Jones sent Neal Coldwell and his Company E, accompanied by Company A that was attached temporarily to Coldwell's command, as well as Dolan's Company F to Rio Grande City to work with the local authorities.[52]

In the meantime, Jones returned to Lampasas where its annual fair was under way and from where he issued reorganization orders to his commanders on August 20.[53] At the same time he requested that Sergeant N. O. Reynolds be promoted to second lieutenant, describing him as "a man of splendid courage, active and energetic, has good control of [his] men and has been remarkably successful, both as a scout after Indians and in finding and arresting fugitives from justice."[54] In addition, Steele was asked to supply the Battalion from the new appropriation with various items ranging from thirty packsaddles to 200 pounds of horse shoes and 360 seamless sacks to hold corn, all items necessary to the maintenance of a hard-riding Ranger force.[55] Company E was ordered to Lampasas from Frio City to be commanded by the newly-promoted Reynolds, leaving Coldwell now in command of Company A.[56] It had been Jones' intention to have Sergeant George W. Arrington promoted to head up Company A, but Arrington had announced his intention to resign and been replaced by Coldwell as First Sergeant by Corporal J. M. Baker;[57] Arrington subsequently did not resign and resumed his original rank.

The summer of 1877 was a breakthrough period for the State of Texas in terms of nabbing its most wanted criminals. In June, William Preston "Bill" Longley was captured in Louisiana by the Nacogdoches County, Texas, sheriff and returned to Lee County where he was wanted for murder. Longley promptly launched an "autobiography" in local media in which he claimed thirty-two killings and declared himself the worst outlaw in Texas. He had cause to recant his boasts when he was sentenced to hang, an execution carried out in Giddings in October 1878.[58] The title sought by Longley belonged to the vaunted John Wesley Hardin.

In August of 1877, Lieutenant John B. Armstrong of Hall's force, accompanied by Jack Duncan, a Dallas detective recruited by the Rangers to go undercover to learn Hardin's whereabouts, surprised and arrested the Texas badman on a train at Pensacola, Florida, returning him in chains to Austin where a reward of $4,000 was outstanding.[59] A detachment of Rangers was assigned to help Travis County Sheriff Dennis Corwin guard the jail.[60] Although the Frontier Battalion was not directly involved in these important arrests, they reflect the increased prominence of law and order in the state, in contrast to the post-Civil War days. The time of the deadly freewheeling Texas gunfighter, which sprang up during and after Reconstruction, was now fading into history. Crime and criminals would become more mundane, although no less serious. In September, Hardin was escorted by Rangers back to Comanche where he was found guilty of murder and sentenced to twenty-five years in the penitentiary.[61]

Hall and the federal troops were still having problems with Mexican bandit incursions along the Rio Grande. Warnings issued from the American side were perceived by the Mexican government as a threat that Americans would illegally invade their territory after bandits. On August 27, Steele asked Jones, who was on another inspection tour, to consult with Governor Hubbard in Austin about overseeing a contingent of the Battalion in the Rio Grande area.[62] Perhaps feeling a little out of the loop, Steele also asked Jones to disseminate a general order requiring members of the Battalion, when passing through Austin, to report to the adjutant general's office there.[63] Jones responded to Steele's request to report to the governor that he would be delayed because he was awaiting the return of Company C and was leaving for Burnet to head off some expected jailbreakers. He was the only suitable officer there to reorganize the company, but thought he could be in Austin by September 1.[64] Steele urged him to come "without loss of time."[65]

Friends of two prisoners in the newly-constructed Burnet County jail had approached Sheriff J. J. Strickland and paid him a bribe totaling $1,000—$700 in horses and a note for the balance—to release the two when the jailbreakers came. Strickland immediately consulted with Jones, who advised him to agree to the plot and accept the bribe. On August 27, Jones and Reynolds rode to Burnet to talk with Strickland and work up a plan to nab the jailbreakers. They returned to camp in Lampasas the next day, then on the 30th returned to Burnet with a detachment of Companies A and E. Jones and the men stationed themselves around the jail. The Rangers expected two separate parties, but, instead, only one group of three men came. Thinking that Jones and his men were the other party, the three—Bob Sneed, William Van Winkle, and Andrew Murchison— entered the jail where they were promptly arrested.[66]

According to Jim Gillett, Jones allowed Reynolds to pick the best men from both Companies C and E for his new command. One man he requested was Gillett, who at that time was assigned to Coldwell's command in Frio City. Gillett got the news and promptly made his way to Lampasas, stopping briefly in Austin to meet with Major Jones. Gillett said that when he rode into the Company E camp, he attracted immediate attention because of his big Mexican hat mounted with silver, a fringed buckskin jacket braided with flowers in highly colored silk, and enormous Mexican spurs, attire perhaps suitable for the border, but not for Central Texas, and he promptly adopted more conventional wear.[67]

As August ended, Lieutenant Frank Moore of Company D indicated that he intended to resign from the Battalion. Nineteen members of his company petitioned Major Jones on August 30 recommending that their first sergeant, Warren W. Worcester, be appointed to replace him.[68] Worcester, in camp with them in Kimble County, also requested the appointment, along with eight local citizens who submitted a petition on his behalf from Kerr and Kendall Counties.[69] Moore sent Jones his resignation on September 6 with a recommendation that Worcester replace him.[70] However, at the same time, sixty-one citizens of Mason County urged appointment of Ranger L. P. "Lam" Sieker as commander, who himself applied for the slot.[71] Sieker even enlisted the support of former Captain Dan W. Roberts, who

John B. Armstrong *(Courtesy of Chuck Parsons, Luling, Texas)*

thought Sieker "would be ambitious enough to try to merit your esteem, which would force him to do his whole duty."[72]

Jones mulled over his decision, then on September 17 notified Worcester that he would temporarily command Company D. He was determined to take his own time to find a permanent commander that he believed to be "sufficiently well qualified,"[73] he apparently not having enough confidence in the two candidates. Jones then temporarily assigned Company D to Coldwell's command at Frio City.[74] Coldwell was ordered to take both companies, along with Dr. Nicholson, to Rio Grande City, learn which officials could be trusted, and then see to the peace and quiet of the area, clear down to Brownsville.[75]

On September 13, Jones had gone up to Waco to investigate the August 24 mob lynching of brothers Jim and Bill Green in Coryell County. The brothers had long been suspected of being stock thieves, but efforts at prosecution had been fruitless. Since no members of the mob could be identified, no indictments resulted and the lynching went unsolved.[76]

Some concern was registered at the state capitol in early September when a letter was received by General Steele from William A. Bridges, an escaped convict who had been recaptured and jailed in Austin. Bridges related that he had seen a letter that threatened an "outburst of marauders in West Texas" that would release prisoners from various county jails until there was a force of criminals sufficiently strong to take both the Austin jail and the state penitentiary at Huntsville. The group was then supposed to kill Jones and other prominent Rangers.[77] The information was considered preposterous and the matter was forgotten while Jones and others attended to more important matters, including a brief return to Navarro County for a short rest.[78]

On September 15, Bone Wilson, the slayer of Sheriff James Martin at Stephenville in June, was located by Sergeant Thomas M. Sparks and ten men from Company C about twenty miles from Fort Chadbourne in northeastern Coke County. Sparks had received information about Wilson's whereabouts and had been camping in the thicket near the suspected Wilson camp. Two of Wilson's brothers had already been arrested. The entire Wilson family was preparing to go on a buffalo hunt, but Bone Wilson had left temporarily to visit his wife. As Wilson rode back into his camp, the Rangers moved in and he was ordered to raise his hands. Instead, Wilson reined his horse around and attempted to draw his pistol. The lawmen fired, hitting both Wilson and his horse. The wanted man fell with his horse, and, attempting to use the struggling steed for cover, leveled his pistol at his pursuers. The horse struggled to its feet, throwing off Wilson's aim. Wilson got to his feet and ran about ten feet to his horse and again took aim at the Rangers. Another shot hit him in the right breast, and, after taking about five steps, he fell dead still clutching his cocked pistol. The body was taken to Coleman where an inquest was held and subscribers gladly turned over to the Rangers an offered $600 reward.[79]

The question of who would command Company D was finally resolved when Jones wrote to Dan Roberts, then living in Houston, asking him to reassume his old command at the rank of captain and with better pay. Roberts went to Austin to receive his new commission, then was promptly ordered to join his company on the Rio Grande where it was being overseen by Captain Neal Coldwell.[80]

In October, an issue flared in far-flung West Texas that threatened to tarnish the hardwon reputation of the Frontier Battalion. For decades, the Hispanic occupants in the vicinity of El Paso County had trekked to the salt lakes at the base of the Guadalupe Mountains and freely dug in the deposits there. However, in 1877 Austin businessman George B. Zimpelman, a former Travis County sheriff, staked a legal claim to the lakes and designated his son-in-law, District Judge Charles Howard, as his agent to protect his rights in the salt.[81] Howard had a long history in the El Paso County area, reflected in his appointment to the Texas Constitutional Convention in 1875.[82] Early on Howard had been a political ally of Italian-born Louis Cardis, a state representative,[83] but that relationship had gradually soured and the two became bitter political and personal enemies, even to the point of at least one physical encounter.[84]

On September 29, 1877, Howard caused an arrest warrant to be issued at San Elizario, the county seat of El Paso County, for several Hispanics who had taken salt from the lakes without permission. Two men were arrested; the case against one was dismissed on his promise not to take any salt again, but the second man was jailed on his refusal to recognize any legal prohibition against going to the salt lakes. That evening, a group of armed Hispanics went to the residence of the county judge, G. N. Garcia, and demanded a warrant for the arrest of Howard. Garcia refused and was held captive while a mob grew in strength.[85] The mob took Howard from the protection of El Paso County Sheriff Charles Kerber and other officials, and threatened to kill him unless he signed papers stating that he had no right to the salt lakes, that he would not prosecute anyone for this action, and also that he would leave the county within twenty-four hours, never to return. Fearing for his life, Howard agreed on October 3 and was released. A $12,000 bond was posted on his behalf.[86]

Sheriff Kerber sent word of the incident to Zimpelman, and District Clerk G. W. Wahl wrote Governor Hubbard.[87] Steele immediately queried Kerber for more details so as to better understand the situation, and Hubbard sent a similar query to A. J. Fountain, a newspaper editor in Mesilla, New Mexico Territory.[88] Kerber escorted Howard out of the county, there being a suspicion that Cardis might have been behind the excitement, Cardis having publicly contended that the salt lakes belonged to the people.[89] However, Howard had no intention of abiding by the agreement. Upon his arrival at Mesilla, he prepared to return to El Paso and San Elizario with an escort of army troops.[90] A detachment of twenty cavalrymen went to San Elizario but insisted that he remain in El Paso lest he set off another mob action by his return.[91] In Austin, Steele reported to the governor that there were no state troops anywhere near there that could be sent to protect lives and property.[92] On October 9, Cardis sent a telegram to Hubbard taking

Louis Cardis (*Courtesy of Texas State Library & Archives Commission, Austin, Texas*)

credit for restoring peace in the vicinity, "though reports may come to you in the contrary."[93]

While the trouble continued to roil in El Paso County, John Sparks of Company C had his own problems. On October 4 he was arrested in Austin for shooting at a lamp in a restaurant within the city limits and fined twenty-five dollars in the police court on his plea of guilty. Upon leaving the courtroom, Sparks used a cane to assault the person who made the complaint against him, resulting in a new charge of assault and battery. Another complaint was made against him for carrying a concealed weapon. When Sparks appeared before the Austin mayor, there was almost another altercation, and the local newspaper termed Sparks a "bull-dozer and a bully."[94] At the same time, Jones wrote to Sergeant Tom Sparks inquiring about reports he had received that some members of Company C had engaged in drunken and riotous conduct at Coleman, firing many shots in town and some into houses. He asked for an immediate report.[95] Judge J. F. Miles of Coleman advised Jones that he did not know if any Rangers had been involved in such conduct, but young men in the area had been getting on "binders," and he suggested that the Rangers "need a lecture in regard to such conduct."[96]

In El Paso County, the turmoil was fanned on October 10 when Howard confronted Louis Cardis in a store in El Paso and shot and killed him.[97] Despite that, reports were made to the governor that all was quiet in the area, given the presence of a detachment of soldiers.[98] But the death of Cardis, along with the fact of Howard's return, further infuriated the Hispanic populace on both sides of the border, and anger was seething.[99] Kerber was at Mesilla with Howard, but refused to return to El Paso County with him for fear the judge would be killed by a mob.[100] The state government would have to respond in some manner, so a decision was made by the governor on October 22 to send Jones to the area to determine just what that response should be.[101] Jones' last official act in Austin prior to leaving for El Paso County was to issue an order directing the companies to go into winter quarters, and dictating what amount of corn would be fed to horses from November through the following March.[102]

11

HERE COMES THE RANGERS!

MAJOR JONES LEFT AUSTIN for El Paso County by stage-coach on the morning of October 24, 1877. A detachment of Rangers was readied to proceed separately to El Paso, but, if Jones was able to reach an "amicable adjustment" of the affair before their arrival, the troops were to return to their original assignment.[1] Judge Howard wrote Steele that state troops were necessary to restore order,[2] and officials and merchants in San Elizario wrote Governor Hubbard for relief from an "ignorant, prejudiced, and blood-thirsty Mexican mob."[3] Jones arrived at Mesilla, in the New Mexican Territory, not far from El Paso, on November 3 and conversed for several days with Howard and A. J. Fountain.[4] Finding that the mob at San Elizario had not disbanded and that violence was still threatened against "Americans," Jones went there from El Paso on the 7th.[5] Sheriff Kerber warned him to be on the lookout because "these greasers are very treacherous."[6]

On November 8, Jones met with the leaders of the mob, who sent a delegation to visit him in San Elizario. The mob had surrounded the men who had posted Howard's bond, and with Father Pierre Bourgade as interpreter, Jones inquired as to their intention. They didn't answer, arguing only that they had a constitutional right to assemble and bear arms.

He urged them to obey the law and quietly disband. Jones made sure they understood that he had not come to resolve the question of the salt lakes; that was a matter for the courts. His only concern was to keep the peace.[7] The delegation promised to keep quiet, disband, and not to give cause for any more complaints. However, after they held a meeting, Jones was asked to meet with them again that evening. The mob had heard that Jones intended to raise a company of Rangers there and objected to his enlisting any Hispanics, preferring to raise their own company and elect their own officers. It was again promised that there would be no more violence and that the group would abide by the decision of the courts, although side remarks hinted that the promises were insincere.[8]

During other conversations in the area, Jones received a report that a former lieutenant of the Mexican army, along with other former Mexican soldiers, had been on the Texas side of the Rio Grande drilling mob members. It became his belief that some members of the San Elizario mob were Mexican citizens, perhaps involving some covert influence by the Mexican government.[9]

On November 9, Jones wired Steele that despite the serious trouble there, he thought he could "control the mob in a few days," and that he had decided to organize a minute company for a three-month duration.[10] In anticipation that some form of armed force would have to be organized, Steele had been unsuccessfully trying to procure arms and ammunition from the army.[11] Steele authorized Jones to raise all the men he thought he might need, but Jones changed his mind, deciding on November 12 to instead organize a twenty-man detachment of Company C at San Elizario rather than a minute company.[12] Likely this was decided so that Jones could retain command of the detachment's activities, rather than turn it over to county authorities.

According to Jones, he had at first approached the county judge, Gregorio Garcia, the well-respected leader of a small band of moderate Hispanics who opposed the mob and who stood ready to protect Jones while he was there. It was Jones' proposition that Hispanic citizens have the privilege of forming a company, arms to be provided by the state. However, there was an immediate loss of interest and the proposal died when Jones emphasized that such a company would be expected to join in the suppression of any invasion from Mexico.[13] Ignoring the offer of help from Garcia's faction, Jones went ahead with the formation of the Ranger detachment. As commander, Jones selected John B. Tays to serve as a second lieutenant. Tays was approved by prominent citizens that Jones had consulted, and he asked Steele to send a commission for him.[14]

Judge Howard commended Jones on his selection, stating that Tays was a good man, "but he is very slow."[15] Tays, 35, was born in Nova Scotia and had labored in the gold fields of British Columbia and Montana, ultimately serving in the Texas state police and smuggling cattle on the side to supplement his income. The brother of an Episcopal missionary, he was uneducated and had no particular skills, other than digging wells and making furniture. However, according to some apparently unaware of his smuggling background, he was said to be of unblemished integrity as well as courageous.[16]

To help fund this new unit, Jones ordered Companies B, C, and E to each discharge four men from their companies by the 30th of November.[17] In recruiting Tays' detachment, Jones was candid:

> When I went out there I tried to organize a company but found it most difficult, as the whole population there are, you may say, Mexican, and I determined not to enlist Mexicans, as I could not trust them. I did succeed in getting twenty-two men to suit me, and then had to accept two men and a half breed. I put them in command of Lieutenant Tays, a white man belonging to the country, and whom I knew to be cool and determined.[18]

Historians have criticized Jones for, first, selecting a lightweight to command the detachment, and, second, allowing Tays to recruit some "hardcases" of questionable character among the members of the new detachment.[19] One of the Rangers most often cited is Jim McDaniels, a New Mexico gunfighter who would ultimately be involved in the infamous Lincoln County War.[20]

On November 15, Jones issued an order designating Tays as commander of the Ranger detachment, directing him to scout throughout

El Paso County and to assist Sheriff Kerber in making arrests and escorting prisoners, such as Judge Howard. In addition, Tays was to observe the same reporting requirements as the other companies of the Battalion and maintain "strict discipline and attention to duty."[21] The only remaining problem for Jones was the necessity of arresting Howard for the shooting of Cardis and bringing him back to San Elizario, where the threat of the mob was still very real.[22] Accompanied by Tays and three or four Rangers from the detachment, Jones consulted at El Paso with Joseph Magoffin, a deputy customs collector and El Paso alderman, and privately told him that he was expecting Howard that evening and wanted Magoffin to accompany them to see a justice of the peace about arrangements, such as bond. The two rode horseback to the magistrate. After Magoffin had written out a complaint charging Howard with murder, the justice of the peace agreed that he would release Howard on bond, although he should be held over by the district court until March, by which time Jones felt that he would have sufficient help to enforce the law.[23]

On November 18, Jones returned to Magoffin's house with Howard, accompanied by Tays and six or eight of the new Rangers. Before the justice of the peace, Magoffin swore out his complaint and Jones made return on the warrant being issued. Howard waived examination and was bound over on $4,000 bond. Magoffin and Jones both urged Howard "for God's sake" to stay away from the area until the court met, and he agreed, musing that he might visit Chihuahua, Mexico.[24] Through the military telegraph, Jones wired Steele that Howard was under bond and that there was "much excitement and many threats in consequence, but do not apprehend collision."[25] From Austin, Steele sent a shipment to Fort Concho, for transfer to Tays' detachment, of ten Winchester carbines, twelve pistols, belts and holsters, and a box of ammunition.[26] Satisfied that the mob had finally disbanded now that Howard had been returned to Mesilla and Tays and his men were operational, an optimistic Jones left for Austin on November 20 via Coleman and Kimble Counties.[27] Unfortunately, this was only a temporary respite from the troubles there, and Jones has been criticized for overlooking what many in Texas familiar with Howard knew instinctively: Howard's pride would not allow him to stay away.[28]

The rest of the Frontier Battalion had continued to operate in the major's absence. The thieving Dublin brothers, who escaped the Kimble County roundup in April, had been a thorn in the Rangers' side for several years, even before the Kimble County operation. Repeated scouts that focused on the capture of Dell or Dick Dublin, as well as their cohorts in crime, Mac Potter and Luke Cathey, failed to turn them up. Ranger Jim Gillett of Company E had met Dick Dublin in 1873 when he was working as a cowboy, before he was a Ranger, and knew firsthand just how desperate a man Dublin was.

Roll and Dell Dublin (*Courtesy of David Johnson, Zionsville, Indiana*)

Lieutenant N. O. Reynolds and ten men from his company, including Gillett, set out to locate the Dublin brothers at their father's place in Kimble County. On November 19, 1877, they converged on Luke Stone's place about four miles from Junction and surprised Dell Dublin in a cow pen. Angry at being caught so easily, the prisoner tore his shirt open and dared the Rangers to shoot him. As he was being disarmed, his brother, Dick, rode out of the brush and was approaching the ranch when he spotted the Rangers. Dell yelled at him, "Get out, you damned fool. Don't you see the Rangers have got me?" Dick raced away and escaped, the Rangers vainly in hot pursuit, emptying their carbines at him.[29]

Around this time, John Sparks, the commander of Company C, who was always fond of alcohol, became the subject of yet another complaint about disorderly conduct on his part. On December 4, a citizen at Fort Concho wrote Major Jones that Sparks had broken up a "whorehouse dance" and threatened people with a drawn pistol. The observation was made that citizens of that place were glad twice: when Sparks initially arrived there and when he left.[30] This was apparently the proverbial last straw. On December 10, Sparks submitted his resignation as commander of Company C, effective the 15th, which was accepted by Steele the same day.[31] Steele temporarily revoked the termination, reaccepting it as effective on Christmas Eve.[32]

Jones recommended that First Sergeant George Washington Arrington of Company A be appointed first lieutenant of Company C, declaring that "I have tested him thoroughly in the management of men, in commanding detachments, and in his capacity for business." He also recommended that Pat Dolan be promoted to captain of Company F, "in consideration of the efficient and faithful service rendered" by him in the last sixteen months.[33] On December 29, Steele agreed and so ordered.[34] In sending the promotion to Dolan, Jones remarked that he was led to ask for his promotion because "your zeal and efficiency merited the promotion as well as because the pay of Lieutenant is not a just compensation for the service rendered."[35]

Arrington was a peculiar choice on Jones' part to command a Ranger company. His true name was John C. Orrick, Jr., born in Alabama, and

G. W. Arrington *(Dudley G. Wooten, A Comprehensive History of Texas, 1685 to 1897, Dallas, Texas: William G. Scarff, 1898.)*

wanted in that state for the 1867 killing of a black man. Although no sources are cited, two authors have claimed that Jones was aware of this when he allowed Arrington to enlist in the Battalion in August of 1876.[36] Apparently Arrington's excellent service with the Battalion allowed him to overlook that problem, if, indeed, he was aware of it. However, knowing that Arrington often could be hotheaded and unyielding in discipline, Jones felt called upon to advise him that, in light of the "slack rule" under which men in Sparks' command had been governed, "it will probably be better not to be too rigid in the enforcement of discipline at first, as you are not acquainted with the men . . . As you become better acquainted with them you can draw the reins tighter & gradually bring them to proper discipline & duty."[37]

By November 28, Jones was back in Kimble County. Despite his promise to Jones and Magoffin, Charles Howard stubbornly and arrogantly returned to El Paso County from Mesilla on some personal business. When the men escorting him shot at a dog at a ranch on the way, some fifteen armed men rushed out, apparently of a mind to kill Howard. A payment of $100 and "some nice talk" smoothed things over and the party proceeded.[38] The excitement created by Howard's return to the county was thought to have died down, and Tays noted to Jones that his men had been "sick with chills."[39]

Jones briefly returned to Navarro County in early December, armed with a capias warrant from Travis County to arrest H. V. Hurlock for forgery in a land swindle. He was concerned that Hurlock might disappear as soon as he heard that he was wanted. In addition, Jones was needed in court in Austin the next day, so there was a sense of urgency in making the arrest. He brought with him Ranger A. H. Arnett to assist in transporting the prisoner once he was in custody.

On the evening of Wednesday, December 5, 1877, after dark, the two men arrived at Hurlock's house. Knowing that the family would recognize him and probably realize his business, Jones directed Arnett to knock on the door. If Arnett entered the residence, Jones would know that his target was there and would follow in behind him. When the door opened, Arnett saw both Mr. and Mrs. Hurlock, and he confirmed that the man was indeed Hurlock. Arnett told him that he would like to see him on some business, but the man's wife warned that he was not going out of the house with Arnett. When Hurlock, who had been drinking, rose and put a hand in his pocket, Arnett quickly drew his pistol and told him that he was under arrest. Mrs. Hurlock slammed the door shut and caught hold of the Ranger's pistol, and Hurlock also grabbed for the weapon. The trio fell backwards across a bed, which broke on impact, and two other men and a boy jumped into the fray while Arnett sought to hold his pistol away from them.

When the door slammed and Jones heard the noise of the fracas, he burst through the door and saw the fight. Pulling his pistol, he raised it above his head and commanded everyone to stop. He grabbed Hurlock and jerked him off the writhing humanity. Telling Arnett to be careful with his pistol, Jones placed Hurlock under arrest. The two conveyed their prisoner to Austin where they kept him with the Ranger detachment until he could post a bond.[40] Jones felt that the whole matter was the result of a misunderstanding, not an attempt to escape.

However, Hurlock's wife promptly complained publicly that at about six o'clock in the evening, a man unknown to her and her husband knocked at their door and was invited in. According to Mrs. Hurlock's version of events, the man promptly pointed a pistol at Hurlock without saying anything. Man and wife wrestled with the stranger for the pistol, knocking over a chair and falling onto a bed, which was broken. She claimed that the pistol discharged, narrowly missing Hurlock, and Jones then walked in, pistol in hand. Upon recognizing the major, Hurlock surrendered to him, according to his wife, after Jones explained why he was there. Hurlock supposedly asked why Jones had not come in instead of the "ruffian."[41] Jones didn't blame Mrs. Hurlock for her confusion as to what happened, even as far as believing that a pistol had been fired.

Because of the public complaint, a citizens meeting was called at the Navarro County courthouse on December 10 to protest the manner in which Hurlock was arrested. A committee was appointed to draw up resolutions, Major L. T. Wheeler addressing the meeting "in a forcible manner."[42] The resulting resolutions avowed that the arrest was unwarranted by the laws of Texas "and in total disrespect of the civil authorities" of Navarro County. According to the protest, the "military" should always be subservient to civil authority except in times of insurrection. State troops were solely for frontier protection and in the event of mobs and lawless violence where the civil authorities are unable to execute the law, which was not the case with Hurlock.[43] However, once Jones gave his side of the story from Austin, including an explanation that he, too, was a civil peace officer, the matter was quickly forgotten.[44]

In the meantime, Charles Howard's presence in El Paso County had reignited the violence. On December 12, Lieutenant Tays and a number of men escorted the judge from Ysleta to San Elizario, arriving after dark. Tays was under the impression that an army detachment would be there for protection, but it had unexplainably turned back when confronted by some of the mob,[45] an action that in effect allowed the subsequent violence to occur. Howard was quartered with the Ranger detachment in its one-story adobe building used for a barracks, but he brazenly walked freely through town. The tension accelerated, as did the crowds throughout the small village. When a storekeeper named Charles Ellis suddenly disappeared and his body later turned up with its throat cut, Tays decided that the prudent move was to barricade his men with Howard and others in the barracks and other nearby buildings.[46]

In light of the reports of a near outbreak of violence at San Elizario, Governor Hubbard authorized Sheriff Kerber to raise up to 100 men to back up the Rangers, at the same time notifying the Secretary of War, which resulted in a promise to send troops.[47] Jones was in Houston at the annual meeting of the Masonic Grand Lodge of Texas where he was elected a Deputy Grand Master.[48] The *Houston Telegram* carried a flattering portrait of Jones:

> By birth and education a gentleman, and by profession a lawyer [*sic*], this daring chief of the lawless border as he appears on our streets and as a guest in the best houses, is a small man scarcely of medium height and stature, whose conventional dress of black broadcloth, spotless linen and dainty boot on a small foot, would not distinguish him from any other citizen, while in his quiet, easy manner, almost free from gesticulation, his soft and modulated voice, his grave but genial conversation, one would look in vain for the marks of a frontier bravo.[49]

> If his face were consulted one would see a mask of bronzed [*sic*] seasoned and embrowned by a semi-tropical sun and by the war of wind and weather and the storm of battle. Quiet, serious, but always ready to smile, determination, resolution, self-possession and intrepidity would be seen in every feature, and especially in the firm mouth and dark-eyes with their steady concentrated gaze; but it would require a good deal of penetration to see in this quiet, affable gentleman the leader of the celebrated Texas Rangers and the hero of many a daring assault and wild melee, and the bulwark of the border and the terror of the frontier foragers.[50]

"Bulwark of the border" notwithstanding, in San Elizario, Ranger Sergeant C. E. Mortimer left the Ranger's barracks on Thursday morning, December 13, to walk to Ellis' store. A sniper's round hit him in the back, mortally wounding him. Tays bravely ran to him and, under gunfire from the mob, dragged the sergeant back to the barracks where he later died.[51] At this point, it was open warfare and gunfire poured in against the hunkered Rangers. That afternoon a truce was agreed to, but it didn't hold. The firing continued through the next day. Although the mob made several charges, the Rangers continued to repel them. On Saturday, December 15, with Governor Hubbard requesting federal troops of the President, the firing remained heavy.

The next day, Sunday, December 16, Tays met with Chico Barela, one of the leaders of the mob, and they agreed to another truce until the next morning; this truce held, although the mob continued to erect fortifications and dig rifle pits during the night. A deputy sheriff of Pecos County, Andrew Loomis, was holed up with the Rangers, and the mob leaders agreed to let him go. Kerber wired the governor that all were "doomed" and would be murdered unless Howard was delivered to the mob to be beheaded.[52]

The next morning, accompanied by John G. Atkinson, a local merchant and one of Howard's bondsmen who was along to translate, and one of his Rangers, the nefarious Jim McDaniels,[53] Tays met with Barela, who threatened to blow up the barracks if Howard was not turned over. Barela promised that Howard would not be hurt if he again relinquished any rights to the salt lakes. Tays returned to the barracks and consulted with Howard, who well knew that to surrender meant certain death. Even though Tays promised to continue to protect him, Howard recognized that their situation was a desperate one; despite this realization, he consented to go in order to save the others. In addition, there was no reason to believe that army troops would be forthcoming.

Tays and Howard ventured out to meet Barela, and, once in the building with the mob leader, Tays sent for Atkinson to once again act as interpreter. Atkinson was not allowed to see Tays and Howard, however, and after Barela promised Atkinson that all would turn out well if the

Rangers surrendered, Atkinson returned alone to the barracks. Perhaps to save his own life, the merchant told the waiting Rangers that everything had been peacefully arranged and that Tays, not Barela, had ordered them to surrender with their arms. The Rangers marched out dutifully and were quickly disarmed by the mob. They were then held prisoner, many falling immediately asleep after so many days under siege.[54]

The mob wasted no time in exacting its revenge. Howard was marched out before a nine-man firing squad. He stood erect and pronounced, "You are now about to execute 300 men," and was said to have ripped open his shirt and hollered "fire!" The guns exploded and Howard fell to the ground, squirming. Jesus Telles ran up with a machete and hacked him to death, after which his body was thrown into a well. Then Atkinson and Ranger Sergeant John E. McBride were brought out and also executed.[55] The next morning, Barela had stopped the mob from further bloodlust and the Rangers were given their horses and saddles and released, but all other equipment was kept by the mob.[56] Tays subsequently retrieved the bodies of Atkinson, Mortimer, and McBride and buried them at San Elizario. Howard's mutilated body was removed from the well and taken to El Paso.[57]

Leaving Houston for Austin on Tuesday, December 18, Jones was interviewed by local reporters and reiterated his opinion that the San Elizario mob contained a healthy contingent of Mexicans from the other side of the river, and that the mob had been drilled by a former member of the Mexican army. He blamed the return of Howard as the immediate cause of the renewed violence, but praised Tays as a man "of coolness and nerve."[58] When Jones arrived in Austin on the 20th, a *St. Louis Globe-Democrat* reporter noted the major's slight build, black hair, piercing black eyes, and heavy moustache slightly tinged with gray. According to the reporter, Jones gave the same information about his suspicion of involvement by Mexican authorities, but also made the offhand remark that "prominent Texans" who knew Howard considered him an "unscrupulous, bad man, generally despised—a cutthroat and a desperado."[59] When this quote was published, Jones quickly denied that he ever gave such an interview or made any such statements, insisting that he found

Howard to be "very prudent, cautious, honorable and reliable," as well as a man of courage.[60]

Even though the San Elizario mob had dispersed, violence nevertheless continued in El Paso County. The violence was ultimately laid at the feet of "volunteers" recruited by Sheriff Kerber from Silver City, New Mexico Territory. Thirty men commanded by a Silver City deputy sheriff, Dan Tucker, had arrived at San Elizario on December 21 and immediately engaged in episodes of murder, rape, and robbery.[61] Tays' men were not believed involved, although there is some evidence that Jim McDaniels may have joined his New Mexico cohorts in some of the violence.[62] However, Tays could be properly criticized for not stepping up against the excesses being carried out by such "volunteers" against Hispanics in the name of law and order.[63] Tays' detachment continued in service, increased to thirty men,[64] but the Salt War was at an end.

Subsequent historians have criticized Jones' actions as shortsighted in responding to the San Elizario violence. The fact that a Ranger unit had been forced to surrender was bad enough, but Jones was accused of placing too much trust in Howard and of leaving the county before fully reconciling the parties and seeing the matter through, if such a thing was possible. In addition, it has been argued that Jones certainly did the situation no favor by appointing Tays rather than working out an arrangement with Gregorio Garcia, perhaps displaying a cultural bias on his part that clouded his better judgment.[65] Jones' failure to keep Howard from returning, as well as not effectively instructing Tays as to the role and specific mission of his detachment, were factors seen as an omission on the major's part.[66]

Of course, as the bromide goes, hindsight is always twenty-twenty. Jones went to El Paso County with very little idea as to the extent or nature of the problem there. He could have perhaps urged that experienced state troops ordered to go there continue on to join him, but in the face of considerable budget problems and with the difficult logistics of moving such a force, Jones faced hard decisions in regard to a still-undefined problem. He also could have taken along just one or two experienced Rangers to help arrive at an appropriate decision. But perhaps it was a better idea to first get the lay of the land and an understanding of the problem before committing any resources.

Clearly, Jones initially thought he could bring the parties to reason, much as he had done with the Horrell-Higgins feud at Lampasas, especially when he was under the impression that he had Howard's pledge of cooperation. Also, John Tays came highly recommended, and there was no reason to believe that he couldn't recruit twenty-odd good men to staff the detachment, which, for the most part, he did. But for Howard precipitously forcing himself back on the scene, the matter might have been properly handled by the courts and the matter of the salt lakes quietly resolved. Tays remained at all times ready to protect Howard, and without his separation from his men and the alleged treachery of Atkinson, no surrender would have occurred. Likewise, if the army had not backed off entering San Elizario, the mob would have been dealt with more effectively. On review, Jones does not deserve as much criticism as has been directed toward him, although the episode certainly remains a sad one in Ranger history.

At the request of Jones' brother-in-law, Congressman Roger Q. Mills, President Hayes ordered the creation of a commission to investigate and report the facts of the San Elizario violence. General E. O. C. Ord was to detail from army ranks two members of the commission, and Governor Hubbard was to designate a representative. Of key concern to Texas authorities was whether or not Mexican citizens had crossed the border to participate with the mob.[67] The army appointed Colonel John H. King of the Ninth Infantry and Lieutenant Colonel William H. Lewis of the Nineteenth Infantry to convene at Fort Bliss on January 16 to begin its hearings.[68] At the same time, Jones and Steele were summoned to Washington to testify as soon as January 10 before the House Committee on Foreign Affairs about border problems in Texas.[69]

As a peculiar aftermath to the troubles at San Elizario, in an incident that perhaps questions Tays' ability to select appropriate men for his detachment, one Ranger in the detachment killed another in January. Sam Frazier had been appointed second sergeant of Tays' detachment, but became upset when John C. Ford was appointed over him as first sergeant, even threatening to kill Ford before Tays smoothed things over. When an order came down that members of the detachment were not to carry guns outside camp without Tays' permission, Ford asked for Frazier's pistol when the latter was preparing on January 29 to go to El Paso from the camp at Ysleta. That evening Frazier was heard to say that the company was not "big enough to hold both of us," and again threatening to kill Ford. Both Frazier and Ford were considered good shots. When Frazier rode into the detachment's corral and was dismounting, Ford came up behind him with a double-barreled shotgun and called out "Sam" in an ordinary voice.

Frazier turned around and screamed when he saw the shotgun. Ford fired, hitting his enemy in the right side, and missing with a blast from the second barrel. Frazier staggered, then fell to a sitting position, saying, "Don't shoot any more." Ford calmly walked up to him and emptied six pistol shots into the wounded man, five in the head.[70] Apparently the reported aggressiveness of Frazier satisfied a jury of inquest, it finding that the killing was justified, and Ford no longer had to look over his shoulder as he went about his duties.[71] Interestingly, Ford was appointed as George Zimpelman's agent for the salt lakes, and he claimed that the "Mexicans" recognized his authority and were now asking permission to get salt.[72]

New Year's Day of 1878 saw another Ranger downed in the line of duty. On December 31, Lieutenant N. O. Reynolds and five men of Companies E and A, returning from a scout to Menard County, arrived at Fort McKavett to assist county officers in keeping the peace during New Year's celebrations. Along with the scout were two black men, Ben Johnson and George Stevenson, who drove the detachment's wagon and cooked, and both of whom were required to carry pistols. Johnson was carrying a revolver belonging to twenty-seven-year-old Ranger Tim McCarty, who was formerly assigned to Coldwell's Company A. The two teamsters found themselves caught up in a crowd of reveling, drunken black men at a dance in "Scabtown" near the fort; most of the men were former soldiers, including Charles Miller, Henry Clay, and Steve Saunders. The two men were forced at gunpoint to hand over their pistols. There may have been some resentment of the light-skinned Stevenson, who could have been mistaken for white, and there was also the damning fact that both men were a part of the Ranger scout.

At about eleven o'clock, the two teamsters returned to the Ranger camp and reported what had happened. Reynolds was awakened at a store where he had bunked, and he gathered the two black men plus four Rangers—Sergeant Henry McGhee, and Rangers Tom Gillespie, Dick Harrison, and Tim McCarty. The party went to Miller's house where Reynolds identified himself and demanded return of the pistols. Miller refused, threatening to kill the first "white-livered son of a bitch" who attempted to enter. Reynolds again directed them to surrender and allow a search of the house. Miller responded that if the black men in the house died, they died right there. Miller's wife, Ida, looking for an out, excitedly shouted to Reynolds that they could have the pistols, and her husband then agreed. But as McCarty stepped forward to retrieve one of the pistols, Miller fired, missing the Ranger. McCarty returned the fire, but Miller's next shot hit him below his left nipple and he went down, mortally wounded, calling out to Reynolds, "Lieutenant, I am killed." The Rangers opened up on Miller, killing him. When the remaining inhabitants then refused to surrender and opened fire, the Rangers shot through the doors and windows of the house. McGhee got off some ten shots with his Winchester.

When the gunsmoke cleared, the Rangers entered the house and found three dead black men—Miller, Saunders, and Clay—and a dead black girl, who was "accidentally shot." McCarty died the next evening and was buried at the fort. An inquest was held and the justice of the peace ruled that the black men came to their death by resisting officers discharging their official duty. Reynolds reported that "the citizens are jubilant over the killing of the Negroes."[73] In Austin the Washington Steam Engine Company Number One, of which McCarty had been a member, met on January 6 and passed a resolution of regret at McCarty's passing.[74] However there was some criticism in the media of Reynolds and his men for being too cavalier with their firearms in this incident, so Jones directed Reynolds to provide him with a copy of the inquest verdict so that it could be publicly disseminated.[75]

Miller's wife, Ida, did not remain silent. She complained that her daughter's head was shot to pieces, her husband was shot in four places, and the other two men were shot and fell in the fire. The following March she pleaded publicly for the murderers of her family to be brought to justice.[76] Perhaps this was the criticism that came to Jones' attention.

The three dead men at Fort McKavett were not the only ones out on a spree for New Year's. In Austin, after delivering prisoners, Sergeant T. M. Sparks and Privates W. H. Taylor and Jerry Geren of Company C got caught up in a disturbance at the Casino Theater and were immediately discharged by Jones. But members of the company petitioned Jones to reinstate them, and Jones did so, "in consideration of their repentance for past offenses and their promises of good deportment in the future."[77]

Jones and Steele both left Austin for Washington on Wednesday, January 9, 1878.[78] It was not until after he had left Texas that Governor Hubbard appointed Jones to be the Texas representative on the San Elizario commission. Some saw this appointment as creating a conflict of interest, given the fact that Jones' Rangers were involved.[79] On January 19, Jones gave his testimony to the House Committee on Foreign Affairs, speaking generally about Indian and Mexican bandit problems on the Texas border.[80]

Of course, while the Salt War raged and the aftermath saw Jones caught up in investigations and testimony, the Battalion continued to vigorously pursue outlaws. One old adversary, Dick Dublin, had continued to plague Kimble and Menard Counties. In January of 1878, Corporal Jim Gillett of Company E was on a five-day scout after the elusive Dublin brothers, accompanied by brothers John and Will Banister, Tom Gillespie, Dave Ligon, and Ben Carter. After several days of fruitless search, on the evening of January 18, the scout approached the ranch of "Old Man" Tom Potter, a known ally of the Dublins. The Rangers dismounted and prepared to surround the house, leaving John Banister and Ligon to guard their horses.

As the Rangers approached on foot, remaining hidden in the brush about fifty yards from the one-room house, they observed a lone rider approaching. Old Man Potter and one of his sons were unloading some hogs from a wagon into a pen. The lawmen decided to rush the house and try to take the Potters and the rider by surprise. As they ran toward the men, the old man yelled, "Run, Dick, run! Here comes the rangers!" Dublin, who had dismounted, made a dash on foot for the brush, ignoring Gillett's call for him to halt and surrender. Running after the fleeing man, Gillett saw him climbing up a small ravine. Drawing a bead, Gillett again ordered him to halt. When Dublin reached inside his coat as if to draw a weapon, the Ranger fired, killing him instantly. It turned out that he was unarmed. The latter was Gillett's account written years later.[81] A more contemporary account, from a letter by Corporal J. W. Warren, also of Company E, said that Dublin fired at the pursuing Rangers after a number of warning shots were fired over his head, and that he was brought down by two rifle shots.[82]

N. O. Reynolds' report stated that Dublin was eating supper at a table when the Rangers ran up, the outlaw then choosing to run for it.

> The Corporal states that he halted him three or four times but he paid no attention to him. Several shots were then fired at random to intimidate him. He still kept running and gaining ground on them. After being thoroughly satisfied that they could not capture him without shooting, they commenced firing in earnest to cripple him, if possible. He received two dead shots and died instantly about two hundred yards from the house.[83]

However it happened, another bad man had been tracked down by the Texas Rangers.

The board to hear evidence on the El Paso County violence first convened at Fort Bliss on January 22, although Jones had yet to report, still being in Washington.[84] The major returned to Austin, briefly catching up on administrative Battalion business, then left for El Paso by stage on February 9, anticipating an absence of a month to six weeks, after which he wanted to make another tour of inspection.[85] In the meantime, Steele would be responsible for the day-to-day oversight of the Battalion. The general formally charged Jones, in taking his position on the commission, to be "governed by the instructions you have personally received from . . . Governor Hubbard."

> The instructions which have been given to other members of this commission not being known, much discretion must necessarily be given you in your action, bearing in mind that as the representative of Texas, you are expected to urge a full investigation of the troubles referred to, and to be satisfied with nothing else.[86]

When Jones arrived at Fort Bliss and took his seat on the commission on February 19, he found that the other two commissioners planned to investigate the conduct of county and state officials in the matter. He inquired of Steele if he should do likewise. Steele responded that the commission was intended only "to settle the question of invasion from Mexico," and Jones was not to take part in any matter not relating to that subject.[87]

As an aid to the members of the Frontier Battalion, General Steele distributed copies of the 1878 *List of Fugitives*, a 225-page book with the names and descriptions of wanted fugitives from all parts of the state, although some counties had failed to submit lists from their jurisdictions. A total of 4,402 names were included from 108 counties, including some 300 for whom a reward had been offered by the governor. Past editions of the list had proven invaluable to lawmen across the state, not just the Rangers. One newspaper estimated that there were fifty percent fewer fugitives in Texas than two years before when the list was first promulgated, and "the State, in fact, is now rid of nearly every prominent desperado."[88] That comment was a bit premature, as at that very moment one of the most notorious outlaws in Texas was beginning his own saga.

12

A MANLY AND VIGOROUS EFFORT

JONES FOUND HIMSELF at Fort Bliss in February of 1878, jousting with his fellow commission members as they took testimony from witnesses such as Tays, Kerber, and others, and collected all available documentation. In the interior of the state, the Frontier Battalion continued as usual with its daily scouting activities, arrests, reports, and keeping up with supplies and livestock. Steele promulgated an order directing Rangers to "lay aside their arms when in cities or towns, unless in the discharge of some specific duty." Going into saloons, circuses, "or other places of amusement" while armed was strictly forbidden unless under orders for a specific purpose.[1] A wanted horse thief, Stark Reynolds, was captured by Jim Gillett and others on February 21 after a furious pursuit.[2]

In following the governor's orders not to delve into the acts of local and state officials, Jones was criticized in the media for obstructing a legitimate examination of the causes of the disturbance at San Elizario. The complaint was, "Without looking into their acts, it would be impossible to determine the nature of the disturbance." It was charged that Jones' position would damage him politically and give his enemies room to charge that he "shrank from a full investigation of his own acts, for fear of damaging revelations." There was a wide opinion that Texas officials had a desire to provoke a war with Mexico by concentrating only on who was involved in the violence.[3] However, criticism notwithstanding, on February 23 Governor Hubbard instructed Jones to act only in a limited fashion with the other two commissioners, taking testimony only as to facts, not opinions or suggestions.[4]

On the 27th, Jones filed with the commission a protest complaining that Commissioners King and Lewis were taking testimony regarding acts of violence allegedly committed by "Rangers," which had occurred in El Paso County since December 17, in the aftermath of the San Elizario violence. He contended that such evidence was irrelevant to the charter of the commission, and, if true, should be left to civil courts to handle. He also objected to the admission of various newspaper editorials written about the commission.[5] To Steele, Jones explained that, in light of the intent of the other two commissioners to "investigate everything," he would attempt to introduce rebutting and explanatory testimony if possible.[6] The commission also traveled to Ysleta, San Elizario, and Socorro to take testimony.

Some five months earlier, on the evening of September 18, 1877, at a small watering station at Big Springs, Nebraska, six masked men held up the eastbound Union Pacific train and liberated it of $60,000 in newly-minted twenty-dollar gold pieces. The gang, headed up by a former Dallas man, Joel Collins, included an Indiana native, Sam Bass. Bass had taken up with Collins in San Antonio and the two ended up hustling in the Deadwood, Dakota Territory, area of the Black Hills. Running out of money, the two had formed a gang and sought to enrich themselves through stage robbery. When that endeavor proved largely unsuccessful, they struck it rich with the Union Pacific robbery.[7] The gang quickly dispersed and Collins and another robber were killed in Kansas and others were tracked down, but Bass made it back to Denton County, north of Dallas, where he had previously worked for the sheriff, William Egan.

Names and descriptions of the train robbers, along with reward offers by Union Pacific and express companies, were quickly disseminated throughout Texas. Bass, in possession of a princely sum of the train loot, did not dare go about publicly, so he hid out in and around Denton

County, relying on two companions, Henry Underwood and Frank Jackson, to keep him supplied with provisions and news.[8] After languishing in the underbrush and woods for several months, Bass decided that train robbery could be just as lucrative in Texas as in Nebraska.

After a few stagecoach robberies by Bass and companions near Fort Worth in December 1877, however, Underwood was arrested as a suspect in the Nebraska train robbery and hauled back to that territory. Bass and Jackson recruited a young tough, Seaborn Barnes, and Missouri mankiller Tom Spotswood as part of their gang. They struck for the first time on February 22, 1878, holding up the southbound train at the small station of Allen, just north of Dallas, making away with a very small amount of loot. A reward was offered by Governor Hubbard for the capture of the

Sam Bass (Author's Photo)

bandits,[9] and Spotswood was quickly tracked down and arrested by railroad detectives. However, the robbery soon disappeared as a major topic of discussion. A few Rangers from Hall's Special Troops traveled north briefly to nose around through the area for any sign of the outlaws, but with no luck.[10] But Bass was just getting warmed up. This was the forerunner of a series of crimes and a Ranger manhunt that would result in a Texas legend.

In the meantime, sitting on the commission at Fort Bliss, Jones, while remaining polite and patient, focused his questioning on who was actually involved in the mob at San Elizario. One witness, Judge Allen Blacker, estimated that there were not less than 150 Mexican citizens within the mob.[11] Governor Hubbard sent some documents to Jones that he wished incorporated into the commission's final report. It was understood that if any objection was made by the other commission members, Jones was to embody those documents in a minority report.[12] Finally, on March 16, and with Major Jones dissenting, the commission issued its preliminary final report.

The majority report estimated that the mob was about 400 strong, of which not less than one-third were Mexican citizens. However, it was concluded that the evidence did not support a conclusion that the mob was drilled and disciplined by Mexican military figures. The report recognized the close, intimate connection between citizens on both sides of the Rio Grande, willing to support each other in whatever cause. As to what led to the outbreak, the report focused first on the feud between Judge Howard and Louis Cardis and concluded the premeditated murder of Cardis, who was well thought of in the Hispanic community, was a large factor. Of course, the dispute over access to the salt lakes played a major role. The report also delved into what it considered the inexcusable violence occurring after the riot had ended, laying it at the feet of unnamed "rangers," although the reference was actually to the contingent force brought from Silver City at Sheriff Kerber's request, not the members of Tays' detachment. The majority recommended the establishment of a military post in the area, as well as improvements in irrigation. In addition, the report suggested firm demand should be made on Mexico to surrender those who played a part in the riot and to pay reparations.[13]

While concurring with much in the majority report, Jones nevertheless took issue with some of the "opinions and inferences" with which he could not agree. Since the other commission members were leaving the next day, he resolved to draft a minority report to be forwarded later by mail.[14]

On March 18, Sam Bass and his gang struck again, this time attacking the train at the Hutchins station, just south of Dallas, engaging in a brief gunfight with passengers, but again making away with only a nominal amount of loot.[15] At about the same time, Underwood escaped his Nebraska jail cell to return to Texas, bringing with him another bad man, possibly named Huckston, who called himself Arkansas Johnson. This second robbery, so close on the heels of the Allen holdup three weeks earlier, began to generate excitement among local officials as well as the media.

Jones, likely unaware of the train robberies, wired Steele from El Paso on March 19 that he would be staying about a week longer, and that he was continuing Tays' detachment in service there.[16] He received a petition from citizens of Ysleta, in El Paso County, asking that Tays' detachment not be disbanded.[17] On March 22, he forwarded his lengthy minority report, pointing out those portions of the majority report with which he disagreed. Specifically addressing a number of what he considered inconsistencies between the majority's conclusions and the evidence, he asserted that the evidence taken showed some military leadership of the mob and a military structure with a strong Mexican influence. He again objected to any portions of the report that dealt with violence in the county after the riot had subsided, such matters, in his opinion, being beyond the charge given the commission and properly belonging before a grand jury. In summarizing the causes of the trouble, Jones laid the blame on Cardis for trying to obstruct Howard in legally controlling the salt lakes. The failure of the United States Army to act promptly was also a factor. He was also critical of Mexico for not taking steps to control its side of the border and preventing persons from crossing to join the mob.

He concurred with the majority that federal troops should be stationed in the area, but he further recommended that "such steps as are deemed just and proper" be taken to require Mexico to bring to justice and punish the approximate 150 Mexicans who were in the mob, about fifty of whom had been identified. If Mexico took no action, those persons should be handed over to the United States for trial.[18]

John Tays submitted his resignation from the Ranger detachment on March 25, which Jones accepted. In his place, Jones recommended James A. Tays, his brother, effective April 1.[19] Such appointment reflects Jones' belief that both men were qualified to command the detachment, and the major left El Paso, never to return. It was later reported that the El Paso grand jury found 285 indictments, and extradition from Mexico of 180 nationals was demanded, but with no response noted.[20] The following May, Jones retained Tays' detachment until the following August,[21] and Governor Hubbard offered a $250 reward for eight mob leaders for the murder of Charles Howard.[22]

In the meantime, the Bass gang had again become front page news. James E. Lucy of Hall's Special Troops was dispatched north to work undercover and see what he could find.[23] A. L. Parrott, another member of Hall's troops, was also scouring the area and following any leads that could be developed. Sam Bass was now identified as being involved in the robberies.[24] Railroad executives requested to be allowed to arm their employees, but Governor Hubbard asserted that he did not have the authority to authorize that.[25] Two of Joel Collins' brothers, Billy and Henry, also joined the Bass gang.

On the same day that Jones returned to Austin from El Paso, April 4, a third robbery was pulled off by the gang, this time at Eagle Ford, just west of Dallas. Again, very little loot was gained.[26] Statewide concern over the robberies now became much more pronounced, especially from railroad and express companies, as well as postal officials. Governor Hubbard offered a $500 reward for each of the train robbers.[27] On Wednesday, April 10, just six days after the Eagle Ford robbery and forty-seven days after the Allen robbery, the gang struck for a fourth time at Mesquite, east of Dallas. Two new members of the gang from Dallas joined in, Albert Herndon and Sam Pipes. This time the outlaws met armed resistance from a plucky conductor, Jules Alvord, a Union veteran, who wounded Sam Pipes before he himself was wounded severely in the arm. But, again, the gang made off with only a paltry sum.[28] Now, with railroad and express company officials camped on his Austin doorstep, Governor Hubbard doubled the reward for each robber.[29] Thus was launched one of the biggest manhunts in Texas history.

Steele ordered Jones to go at once to Dallas to determine what needed to be done to run down this gang. Steele proposed that Companies A, D, and E report to Austin and then be transported to Dallas. "I wish you to post yourself so that you can proceed in a legal manner to arrest as many felons as possible, the RR robbers being the ones that are most required."[30] Jones had been subpoenaed to testify in the federal court at Galveston regarding some land fraud cases, so Steele wrote the court asking if the major could be excused from attendance there.[31] On the way to Dallas, Jones stopped off briefly in Waco to retain a lawyer to represent Jim Gillett and others in Kimble County in the event they were indicted for killing Dick Dublin, followed by a short visit to Corsicana.[32]

On April 12, Governor Hubbard, recognizing the difficulty of immediately sending experienced Rangers to Dallas, determined that the best course of action was to instead raise a force of thirty men there to go after the Bass gang. The company was to be activated for no more than thirty days. Jones was to muster them in and direct them to work closely with United States Marshal Stilwell Russell, who was heading the investigation.[33] The state government was already under strong criticism for not sending a contingent of Rangers right after the Allen robbery. "Let General Steele and Governor Hubbard forget legal and executive formalities and the red tapery of Austin for a few days, and make a manly and vigorous effort to catch and punish the train robbers."[34] Jones arrived in Dallas on April 14, publicly proclaiming that he was there only on routine business, not after the train robbers.[35] The trains were now well guarded. Privately, Jones consulted with Marshal Russell and with prominent Dallas leader Col. E. G. Bower, who provided him with the names of some half dozen men who could command the new company.

Without hesitation, Jones selected Junius "June" Peak as the commander of the temporary company, and asked that he be commissioned as a second lieutenant.[36] Peak, currently the city recorder and a former deputy sheriff and city marshal, accepted the position and immediately set about recruiting men for the company. Fifteen signed up immediately. Jones described Peak as "very popular, is regarded as a terror to evil doers, is a man of fine courage, active, energetic and efficient in finding violators of the law."[37] On the 17th, after swearing in the initial eighteen members of the company, Jones went to Denton County incognito just to get a feel for the area, there being rumors that citizens of Denton County were protecting the gang.[38] He returned to Dallas the next day, having gained a little more information about the gang, but satisfied that a number of Denton County citizens deplored the presence of the train robbers in their midst.[39]

Two would-be detectives, William "Billy" Scott and E. W. "Jack" Smith, approached Jones with a scheme, and it was agreed that they would get a share of any reward if their efforts led to the capture of the gang. Scott had made contact with members of the gang and fed the information to Jones. It was their plan to set up a hoax holdup where the gang could be trapped.[40] Peak's company was finally fully staffed and organized, and in the early morning hours of April 21, Jones, Peak, and the company arrested Albert Herndon and Sam Pipes near Duck Creek in the northeast part of Dallas County, finding Pipes asleep at the house of the father of Joel, Billy, and Henry Collins.[41] Another close friend of Bass, Scott Mayes, was also arrested, believed to be acting as a courier for the gang.[42]

Jones and Marshal Russell wanted to transfer their prisoners to the federal court at Tyler, but Pipes and Herndon gave bail in Dallas on April 24 and were unexpectedly released by the United States Commissioner. Russell was adamant that the action of the commissioner was void and that the two should be rearrested and sent on to Tyler. Jones went briefly to Fort Worth to investigate a claim that some of the Union Pacific gold was in a bank there. Pipes and Herndon were rearrested and arraigned on state charges on April 26, then rearrested on federal charges. This time they were taken before a different commissioner who set a bond too high for them to make, and they were subsequently hustled off to jail at Tyler to await the action of the federal grand jury.[43]

Jones wrote Denton County Sheriff W. F. Egan on April 28, just before leaving Dallas to appear before the grand jury at Tyler. The major was concerned that local authorities in Denton County were not making a sufficient effort to corral the Bass gang. He made an earnest appeal asking him to help Peak run down the outlaws.

> These outlaws must be arrested or driven from the country and, as I do not believe they can be caught in "traps," I know of no other way to accomplish the desired objective except to make a drive for them through the woods, scour the country thoroughly, when they will certainly be caught or forced to leave the country . . . I hope and shall expect that you, as well as all good citizens of Denton County, will render us all the assistance in your power to rid the country of these out-laws.[44]

However, Egan was already forming a posse to search for the gang, and on April 29 ran across the fugitives and engaged them in a running gunfight until the gang managed to escape.[45] Near Dallas, Billy Collins was arrested with others as an accessory and sent on to Tyler.[46] Jones returned to Dallas from Tyler on April 30.[47] More prisoners were being rounded up in Denton County and brought to Dallas, believed to be material witnesses or to have harbored the Bass gang in some way; they were then sent on to Tyler to await the action of the grand jury.

Bass and his men remained hidden in the thickly-wooded portions of Denton County, relying on a few friends to bring them provisions and news about the pursuit. Both Egan's and Peak's men were scouring the county in hopes of rousting the outlaws, Egan one time riding up on them and exchanging a few shots until the gang fled. On Wednesday, May 1, when Steele wired him that he had a "proposition to sell out the train robbers," Jones returned from Tyler to Austin with Captain Lee Hall of the Special Troops, the federal grand jury having indicted eight principal actors and six men believed to be accessories.[48] Confident,

Jones telegraphed General Steele: "Will catch them or chase them out of the country."[49]

In the middle of the chase after the Bass gang, another problem for Jones was building in Shackelford County. Lieutenant George W. Campbell and Company B had their camp in that county near the rough-and-tumble community of Fort Griffin. The law enforcement of the county was in the hands of Sheriff Bill Cruger and City Marshal William C. "Big Bill" Gilson.[50] At the same time, however, a vigilante group was taking affairs into its own hands, and a number of hangings of suspected stock thieves dotted the tree line. A well-known desperado, William A. "Hurricane Bill" Martin, the nickname alluding to his propensity for loud talk, was leery of the vigilantes, although he was frequently in trouble in Fort Griffin for such behavioral lapses as drunkenness, pimping, and gambling.[51] Martin subsequently worked with the vigilantes, serving as a guide to track down targeted horse thieves.

Two of the most active thieves in Shackelford County were former Sheriff John Larn and his partner, mankiller John Selman, and rumors of their criminal escapades were widespread.[52] In February Campbell and Company B assisted the local officers in executing a search warrant and arresting Larn and Selman, who were found in possession of stolen hides, although they were apparently released and the prosecution was not pursued.[53] The vigilantes grew alarmed because Larn, as a former vigilante himself, knew far too many of their secrets and the identities of men involved in the movement. When "Hurricane Bill" Martin was arrested in April by Rangers in Castroville after jumping bond on an assault to murder charge, he was returned to Shackelford County.[54] Concerned for his personal safety, Martin offered to tell Campbell all he knew about the vigilantes in return for protection. Campbell posted a guard of four men around him and other prisoners at the county seat of Albany, and wrote Jones that he thought Martin could lead him to important witnesses who would give evidence against the vigilantes.[55] This letter was apparently intercepted when posted at Fort Griffin and immediately created a frenzy of alarm among the vigilantes. Revealing the roles and identities of the vigilantes, many of whom were well-respected members of the community, would be explosive and would certainly subject them to legal consequences if Campbell carried through with his intent to break them up.[56]

On April 15, 1878, when Hurricane Bill came up before District Judge J. R. Fleming, Lieutenant Campbell appeared and tried to introduce evidence against the vigilantes. But the wheels were already in motion. Fleming refused to hear the evidence and also denied Campbell's request for a change of venue to a different court. Fleming then wrote Governor Hubbard, praising Campbell as "perhaps a good man and desires to do his duty," but, "expressing the sentiments of the people of Shackelford County," accused him of falling under the influence of Hurricane Bill, "a man utterly devoid of principle . . . interested in maligning and traducing the character of the good citizens of that county." He criticized Campbell for believing everything Martin said, suggesting that the Ranger company's usefulness in Shackelford County had been destroyed and that the company should be removed to another county.[57]

Jones returned to Austin on May 2 where he caught up on Battalion business while Peak continued the chase after the Bass gang in North Texas. He moved Lieutenant N. O. Reynolds and Company E to Burnet County.[58] On May 7, no doubt having heard from Governor Hubbard and General Steele about Judge Fleming's complaint, and perhaps acting under their orders, Jones notified Campbell that Company B would be disbanded at the end of the month, leaving behind only a token force familiar with that area which could guide another Ranger company that might need to work there.[59] Campbell was likely unaware of the political controversy he had stirred up by threatening to go after "respectable" citizens involved in vigilante violence.[60] Jones expressed to Fleming that Campbell might have been influenced by someone else to take the actions that he did.[61]

Jones issued a special order on May 18 reducing Company B to a token force of five men under the command of Sergeant J. E. Van Riper.[62] In notifying Campbell, Jones blamed the necessity of reducing Company B on the expenses incurred in sustaining the company of Rangers in El Paso County and other Battalion operations, but did not include a word about the conflicts in Shackelford County.[63] He also advised Steele that the action was justified by "the necessity for reducing the force of the command to bring its expenditures within the existing appropriation for frontier defense," and that he thought that the company "could be dispensed with at less detriment to the service than any other."[64]

The "coincidence" of the complaint by Fleming followed immediately by Jones making what is alleged to be a move necessitated by financial concerns is highly questionable. In what appears to be an obvious and purely political decision, i.e., disbanding a viable Ranger company in order to avoid the investigation of a bloody vigilante movement whose members were likely prominent, there is a negative reflection on the moral integrity of all those likely involved: Governor Hubbard, Adjutant General Steele, and Major John B. Jones. Unfortunately, there is no additional correspondence in Ranger or other records reflecting any of the behind-the-scenes discussions that had to have taken place, and which might have injected additional considerations that justified disbanding the company. It may have been that Jones, low man in the hierarchy, was merely carrying out orders from on high. However, the facts as they are demonstrate questionable decision making, with Jones apparently recording no formal protest.

Making the decision even more puzzling, the disbanding of Company B did not sit well with many citizens in the area. Denizens of neighboring Throckmorton County petitioned Jones, asking that the company be retained in service at least until ongoing stock thefts could be investigated.[65] Two doctors at Fort Griffin wired Jones that "nine tenths of the people in this part of the country want Lieut. Campbell's company of Rangers retained here."[66] Nevertheless, the decision had been made and was carried out. A number of the men discharged from Company B volunteered to continue without pay on the hunt for Sam Bass. Jones promised to come to Fort Griffin in June and, if he found the need, send some men there at that time.[67]

Jones returned to Dallas from Austin on Saturday, May 11, to catch up on the hunt for Bass and his gang.[68] Billy Scott and Jack Smith, the two erstwhile spies, were formally enlisted into Arrington's Company C, their undercover usefulness at an end with the Bass gang fleeing to western counties under heavy pursuit by multiple posses.[69] Jones took a train to Tyler on the 14th with the intent of attending the trial of Sam Pipes and Albert Herndon. However, the trial was subsequently continued, and he returned to Dallas on the 17th.[70] Sixteen men of Peak's company were then discharged; the remainder kept after Bass in Dallas and adjoining counties.[71]

An original Denton County settler, Henderson Murphy, had been one of those rounded up and arrested under suspicion of harboring the gang, along with his sons Robert and Jim, all of them having been transferred to Tyler. Jim Murphy, out on bond and chagrined that his elderly father had been swooped up in the Ranger haul, approached Marshal Russell, Lieutenant Peak, and Jones. Conferring with them in Jones' hotel room, Murphy told the lawmen that he thought he could join the Bass gang and lure them into a position where they could be captured. After hearing the proposition, Jones consulted with the United States Attorney, Andrew J. Evans. Returning a half hour later, he told Murphy that Evans had agreed and a formal agreement was drawn up by Evans. If he made a good faith effort to follow through, Evans promised to dismiss the cases against him and his father.[72] The next morning, May 22, before court met, Murphy secretly left Tyler, "jumping bond," and began making his way back to Denton County to locate the Bass gang. The cases in Tyler against the indicted prisoners were continued and the federal court, having completed its term, transferred the train robbery cases to the federal court at Austin. Jones left Tyler to attend court in Galveston.[73]

Jones was interviewed in Galveston by the *Daily News*. The newspaper described him as bearing "the marks of hard service in his face, which is thoroughly tanned by contact with the winds and rains through which he travels in total disregard of their existence." He gave the reporter no real information about the hunt for Bass, although he did share a telegram advising that Jim Murphy was missing from Tyler.[74] On May 25, Jones returned to Austin at the same time that the prisoners from Tyler were arriving.[75] One of his first actions was to recommend the promotion of June Peak to captain, which was completed.[76]

While Murphy was furtively making his way to Denton County, another episode occurred that would require the Frontier Battalion, this time in San Saba County. On Tuesday, May 21, the justice court in San Saba was conducting a trial of William A. Brown, a local saloon keeper, for violating the local option liquor law. While the jury was deliberating its verdict, Brown, reportedly under the influence of "benzene," and the prosecutor, County Attorney S. S. Brooks, got into an argument. Brown pulled out a pistol and fired at and missed Brooks. An attorney assisting Brooks, Dallas attorney Thomas G. T. Kendall, pulled his pistol and mortally wounded Brown, who died in a few hours. Brooks and Kendall were kept prisoners through the night, then Brooks was released.[77]

The San Saba County Judge, John T. Guinn, got off an urgent letter to the Rangers "in the name of law and humanity," asking for a detachment to be sent there immediately to protect Kendall from an expected mob.[78] Lieutenant Arrington and his men were soon on the scene, and Jones immediately ordered N. O. Reynolds and his company to move to San Saba without delay and take charge of Kendall from Arrington. Reynolds was to bring Kendall to Austin and leave a detachment at San Saba to preserve order.[79] Before Reynolds and his men arrived, a number of San Saba citizens, including the county judge and district attorney, wrote Jones that they were satisfied with the services of Arrington and his men and feared a renewal of trouble if they were withdrawn.[80]

Reynolds and his men arrived and prepared to transport Kendall to Austin. Ranger Jim Gillett wrote years later that William Brown's brother, a heavily-armed James Madison Brown, the sheriff of Lee County and a former Ranger under McNelly, made his appearance among the watching crowd, sitting on his horse within ten feet of the jail door. Reynolds ordered the crowd back, but Jim Brown refused to move. Reynolds then ordered his men to draw their weapons and move everyone at least fifty yards from the jail. Brown told Reynolds that he was going to Austin with the detachment, and Reynolds reportedly responded, "If you do, you will go in irons. Move back."

Without saying a word, Brown turned and rode away. A scout under Sergeant Charles Nevill was sent after him, and a member of that scout, W.

James Madison Brown *(Courtesy of Chuck Parsons, Luling, Texas)*

L. Banister, tried to halt Brown, but the sheriff eluded him. An infuriated Reynolds immediately discharged Banister from the service, but rescinded the order at the request of some citizens, although he ordered forfeiture of one month's pay for the Ranger.[81] In Austin, Jim Brown reportedly apologized to Reynolds, telling the Ranger that his plan to assassinate Kendall dissolved in the face of the armed and determined lawmen. Reynolds told him that he had anticipated as much, and had ordered his men to "shoot Brown into doll rags at his first move."[82] There is no official record of this occurrence. On May 30, Jones left Austin for San Saba.[83] While there, he met with local liquor dealers and suggested that all of the prosecutions cease upon payment of back liquor taxes. This was not acceptable, and no agreement was reached. Jones returned to Austin on June 2.[84]

In Bell County, Belton Mayor W. H. Estill wrote Governor Hubbard on May 31 for a detachment of Rangers, complaining that local law enforcement was overwhelmed by a "lawless element" that was depredating with impunity.[85] This claim was backed up by another letter from Belton merchant J. W. Embree complaining of an infestation of thieves that local law enforcement could not control.[86] Back in Austin on June 4, Jones responded that he would send some men to Belton as soon as some were available.[87] Upon transporting T. G. T. Kendall from San Saba to Austin, Corporal J. W. Warren, whom Jones described as "a man of cool and resolute courage and good judgment," and five men were dispatched by Jones to Belton's aid.[88] However, by June 9, the leading citizens of Belton had heard about Estill's request for Ranger assistance and, concerned about the community image, convinced him that maybe things weren't so lawless after all. Although Warren and his men had arrived in town, Estill now felt that they weren't needed as the local officials had everything well in hand.[89] The mayor followed this up with another letter the next day, an "anonymous" one, detailing all of the violence in Bell County that had led to his request.[90]

While all of these distractions occupied Jones, the hunt for Sam Bass and his gang was still the foremost matter facing the Frontier Battalion.

13

AGIN' MY PROFESSION

CONFRONTED IN THE UNDERBRUSH of Denton County by running gunbattles with various posses, including Peak and his men, Sam Bass and his gang—Henry Underwood, Seaborn Barnes, Frank Jackson, Arkansas Johnson, Henry Collins, and Charles Carter—fled to the west. Stephens County lawmen attempted to surround the outlaws in a mountainous area in that county, but the elusive gang slipped away. The gang then surprised a party of farmers on their way to join the posse, and treated them to beer at a store until they were intoxicated, further cementing Bass' legend as a Robin Hood sort. The Rangers tracked the gang back through Jack and Palo Pinto Counties.[1]

Bass returned to his old haunts in Denton County, even liberating from a local stable some horses previously seized from the gang in a prior confrontation.[2] Posses led by Denton Sheriff Egan and Grayson County Sheriff Bill Everheart chased after the gang, occasionally running across them and engaging in brief but distant gunfire, but were unable to nab them. Peak and his men traded shots with the gang at one point on June 11, 1878, but, unfamiliar with the terrain, they were unable to track the fleeing outlaws. The gang, forced by the pressure of the persistent manhunt, fled once more to the west. They found a campsite on Salt Creek near the little town of Cottondale in Wise County. Hobbling their horses, they tried to relax and let the adrenalin die down.[3]

Joining a posse led by Wise County Sheriff George W. Stevens, the first commander of the Battalion's Company B, Peak and his men, along with lawmen from Tarrant and Denton Counties, received a tip from a cowboy out hunting strays about a group of men by the creek. Stealthily moving in, the lawmen caught the bandits by surprise on June 13, opening a withering fire. The gang fled on foot, unable to reach their horses grazing nearby. Arkansas Johnson was shot dead on the spot by Sergeant Thomas Floyd, and the other gang members scattered and disappeared in the underbrush.[4] The fleeing bandits were able to steal some horses and rode back to Denton County.

Jim Murphy had made his way from Tyler back to Denton County, spending several weeks trying to make contact with Bass. On June 15, after scurrying back from Wise County, Bass contacted Murphy at his residence, and Murphy "agreed" to join the gang. Now he had to find a way to contact lawmen without his efforts being noticed by Bass and the others.

The violence in Shackelford County had continued in the absence of the disbanded Ranger company. Sergeant J. E. Van Riper, in charge of the small remaining squad of Rangers, reported to Jones, asking him to come to the area, because the state of affairs was "in a terrible stage—armed parties of men continually riding the country—riding at midnight into the door yards of peaceable citizens and discharging their firearms." He described citizens being forced to abandon their property; John Larn and John Selman, having escaped prosecution, were continuing to steal stock from their neighbors; cows and calves were being shot down; and vigilantes were taking up arms in defense.[5] Bodies were turning up, and Larn was reportedly making threats against Lieutenant Campbell and Sergeant Van Riper. Knowing that the mail was being tampered with at Fort Griffin, Van Riper posted his letter from Breckenridge in Stephens County.[6] Campbell also advised Jones that affairs there were even worse than before the company was disbanded. "You have no idea how bad your presence is needed here, at the present time, and now the citizens look to you and will flock to you for relief." At the same time, Campbell defended his actions that had led to Judge Fleming's complaint and asked Jones to make it public that the company was not discharged for dishonest actions.[7]

On June 23, a Shackelford County posse rearrested John Larn and took him to the county seat, Albany, where he was shackled and placed in a picket building that was serving as the county jail. Sometime after midnight, a group of vigilantes overpowered the guards and riddled Larn with bullets.[8] Hurricane Bill Martin, also being held in custody, was given a reprieve by the mob and hastily departed the neighborhood. John Selman avoided arrest and also fled, knowing that he would be assassinated if caught.[9] The violence only heightened the local sense that Jones should come personally to the county, and the governor was asked to send him.[10] Major Jones during this time was back home in Corsicana where, on June 26, he presided as Deputy Grand Master over the laying of a cornerstone of the Presbyterian church.[11] The skeleton crew of Rangers remaining in Shackelford County, continuing to be thwarted by the vigilantes and their supporters, became frustrated with their inability to meaningfully deal with the ongoing crimes and left on their own volition for Austin and other duties.[12]

Back in Austin on July 6, Jones issued an order requiring company commanders to report the names, dates of discharges, transfers, enlistments, deaths, or desertions, as well as changes in officers and non-commissioned troops. Apparently there had been slack bookkeeping in Austin and this was an effort to correct the Battalion rolls.[13] Jones also wrote to Sergeant Van Riper asking for particulars in the killing of Larn, as well as other episodes of violence, and committed himself to visiting Shackelford County as soon as he could get free.[14] He ordered Lieutenant Arrington to move Company C to within five or six miles of Fort Griffin and make himself available to the local officers in giving "protection to the lives and property of all citizens." Arrington was to contact a number of noted citizens in the community to gather more information about the troubles there. In effect, Jones negated his own reasons for disbanding Campbell's company only six weeks before.

Now, perhaps mindful of the Mason County and El Paso conflicts, Jones cautioned Arrington:

> You will, however, be particularly careful to avoid and guard your men against any undue sympathy with or prejudice against any of the parties to [the] feud which exists in that section, and will do all that is in your power to prevent any further violations of law by any of the parties to this feud and to restore peace and quiet to the community.[15]

This assignment to the Fort Griffin area was later made permanent.[16]

Shaking free from Austin was not going to be easy. The trials of the Dallas area train robbery suspects, the venue of which had been transferred from Tyler to the court in Austin, were commencing. On July 11, Jones testified about how the Rangers had come to arrest Sam Pipes and Albert Herndon, the two principal robbers of the Bass gang in custody.[17] He also took time to write Lieutenant James Tays, commander of the Company C detachment in El Paso County, that he was continuing that unit until at least January, and advising as to his policy for distributing rewards to Rangers:

> In regard to who is entitled to rewards for the arrest of fugitives from justice, my rule is to give the reward to the men who work up the case and who are present and assist in making the arrest, and to divide it between the officers, non-commissioned officers and privates in the ratio of their pay. This is right; has always given satisfaction to the men, and stimulates them to make personal and individual exertion to find and arrest parties for whom rewards are offered.[18]

After the Wise County attack, the chase for Sam Bass quieted and the bandits dropped out of sight. Jim Murphy, now ensconced with the gang, attempted to set up a trap in collaboration with Assistant United States Marshal Walter Johnson in Denton County, but the lawman did not follow through. The remaining members of the gang had decided to flee to safety from pursuit and planned to work their way south to Mexico. Unfortunately, Sherman and Fort Worth newspapers printed a report quoting Johnson as saying that a spy named Murphy was working with the lawmen.[19] While Sam Bass was illiterate and could not read, Seaborn Barnes could and convinced the bandit leader that Murphy had to be killed. Frank Jackson stepped forward to protect Murphy, and, thinking fast, Murphy assured the gang that he had made a deal but had no intention of carrying it out; he just wanted to get free from Tyler and the threat of prison.[20] Not convinced, Barnes and Bass backed off for the time being, and Murphy stuck close to Jackson. "We then left Denton and the party was so suspicious of me and watched me so closely—having heard that I was a spy—that I had no opportunity to communicate with anyone who could arrest them."[21]

The gang wended its way south—Sam Bass, Seaborn Barnes, Frank Jackson, and Murphy—and briefly considered robbing a bank at Waco until Murphy managed to talk them out of it. They then rode south to Belton in mid-July where Murphy was finally able to get a message off to the lawmen that they were on their way to Round Rock, in Williamson County, to rob the bank or the railroad, and "for God's sake to be there in time to prevent them from doing it." At Georgetown, just north of Round Rock, he was able to get off another message on July 16, this time to Major Jones, alerting him that the gang planned to rest its horses for four or five days, then rob the bank at Round Rock or a train. The gang camped a few miles west of Round Rock.[22] The plan decided on was to rob the Williamson County Bank in Round Rock on Saturday, July 20, then, with their horses fed and rested, make a dash for Mexico.[23]

Alerted by Murphy's message on Thursday, July 18, Jones sent three Rangers from his escort—Dick Ware, Chris Connor, and George Herold—to Round Rock with instructions to stay out of sight but to be alert for suspicious men who might be the Bass gang. Jones then dispatched Ranger Vernon C. Wilson to ride from Austin to Lampasas to summon Lieutenant N. O. Reynolds and his Rangers to Round Rock as quickly as possible. Wilson sped off on his horse, which was fat and soft from several months of stable life. On his way to the train station to go to Round Rock, Jones ran into Travis County Deputy Sheriff Maurice B. Moore, a former Ranger, and invited him to go along, which the deputy did.[24]

Once at Round Rock on the 18th, Jones sent out several telegrams from the railroad station depot south of town. He notified Lee Hall in Austin that Bass was in the area, maybe even in Austin. Telegrams went out to the railroads admonishing them to "Guard trains against robbers."[25] The next day, Friday the 19th, more telegrams went out. He asked General Steele to send Hall there, then advised Steele that there were reports of parties in the area fitting Bass' description, but cautioned that the bandits may have ridden on to Austin. He warned that Billy Collins, who had jumped bond at Tyler, may be headed that way, and a flurry of telegrams pondered the identity of a Grayson County deputy sheriff on his way to Round Rock.[26]

In the meantime, Ranger Wilson raced his horse to Lampasas, arriving there at daylight Thursday morning, only to have his overworked mount collapse and die. Wilson was shocked to find that Lieutenant Reynolds had moved his company to San Saba, so he had to take a stagecoach to the Ranger camp, arriving there Thursday evening. Reynolds quickly rounded up his men, and they were soon in the saddle racing for Round Rock.[27]

On Friday afternoon, July 19, Bass, Jackson, and Barnes decided to ride into Round Rock to buy some tobacco and to take one more look around. As they headed toward town, Murphy convinced them to let him stop off at a store on the way to see if he could learn any information about Rangers in the area.[28] The three outlaws then rode into Round Rock, hitching their horses in an alley behind the bank and the stable of Henry Highsmith. They were unaware that Herold and Connor were at the stable, while Dick Ware was in a barber shop across the street, keeping watch through the window on any traffic coming down the main street. While Jones was down at the train depot, Maurice Moore was out in the street with Williamson County Deputy Sheriff A. W. Grimes, another former Ranger.[29] Hall had arrived from Austin, but was lying down and resting in a hotel room. The scene was set for one of the Old West's most renowned gunfights.

At about four in the afternoon, Bass, Jackson, and Barnes walked around the corner and headed toward Henry Koppel's store, passing Moore and Grimes. Highsmith mentioned to Moore that they were strangers, and Moore thought he saw a pistol under the coat of one of the men. Moore told of his suspicion to Grimes, and the two lawmen followed the three strangers into Koppel's store. Moore hung back by the door while Grimes approached the three men at the counter talking with the clerk.

No sooner had Grimes inquired about a pistol than guns were drawn and Grimes, his pistol still in its holster, ran for the door, bullets tattooing his back. He fell dead outside the door. Smoke filled the store and Moore fired in the direction of the three outlaws. An answering bullet tunneled through one of Moore's lungs and out his shoulder. As he slumped against the door, the men rushed out past him, one of them—Bass—holding up his right hand, the ring and middle fingers having been taken off by Moore's shot. Moore would survive his wound. The outlaws raced across the street, aiming for the head of the alley to reach where their horses were hitched.

Koppel's Store as it appears today, Round Rock, Texas (*Author's Photo*)

Dick Ware came out of the barber shop, firing and ducking as the outlaws responded in kind. Connor and Herold, not near the action, ducked back into Highsmith's stable to retrieve their Winchesters. Jones was coming up from the telegraph office at the depot with station agent J. F. Tubbs, who was missing his left hand. The major drew his pistol and joined Ware in the fight. Tubbs retrieved Grimes' holstered pistol and also fired at the retreating bandits. Jones, Ware, and Tubbs steadily advanced on the retreating outlaws as they backed down the alley toward their horses. Barnes reached his horse, and as he mounted Ware took aim and killed him with a shot to the head. Bass had emptied his pistol as George Herold, in the stable, called on him to surrender. Holding his pistol in his left hand, Bass pointed it at Herold, and as his horse likely turned him around in the confusion or Bass started to mount, Herold let loose with his Winchester, the bullet entering to the left of Bass' spine and exiting to the left of his naval. Bass clung to the top of the stable fence for support, and Frank Jackson raced to his aid, fending off the approaching lawmen while helping Bass into the saddle. Jackson managed to climb on his horse and the two raced off, Jackson remarkably unscathed. Murphy later recalled seeing the two ride by him, Jackson holding a deathly pale Bass in the saddle.[30]

A feeble attempt was made by the Rangers to pursue, but only jaded horses were around to be commandeered, and the Rangers decided to wait and go after the pair the first thing in the morning, as a wounded man would not be hard to track. Reynolds and his men arrived about two hours later, too late to get in on the action. Early Saturday morning, July 20, a detachment led by Sergeant Charles Nevill came across a man sitting under a tree, and it was quickly established that it was the seriously wounded Bass. Frank Jackson was gone. A wagon was brought and Bass was returned to Round Rock where he was installed on a borrowed cot in a tin shop with a nurse, his wounds pronounced by doctors as fatal. Jones wired Steele that Bass had been captured, and Steele responded that members then attending the Democratic state convention in Austin thought it was an election trick. He advised him to bring Bass to Austin if possible, then countermanded his order.[31]

Alley of the Bass shootout as it appears today, Round Rock, Texas *(Author's Photo)*

Jones stationed a stenographer by Bass' bedside to take down any statement the outlaw might make, but Bass proclaimed: "It's agin' my profession to blow on my pals. If a man knows anything he ought to die with it in him." At about four Sunday afternoon, July 21, on his 27th birthday, Bass breathed his last, and he and Barnes were buried near their camp west of Round Rock in a far corner of the cemetery.[32] Frank Jackson made his way back to Denton County, where he later implored Jim Murphy to intercede with the authorities on his behalf.[33] When legal relief was not forthcoming, Jackson disappeared and the murder case against him remained pending in Williamson County until 1936.

Jones returned to Austin from Round Rock by horseback on the evening of July 22. He promptly fired off letters to railroad and express companies inquiring about rewards for his men. All charges against Jim Murphy were dismissed per the agreement with him. Pipes and Herndon were found guilty and sentenced to ninety-nine years in the penitentiary.[34] Rewards offered by the state were sent to Peak to share with his men, including Scott and Smith. Jones also directed Peak, now that it was fairly certain that Frank Jackson had left for parts unknown, to move what was now designated as Company B to Coleman for service from that point.[35] Jones also reenlisted Maurice Moore as third sergeant in Coldwell's Company A, although he was still recovering from his wound.[36]

Jim Murphy did not fade away with the demise of the Bass gang. He complained to Jones that Grayson County Sheriff Bill Everheart had jailed him in May and took his horse without returning it when he was shipped to Tyler.[37] When Murphy returned to Denton, he complained to Jones that Peak now had his horse and wouldn't give it up, his accusations apparently angering Jones.[38] When Murphy wrote Jones, making demand for a significant reward, Jones responded that he was "insulted," leading Murphy to abandon his demands and to beg forgiveness.[39]

O. M. Roberts was nominated as the Democratic candidate for governor to replace Richard Hubbard. Even before the election, which was a sure thing in Texas for a Democrat, applications for governmental appointments came flooding in. Walter P. Layne of Harrison County, who had fought in the Texas Revolution and Civil War, argued that he was "entitled" to appointment as adjutant general because of the services he had rendered and begged others to write on his behalf.[40] But William Steele wanted to keep his job, and friends also wrote in on his behalf.[41]

On August 4, Jones again ordered his commanders to honorably discharge their men on the 31st, then reorganize on September 1. Each company was to have, in addition to the commanding officer, two sergeants, two corporals, and twenty men.[42] Tays, however, was to have only sixteen privates in his detachment at El Paso, a slight increase from his previous manpower authorization.[43] Jones urged his commanders to drop any man thought to be inefficient or unsuitable.[44] The next day Jones went to Dallas, then went home to Corsicana for a brief visit with his father.[45] While Jones was there, Neal Coldwell submitted his intent to resign from the service no later than November 1, feeling it his duty to find some other occupation that would not require continued absence from his family. He was also a candidate for Kerr County sheriff.[46] Jones responded with his regrets, which were unusually formal and stiff, given Coldwell's faithful service:

> You have always proven faithful, prompt & efficient in the discharge of every duty and our association, both official & social, has been entirely pleasant and agreeable to me.[47]

Coldwell subsequently decided to resign on September 30 in order to run an active campaign for the sheriff's office, "repugnant" as the idea of electioneering was to him. "If you still wish me to remain [until November 1], I will do so, although it may defeat my aspirations for civic honors." Jones accepted the resignation, but to be effective on October 15.[48] In a later letter to Coldwell on October 8, explaining why the resignation was held up, he again expressed his regret, but with a little more compassion:

> I regret to lose so efficient an officer as yourself from my command, and more especially one with whom my intercourse, both official and social, has always been so pleasant. You have my best wishes for your success in your new undertaking and I shall be glad to render you any service that I can at any time.[49]

James Tays reported to Jones that he had taken five men of his detachment to escort the transportation of some livestock. In actuality, he had personally bought thirty-four head of cattle, and a friend who owned a ranch in the Guadalupe Mountains agreed, in return for an escort for his sheep, to take Tays' cattle and keep them for him. Returning on August 10 from that escort to their post, Tays' Rangers came under attack by Indians believed to be from the Fort Stanton reservation in the New Mexico Territory. Caught in the open, Tays and his men fought back, using their horses for cover, two of which were killed. They retreated some 400 yards to the adobe wall of an old station. The Indians tried to surround them and a battle raged for about ten minutes. One of Tays' men, a Russian named A. A. Ruzin, was killed and his horse and arms taken by the Indians. The slain Ranger, described as a "nobleman and nihilist," was from

Siberia and had only been in the United States for eighteen months, enlisting in Tays' detachment on June 1. "I considered him one of the best men in the company . . . His bravery killed him."[50] Jones' response was oddly detached: "I regret the loss of your man in the Indian fight, but, of course, he only met the fate to which all good soldiers are liable."[51]

The matter of Tays using his Rangers to escort his own cattle prompted a complaint from the El Paso District Clerk, G. W. Wahl, that it was a grave impropriety. Upon hearing about the complaint, Tays branded Wahl as his "deadly enemy" of long standing.[52] Jones wrote Wahl in October that he had mislaid his letter and asked him to again send the complaint.[53] On the same day, however, he also wrote Tays that he found nothing wrong in him sending his own stock along with that of his friend.[54]

Gov. O. M. Roberts *(Clarence R. Wharton,* Texas Under Many Flags, *Chicago: American Historical Society, 1930.)*

On August 7, a day before Jones left for Navarro County to help his father send off a herd of horses to Louisiana,[55] officials of Atascosa County petitioned him to appoint one of their deputy sheriffs, D. M. Young, as a company commander upon reorganization of the Battalion. They expressed "implicit confidence in his integrity," and proclaimed him a "living terror" to outlaws.[56] These accolades were followed by another petition from Castroville recommending Young as a suitable candidate for any position in the Battalion.[57] Young himself wrote Jones and asserted that Coldwell and Lee Hall would stand up for him, and "I believe that I could command a company and work to an advantage."[58] Although Frontier Battalion records do not reflect it, Jones apparently decided to enlist Young and assign him as first sergeant of Coldwell's Company A. Upon receiving word of the appointment, Coldwell was quick to respond with his regret, obviously not willing to "stand up" for the man. He had entertained the idea of enlisting Young a year earlier, but decided he was unsuitable.

> I will say, however, that he is better posted on the fugitive list than any Shff that I know of, and that he has considerable detective capacity. But as a man I believe him to be unreliable and know that he is untruthful and a coward.[59]

When Young arrived at the camp and had a talk with Coldwell, he decided not to enlist in the company, a prudent decision under the circumstances.[60]

Coldwell had a more serious tragedy occur. On August 23, Melvin E. Beauman, a private in Company A since his enlistment on June 3, accidentally shot himself in the abdomen while practicing with his pistol. The bullet was cut out near his backbone. He was kept in bed in Pleasanton for medical care. Since it was thought initially that Beauman would recover, Coldwell held his position open at reorganization. But the Ranger died of his wound in September about three weeks after being wounded. When a bill of some $150 was presented for the expenses of medical attention, funeral, and room and board, all occurring after August 31 when the Ranger's enlistment was shown as terminated, it was refused by the state.[61]

Mishaps with firearms were not uncommon in Ranger camps. Lieutenant John Armstrong of the Special Troops wounded himself in the groin prior to his participation in the capture of John Wesley Hardin in 1877.[62] Corporal J. E. Hines' foot was shattered when a "comrade" accidentally shot him in September, although he remained on Ranger rolls for almost another year.[63] James Tays reported that on October 13, 1878, one of his enlisted men, 28-year-old Henry Crist, was mortally wounded when the pistol of another man discharged after falling from its holster, the bullet "cutting the bowels."[64] In December 1878, a Ranger named Alston in Company A accidentally shot himself in the foot.[65]

At the same time, after an incident in which N. O. Reynolds personally thrashed John Binford, a drunken and insubordinate Ranger teamster, Reynolds had to respond to a riotous situation in San Saba. Jones gave the company commander his neutrality sermon.

> [B]ut [I] must urge upon you, as I have heretofore done, the imperative necessity of avoiding and guarding your men against any undue sympathy with, or prejudice against any of the parties to the trouble in localities where you are operating, or the expression of any opinion as to the guilt or innocence of parties against whom there are charges in court, always bearing in mind that it is our duty to put down strife, preserve the peace, assist in the enforcement of the law, and give protection alike to all citizens, good or bad, and that we must not allow our personal feelings to interfere with our official duty.[66]

John Wesley Hardin had basked in the Travis County jail ever since his capture in August of 1877. When his sentencing was scheduled in Comanche for the murder of Charles Webb, Jones ordered N. O. Reynolds to bring half of his company to Austin to escort Hardin to Comanche. This was an extraordinary guard, but reasonable given the thought that Hardin had a number of friends who might try to rescue him. Hardin was handcuffed, shackled, and transported in a two-horse wagon by his escort of some twenty men.[67] He was subsequently sentenced to twenty-five years in the penitentiary at Huntsville, where Reynolds and his men delivered him on October 5.[68]

After a short visit to Corsicana on September 9 and 10,[69] Jones finally headed to Fort Griffin to investigate affairs there,[70] then went on to Stephens County on September 18,[71] deciding to leave Arrington's company in Shackelford county.[72] He was back in Corsicana on September 20 to attend to personal business on behalf of his sister, Fannie Halbert, delaying his return to Austin, where he arrived on October 2.[73] On the 7th, Jones ordered the companies into winter quarters, each commander to select a site close to their present camps, "having in view protection from Northers, water, grass, & firewood," and promising to send any additional tents that may be needed.[74] Jones continued to testify as a witness in trials involving land thieves.

Preparatory to returning to Shackelford County, Jones directed Lieutenant Arrington to take fifteen of his men to Albany to attend court and keep the peace while Judge Fleming was there.[75] On October 11, Jones left Austin for Fort Griffin.[76] Once there, he found affairs all quiet and moved on to Coleman. While there he ordered Reynolds to move his company from San Saba to report to Captain Dan Roberts at Kerr and Kimble Counties. Peak's Company B was moved to the Colorado River in Runnels County where Indian activity had recently been reported.[77]

During this period General Steele sent inquiries to district judges, county judges, and sheriffs in various western Texas counties, asking if state troops had been effective in protecting lives and property, and if it was possible to remove some of these troops. The response was dramatic, all jurisdictions adamantly (and predictably) insisting that conditions there mandated the maintenance of such protection. Aransas County was concerned about the depredations of stock thieves, claiming that actions of the lone sheriff in organizing a posse to go after them was a "nullity." Twenty-third District Judge H. Clay Pleasants wrote that the presence of state troops "has been indispensable in this and other counties to the peace and tranquility of society." Sheriff Albertus Sweet of Lampasas County, mindful of the Horrell-Higgins violence, touted the Rangers as helping to keep counties such as his from being sanctuaries for "bad men and fugitives." Common sentiments were also heard from Gillespie, Bee, Tom Green, McCulloch, Coryell, San Saba, Burnet, Atascosa, Frio, Goliad,

Nueces, Llano, and Coleman Counties.[78] At the same time, Steele offered a ten-dollar reward to anyone who brought information to a Ranger commander of "a raid," to be paid once the report was established not to be a false alarm and only if the report was provided within twenty-four hours of the occurrence.[79]

Leaving Fort Griffin, Jones traveled through Fort Concho on October 22 on his way to Kimble and Kerr Counties to consult with Roberts and Reynolds.[80] Once in Kimble County, he redirected Reynolds' command to the head of Johnson Creek in Kerr County in order to intercept any raiding Indians, urging him to continue to work closely with Roberts.[81] Jones was back in Austin on October 29, reporting that citizens in the frontier counties were "much excited and discouraged over the prospect of reducing the State troops," it being claimed that where Rangers had been temporarily removed, settlers had been forced to move back to more civilized areas.[82] On November 1, Jones recommended to Steele that Guy B. Broadwater be appointed a first lieutenant to replace Neal Coldwell as commander of Company A, which was ordered.[83] He also ordered Lieutenant James Tays to reduce his detachment at El Paso by five men to fifteen, blaming "the small appropriation for frontier defense & the great expense of maintaining troops" there.[84]

Tays did as instructed, then submitted his resignation, effective December 1. He had been appointed deputy collector of customs at El Paso, "which is better pay and easier work." Tays recommended another brother, Alexander, to take his place.[85] Strangely, two former members of Tays' detachment, Jack Irving and A. G. "Guss" Moore, were found dead on December 10, 1878, near Tularosa in the New Mexico Territory. They reportedly had been stealing cattle, arrested, and briefly jailed at Lincoln. It was supposed that vigilantes from Lincoln County caught up with them after their release.[86] The men of Tays' detachment petitioned Jones to appoint as commander their reliable first sergeant, M. Ludwick.[87] Jones took no immediate action to name a commander, leaving Ludwick temporarily in charge. Also resigning again and for the last time, on December 1, was the Battalion surgeon, Dr. E. G. Nicholson, "the visit of a relative rendering it imperative that I should cease meandering."[88]

Oran M. Roberts was elected governor in late 1878 and applications again poured in for political appointments prior to his succeed-
ing the outgoing Hubbard. Steele submitted his application to Roberts
on November 11, 1878, for reappointment as Texas adjutant general,
citing "a military education and a service of many years in the regular
army . . . supplemented with experience under the administrations
of Governors Coke and Hubbard."[89] A San Antonio newspaper even
endorsed his reappointment.[90] While that position was being considered,
Jones went to San Antonio where Steele wired him that "outlaws driven
out of New Mexico are playing the devil in Pecos County," asking if anything could be done.[91] Jones responded that there was no greater necessity
for Rangers in Pecos than anywhere else, and that the United States Army
could also do nothing there.[92] However, in Pecos County there was considerable agitation about the number of armed men camped throughout
the area, creating a general foreboding about coming lawlessness that led
to a request for troops.[93]

On December 2, 1878, Steele submitted his annual report to Governor Hubbard, noting that the Frontier Battalion now averaged about
twenty-five men in each of the companies. He pointed proudly to the 826
arrests made by the Battalion in the last year, including 147 for murder, 71
for assault to kill, and 310 stock thieves. The Rangers went on 809 scouts,
conducted 191 escorts, and returned 82 stolen horses and cattle to their
owners. Sadly, he had to report that five Rangers were killed on duty, two
were wounded, and complaints of problems in Pecos County still plagued
him.[94] The current annual amount appropriated to sustain the Battalion
was $150,000, plus an additional one-third of that amount for the final
four months of 1878. The average number of men kept in the field was 164,
each man in the Battalion representing an expense of $726.09 for sixteen
months, including salary and subsistence.[95]

Jones left Austin at the end of November for Kerrville, accompanied
by Lieutenant Guy Broadwater and men of Company A, which was being
restationed from Frio City to near Fort Ewell. Regarding an October massacre of four children in a family named Dowdy by Mexican bandits, the
major could only tell a local newspaper that he regretted "that the state

force was so weak that a perfect line of defense could not be made to check the periodical inroads made by the Mexicans and the Indians, but hoped that the next legislature would provide such means as were in their power to alleviate the evils to which our border has so long been subjected."[96]

Back in Austin on December 10, 1878, Jones issued an order directing the company commanders to again honorably discharge at the end of the year those who were unwilling to remain in the service dependent on the hope that the next legislature would continue funding for the Battalion, which Jones believed would occur.[97] Jones received a letter from John C. Sparks, the former commander of Company C who left under a cloud as a result of his repeated drunken conduct, asking again to command a company of Rangers. "I deem it proper, and am proud to say, that I am no longer a victim of the accursed habit of occasional sprees, and by total abstinence for a period of three months am prepared to say that I never will become intoxicated again."[98] He was not reinstated. Jones fully expected that although funding by the legislature would happen, there would have to be another reduction of the force after the first of the year, maybe even disbandment of one or more companies.[99] Underscoring that concern, Governor Hubbard ordered the disbandment of Lee Hall's Special Troops on December 31.[100]

On the night of December 12, several hundred bullets were fired at storefronts at Buffalo Gap in Taylor County. Steele ordered Captain Peak to proceed there with a strong detachment.[101] John Mann, who had just been elected sheriff of Taylor County, wrote Peak that the trouble was the work of J. W. Carter, the first sheriff of the newly-organized county, who had served for only about four months. "Our town constantly resounds to their random shots fired in bravado and which perforate our business and dwelling houses, and imperil the lives of peaceable citizens and helpless women and children."[102] Peak led a detachment there and peace was quickly restored.

Jones had seriously begun to entertain the idea of leaving state service and returning to his horses in Navarro County. Judge McFarland of Kerrville, a friend to whom Jones had confided these thoughts, expressed his admiration:

I regret to hear that you think of leaving the service, and, judging from my own feelings, I believe this fact alone will weaken the interest that the frontier people will feel in the future of the command. As a soldier, a lawyer and an accomplished man of business, no one knows better than yourself the full value of the service you render . . . I express but the feeling of the native frontier people when I say that I cannot conjecture where in the whole State a man can be found who will prove himself your worthy successor.[103]

Jones resolved to stay on as commander of the Frontier Battalion, and 1879 loomed as a significant year in his life.

14

STATELY AS A QUEEN

ALTHOUGH IT HAD BEEN PROCLAIMED that the problem of raiding Indians had been diminished by the state troops, companies continued to scout for their presence. Usually all they found was evidence of the Indians' presence in an area, but occasionally there was a confrontation, sometimes with unexpected results. On January 1, 1879, Lieutenant George Arrington, the new Company C commander, along with seventeen men and fifteen days' rations and six pack mules, left the camp near Fort Griffin to investigate the report of Indians along the Pease River. Four inches of snow and sleet fell on the Rangers on the 4th, and they had to walk their horses to keep the blood flowing in their own feet. Camping briefly in a canyon, they cut down cottonwood trees to feed their horses.

The cold, wind, and heavy snow slowed their progress, and they finally had to turn back to a nearby ranch where one of their horses froze to death. On January 14, the weather cleared sufficiently for the scout to resume. The next day they ran across fresh signs of about fifteen ponies. Accompanied by one Ranger and a guide, Arrington rode ahead of his group about a mile or two. The party to the rear spotted an Indian on foot running for a pile of boulders, and thinking that more

Indians may be hidden there, Sergeant W. C. Bradley ordered his men to charge the rocks. With pistol in hand, Bradley confronted the sole Indian, later identified as a Kiowa named Gun Boys, who was brandishing a carbine. The Ranger shot him twice in the heart and the arm, and gunfire from other Rangers made sure he was finished. Then another Indian was spotted, and the Rangers on horseback raced after him, but the Indian escaped. Arrington returned to his men, reporting that he had spotted a nearby Indian camp. Stealthily, the scout approached a small valley containing fourteen tepees, with about 150 to 200 horses grazing nearby. A scene of peacefulness presented itself, Indian women and children unaware of the violence that had just occurred or of the Rangers' quiet approach.

The Rangers' plan was for Bradley to take seven Rangers to attack the camp, while Arrington and men went after the horses. However, as they approached, Indians on horseback began yelling "Heap Texas! Heap Texas!" and tried to round up the horses. Indians in the camp began running amidst much confusion. The Rangers held their fire as they advanced closer to the camp, but as they were about to charge, six soldiers of the Tenth United States Cavalry rode up on horses bareback and called on the Texans to hold their fire. The camp was protected by regular soldiers who had escorted the Indians there to hunt. The carbine carried by the Indian who was killed was returned to the soldier who had loaned it to him. Disappointed, Arrington and his men retraced their route, arriving back at their camp on the 21st, their trek having extended about 300 miles. As one of the Rangers expressed it, "We suffered considerably, yet we have but one regret, and that is that we did not catch more of those Indians before we got to the camp."[1]

The army was upset with the killing of the Indian, reportedly shot four times and scalped. Captain John A. Wilcox, commander of the Fourth United States Cavalry, wrote Steele complaining that the Indians had not committed any depredations and that the attack by the Rangers was unprovoked. "On the contrary, I think they [the Indians] have evinced more than usual forbearance," he proclaimed. After the attack, the Indians, described as despondent, were induced to return to the reservation at

Fort Sill in the Indian Territory.[2] This did not prevent Governor Roberts from writing the army in February:

> I have the honor to inform you that there are now over one thousand Indians within the State of Texas, said to have come from Fort Sill Reservation, with permission to hunt in Texas. They are now roving about in small bands on the upper waters of the Brazos, Wichita & Pease Rivers. They are depredating on the property of the citizens of that sparsely settled region and our citizens are apprehending serious damage from them . . . I deem it my duty to call your attention to these facts and to request that you will at once take measures to have them removed from the Territory of Texas.[3]

At the same time, the governor asked the state legislature to authorize an agent to work with Texas congressional representatives to seek reimbursement from the federal government for expenditures the state had to make in defending itself against Indian incursions. He also asked that a law be enacted making it a felony offense for an Indian, or those cooperating with them, to be found within the state's limits.[4] In support of the governor's message, one representative even filed a bill to disband the Frontier Battalion, supposedly the idea being that the federal government would then be forced to do more to protect the state's borders.[5] Jones submitted to the governor an estimate of 2,000 Indians in Texas, primarily occupied with the stealing of cattle, horses, and mules. "The small force now in the service of the state, distributed, as it necessarily is on more than one thousand miles of our frontier cannot possibly give the protection that is asked for by the settlers in the section of country where these Indians now are."[6] The army, however, continued to deny that any depredations had taken place and insisted that the Indians, with army permission, were only in Texas to hunt.[7]

All of the companies of the Battalion reorganized at the first of the year, and the men were again sworn in. However, the status of William Steele as adjutant general was still not settled. It was reported that the new governor contemplated consolidating Steele's duties with those of Jones. Steele argued that the positions being separate allowed them to act as a check on the authority of each other to order vouchers from vendors to be paid. Also, Steele pointed out, the success of the Frontier Battalion was in large part due to Jones' ability to spend time with his companies, away from the day-to-day distractions of administrative noise. As adjutant general, Jones would not be able to get away very frequently, if at all.[8]

June Peak wrote Jones about his concern that the major's position might be the one abolished: "Your loss I feel would be a great one to Texas as well as the officers of your command, and one from which the Battalion would in all probability scarcely recover during its existence." Peak volunteered to work for the defeat of such a measure.[9] In response, Jones, who was apparently already aware of what the governor intended to do, stated simply that the matter "will be arranged to my entire satisfaction," and urged Peak to bring whatever political influence he could to bear on the legislature to procure a "liberal appropriation" for the Battalion.[10]

The state legislature convened in Austin on January 14, 1879. In his first message to the legislators, Governor Roberts praised the record of the Frontier Battalion and recommended its continuation: "All honor is due to these gallant and faithful officers and men for the soldierly service they have performed for the state."[11] At the same time, Texas sheriffs were holding their annual convention in Austin, and Jones proposed that they urge a statute authorizing the taking of depositions of witnesses for defendants in felony cases so as not to allow defendants to delay trials because of such witnesses being absent.[12]

Lieutenant Broadwater of Company A imprudently wrote Jones from Fort Ewell that the company had received assistance in "finding out fugitives" from a man named Baylor, a son of John R. Baylor of San Antonio, who lived near the fort. "He has a brother who wants to join my company & while I am aware of the fact that you & the old Gen. are not on the best of terms, I thought that I would mention the subject of young Baylor joining the company to you."[13] A former state legislator, Indian fighter, and a controversial Confederate officer, John R. Baylor was noted for his cantankerous personality and his repeated involvement in violent confrontations.[14] Broadwater's letter led to a rebuke from Jones:

You are mistaken in supposing that Gen'l Baylor and I are not on good terms, or that I would not want one of his sons in my command. Officially, I have no feeling against any family or citizen in Texas and would as soon have a member of the Baylor family as any other, provided he is fitted for the service. Many members of that family have been my warm personal friends for years, and on that account and also on account of the distinguished services rendered by Gen'l Baylor to the State heretofore, I shall be glad to have his son in my command, and, therefore, although I had determined not to enlist any more men at present, you will enlist young Baylor at once. I have no doubt from what you say of him that he will make an efficient man and render valuable service to the State.[15]

Broadwater apologized to Jones, emphasizing that he had heard about the alleged enmity at Fort Ewell from some parties there, but that he had not mentioned it to anyone except in the letter to Jones. A request had been made of Broadwater to enlist the Baylor brother, and that was the primary reason for the letter.[16] On February 3, 1879, George W. Baylor requested appointment as a company commander in the Battalion, accompanied by numerous letters of support from prominent citizens and politicians. There were no such vacancies, but Jones promised that he would make such appointment should there be an opening, as he believed Baylor "well qualified for the position."[17]

In Uvalde County, Captain Pat Dolan of Company F was confronted with a potential serial murder. Early in January a man named Thompson was killed, supposedly by two shepherds who worked for him. However, they were found dead a few days later, likely killed by the same person or persons who slew Thompson. All had been shot in the back. Dolan received a report of three Mexicans who had been seen in the vicinity of the killings, traveling west from Sabinal Canyon with a small herd of horses. He sent two squads in different directions to try and intercept them.

One of the squads, three men under the command of Sergeant Richard Jones, came upon a sheep camp and approached it to inquire if the

Mexicans might be there. One of the Mexicans in the camp, Roman Gonzales, unexpectedly opened fire at the Rangers, and the sergeant and his men called out in English and Spanish that they were Rangers. The Mexican tried to fire again, but the lawmen responded in force, killing Gonzales and wounding Cosmo Gonzales, the other Mexican at the camp, in the leg. A justice of the peace quickly summoned a coroners' jury, which found that the Rangers had acted in self-defense. The other squad of Rangers, led by Sergeant G. K. Chinn, apprehended the three suspected Mexican horse thieves.[18] The murderers of Thompson and his shepherds, however, turned out to be three white outlaws—Reese Gobles, James Irvin, and Walter Clark—who were never apprehended.[19]

The ongoing question of consolidating Jones' position with that of the adjutant general underwent legislative scrutiny. A question arose about the efficacy of Jones acting as both commander and quartermaster of the Battalion. Jones wrote Senator Charles Stewart about the current arrangement, in place since March of 1875, pointing out that he had seldom asked to be reimbursed for personal expenses, the primary exceptions being his travel to El Paso and the hunt for the Sam Bass gang. He told the senator that the arrangement had led to a savings to the state of nearly $5,000, as well as a twenty-five percent savings accrued from the method by which he purchased supplies from larger markets, rather than from individual, local contractors.[20] Steele also reported to the legislature that when Jones was made quartermaster, it was understood that payment for any vouchers sent for purchase of supplies ordered by Jones would be reviewed by the adjutant general's office for payment, not by Jones.[21]

On January 22, 1879, among other appointments, Governor Roberts nominated Jones to replace Steele as adjutant general of Texas.[22] The senate went immediately into executive session and engaged in heated discussions. Some legislators questioned Jones drawing payment for two offices—Battalion commander and quartermaster—and it was rumored that some legislators preferred Walter P. Layne, a veteran of the Mexican War and a brigadier general in the Civil War, to command the Battalion. Lane had even drawn some media recommendations for the post.[23] Jones' letter to the senate explaining the double payment was reviewed in the executive session, and it was revealed that the opposition to his appointment as adjutant general arose "out of circumstances of the past involving defeat for offices in the frontier battalion, of persons who have apparently some influence in the councils of the senate." Steele confirmed Jones' account of his duties and was instrumental in magnanimously removing opposition to Jones' confirmation.[24]

Nevertheless, opposition to Jones' appointment continued, and it was speculated that, in order to dilute the political acrimony and discord, the senate and the governor might choose to compromise with the appointment of someone else.[25] The *Austin State Gazette* editorialized that the ongoing controversy involving Jones was "an act of injustice to a faithful and efficient public officer," but nevertheless endorsed Steele for reappointment to the position.[26]

Finally, on January 25, Jones' appointment as adjutant general was confirmed by the state senate with a vote of twenty-one to eight. It was reported that "the contest has engendered personal feeling, and may be considered, the entering wedge to much contention in the future."[27] A German-language newspaper, the *San Antonio Freie Presse*, criticized the governor for turning out Steele, a "worthy officer," based solely on the governor's "personal regard" for Jones.[28]

Jones took his oath of office on January 27 and posted a $10,000 bond the next day.[29] Now the issue of an appropriation for the Frontier Battalion remained. Incredibly, the *Sherman Register* editorialized that the services of the Battalion "have been utterly insignificant when the cost is considered," recommending disbandment of the Battalion, perhaps leaving one company for a short time for some protection.[30] The state senate committee on Indian affairs and frontier protection reviewed in depth the cost and extent of the operations of the Frontier Battalion, but observed a more intrinsic worth:

> The value of the services of this command cannot be measured by computing the number of arrests it has made, the miles marched, the scouts performed, or by the number of Indians it has killed; but the true measure of its worth is the confidence it has inspired in the breast

of the law-abiding citizens, not only on the frontier, but in the older counties, that the offender against the laws cannot escape as he has heretofore done, the cessation of Indian raids with their accompanying robberies, murders and crimes too hideous to name, perpetrated on innocent girls and women; and the feeling of security that it has instilled into the brave and hardy pioneer, who, emboldened by its presence, is willing to settle, not only in his immediate neighborhood, but even to go beyond it.[31]

The committee recommended to the senate that another appropriation of $150,000 per fiscal year be made for frontier defense and the suppression of lawlessness and crime.[32]

Jones assumed duties in addition to those involved in overseeing the Frontier Battalion, the position of major remaining unfilled. He now oversaw the maintenance and arming of the various militia companies organized in many cities and towns, as well as the operation of the commissary general, paymaster general, and chief of ordnance.[33] One of Jones' first official acts as adjutant general was to appoint Thomas P. Martinez as his chief clerk in Austin.[34]

Governor Roberts revoked all existing state rewards for fugitives, it having proven difficult to successfully prosecute those for whom rewards had been offered years before. He laid down new procedural rules to be followed when requesting the offering of a reward by the state for the arrest of a criminal, stating that "rewards will be offered only in extraordinary cases, where it is absolutely necessary for a proper execution and administration of the criminal laws."[35] Roberts also asked his department heads, including Jones, to make recommendations that could lead to budget improvements. Jones was quick to respond that any reductions in his operations could only be minimal, weakly suggesting that maybe there could be some savings in reducing the expense of storing ammunition.

I shall take great pleasure in seconding any effort on the part of your Excellency in reducing the expenses of the government, and in the management of my department will promise to be diligent in observing that no expense is incurred, and that no appropriation that may be needed, shall be expended unless absolutely necessary for the proper management of the office and the good of the State.[36]

Understandably, Jones devoted the majority of his time to the operations of the Frontier Battalion. On February 5, he sent W. L. Banister of Company E to Guadalupe County in an undercover capacity to look for some wanted fugitives believed to be at Kingsbury, although the effort was not fruitful.[37] A petition to the governor from Kerr County to have Neal Coldwell appointed as major of the Frontier Battalion went nowhere.[38] At the same time, Lieutenant N. O. Reynolds, commander of Company E, pleading ill health and having been "patched up by first one doctor and another," submitted his resignation from the Battalion on February 14, to take effect at the end of the month. Reynolds felt that the constant horseback riding was what kept him from getting well.[39] The members of his company, including Reynolds himself, petitioned General Jones to promote Sergeant Charles L. Nevill to take the commander's place.[40] The same company passed a resolution honoring their "highly esteemed and much loved friend and officer," Reynolds, as a gentleman who was "good, noble, kind, just and impartial, brave and true as steel."[41]

Numerous petitions from the various frontier counties continued to bombard state government, all pleading for continuation of Ranger protection in their specific locale, some concerned that the Frontier Battalion may be disbanded. One newspaper editorialized that, with the army now requiring troops to accompany Fort Sill reservation Indians on their hunting expeditions into Texas, the threat of depredations was greatly diminished, bringing into question the need to spend $150,000 each year for the Battalion. However, the same source recognized that there still remained the problem of "skulking criminals" in the interior and suggested the expenditures for an effective police force should not be begrudged.[42] But the reluctance to raise taxes led to further government retrenchment efforts, and one legislative committee even suggested the abolishment of the adjutant general's office (and Jones' annual salary of $1,500) and the absorption of its duties by the governor.[43]

Charles Nevill   (*Courtesy of Texas State Library & Archives Commission, Austin, Texas*)

Governmental problems aside, General Jones, whose life to this point had been solely and single-mindedly dedicated to the Frontier Battalion, now took on a wife and an instant family. On February 25, 1879, he married Ann Holliday Anderson in a ceremony conducted by the Reverend C. C. Chaplin, a Baptist minister. The wedding took place at the bride's residence on San Jacinto Street in Austin.[44] The new Mrs. Jones was born on November 20, 1833, in Tennessee to Samuel Holliday, now a prominent Brazos county planter.[45] She was reportedly educated at the Judson Institute at Marion, Alabama, and emigrated from Tennessee to Texas with her father at an early age.[46] She had first married Thomas J. H. Anderson, a prominent farmer of Robertson County and Grand Master of the Masonic Lodge of Texas.[47] One description was given of her many years later by one of her daughters:

Mrs. Jones was described as a combination of the social and executive type. She was beautiful, charming and fascinating in the drawing room; yet she was able to supervise successfully her large business interests, She was stately as a queen, but was not the type to be interested in clubs of a political nature.[48]

After the death of Anderson, the affluent Mrs. Anderson moved to Austin with her five daughters and two sons, where she constructed an elegant two-story house. The house was the center of a number of social activities, but she was quite religious, leading to her friendship with Jones at the Baptist church they both attended. The wedding was held at her house, and the two made a "regal looking couple."[49] Since Jones had no permanent home of his own, he moved into the house with his bride and her children.

In his new role as a stepfather, Jones was apparently successful, for, as described by one of his stepdaughters, he was

a person you were proud to know, a person you liked to be with and to talk to, a man in whom you had great confidence, a person who commanded the attention of everyone in the room . . . [He] was always considerate of the wishes of others. Although he was small in stature, . . . yet he had such dignity and bearing that one was unaware that he was not a much taller person. He was always immaculate, and the long coats which he wore so gracefully gave him a "kingly appearance." His wisdom, tact, good judgment and elegant manners caused him to fit happily into his new family.[50]

One of Ann Jones' sons, Reuben T. "Rube" Anderson, was a member of Dan Roberts' Company D, the young Ranger having been enlisted by Jones in October of 1878, no doubt after Jones' association with his future wife. Jones granted his stepson a two-week furlough so that he could attend the wedding in Austin.[51]

But the business of frontier protection went on, and an initial appropriation of $16,000 was authorized for Battalion payrolls for just the first two months of 1879.[52] At the same time, Governor Roberts, who had revoked standing rewards for criminals then on the books when he was inaugurated, asked that money again be appropriated for another state reward pool. He also asked for money with which to employ detectives on occasion as needed.[53] But the biannual battle for money was on once more. Again, $150,000 was proposed by the state senate, but rejected by the house finance committee and by the *Sherman Register*, which preferred just one small company of Rangers.[54] It was necessary to again reduce the number of men in the Battalion, and on March 25, 1879, General Jones issued an order directing commanders to reduce their companies by from two to four men each, for a total of seventeen fewer men.[55] Jones despaired of even receiving the same appropriation as before, and he was perplexed as to what was going to happen. He wrote former Captain Neal Coldwell, saying he would "be glad to have the benefit of your services in some capacity if the Frontier Battalion is kept in the service," but that he had no definite proposition because of the uncertainty.[56]

The reduction in force allowed a small surplus of supplies to accumulate, but only until about the middle of April. Since no appropriation was yet forthcoming from the legislature at the beginning of April, there were no funds on hand to purchase additional supplies for the Battalion's five officers and 125 men, now stationed in Throckmorton, Runnels, Kimble, El Paso, Kerr, Uvalde, and LaSalle Counties.[57] Nevertheless, Jones continued to order supplies, promising payment when an appropriation was made. For example, for Dan Roberts' Company D he ordered 250 pounds of bacon, sixty-five pounds of coffee, ten pounds of soap, 400 pounds of flour, sixty-five pounds of sugar, thirty pounds of salt, fifty pounds of beans, four pounds of candles, and three pounds of baking soda, all on credit.[58]

As part of his duties as adjutant general, Jones had to oversee the growing number of militia companies in the state, as well as see to the provision of arms to those companies from the state arsenal. Remarking that "quite a military (militia) spirit has suddenly seized upon our people," Jones wrote his brother-in-law, Roger Q. Mills in Washington, that twenty new militia companies had applied for arms in the last two months, which the state was unable to provide. The state legislature passed a joint resolution asking the federal government for a loan of four batteries of artillery with which to arm two existing companies in Galveston and Houston, although the state needed "ten times more in small arms."[59] At the same time, the legislature provided that pre-emption settlers, i.e., those who were given state lands if they occupied the same plot for at least three years in order to gain title, were allowed extra time if, during the three years, they joined the Frontier Battalion.[60] Jones appointed F. W. James, an Austin attorney, as Inspecting Officer of the State Militia, with the rank of brigadier general, his duties to see that all militia companies in the state were properly organized in accordance with the law and meeting all administrative requirements.[61]

Finally, only $80,000 was authorized by the legislature for frontier defense, and Jones was faced with making even further reductions in the manpower of the Battalion. In Company A, not only did he discharge four privates, he dismissed Lieutenant Broadwater, leaving Sergeant T. L. Oglesby in charge of the company. Likewise, in Company F, he dismissed Captain Pat Dolan and all of the company except Sergeant Richard Jones and two privates. Company E was reduced by five privates.[62] Interestingly, none of the correspondence from Jones to his terminated commanders gave any hint of appreciation or wishes of good fortune. He did, however, recommend that Arrington be promoted to captain, because, "I thought your faithful and efficient service to the State heretofore and the important position which you hold, having to operate in so large a territory entitled you to the promotion and rank and pay." At the same time, Neal Coldwell was once again on the rolls of the Battalion as captain and quartermaster, commencing May 4, 1879, thereby relieving Jones of that responsibility and becoming Jones' eyes and ears in the field.[63] With Coldwell acting essentially as inspector, Jones no longer had to continually go "up the line."[64]

Jones also notified Sergeant Ludwick of the Company C detachment in El Paso that, because of the reduced appropriation, a rent of more than ten dollars per month for shelter for the detachment was out of the question. If needed, Jones would send tents.[65] Further denoting the reduction in funding, Jones also ordered that the ration of corn for horses throughout the Battalion be reduced to six pounds per day.[66] Jones had delayed appointing a new commander for the El Paso detachment, preferring to leave Ludwick temporarily in charge. On May 17, Jones wrote Judge Blacker asking his candid opinion on Ludwick's fitness for the job. "I know nothing of him except the record he has made since Tays resigned, and he seems to have done very well, but I have thought it would be better to send a new man there, one of some established character and who could set in free from any local 'entangling alliances' or influences."[67] He continued to hold off making any command appointment for the detachment.

At the direction of Governor Roberts, Jones laid plans to send a man undercover into Navarro, Hill, and Ellis Counties to ferret out information on violators of the law. Private Peter C. Jackson of Company E was summoned to Austin and given an open letter establishing his assignment, to be shown only to local authorities whenever necessary.[68] At the same time, Arrington was directed to take Company C to newly-organized Wheeler County and help get law enforcement officials there on an even keel.[69]

Jackson went promptly to work, assisting a hide inspector at Waco in arresting two cattle thieves on May 24 (one of whom immediately escaped), then making another arrest in Hill County.[70] Jackson then met in Navarro County with Jones' father, who grandly introduced him to appropriate persons in the county to facilitate his mission, setting up a meeting with various officials from surrounding counties.[71] Jones received the information from Jackson and was not too happy:

> I have been quite surprised by your two letters, informing me of your arresting two men at Waco and one in Hill County. You were not sent on duty of that kind but on secret service with specific instructions to go secretly and without making yourself known to any one or allowing any one to know that you were expected to get information in regard to the parties you were after. It was not expected that you would make any arrests at all, but would merely find out who the guilty parties were and give the information to the officers of the county where they were found.

John B. and Ann Holliday Jones *(PICA 09058, Austin History Center, Austin Public Library)*

Since Jackson had overtly revealed his identity, his usefulness in Hill and Navarro Counties was over. Jones directed him to move on to Comanche County and remain there until court started up, then return to his company.[72] Jones gave the same sort of assignment to Company E's Henry Maltimore, who was to do his secret service in Bell, Milam, and Falls Counties.[73] Likewise, A. Anglin, also of Company E, was sent back to Hill, Navarro, Ellis, and Johnson Counties, this time to do the job correctly.[74]

At Fort Griffin in Shackelford County, a wanted desperado met his end before the guns of two Rangers. August Erps had been indicted in Medina County for horse theft, but jumped his bond, and a warrant for his arrest was outstanding. Some local citizens, aware of the warrant, pointed the fugitive out to Rangers C. F. Brown and P. H. Clifton of Arrington's Company C. On Sunday, May 23, with warrant in hand, the two Rangers walked toward Erps, but he spotted them and jumped on his horse to leave town. Brown and Clifton raced to their horses and started after him. Seeing them in pursuit, Erps stopped, dismounted, and ran inside a shoe shop. The Rangers were close behind him and told him that he was under arrest. Erps went for his pistol, but the Rangers were faster. They both fired, hitting Erps in the hand and the breast. Erps dropped his pistol, then fell to the floor, living only a few minutes. A coroner's jury ruled that Erps had come to his end by resisting arrest. Most onlookers familiar with the outlaw did not think it a great loss.[75]

Among the highest Masonic honors in Texas, Jones was elevated in 1879 to Grand Master of the state's Masonic Lodge. Thus, in addition to his state duties, Jones had to find time to attend to the functions of his Masonic office. For example, on June 7, he attended the installation of officers of two lodges at Austin's Masonic Hall, an event also attended by a number of state dignitaries, including the state's lieutenant governor.[76] On the 23rd of June, accompanied by his wife and stepdaughter, Tilly Anderson, Jones left Austin by train for Palestine and the dedication there the next day of a Masonic temple. He declared the structure "by far the handsomest Masonic building in the State."[77]

Jones also installed the officers of an Austin lodge on June 27, which was followed by a sumptuous banquet.[78]

In the meantime, arriving at Sweetwater in Wheeler County on June 12, Arrington wasted no time in provoking a controversy. Two local sutlers, Lee and Reynolds, were opposed to the organization of the new county, calling on Lieutenant Colonel J. W. Davidson, commander of the Tenth Cavalry at Fort Elliott, to not allow his troops to come to Sweetwater. Arrington had no sooner unsaddled on arrival than Davidson sought him out and asked his intentions toward the Indians. Upon pointed questioning, Arrington admitted that he would kill any Indians if they were armed and likely committing depredations. As it was, Indians were reported going in houses for food, as well as killing hogs and stealing cattle. After several scouts, Arrington had the distinct impression that Davidson was warning the Indians as to the Rangers' whereabouts. Local citizens, tired of the damage caused by Indians, were ready to go out with their own scouting parties and put a stop to it. On June 18, Arrington was told that John Donnelly, a clerk at the local post trader's store as well as a county commissioner, had said that Colonel Davidson stated that he would order his men to open fire on the Rangers or put them in irons if they killed or molested any Indian in the Texas Panhandle. Although Donnelly denied making the statement, Arrington wrote Davidson asking clarification, "not that I have any fears of you in the escalation of the enterprise, but for the purpose of laying the matter before the Governor and the legislature." Davidson did not dignify the request with a reply.[79]

15

SCARED ON OUR ARRIVAL

PEGLEG CROSSING SAT ON the San Saba River about twelve miles east of Menard in Menard County for many decades. A relay station was constructed there to accommodate a stage line running between Fort McKavett, Fort Mason, and San Antonio.[1] The fact that horses pulling coaches had to slow a mile west of the station to climb a steep hill made it a convenient stopping point for robbers. As early as January 1877, the stage was robbed there and $300 taken from passengers.[2]

On December 14, 1877, the stage was again held up. Among the passengers were Judge Allen Blacker and Army Lieutenant Harry Kirby, fresh out of West Point. The young lieutenant had purchased a large revolver upon commencing the journey to Fort McKavett from the Academy after hearing about violence in Texas. When the stage was suddenly stopped, the judge had to talk Kirby out of opening fire on the bandits lest all of them would be killed. The lieutenant instead hid his money in his boot. After the robbers had taken what loot they could find, Judge Blacker said that the "boss" of the gang identified himself as Dick Dublin, who claimed he "has come back to stay a while."[3] On July 5 of the following year, three men once more held up the stage at Pegleg Crossing, rifling the mail sacks.[4]

Captain Dan Roberts of Company D, in September 1878, had even sent new Ranger C. H. Elliott to mingle among suspected robbers, representing himself as a stockbuyer. He carried a letter that had been prepared indicating that a "brother" would leave San Antonio for Menard on September 30, supposedly carrying $1,500 with which to buy stock. Roberts planned to have men in the vicinity lay in wait for the robbers, but the bandits didn't bite.[5] Another stage robbery occurred at Pegleg on November 23, 1878, when two men again took the mail sack.[6] A fifth robbery occurred there four months later, on February 26, 1879, when two men took some thirty dollars off the four passengers and again went through the mail sacks.[7]

Efforts to track the robbers each time were stymied by the mountainous countryside, and the trail was always quickly lost. Roberts even sneaked a Ranger with a double-barreled shotgun aboard the stage, but the man was called off under the assumption that the robbers had heard about the scheme.[8] Lawmen were frustrated by their inability to even identify the culprits, although the Dublin brothers were high on their list. It was even suspected that one of the robbers might be a woman because of "exceedingly small footprints" found at the site of each robbery.

While out on a scout in May of 1878, Sergeant Charles L. Nevill had arrested Bill Allison, a member of the Dublin gang and deposited him in the Travis County jail, where he languished for over a year without being able to be released on bond. His resentment toward his former colleagues festered because of the gang's failure to get him out, and he determined to get even, maybe even helping himself at the same time.

Rangers Jim Gillett and Dick Ware were delivering some prisoners to the jail in June of 1879 when Allison called out to them and offered to give up the Dublins as the Pegleg robbers. Arrangements were made for Allison to be taken to Jones' office where the general talked to him alone for over an hour.[9] Allison told Jones that the Dublins had "gone back" on him and claimed that they had wanted him to join them in robbing the stage at Pegleg, afterwards showing him the loot. He offered, if he could be released, to find another witness who could corroborate what he said. Jones entertained the idea of posting Allison's bond himself and releasing him to find the witness and convince that person to come forward. It would also be arranged that if Allison ran off, the bond would not have to be paid. "If he runs away we will miss a mere chance to convict a petty thief. If he does what he says he can and will do, we have a pretty good chance to catch or break up the most daring and successful band of stage robbers that has ever infested the State."[10] There is no record that this plan was carried out, but Rangers were sent to Kimble County, where the Dublins resided, to try and round up the gang.

At the same time, another Ranger fell in the line of duty. On June 29, 1879, Captain June Peak of Company B, in the vicinity of Tom Green County, sent Corporal Y. E. Douglass and six men to the head of the North Concho River to establish a camp for the company, there being some concern that Indians would be coming into the area. About twenty miles northwest of Fort Concho, Douglass and his men were informed by ranchers that Indians were indeed in the vicinity. The Rangers found the Indian trail and followed it for about twenty miles, coming up on the Indians' horses staked out near their camp. Stealthily, Douglass and his men cut the horses loose, drawing gunfire from the camp. Two of the Rangers' horses were killed, one from under a Private Gibson, and a third horse, belonging to Tom McConnell, was wounded. Douglass and McConnell tried to maneuver behind the Indians to catch them in a crossfire, but the Indians took refuge behind a high rock bluff. In the ensuing fight, two Indians were killed and one was wounded. As darkness enveloped the scene, the exposed Rangers retreated to a temporary camp, taking with them eight of the Indians' horses, saddles, and bridles. However, two of the pack mules the Rangers had brought got loose during the encounter and went straight to the Indian camp. Around midnight, the Indians attacked the Ranger camp but were driven off.

At daybreak, the Rangers renewed their pursuit of the Indians, who had ridden off in a westerly course, taking with them the Ranger mules. After several days and having ridden a distance of about 100 miles, on July 1, Douglass and his men ran up on the two mules "upon a small eminence in the prairie." There were no signs of any Indians or any likely hiding places where they could be concealed. Leading the Ranger scout by several yards was Virginia-born W. B. Anglin, riding in leisurely fashion following the Indian trail. At this point there are two versions of what happened next.

In Peak's report to General Jones, he said that Douglass directed his men to check out the "eminence." Suddenly, Anglin wheeled his horse around as shots rang out from Indians concealed in a sink hole in the prairie. The volley knocked Anglin from his horse, but he rose to his feet, both hands clasped to his chest. Another volley from the Indians killed him. Outnumbered and in the face of heavy fire with no cover, Douglass was forced to order his remaining men to retreat, and they retraced their steps over 100 miles to get reinforcements.[11]

In another version, Peak was quoted in a Fort Worth newspaper as saying that as Anglin rode along ahead of his companions, he spotted a moccasin on the ground, and dismounted to pick it up. He was suddenly riddled with bullets by fifteen Indians concealed in a sink hole not ten paces in front of him. The Rangers responded with gunfire but were driven back, then forced to watch as the Indians scalped their fallen comrade and "brandished it in the visage of his helpless friends."[12] In the fight, Anglin's horse was also killed, as was a horse belonging to a Private Manning. With three men afoot and 100 miles from camp and water, Douglass had no choice but to retreat from the scene, leaving Anglin's mutilated body behind.

The scout encountered an army scouting party from the Tenth Cavalry, and Douglass assigned two Rangers to take the troopers back to where Anglin was killed and recover the body. On Anglin was found an unopened letter from his longtime fiancé in Virginia, their wedding date set for the following October. Peak wrote the would-be bride a letter of sympathy. It was later determined that the Indians had come from the Fort Sill reservation, the army having issued them ammunition and supplies upon their promise to return to the reservation, which they did not do. Peak wrote: "The blood of this man calls aloud for retribution."[13]

In Austin, the deskbound General Jones continued with his administrative duties. On July 3, he issued an order authorizing company commanders to assign men to extra duty for disciplinary purposes.

Dishonorable discharges or stoppage of pay by a company commander would be subject to amendment by the adjutant general, to whom any Ranger thinking himself unjustly treated could appeal.[14] Captain Arrington of Company C, had discharged Private John Birdwell for drunkenness, but Jones authorized him to reenlist Birdwell, if he so desired, based on the private's heretofore excellent record.[15] Jones philosophized about discipline:

> Any man who does not come up to all the requirements of the service must be discharged. It sometimes happens, however, that hot headed impetuous young men who have never been subject to control by judicious management are brought into a proper state of discipline, and when that is accomplished their very characteristics which rendered them obnoxious at first make them the best soldiers we have.[16]

Jones also congratulated Arrington for standing his ground against the army in Wheeler County. While no conflict between the state troops and the army was welcome, he observed that the army still had no right to interfere in state duties.[17] However, "the only way to impress it upon them [the Indians] effectively that they must not depredate upon us is to kill them when they do it."[18] Nevertheless, Wheeler County commissioners, including John Donnelly, petitioned Governor Roberts to withdraw Arrington's company from there before the Rangers "provoked" the Indians into a "merciless and useless war" by their policy of "killing any or all Indians that may be found within the limits of the Panhandle."[19]

Arrington's response was to reiterate that any comments he made about killing Indians were to the effect that the Rangers were there to protect life and property, whether against depredating Indians or white men. He also warned that he had received information that about 3,000 half-starved Comanches, Kiowas, Apaches, and others were in the Indian Nation holding a medicine dance to determine whether or not to go on the warpath. "I am not going to be indiscreet and kill Indians near the line, as at this present time there is great danger of an Indian war, but if I find a raiding party I will attack them."[20] Quartermaster Neal Coldwell, making an inspection of Company C, noted that Arrington "has won golden opinions of the people wherever he goes. I hear him well spoken of by all who know him. From what I can see he is a most efficient commander."[21] In the Blanco Canyon area, stockmen promised to aid Arrington if needed, they being able to quickly call up seventy-five to 100 armed men to head off white thieves and rampaging Indians.[22]

The command of the detachment at El Paso had been left unfilled ever since James Tays' resignation. Jones now offered command of the detachment of ten men to George W. Baylor, with the rank of lieutenant. "I have been trying to find something better than that for you, but as yet have not been able to do so." He hoped that Baylor, if he accepted, would start to El Paso by the end of July, and Jones would furnish him with a wagon and two mules, as well as two men for escort.[23]

The forty-seven-year-old Baylor had fought Indians, served as a colonel in the Confederate Army, and, in 1865, shot and killed a fellow staff officer in Galveston after an argument. A teetotaler who also did not use tobacco, a major fault was his "tender-heartedness" with his men, not being willing to readily enforce discipline in his camp. That would come back to haunt him as his Ranger career progressed.[24] Baylor, anxious to swap "raising cabbages and onions" for killing and scalping Indians, accepted the offer, and Jones had him come to Austin so that the adjutant general could explain in depth the situation in El Paso.[25] Jones directed the new commander to discharge the present company on August 31, then reenlist them to compose a detachment of two sergeants and eight privates. He urged Baylor to retain Ludwick as sergeant and to make Jim Gillett his second sergeant, although Ludwick had made known his wish to resign about the same time.[26]

On August 2, accompanied by Rangers Gillett, Henry Maltimore, Dick Head, Gus Small, Gus Krempkau, and George Herold, Baylor and his wife, along with two children and a sister-in-law, set out for El Paso from San Antonio. One wagon was heaped with such items as a grand piano, game chickens, and household goods, while the women and children rode in a hack. Two men on their way to New Mexico in a two-wheeled cart also ride along for protection. The party arrived at Ysleta on September 12, and Gillett was promptly promoted to first sergeant.[27]

George W. Baylor (*Dudley G. Wooten*, A Comprehensive History of Texas, *1685 to 1897, Dallas, Texas: William G. Scarff, 1898.*)

The state legislature, always tight with tax dollars, reduced the pay of the men of the Frontier Battalion on July 4, 1879. Captains would receive monthly pay of $100, lieutenants seventy-five, first sergeants fifty dollars, with forty dollars for other duty sergeants, thirty-five for corporals, and thirty for privates. Jones instructed his commanders to give a discharge to any man who was dissatisfied with the reduction in pay.[28]

The pursuit of the Pegleg robbers was not forgotten. On July 14, Jones wired the United States Attorney in Waco asking if the United States commissioner could authorize a Ranger to "arrest the mail robbers," indicating an apparent preference to file federal mail robbery rather than state robbery charges against the culprits once they were apprehended.[29] On

July 3, Henry Carson, a school teacher in Menard County, approached Sheriff J. H. Comstock and offered to betray the robbers in return for half of any reward offered. The sheriff agreed, but Carson got cold feet and backed out and fled, afraid of retribution by the gang. Comstock and postal agent W. E. Smith, however, quickly overtook Carson, and his information was passed on to the Rangers, corroborating the information given Jones by Bill Allison as to the Dublins. Within a few days, men from Captain Roberts' Company D (he was absent from camp taking his wife to Burnet), along with the Mason and Menard County sheriffs, were blanketing Kimble County for the robbers. By the 21st of July, twelve suspected stage robbers had been taken into custody.

On Wednesday, July 23, a squad of Rangers rode into Austin with Roll Dublin, William Patton, Reuben "Rube" Boyce, and a man named Burt, all of whom were placed in the Travis County jail for safekeeping.[30] On August 1, a scout of three Rangers under Corporal H. T. Ashburn, Company D, came within 200 yards of the Dublin house on the South Llano River in Kimble County and spotted Dell Dublin and Mac Potter trying to ride off. The Rangers opened fire, inflicting a wound on Dublin and capturing his horse, which had been recently stolen. One bullet shattered a knife that Dublin kept in his rear pocket, a piece of that knife inflicting a serious wound in the outlaw.[31] After the shooting subsided, the outlaws having escaped into the underbrush, a woman ran from the Dublin residence and berated the lawmen for "killing" the two men.[32]

Early the next morning, Dublin had a Doctor Donnan (or Dolan) of Junction brought to him, complaining that he had accidentally shot himself and asking for treatment of the wound in his backside. Dublin and Potter then disappeared while Roberts' men spent over a week scouting for them. Finally, Roberts was notified that H. J. Garland, a deputy sheriff in Kimble County, and a posse had arrested the two fugitives, and the Rangers took them into custody.[33] They were taken to Austin to join their cohorts. On August 18, Roll and Dell Dublin, along with William and Mac Potter, Rube Boyce, and M. Wilkins (who had also been arrested for bigamy) were examined before the United States Commissioner.[34] At a subsequent hearing, Bill Allison testified for the state, telling of the gang's operations, and the commissioner set a bond for each prisoner of $8,000.[35]

On the Texas-Mexican border, Rangers Oscar Oberwetter and J. M. Sedberry of Company E, were some fifteen miles from the village of Presidio on July 31 tracking a Mexican horse thief. At about midnight they ran into the thief who had two horses with him. When the Rangers halted him, he cut loose the horses and opened fire with a six-shooter. The Rangers "riddled him with bullets and he fell dead without a groan." The horses were returned promptly to their owners in Presidio.[36]

In another shooting incident, William A. "Red" Brown was arrested on a warrant from Baylor County by Throckmorton County Sheriff Glenn Reynolds and two Rangers. In chains at the Ranger camp on August 2, Brown asked that his shackles be removed so that he could take off his clothes and go to sleep. The guard initially declined, then relented, telling the prisoner that if he tried to run for it he would be shot. When the chains were removed, Brown struck the guard a hard blow and made a dash for it. As he had promised, the guard unlimbered his firearm and sent one bullet through Brown's back, mortally wounding him. While dying, he admitted not only to horse theft but also to the murder of a man in South Texas.[37]

In 1879, the state legislature, in addition to continuing to fund the Frontier Battalion, also created a "special force for suppression of lawlessness and crime," the new company of twenty-five men designated to police southwest Texas. The special troops originally commanded by Leander McNelly and then Lee Hall had been disbanded, but Hall was now named as captain of the new unit, reporting directly to Jones.[38] Jones moved Company A to support Hall's Special Force, naming T. L. Oglesby as first lieutenant under Hall, and telling the new lieutenant, "I have assumed the responsibility of your fitness for the position and I trust that your conduct hereafter will be such that I shall never have cause to regret having done so."[39] Oglesby was quick to respond that he would "enter upon my new duties with a ferocity and zeal worthy of the cause engaged in."[40]

When Hall's new company organized at San Antonio, it was observed that Hall "[didn't] want his men to sport ivory-handled pistols, or to wear spurs that look like they were built for a horse 27 feet high."[41] The company subsequently headquartered at Carrizo Springs in Dimmit County. Very quickly, Hall was embarrassed when noted desperado John King Fisher escaped from a Ranger guard in September, the outlaw dashing off through the brush just eight miles from Laredo. "I have ordered the corporal and men who allowed him to escape to report to San Diego, where I will discharge them, unless there is some excuse more than I have heard for his escape, as I am now satisfied it was through carelessness."[42] In discharging Ranger W. F. Bentley, Jones agreed with Hall that it was "inexcusable carelessness."[43]

Jones also reorganized Arrington's Company C to three sergeants, three corporals, and twenty-four privates.[44] Prior to relocation of the

Thomas L. Oglesby (*Dudley G. Wooten*, A Comprehensive History of Texas, 1685 to 1897, *Dallas, Texas: William G. Scarff, 1898.*)

company from the Fort Griffin area to Blanco Canyon in Crosby County, a group of citizens, with bottles of beer and boxes of cigars, descended on the camp to wish the Rangers a fond farewell. "Not many minutes elapsed ere the popping of corks was heard and the air made fragrant from forty odd Havanas." Songs, instrumentals, and short speeches were presented, the party finally breaking up at 3:30 the next morning. On August 21, the company made its move.[45] Jones also promoted Charles L. Nevill to second lieutenant and placed him in command of Company E on September 1, 1879.[46] Nevill promptly took charge, prohibiting his men from playing cards in camp and requiring them to leave their firearms in camp unless detailed for some specific purpose.[47]

Taking a break from his duties, Jones and his family visited Navarro County. On Tuesday, August 19, a grand ball was held in their honor at the Corsicana Opera House before their return to Austin on the 22nd.[48] Jones' apparent frailty came as a stark shock to a correspondent for the *Galveston Daily News* when he visited his old wartime comrade at his Austin office. The reporter was "astonished and shocked" on seeing that Jones was "as gray as a fox."

> I asked my old friend how old he was. He said he was only 44, and began to apologize for his grayness, saying that his hair was at first, as I recollected, very black, and very black-headed people often turn gray very soon . . . He was not sorrowful that I looked so young, but that he looked so old. I asked him how he felt physically—how age affected his limbs, his eyes and mind. He replied that he felt all right all over, and was as straight as a shingle in all respects except in his gray hairs.[49]

Lieutenant George Baylor did not let any grass grow under his feet once his company was organized in El Paso County. The Apaches remained a major problem there. On October 5, he received word that a band of Apaches had attacked a camp and were thought to have killed five Mexicans who were cutting hay for the stage company, although it was later learned the Mexicans had scattered and survived. Baylor led Sergeant Jim Gillett and a scout to investigate, getting the details from a survivor of the attack. The Rangers followed the Indian trail as it led south to the

Rio Grande. Baylor received permission from local authorities to cross into Mexico. The Apaches had murdered a Mexican herder, and Mexican volunteers willingly joined with Baylor in tracking them. Coming to a large canyon, Baylor and his Mexican counterpart determined that the Apaches were set up there to ambush them.

It was quickly agreed the Rangers would scale the mountain and gain the top so they could get behind the waiting Indians. Baylor stuck grass in his hatband to help camouflage himself. Suddenly gunfire erupted and Gillett spit out some cheese he was chewing. Rather than hunker down behind cover, Baylor ordered a charge, but the responding gunfire forced the Rangers to seek cover behind rocks. Gillett's hat brim was torn off by a bullet, but he was able to take out the offending Indian before he could fire again. Baylor ordered another charge, but George Herold talked him out of it. A siege set in and desultory fire continued through the day. When the Indians began to focus their fire on the Rangers' horses, killing one, Baylor had them moved out of range. That night, after a day without water, Baylor decided they should withdraw, and the Rangers rode to a nearby ranch where they rested before returning to their headquarters at Ysleta.[50] Baylor later lamented, "If I had fifteen more men, I could make something of a fight." Of the fight in Mexico he said:

> Here all you see is the flash and then the smoke arising from a pile of rocks. An Indian shot at me twice not over twenty-five yards distant. One shot knocked the leaves on a Spanish Dagger behind which I stood in my eyes, and the other went over my head. Yet nary any Indians could I see.[51]

Jones gently admonished Baylor about pursuing Indians into Mexico, suggesting that to supplement his efforts he could oversee the organization of a militia company in the area, perhaps under the command of Telesforo Montes, for which the state could provide arms.[52] In December, he authorized Baylor to increase his force to fifteen men. "I shall have to cut very close in other quarters to allow you this increase and shall expect you to economize as much as possible in the use of forage and subsistence."[53]

Jones wasn't finished with the Pegleg stage robbers. On October 9, he sent a search warrant to Captain Dan Roberts to look through the premises in Kimble County of the Dublins, Potters, and one Byers for any watches or other loot taken in the robberies. In August, Roberts had advised Jones that he had been told that the Dublin family was secreting a fine gold watch taken in one of the robberies.[54] Time was of the essence as court was then in session and trials of the robbers could be anticipated. Jones sent a description of the watch, watch chain, and gold shirt studs that had been taken from Lieutenant Kirby in the December 1877 robbery.[55]

Roberts made a search of the places named in the warrant but found nothing. When he received a followup letter from Jones with a description of the watch and stud buttons, he recalled that during a search of the Dublin place the Rangers had found a sealed envelope with two "fine looking studs, spiral fastenings, evidently gold," as well as finding three watches.[56] Roberts sent some Rangers back to the residence to seize the studs and rush them to Austin to turn them over to the prosecutor.[57] Awaiting trial, the prisoners plotted to induce compatriots on the outside to pull off some robberies to make it appear that the wrong gang had been arrested. An informant, John Miller, an Englishman, passed the information on to Jones, corroborating what Jones had already heard from other prisoners confined in the jail with the gang.[58] No such robberies took place.

Santa Maria was a large ranch approximately thirty miles above Brownsville in South Texas, consisting of three or four stores, where a large quantity of corn, cotton, and other crops were grown. Across the Rio Grande in Mexico was the Bolza Ranch, which was headquarters for a group of stock thieves. A petition to Colonel John S. "Rip" Ford, an old Texas Ranger of note, asking for protection came from citizens at Santa Maria citing the criminal problems in the area and the recent removal of federal troops.[59] Contacted by Ford, Jones ordered Lee Hall to take "a few men" to Santa Maria and render whatever assistance he could to the local authorities.[60]

When Hall and his men arrived on October 27, it was just in time to thwart a contemplated raid by the thieves and cutthroats. "A Mexican has more fear of fighting the rangers than soldiers, for McNelly's lesson to them, some years past, will never be forgotten."[61] Very shortly it could be reported that the area was calm: "Those parties all got scared on our arrival & they have not completely recovered from it yet."[62] Brigadier General E. O. C. Ord, explaining to Governor Roberts that he could only put a token number of federal troops in the area, complimented Hall's men, "whose presence has had an excellent effect in restraining the large lawless element in the population."[63] In return, the governor asked the general's cooperation in support of a bill pending before congress asking federal reimbursement to Texas for expenses incurred in defending the state's borders since 1855.[64]

In another part of the area, Atascosa County, Hall received word that five men had been acting suspiciously at Campbell's store, about twenty miles southeast of Pleasanton, and it was believed that they were planning a robbery. On November 4, Hall went to the store with two men just after dark, finding Dave Young and a posse of armed citizens, and they all concealed themselves. Some ten minutes later, at about 8:30, five men rode up to the store, two of them seizing the clerk and forcing him outside, while the other three began to loot the store. The men in hiding stepped out and ordered their surrender. The robbers dropped to the floor and one of them, a Mexican named Louis, opened fire. A gunfight broke out. One citizen, Charles Westerman, was slightly wounded in the leg, and Louis was killed, riddled with bullets. Another bandit, John Smith (alias Alexander), was mortally wounded, and a third, Archie Huir, was seriously wounded. All were from Frio County. The other two would-be robbers escaped.[65] Hall subsequently privately revealed to Jones that the two who got away had actually worked with him to set up the trap and the Ranger captain felt that they could be of use in similar undercover fashion to lure other unwary outlaws to justice.[66]

On November 6, Jones left Austin for Dallas to tackle another problem. In Wheeler County in the Panhandle, the local citizenry was "in a great rage" from the alleged actions of Deputy United States Marshal Walter Johnson, the same lawman who had participated in the search for the Bass gang. Arrington facetiously observed, Johnson was "arresting and imprisoning nearly all the county officers on some little charge, and he [was] trying to arrest all the cowmen on charge of letting their cowboys have tobacco."[67] A general complaint had been made that persons in Wheeler County were violating the internal revenue law relating to liquor sales, and some twenty blank warrants were given to Johnson by the federal commissioner in Dallas to execute.

Near Fort Elliott, Johnson located some individuals not described in the warrants and arrested them anyway. Concerned about the amount of fees that he would earn from such arrests, Johnson took additional persons into custody. The county judge was immediately petitioned to issue writs of habeas corpus for the illegal arrests, and he released some of the prisoners. When Johnson tried to transport the remaining prisoners into the Indian Territory, the sheriff was able to overtake the party and bring the prisoners back. Johnson rearrested those that had been released and was promptly fined for contempt of court, then arrested for false imprisonment. He bonded out, returned to Dallas, and procured warrants for the county judge, sheriff, and county attorney, then returned and made the arrests of those officials.[68] Threats of mayhem were directed toward Johnson, which alerted Jones to the possible need for state intervention.

However, Jones was assured in Dallas by United States Marshal A. B. Norton that he would go to Wheeler County and discharge Johnson if he found the stories were correct that the deputy was using warrants made out and signed in blank. Jones returned to Austin on November 8 after giving the marshal a general letter attesting that Norton would "do justice" to all parties.[69] Johnson was subsequently found guilty of false imprisonment and fined $500.[70] Norton investigated the matter and Johnson was dismissed as a deputy.[71]

Another outlaw fell to Ranger gunfire in November. Corporal L. R. Hughes and Private W. L. Banister of Company E, along with several other Rangers, were looking for a gang of robbers in western Travis County, not far from the small town of Bagdad. They held a warrant for one Dick Tutt of that gang and located his camp, although no one was there. The Rangers hid and waited for someone to return. About dark on Monday, November 24, Tutt rode up and was about twenty feet from the camp when the Rangers called on him to halt. He tried to pull up his Winchester, but the lawmen shot at him. Tutt wheeled his horse and rode off into the brush. It being too dark to trail the bandit, and convinced the outlaw was wounded, the Rangers waited until the next morning to go looking for him. Tutt's body was found about a mile from the camp.[72]

The irrepressible George Baylor, flush with excitement after his foray after Indians in Mexico, now took up the task of tracking down the noted Apache warrior Victorio. In August, upset over the treatment he and his people were receiving by the officials there, the Indian chief had bolted from the Mescalero reservation, taking about sixty warriors with him. Just the month before, the chief was indicted by a Grant County, New Mexico grand jury for murder and horse theft.[73] His group was later augmented by several hundred other Mescaleros, Lipans, and Comanches.[74] Soldiers attempted to track down the elusive party, which slipped back and forth across the border, and several conflicts ensued, most of which resulted in American casualties, and all of which enhanced "Old Vic's" reputation as a wily strategist and bloody foe. With continuing violence, New Mexican settlers painted the Indians as bloodthirsty, creating panicky concern that Victorio and his band had to be stopped at all costs. By late November of 1879, Baylor was working with the army searching for the Indians. Baylor and his Rangers inspected the scene of an Indian ambush in the Candelaria Mountains where some fifteen Mexicans had been massacred, followed by the killing of another dozen or so in a rescue party that had been sent out.[75]

General Jones, as the Grand Master of the Texas Masonic Lodge during 1879, attended the Grand Lodge's annual convocation in Houston on December 11, attended by some 400 delegates.[76] In a lengthy speech to the assembly, Jones reviewed his activities on behalf of Texas Masons during the past year. Referring to reports of disorderly conduct by members in some lodges, he called on those who would serve as Worshipful Masters of their respective lodges to "preserve order and decorum" while their lodges were in session. Referring to the gavel each leader wielded, Jones, bringing his lawman background to bear, admonished:

All confusion must cease at its sound. If any should fail to obey it promptly, the Master has the authority, and should command the unruly member to retire from the Lodge, and, in the event of great confusion, can close the Lodge peremptorily. It is his duty to enforce discipline and have the guilty punished.[77]

Jones lamented that the growth of the Lodge in Texas was not as great as years before, which he said might be blamed on the hard economic times and drought that plagued the state.[78] He also paid homage to the late J. J. McBride, whom he credited with being his first mentor in Freemasonry, and from whom he received "my first instruction whereon to erect my moral and Masonic edifice."[79] In concluding his remarks, Jones expressed his gratitude for the honor of being named Grand Worshipful Master of the Lodge, "as well as for the many favors I have received at your hands during a membership of twenty years in this Grand Body."[80] On the 15th, Jones presided over a ceremony honoring departed Masons, and the convocation adjourned the next day.[81] Jones, his wife, and stepdaughter Tillie Anderson then visited Galveston, staying at the Tremont Hotel and returning to Austin on December 20.[82]

With the advent of the 1880s, Jones, with a new family and a secure position as adjutant general of Texas, could only presume that his bountiful life would continue to prosper.

16

PROMPTNESS AND FIDELITY

JANUARY 1880 BEGAN with a bizarre conflict between two Rangers and two company commanders in which Jones had to ultimately intervene, although the details are murky as some of the essential correspondence is not in Ranger records. In October of 1879, Sergeant Ed Hagerman of Company B boastfully told others, because of some unknown situation, that he intended to "round up" Captain Arrington of Company C.[1] The two men had experienced a personal difficulty of some sort several years before, which had supposedly been long settled. Hearing of the boast, Arrington complained to Jones, who summoned Hagerman to Austin for a full explanation. Around this time, in November, Hagerman took a thirty-day leave to obtain an artificial eye.[2] Arrington also contacted former Sergeant J. E. Van Riper, now a saddle dealer at Buffalo Gap, who recalled Hagerman making derogatory remarks about the captain in the fall and winter of 1878.[3] Jones expressed some surprise at the situation, having "always regarded him [Hagerman] as understanding the duty of a soldier too well to be guilty of such conduct as that indicated in these reports.[4]

At the same time, Corporal William Scott of Arrington's command, who had acted as a detective in the search for the Bass gang, also became involved in the imbroglio. Responding to comments that Hagerman had reportedly made to Hagerman's own commander, June Peak, to the effect that Scott intended to refer Hagerman on charges for some unknown offense, Scott allegedly told others Hagerman had lied about him and that he was going to "straighten things" with Hagerman.[5] Word got back to Hagerman and he fired off a letter to Scott, interpreting Scott's remarks as a threat to kill him. Hagerman stated he thought Scott's role in befriending Bass and then "betraying" him was treacherous, and "ever since on that account, I have experience [*sic*] some ill feeling towards you." He also admitted he had told Peak of incidents about Scott that were negative, including comments supposedly made by Scott about Peak himself, including that the captain had sold off state property and kept the proceeds. Hagerman also accused Scott of planning a robbery,

William Scott (*Dudley G. Wooten*, A Comprehensive History of Texas, 1685 to 1897, *Dallas, Texas: William G. Scarff, 1898.*)

of taking a horse that didn't belong to him, and of saying he thought the appropriation for the Battalion could be reduced. Hagerman concluded: "If you should decline [to make an explanation] or you are hell bound on having a difficulty between you and I, just crack your whip. You will always find me prepared to meet you on any ground and on any way."[6]

Meeting with Jones, Hagerman denied making any threats toward either Arrington or Scott. He told Jones when he was appointed first sergeant of Company B in January 1879, Arrington was supposed to have said in the presence of some of his men he did not know why Peak wanted that "damned Dutchman" as he was "no account anyway." In a letter on January 6, Jones admonished Arrington for making any such comments in the presence of his men, thus failing to recognize the dignity of the position he held and rendering himself "liable to a personal controversy with a subordinate." Jones accused Peak of the same indiscretion. Peak was under the impression Arrington had sought arrests in the vicinity of Peak's camp without contacting him, establishing yet another conflict. Jones urged Arrington to work with Peak. "In this service we must have no strife, or contention, or envy, or jealousy, and I hope that there will be no more of it in the future." Jones was also quick to add that this letter was not a censure or reprimand, but to give him "a hint of the rumors that have reached me and to warn you of the impropriety of such things if they do exist."[7] Jones wrote a similar letter to Peak urging that any conflict between his and Arrington's company be immediately resolved.[8]

Scott subsequently attempted to defend himself to Jones and denied Hagerman's accusations.[9] Arrington also wrote Jones admitting he spoke of Hagerman in a derogatory fashion, finding the sergeant boastful and stating that he "had no use for him," but Arrington promised to be more guarded in his comments in the future. He denied any report about arrests near Peak's camp and pledged his full cooperation with any company, although he stated, "I would prefer to operate alone."[10] Arrington also wrote Captain Peak, "as I regret that you are laboring under the idea that I do not wish to co-operate with you."[11] With this exchange, the matter ended. However, on February 29, Arrington honorably discharged Scott from Company C for "not being properly mounted" and refusing to get a larger pony. Jones immediately enlisted him in Hall's company.[12]

In January 1880, Jones and family became the proud owners of a two-seated phaeton, a light four-wheeled carriage pulled by two horses.[13] However, January also saw more activity related to the Pegleg robbers. One of the gang, Rube Boyce, was still in the Travis County jail unable to make the $8,000 bond. He was visited on Saturday, January 4, by his wife and a brother. Her request to stay all night in jail with her husband was turned down, and she was told she could come back the next morning at ten, at which time she could stay with him part of the day. She arrived promptly toting a basket containing clothes and provisions for Boyce. Admitted to his cell, she stayed until 2:30 that afternoon. Both she and her husband came to the cell door and asked Jailer Nichols to let her out, Boyce holding her basket for her. When the door was opened, Boyce produced a six-shooter and took the keys from Nichols, the jailer readily dropping the Winchester carbine he was carrying. With the jailer locked up, Boyce made his escape on a horse that had been left for him. When Nichols tried to call out for help, the other prisoners raised a ruckus to drown him out. During the confusion, Mrs. Boyce quietly rode off in a wagon. Officers and Rangers tried to find his trail but he was well mounted and escaped into the hills west of Austin.[14] Boyce robbed a store of $100 at Junction, in Kimble County, on March 19, and local lawmen chased after him in May, almost nabbing him.[15] It was not until August 1881 when he would be captured in Socorro, New Mexico Territory.[16]

In assessing the cost to the state of protection against Indians, Jones reported to Governor Roberts on January 12, detailing the operations of the Frontier Battalion since its organization in 1874. He pointed out that, from the original organization of six companies of seventy-five men each, the Battalion now numbered just 110 officers and men, guarding an area from Eagle Pass on the Rio Grande to the mouth of the Pease River on the Red River. Since its organization through November of 1879, a total of $870,775.11 had been expended to sustain operations. He observed that Indians continued to raid into Texas, there being fifteen or twenty raiding parties during 1879, during which the Rangers had six engagements and an additional twelve unsuccessful pursuits. Since 1874 the Battalion had twenty-six engagements; killed seventy-seven Indians, wounded twenty-nine, and captured three; killed twenty-six Mexican bandits and wounded three; and recovered a total of 6,871 stolen horses and cattle.[17] The governor sent a copy of the letter to United States Senator Richard Coke asserting that the United States was indebted to Texas for all sums expended in protection of the state against Indian incursions.[18]

On January 13, Jones reviewed the names of men enrolled by Baylor for a militia unit at Ysleta, in El Paso County, the unit having been organized at Jones' suggestion to supplement the operations of Baylor's detachment. However, Jones noted some of the names on the militia rolls were strikingly similar to those of men who had participated in the siege of the Rangers at San Elizario and the assassination of Judge Howard.[19] An attorney at Ysleta, F. K. Andrews, informed him that the names did indeed belong to the same men, and he asked Jones to reconsider those appointments, it being his opinion the enlistees wanted to draw arms and ammunition from Texas in order to further their lawlessness.[20] The El Paso county clerk later informed Jones that a bond sent for the arms from the state was not valid because it was signed by a claimant to the office of county judge who was not legally recognized as such.[21] Presumably the arms were never sent, nor was the unit formally enlisted.

Winter months often presented a formidable ordeal for a Ranger company in the field. For example, on January 10, 1880, a runner informed Captain Peak's Company B at Hackberry Springs in the northwest corner of Tom Green County that there was an Indian camp some 100 miles off. Peak led a scout out, going all the way to the New Mexico line where he found a trail. Peak decided to remain there with nine men to await the Indians' return, and he sent the rest of his scout back to their camp. A cold norther blew in, but the Rangers continued to ride looking for sign. After three days without eating, with their horses also suffering from the cold, they continued to ride. When sleet began to fall, the Rangers finally camped and built a fire. The next day, one of the men was able to kill an antelope, and they had their first meal in three days. The weather grew even colder with blankets of snow fast covering the ground and any possible trail. They returned, and within ten miles of the Ranger camp, one of the horses could go no further and sank down in the snow. The Ranger put his blanket around the animal and forged ahead on foot. He finally caught up with his comrades at their camp, described as the "happiest boys on earth."[22] The animal survived and was later recovered.

On February 25, near Fort Ewell, a squad of Hall's Rangers were looking for a horse thief named Manuel Martinez, for whom they were carrying a warrant. They spotted a man on horseback who the guide with them identified as the man they were after. The Rangers ordered the horseman to halt, whereupon the man wheeled his horse to ride off and fired at the lawmen. The Rangers returned fire, killing the man, who turned out to be Miguel Martinez, the wrong man.[23] It was initially believed the young man, reported as a "quiet, law-abiding citizen," presumed the Rangers were robbers. While the Rangers were not blamed for the mistake, it was observed that "as men of heart they will be lashed inwardly by the remorse that must follow such an agonizing incident."[24] It turned out, however, that Miguel Martinez had been at the spot to warn Manuel Martinez and others that Hall's men were in the area and to postpone a planned selling of stolen horses to one of Hall's men, working undercover in the role of a buyer of stolen stock.[25]

June Peak sent Jones a resignation letter as commander of Company B, effective on April 15, 1880, purportedly because the reduction in force made it "almost impossible to effect very satisfactory service from the mere handful of men employed."[26] On March 6, Jones wired Ira Long, who had resigned in 1876, asking if he would be willing to serve as captain of Company B.[27] Long accepted, provided that Jones allow him to pick a sergeant of his choosing, and that he receive a small loan of $150 to outfit himself, all of his assets being currently invested in his farm and crops at Decatur.[28] On April 10, the members of Company B assembled in camp and passed a resolution of respect for their departing captain:

> That in parting with Captain June Peak, we desire to say that during the two years that he has been the Commander of our Company, he has performed every duty to the State with promptness and fidelity; That

he has shared with us every hardship and danger fearlessly and unhesitatingly. In the camp and on the field he has always been prompted by a stern sense of duty, ever ready, ever willing; That he was ever courteous, polite, and gentlemanly; Ever eager and bold, keen, and quiet, urgent and energetic; Never daunted, never uncertain, fearless in all things.[29]

In addition, the Colorado and Concho Stock Association resolved its best wishes to Peak for his service.[30] Peak, however, also ran into some criticism. In June 1880, Jones received a letter from prominent Dallas cattleman C. C. Slaughter, complaining that Peak had recovered one of his stolen horses and then sold it to one of Peak's Rangers. Slaughter's demand for return of the horse had been allegedly refused. "I felt no little provoked to have the State mounted on my horse when I knew they were intended to protect one."[31] When Quartermaster Coldwell inquired of Peak about the matter, the former captain merely responded that if the horse did belong to Slaughter, then he should be reimbursed by the state.[32]

When Long arrived to take command of the company, he found the unit's horses in bad condition because of the winter scouts without sufficient feed.[33] On his return home to Dallas, Peak gave a lengthy interview about the Frontier Battalion. He recommended that the federal government develop a force of some 500 to 600 experienced frontiersmen, divide them into companies of fifty men each, and station them on the frontier. In addition, he opined that every Ranger ought to be allowed to have three horses rather than just one.[34]

Jones ordered Arrington to provide an escort of two or three months for a state surveying party in the Panhandle.[35] In response to a plea by the county judge of a recently organized Baylor County for help because of lawlessness, which included an accusation that the sheriff was in league with the "rowdies," Jones also dispatched Arrington to go to Baylor County with some men and help the local authorities. Peace was soon restored.[36] The county judge wrote Jones thanking him, noting that once the whiskey had given out, the malefactors had moved on.[37] Arrington wryly noted: "The citizens of Seymour are about the contrarist [sic] set I have ever met. Each man pulls against his neighbor and no one takes any interest in the town or its officers, expecting us to do everything."[38]

On March 29, while in camp at San Diego in Duval County, Corporal C. B. McKinney, a member of Hall's company, received a note from Pierce Johnson, later the first county judge of LaSalle County, asking him to come to that county to serve a warrant on a Mexican, Marcus Sabata, who had shot a sheepherder and stolen a horse. McKinney went to LaSalle County alone. Peter Johnson, a brother of Pierce Johnson, then accompanied McKinney to a sheep ranch in the southeastern portion of the county to point out the fugitive and to interpret. When the two approached the suspect, who was holding a Winchester, three other Mexicans ordered them to leave. When it was apparent that McKinney was not leaving, a man named Jose Gonzales opened fire from a doorway, mortally wounding Johnson. McKinney shot and killed Sabata and severely wounded Gonzales. One bullet went through the lapel of the Ranger's coat, but his life was saved when a memorandum book that he was carrying in his jacket deflected the bullet.[39]

Jones made his first annual report as adjutant general in April. While Neal Coldwell acted as quartermaster and inspector of the Frontier Battalion, Jones had continued to buy supplies for Hall's "Special Force." Because of the decreased appropriation, the Battalion now averaged 107 officers and men in five companies. Companies B, C, and D under Peak, Arrington, and Roberts, respectively, had been primarily scouting for Indians and outlaws and guarding or escorting prisoners, their jurisdiction ranging from Dimmit County on the Nueces River to Fort Elliott in Wheeler County, and as far west as Fort Stockton and the New Mexico line. Jones praised Baylor's company at Ysleta in El Paso County for exemplary efforts in protecting settlements from Indian raids and lawless white men. Near Austin, Lieutenant C. L. Nevill's Company E was kept busy tracking down fugitives and guarding prisoners and jails.

Jones noted that Hall's troops, headquartered in Duval County and numbering about twenty-seven men, operated in small detachments throughout southwest Texas. He credited the unit with breaking up a number of gangs and with providing valuable assistance to local officials, especially since federal troops had been removed from the Rio Grande area. For the year ending February 29, 1880, Jones reported 441 scouts; six fights with Indians with two Indians killed; twenty-four Indian trails followed; 348 fugitives arrested; four fugitives killed and eight wounded; 204 fugitives pursued unsuccessfully; forty-eight courts attended; eighty-one jails guarded; ninety-seven civilian escorts; and 575 stolen horses and cattle recovered. The average cost for maintaining the Battalion worked out to $661 per man for the year.[40]

The *Houston Post* responded to Jones' report, contending that the outlay for state police officers was unnecessary, given the existence of established local law enforcement in all areas that Jones named, as well as the presence of federal troops along parts of the border. That observation was answered by the *Dallas Daily Herald*: "To talk about disbanding the rangers until the country is more fully settled up, is to threaten to take from the people of Western Texas a protection they need, and to strike a blow at the interests of the whole State."[41]

The annual report submitted, Jones and his family took a short vacation in Navarro County, arriving there on April 15.[42] Back in Austin during May, and having previously been appointed brigadier general of the militia by Governor Roberts,[43] Jones appointed Austin attorney F. W. James as a major general of the Volunteer Guard to oversee militia activities in Texas.[44] However, this appointment was overshadowed by a bizarre incident. On Saturday, May 8, a man called at Jones' office stating that he was a friend of Charles Buckley, a wanted convict. Buckley had first been sent to the penitentiary at the age of sixteen for killing a black man in Menard County, but was pardoned because of his age. He was then arrested in that county for horse theft but escaped from jail, only to be nabbed by the Rangers and turned over to local authorities. Buckley promptly escaped again until finally captured and sentenced to eight years in prison. While being transported to the penitentiary on a train the previous winter, he and the prisoner to whom he was cuffed jumped out the window and got away.

The visitor waited for Jones to return from lunch and showed him a letter, purportedly from Buckley, promising to turn state's evidence against a number of outlaws, provided that he received a pardon from the governor. The man had already talked with Governor Roberts, who suggested that he talk to Jones. Upon close questioning by the adjutant general, who was familiar with Buckley's deeds, the visitor answered queries that Jones knew could be answered only by the fugitive himself, and Jones concluded that his visitor was indeed Buckley. Excusing himself, Jones went to the governor's office and confirmed the identity of the man. Accompanied by the governor's secretary, Jones returned to his office and confronted the man, arresting him on the spot. The man admitted he was the elusive Buckley, and when he was admitted to jail, authorities found a bowie knife in a boot and a fine saw up his sleeve made from a watch spring. Embarrassed at being caught, Buckley claimed his motivation for such a brash act was that a girl with whom he was enamored would not marry him unless he was pardoned.[45]

On May 18, Jones received word as to the whereabouts of a wanted criminal named Byron Glasscock. He directed several Rangers to a certain point where Glasscock was promptly arrested. Marveling at such a smooth operation, the Austin newspaper observed: "The fact is the Adjutant-General is acquainted with the ways that are dark and things that are crooked pertaining to outlawry, and no desperado engaged in the business is safe for a moment as long as he remains in the state."[46]

Henry Bishop, a merchant in Hidalgo County, had been awakened early in the morning of Sunday, May 16, 1880, by seven armed men. He was struck across the head and then mortally stabbed eleven times in the neck and side. The robbers fled, but not before looting the store, raping a servant girl, and then attempting but failing to rape Bishop's very pregnant wife.[47] The county judge wired Governor Roberts that "thieving and murdering are going on in this county," asking for state troops at once. Five men in possession of some of the loot were arrested across the Rio Grande by Mexican authorities.[48] Jones ordered Hall to send an officer and five men to Edinburg to work with the sheriff.[49] Sergeant W. L. Rudd of the Special Troops wired Jones that he had an individual willing to turn state's evidence if he had a pardon; Jones responded that a pardon couldn't be given, but promised the man would not be prosecuted if he gave such evidence.[50] Rudd was unable to get the Mexican authorities to turn over their prisoners, but had three prisoners on the American side who confessed to the robbery, rape, and murder.[51]

Lee Hall submitted his resignation to Jones on May 24, "owing to private and business engagements of my own."[52] In actuality, he had just visited his family in North Carolina, was planning to marry, and was thinking about ranching in Crockett County.[53] Lieutenant T. L. Oglesby was promoted to captain and S. A. McMurray was named as lieutenant.[54] Jones wrote Hall expressing his and the governor's regret at Hall's decision.

> For myself, in severing official connection with you I have to regret the
> loss of a most faithful and efficient officer whom I have found was intel-
> ligent, energetic, and untiring in the discharge of duty and to assure you
> of my continued personal regard for you and my best wishes for your
> success and happiness in whatever you undertake.[55]

Only a few months earlier, in March, Oglesby had suffered a severe back injury when his horse fell while on a scout, although the Ranger continued on the trail for some fifteen or twenty days. As a result, he was brought to San Diego in a wagon and placed under medical care for several weeks. During that time the rumor was falsely spread, to his chagrin, that he was suffering from a venereal disease.[56]

At the same time, George Baylor relayed word to Jones that a band of outlaws led by Jesse Evans, who had been associated with Billy the Kid and prominent in the Lincoln County War, had robbed several stores at Fort Davis and may be on its way to El Paso.[57] In one robbery, on May 19, Evans and two men held up a store while two others watched from a nearby saloon and invited all in the saloon to drink up until the robbery was over, when they all rode leisurely out of town.[58] The outlaws were then reported in the vicinity of Fort Stockton.[59] Jones ordered Dan Roberts to send ten men from Fort McKavett to Fort Stockton for two weeks and to report to County Judge George M. Frazer.[60] He also ordered Sergeant L. B. Caruthers of Company E to go by stagecoach to Fort Davis to determine the necessity for permanent stationing of state troops in the vicinity, as well as the cost of forage and subsistence and whether five or six good men could be enlisted there.[61]

Before the Rangers arrived on June 5, the local authorities at Fort Stockton managed to arrest a suspected bandit named Bud Graham, alias Ace Carr, after a fight between him and Evans and Charlie Graham, alias Charlie Graves, in which Carr captured the other men's horses, setting the men afoot.[62] When Caruthers arrived at Fort Davis on June 7, he found that all was quiet, but noticed the citizens were watchful for outlaws from both Mexico and the Pecos River area.[63] Caruthers described the quiet as the "suppressed calm of absolute fear." He received word that other robberies were planned by Evans' gang, and learned a little about the gang's operations. In 1879, the gang had numbered as many as twenty men, with agents secretly looking out for their interests at both Fort Davis and Fort Stockton.

Their "agent" at Fort Davis was known as Captain Tyson, which turned out to be an alias for John Selman, the same Selman who had associated with John Larn in Shackelford County and left that county one step ahead of the vigilantes. Although the reasoning is a little difficult to follow, Caruthers convinced the sheriff to appoint Tyson/Selman as deputy sheriff and jailer. The menacing threat of the gang had frightened off any would-be applicants for the position, even to serve in a posse. Carr was being held by the Rangers at Fort Stockton, which meant that the gang would be unlikely to make a raid on the Fort Davis jail. Caruthers was hesitant to arrest Selman for his involvement with the gang because he could not be safely held there, and Caruthers believed the appointment as jailer might serve to keep Selman in town.[64] At Fort Stockton, Sergeant Ed Sieker of Company D was aware of bandits from the gang finding refuge along the Pecos River, and noted that citizens in that area were also worried about raids.[65]

On June 22, Caruthers finally arrested Selman when Sieker showed up at Fort Davis with Ace Carr. Caruthers knew that he couldn't hold the jail without a contingent of Rangers to guard it. Carr had been deliberately brought to Fort Davis as bait to induce the gang to attempt a rescue, but the sheriff got drunk and revealed the plan all over town.

Furious, Caruthers declared the sheriff "totally unfit for office," and the county judge, whom Caruthers had arrested for assault to murder, no better.[66] Inquiry was made about returning Selman to face charges in Shackelford County, but Sheriff W. R. Cruger served notice that the charges couldn't be sustained, and, anyway, "nine chances to one that the mob will hang him."[67]

On June 29, Caruthers and Ed Sieker received word that the gang had been seen near Presidio del Norte, on the border 100 miles south of Fort Davis in Presidio County. The two sergeants, along with Privates Sam A. Henry, George R. "Red" Bingham, R. R. "Dick" Russell, and D. T. "Tom" Carson headed to that area, with a deputy sheriff accompanying them as a guide. Leaving Fort Davis about 9 p.m. on July 1, the party watered their horses about one the next afternoon at Cibola Creek, about eighteen miles north of Presidio. They spotted four men with pack horses some distance off. Refusing to halt for the oncoming Rangers, the outlaws drew their pistols and left the road, engaging in a running gun battle for about a mile and a half as they struck for refuge on a nearby mountain. The bandits reached the mountain and topped its crest, dismounting to wait behind the rocks for the oncoming lawmen. Sieker, Russell, Bingham, and Carson were on stronger horses and came under fire as soon as they reached the crest, Caruthers and Henry lagging behind. Dismounting, the four Rangers took cover a short distance from the outlaws and returned the fire. Unseen by the other Rangers, Bingham was shot through the heart and killed while dismounting and trying to load his rifle. One bullet went through Carson's hat brim and another under his leg, wounding his horse.

Carson took aim and wounded Jesse Graham in the side, but the outlaw continued to fight until a round between his eyes from Ed Sieker finished him off. When that happened, Evans, accompanied by August Gross (alias John Gunter) and Charlie Graham, broke and ran, but Ranger fire changed their minds, and they called out to surrender. The fight had lasted about an hour. The three were taken into custody and as they walked to the party's horses, Red Bingham's body was discovered. Both Sieker and Caruthers later said that had the Rangers known of his death, they never would have permitted the outlaws to surrender. The prisoners were bound with ropes and the two bodies covered with blankets just as a heavy rain fell. A small brush fire was lit to keep them warm that night.

A coroner arrived from Presidio in the morning and conducted an inquest, and both bodies were buried at Rancho Canagres about fifteen miles from Presidio and about two miles from where they fell. The Rangers planned, however, to remove Bingham's body to Fort Davis as soon as a metal casket could be obtained, and the body was moved the following February.[68] The Rangers formed around their colleague's temporary grave and fired three volleys before leaving with their prisoners. The party arrived at Fort Davis on the evening of July 5, and the three outlaws were committed to jail without bail.[69]

Coldwell had gone to Fort Davis to report back to Jones about the need for a Ranger force there. Jones subsequently directed Lieutenant Nevill to move Company E from Austin to Fort Davis and establish a camp there, its mission to cover the vicinity of both Fort Davis and Fort Stockton. Nevill was also to report to Baylor at Ysleta and cooperate with him in his operations.[70] Ed Sieker was ordered to deliver Selman to Fort Concho and turn him over to the Tom Green County sheriff to await transfer to Shackelford County.[71] Area merchants and stockmen gladly pulled together a $500 reward for the Rangers involved in the fight.[72]

When Caruthers' version of the fight was published in the media, indicating he was "assisted" by Sieker, Captain Roberts took great exception. "I see there is a Sergeant Caruthers, of Co. E, out there who is certainly working in the interest of a Caruthers 'boom' from a telegram sent the San Antonio *Express* . . . My Sergeant there is competent, & my men are brave & ready to execute, and they must have the credit of what they do." On the reverse of the letter, someone in Jones' office wryly noted: "Seems annoyed that L. B. Caruthers, Co. E, gets considerable credit in above affair."[73] Jones wrote Roberts, reassuring him that "Sergt. Caruthers makes a very complimentary report of the conduct of Sergt. Sieker and his men in the fight with the robbers of which I presume you have heard the particulars before this time." Jones again made an odd statement: "The death of poor Bingham is much regretted, but, of course, his fate is that which all take the chance of when they enter such service as we are engaged in."[74] Jones advised Caruthers to make sure that Evans was well guarded against attempts to rescue him by his "strong following in New Mexico" and to divide the arms captured from the robbers between the men engaged in the fight.[75]

The 1880 census, taken on June 3, reflected Jones and his wife maintaining a household in Austin with two stepsons, four stepdaughters, and three African-American servants.[76] In late June, one stepdaughter, Attilia "Tillie" Anderson, was reported as "dangerously ill for several days," but soon recovered.[77] This same month, Jones distributed a revised fugitives list, its 245 pages including the names of 6,043 wanted men.[78]

On July 10, Dan Roberts once again submitted his resignation from the Battalion, to take effect on October 15, giving Jones ample time to find a suitable replacement.[79] Jones responded: "I shall regret very much to lose you from the service and had hoped that you would continue in the service as long as I remain connected with it, as I shall be at a loss to find an officer to fill your place as much to my satisfaction as you have."[80]

One person that Jones didn't regret leaving the service was Sergeant Ed Hagerman of Company B, the same Ranger who had been in the dispute with Arrington and Bill Scott. On July 8, a Ranger party captured Sam Horrell, Gus Stanley, and Tom Snow, all wanted on warrants from Lampasas County. The trio was caught by surprise and disarmed by the Rangers, Snow's pistol accidentally discharging and the bullet going through a Ranger's hat brim with powder burning his face.[81] At this point, Captain Ira Long launched an investigation into the conduct of Hagerman the previous October.[82] It was alleged that over eight months earlier, on October 20, 1879, Hagerman was on a scout with three other Rangers looking for the three men. They came upon Horrell and Stanley and began pursuit. Hagerman briefly dropped out of the chase to retrieve a hat dropped by one of the fugitives, then caught up with his men after they had halted the two fugitives. Horrell and Stanley had weapons displayed and were refusing to be arrested. Hagerman surveyed the standoff, then ordered his men not to fire nor arrest them, and after a brief parley, allowed the two men to leave unmolested. On the company's monthly report, he made this entry: "Ran on to Horrell & Stanley, but they succeeded in making their escape." Based on Long's investigation, Jones dishonorably discharged the sergeant for this deceit, although he had "always regarded Hagerman as a man of fine courage and a soldier who came fully up to the measure of his duty in every respect."[83]

Remnants of the Dublin gang from Kimble County still occupied Ranger attention. On July 24, Corporal D. M. Gourley and four men scouted the South Llano River in search of George Cleveland, thought to be coming to Kimble County. For two nights the Rangers watched a camp known to be frequented by Cleveland and "Indian Jim" Potter, during which time a rainstorm continually drenched the hiding lawmen as they watched the comings and goings of various persons. On the second evening, about eight o'clock, they observed a man ride into camp and, thinking it was Cleveland, the Rangers moved in. Potter was sitting by a fire, a rifle across his lap. When ordered to surrender, Potter broke for the brush on foot, and ten Ranger bullets came whizzing in his direction as he disappeared from sight. Another man at the scene fired at the Rangers and then also disappeared, the bullet grazing Private James H. Renick's gunbelt. At daylight the next morning, the only damage appeared to be a bullet hole perforating a milk can, for which the Rangers paid Mrs. Cleveland one dollar.[84]

17

SOBER, STEADY, AND RESPECTABLE MAN

IN EARLY AUGUST 1880, the Sheriff's Association of Texas met at the Dallas Opera House. Sheriff Eugene Glover of Duval County offered a resolution that the Frontier Battalion and Oglesby's Special Troops "were recognized as an auxiliary to the regular constabulary force of Texas indispensable at present to the frontier counties, and in those officers we recognize the right men in the right place." The resolution was unanimously adopted.[1]

Quartermaster Neal Coldwell made an inspection of George Baylor's Company C detachment at Ysleta in El Paso County. He was appalled at the lack of discipline:

> The men do no guard duty at quarters except day guard over the horses while out grazing. On scout the men march as they please, and are generally scattered over the country. No precaution is used on approaching the water holes when Indians are likely to be camped, but the men go along shooting at any game that may be within range.

Coldwell did note that Baylor strictly enforced sobriety among his men, and that he was well liked by the company as well as the citizenry. The company had very little to do, and probably the only reason to maintain it there was to head off a recurrence of the Salt War violence.[2] On August 4, Lieutenant Baylor and thirteen men united with the troops under army Colonel Benjamin Grierson at Eagle Springs for the hunt after Victorio, Jones ordering Nevill and his men to join with them as soon as possible.[3]

Grierson had received information from a patrol that Victorio and his braves were west of Van Horn (in what is now Culberson County) headed north. The colonel had just come off a recent skirmish and defeat at the hands of the Indians. Keeping the mountains between himself and the Indians, Grierson marched his approximately 200 troops to Rattle-snake Springs, arriving ahead of the Indians. The soldiers ambushed the Indians in a canyon on August 5. The Indians attempted a counterat-tack, but were driven off, scattering among the hills and mountains in the area. The Indians were also repulsed in an attack on a nearby wagon train guarded by an escort of soldiers.[4] After another fight on the 11th in which the Indians lost a large number of horses, Victorio retreated back into Mexico.[5]

Baylor and his men accompanied army troops to Quitman, and Nevill went to Eagle Springs, subsequently uniting with Baylor on August 15. They remained camped on the Rio Grande until the 21st, when Nevill returned to his camp at Fort Davis and Baylor returned to Ysleta.[6] Interestingly, Nevill intercepted a letter from the prison-ers at Fort Davis to "Billy Antrim" asking his help to rescue them. "Antrim" was the noted outlaw Billy the Kid. Nevill observed: "If he comes down, and I expect he will, I will enlist him for a while and put him in the same mess with Evans & Co."[7] Evans and his followers were continually trying to escape, even trying to dig out of jail with a spoon. August Gross (alias John Gunter), who was captured and jailed with Evans, pretended that he was suffering from a paralysis of a leg and arm, but Lieutenant Nevill caught him in an off-moment when he was tapping his foot while a violin was being played.[8] Jesse Evans was subsequently convicted in October in the district court of Presidio County and sentenced to two ten-year terms for robbery and murder, although he later escaped from prison and disappeared from history in May of 1882.[9]

In the meantime, other border problems continued to plague Texas. On July 28, Mexican Consul Ornelas directed a letter to Governor Roberts complaining of "outrages" being committed against Mexican citizens in Bee County. He pointed out what he called persecution of Mexican nationals the previous July in the aftermath of the disappearance of a Timothy Heart. "Grounded on these speculations the local authorities have imprisoned several Mexicans, burned their fields & houses, tortured them in the most brutal manner, hung one & left still in prison three men and an elderly woman." The consul inquired as to the protection to be afforded such citizens. Jones sent a copy of the letter to Lieutenant Oglesby and asked him to make a thorough investigation.[10] Oglesby reported on August 31 that Mexicans had been legally jailed for the alleged murder, but no one had been hanged nor had there been any other acts of lawlessness directed at Mexican nationals.[11]

Ornelas had previously complained in June of 1879 about the death of a Mexican youth, as well as the destruction by Rangers of a boat belonging to a Mexican citizen. The issue now being resurrected again, Sergeant W. L. Rudd explained that the boat had been used exclusively for stealing forays across the Rio Grande. Rangers were sent by Rudd to investigate, as he later wrote with apparent tongue in cheek:

> They then asked some men who were standing on the Mexican side to bring the boat over to this side. In answer to this, they abused my men by using very insulting language. Then, one man proceeded to cross and capture the boat. In the meantime the others fired some three or four shots at the boat and all of the shots struck the boat and never went near the parties that were standing by. This was done, I am informed, by the gentleman in charge, not with the intention of hurting any one, but for the purpose of dispersing the parties and to keep them from injuring the young man while crossing. I am well aware of the good feeling that exists between the two countries, and I assure you that this was not done with any bad feeling or evil intent on our part.[12]

Jones and his family left Austin on Thursday, August 5, for a brief visit to Lampasas, likely to bask in the allegedly medicinal springs located there.[13] He returned to Austin on the 9th, followed on September 6 by his wife and two stepdaughters, Tillie and Bessie.[14]

On August 23, after commencement of the trial in federal court of the Pegleg stage robbers, Mack and Bill Potter, Roll Dublin, and Matt Wilkins changed their pleas to guilty and were each sentenced to ten years in the penitentiary. Dell Dublin, however, let his case go to a jury, which promptly found him guilty and sentenced him to ten years.[15]

N. O. Reynolds had resigned from the Battalion in March 1879, but Jones now offered him the captaincy of Company D once Dan Roberts left in October, Roberts' resignation having been submitted the previous July. Reynolds promptly accepted the offer.[16] Strangely, however, business affairs precluded him from rejoining the Rangers,[17] and Roberts continued to command Company D rather than resign.

On September 8, Jones issued a special order redesignating George Baylor's detachment of Company C as Company A. In addition, Baylor was promoted to captain of that company.[18] Given Coldwell's negative report concerning Baylor, it can only be assumed that there likely was some political motive behind the promotion. According to Jones in a letter to Baylor,

> I have taken this step without committing you and without suggestions from anyone on the subject, because I think you deserve the rank and pay, because the position, geographically, which you occupy, is one of importance and prominence, and because it gives you a rank which I would prefer you should have in the event it should become necessary to operate several companies of the Battalion together. I hope and expect that your conduct and management will be such as to justify my action in the premises.[19]

Although the incident is not mentioned in Ranger records, a newspaper story read across the state in September 1880 told of a Ranger in Oglesby's Special Troops by the name of Lynch. The Ranger was reportedly dispatched from San Diego, in Duval County, to Fort Ewell on some mission. He was supposed to have been overtaken by two Mexicans who rode along with him in friendly fashion for some distance.

Suddenly, one of them struck Lynch with a large knife, knocking him to the ground unconscious. Allegedly, the Mexicans carried him about a mile from the road, stripped him down to his underclothing, tied him to a tree and then left, taking his horse, saddle, gun, and valuables. According to the story, he was finally able to get loose and make his way back to the Ranger camp, where he was unceremoniously cashiered from the service.[20] An F. K. Lynch served in Oglesby's command, but there is no record of his dismissal.[21]

In September Jones proposed having J. H. Martin, a cattle thief from Goliad, pardoned so that he could work undercover for the Rangers.[22] Using the alias "John Henry," Martin was sent by Jones to Corporal John McNelly, a member of Oglesby's command at Schulenburg, and McNelly was instructed that even the other men in his detachment should not know who Martin was.[23] However, Jones did reveal Martin's true identity to Dr. W. W. Walker of Schulenburg.[24] The letters written by "John Henry" are almost illegible and indecipherable, making his activities difficult to determine, although he apparently did not live up to Jones' expectations. On November 20, Corporal McNelly wrote Jones that "I fear our man Henry has played himself out as far as his working this case is concerned," his true identity already common knowledge.[25] Jones told McNelly that was not a problem; the cover story was that he had completed his prison term and wanted to return to his former profession of cattle thief. Jones suggested that "Henry" be given a new assignment if the present one was not panning out.[26] Dr. Walker, however, opined that he did not think Henry "has brains enough" to cope with the lawless characters in that area.[27]

Dan Roberts received information on September 25 that horses had been stolen near Fort Terrett, located on the North Llano River in what would become Sutton County, and Corporal R. G. Kimbell led six men in pursuit. On the morning of October 8, near the New Mexico line, Kimbell and two Rangers, accompanied by a cowboy, encountered the thieves, Jim and John Potter, both of whom were familiar with Kimbell, herding the horses. Kimbell pulled his hat down over his face and rode by Jim Potter, who was trailing the horse herd. Drawing abreast from

John Potter, Kimbell drew down on him and demanded their surrender. But weapons were drawn and a fight commenced. John Potter jumped from his horse, pulling at his rifle in its scabbard, and Kimbell shot him through the right lung. At the same time, Jim Potter was shot through the right knee and left hip by the other three, his rifle having jammed after getting off two or three shots, killing one of the Ranger's horses. Near the scene, a brother, Frank Potter, heard the shooting and came on the run to find his two brothers seriously wounded. The two outlaws were taken by wagon to a nearby ranch where Jim Potter died several days later. John was then taken to Fort Davis where he recovered. John Potter was later killed by a mob when he was taken from lawmen transporting him to trial.[28] Dan Roberts surmised that this would end once and for all the problems caused by the Potter clan of Kimble County.[29]

As an incentive for citizens to get more involved in crime fighting, Governor Roberts offered a fifty-dollar reward for a citizen's arrest of a murderer or robber. In addition, such a reward was also available when a citizen provided the information that led to the arrest of a murderer or robber, or when officers failed to do their duty and a citizen went to a prosecutor with the information.[30] In an effort to make it a little easier for members of the Battalion, constantly in the saddle on long scouts, an order was placed by some Rangers for "drawers" manufactured by C. C. Clancy of Dallas, which were "double lined in the seat" and warranted not to rip under any circumstances.[31]

On October 16, Jones left Austin by train for Dodge City, Kansas, his first trip to the frontier in some time; he stopped briefly on the way at the Malloy House in Corsicana with his brother-in-law, Roger Q. Mills. The purpose of this trip was for Jones to "see the country, mingle with the people and learn from their lips all the facts pertaining to its varied expanse and their own condition." Jones returned to Texas, visiting prosperous ranches along the way. Arriving at Fort Elliott, he was met by Coldwell and an escort of five Rangers. Once back in Texas, Jones visited companies of the Battalion on his southward trek.[32]

By November 2, he and Coldwell were at Fort Griffin, just ahead of sleet and snow, to inspect Arrington's Company C. Two days later they left to visit other companies, reaching Fort McKavett on the 9th or 10th of November.[33] On Tuesday, November 16, Jones arrived back home in Austin, reporting that everything on the frontier was "quiet and prosperous, and free from Indian raids."[34]

One of Jones' first orders of business in Austin was to offer command of Company B to Bryan Marsh, replacing Ira Long who was resigning.[35] Marsh, the former sheriff of Smith County right after the Civil War, was agreeable and met with Jones in Austin on November 24.[36] He reportedly had been a colonel in the Confederate Army who had one arm shot off at the shoulder and lost most of his other hand in the war.[37] Marsh was a hard-drinking and hard-fighting man: "Give him two drinks and he would spit in a tiger's eye."[38] Long's resignation and Marsh's appointment were both effective on December 10, 1880.[39]

The general rule was that a private in the Frontier Battalion, unlike commanders, could not serve as such if married. At times, discharges from the Ranger service were sought for matrimonial reasons. One exception, however, was Sergeant Jim Gillett of Baylor's company, who requested that he be allowed to marry Baylor's daughter Helen and remain in the service. "I promise to be as faithful in the discharge of my duty as I have ever been."[40] Jones gave a rather affable approval:

> Although the rule has always been that married men should not be enlisted in the Frontier Battalion, in consideration of the service you have rendered the State during the last five years, and of your uniform good conduct, and of the further fact that from the wild, rattle-brained spend-thrift which you were when you entered the service, you have become a sober, steady and respectable man worthy of the confidence and respect of all good men and women. I shall make an exception to the rule in your case and I hereby give you permission to get married without being discharged from the service and to remain in the service as long as your marital duties do not interfere materially with your duties as a ranger.[41]

Baylor was coming under some criticism at this time. On November 27, Jones wrote him that citizens of El Paso County were complaining his

Bryan Marsh *(Courtesy of Smith County Historical Society, Tyler, Texas)*

company was not using due diligence in rounding up white and Mexican fugitives. He admonished Baylor that it was his duty to use all means in his power to arrest such lawbreakers, the battalion's appropriation being dependent on a good showing to the legislature.[42] Governor Roberts had to reassure the United States Secretary of State that Baylor was up to the task of enforcing the law on the border, observing that the company had been busy with the chase after Victorio, who was tracked down and killed by Mexican forces in October.[43]

The Texas press gave a brief flurry to the news in December that Jones had sent a contingent of Oglesby's troops to Edwards County to deal with lawbreakers.[44] The trouble was initiated on December 4 when John R. Baylor, George Baylor's hot-headed brother, ran into two men who had been killing and stealing his cattle, one of them named Gilcrease. Baylor opened fire on them with his Winchester, and the two raced off on their horses. Baylor seriously wounded and captured Gilcrease, although Baylor proclaimed, "He is not seriously wounded, but won't be able to participate in the hog steal this season." Baylor had written Jones about having a Ranger company stationed in Edwards County, although he actually meant when and if the next legislature granted an additional appropriation, not immediately.[45]

Jones petitioned the state comptroller concerning the anticipated budget of the Frontier Battalion for the year commencing March 1, 1881. In addition to his $2,000 annual salary, and the $1,200 paid to his chief clerk, Duval Beall, Jones proposed $100,000 for "protection of the frontier and suppression of lawlessness and crime." In addition, he sought $1,150 to be spent for such things as postage, stationery, telegraph, fuel expenses, arms and ammunition, repairs to arms, and building a fence around the arsenal.[46] In the meantime, "John Henry" continued to work undercover in the Schulenburg area, but still with little to show for it after three months. Jones advised him: "If you cannot get up with the principle [sic] men you are after, it seems to me you might find some other parties" against whom he could obtain evidence.[47] Martin, alias "Henry," was finally discharged in March of 1881.[48]

At the end of 1880, the Frontier Battalion was composed of 147 men. Baylor's Company A, consisting of seventeen men, remained posted in El Paso County. Company B was in Mitchell County, on the upper waters of the Colorado River, with thirty men. Company C, with thirty-two men, maintained its camp in Blanco Canyon in Crosby County. Dan Roberts' Company D, with twenty-six men, was near Fort McKavett in Menard County at the headwaters of the San Saba River. Company E under Nevill consisted of fifteen men in Presidio County. The Special Troops under Oglesby were in LaSalle County with a strength of twenty-seven men.[49] The city government at El Paso asked that Baylor's company be reposted to that city from Ysleta, and Jones agreed and ordered Baylor to move his company.[50] Since the state budget could not accommodate "extravagant rents charged for houses in El Paso," Jones directed Baylor to take the city up on its offer to furnish quarters for the company.[51]

The move to El Paso didn't include two men hired by Baylor earlier in the fall. John "Red" Holcomb, an Arizona rustler, and James Stallings, a mankiller from Hamilton County, were enlisted into the company, but stayed together rather than freely mixing among the other Rangers. Gillett described Stallings as a troublemaker, mentioning that he threatened the sergeant for posting him on guard with a Mexican scout. Gillett discovered Stalling's name in the fugitive list and notified Baylor. Incredibly, Baylor determined somehow that Stallings was a good Ranger and overlooked the Hamilton County warrant. Baylor didn't even change his mind when a drunken Stallings threatened to shoot another Ranger. Holcomb requested and received a discharge. When Stallings almost became embroiled in another shootout with a fellow Ranger, Baylor finally had him arrested. The outlaw nevertheless managed to escape his guard and find refuge across the river in Mexico.

Both Holcomb and Stallings were arrested after this. Local authorities were unable to prosecute Holcomb and he was released, only to be subsequently shot to death in Deming, New Mexico Territory. Stallings was placed in jail at Fort Davis where he and others later made their escape.[52] Jones ordered Baylor to recruit his company to twenty men and to hire twenty Indian scouts for twenty days, there being reports of Indian movement in the area. Nevill was to join him with fifteen men.[53]

Jones made his annual report to the governor on December 31, 1880. Dealing first with the various militia companies around the state, Jones reported that about forty volunteer companies had been organized, but many were remiss in reporting to the adjutant general as required. During the last two years, only two companies had been called on to assist the local authorities: one in December 1879 at Calvert when a riot was feared, and another at Fredericksburg in September 1880 to help enforce the law. With respect to the Frontier Battalion, Jones reviewed its successes: the pursuit of Indians, including Victorio; capturing the Evans gang; capture of the Pegleg robbers; and other gains. In the two years reviewed, the Battalion had conducted 1,001 scouts; had seven fights with Indians and five with outlaws, killing twelve outlaws and wounding four; arrested 685 fugitives; and recovered 1,917 stolen stock. This was at an average annual cost of $748 per man in 1879, and $661 in 1880. He stressed the growth of the frontier counties since the inception of his command, which was due in large part to the protection afforded by the Battalion.[54]

Governor Roberts' report to the legislature on January 11, 1881, praised the efficiency of the Battalion and other special troops in protecting the frontier counties with a cost savings. He laid part of the credit on a law finally passed by Congress that forbade army officers from permitting Indians to leave their reservation to come into Texas for any reason.[55]

Captain Marsh, the new commander of Company B, faced one of his first disciplinary measures, the problem of Sergeant John W. Adams. Marsh had given Adams a draft in the amount of $150, directing him to get it cashed. Adams did that, but then he went on a "high lonesome" at Fort Concho and gambled the whole amount away. Marsh filed a complaint against the sergeant for embezzlement, and Adams was committed to the county jail in lieu of $500 bond.[56]

On report of a stage being held up and the driver and a passenger killed, perhaps by Indians, Baylor and fifteen men, along with two mules and ten days' rations, left Ysleta on January 16, 1881, to investigate. About twenty-five miles below Quitman, the Rangers struck a trail left by Apaches that crossed into Mexico. The trail meandered back into Texas, headed for the Devil Mountains, with easily found Indian camps along the way. Nevill and his men, along with four Pueblo Indian scouts, joined the party and the Rangers soon discovered a camp occupied by sixteen to eighteen Apaches on a mountain. On the bitterly cold and windy morning of January 29, at sunrise, Baylor and the Rangers crept to within 100 yards of the camp and formed a line. An opening volley of fire from the Rangers surprised the Indians, and, with a second volley, the Rangers charged with a "Texas yell."

In the confusion of battle, the Rangers killed two Indian women, mortally wounded another, and killed two children. According to one Ranger, Baylor tried to stop the shooting of the women, crying out, "Don't kill them. Can't you see they are squaws?" The answer was, "no sir; they all look alike to me."[57] One wounded Indian woman was captured, along with two wounded children. The woman clung to Captain Baylor, afraid of the other men in his company.[58] Six Indian warriors were killed in the battle. Blood on the ground indicated that those who escaped were likely wounded. The Rangers captured seven mules and nine horses, as well as firearms, saddles, and clothing, burning everything they could not carry off. The Rangers took advantage of the Indian fire and ate breakfast, many eating horseflesh for the first time, although most preferred venison or roasted weasel. The only Ranger casualty was a horse accidentally shot by a Ranger.[59] This conflict came to be termed the last Indian fight in Texas.[60]

The joining of Nevill's company with that of Baylor didn't set well with Nevill. He took exception to Baylor's loose form of leadership, asserting Baylor refused to discipline men who, in Nevill's opinion, were out of control. Nevill submitted proposed rules of discipline for Jones' consideration, suggesting they be promulgated throughout the battalion.

> I do not wish to be understood to cast any insinuations on Capt. Baylor, only that he is too good to his men, so much so that they impose on him. He is anxious to be efficient and to give satisfaction to yourself and the Governor, and I think the evil can be remedied by my suggestion, and if it is done, I would like to cooperate with Capt. Baylor.[61]

Nevill had to be doubly irked when some of his own men asked for transfers to Baylor's company because "they say they would have an easier time."[62]

Jones himself was "exceedingly annoyed" by the number of new applicants for positions in Roberts' Company D, brought about by a flood of Rangers in that unit who had announced they were going to quit the service on March 1. He promptly notified Roberts:

> Now so far as I am informed there is no such word in the military vocabulary as "quit." Men are sometimes discharged, but I never heard of a military [illegible word] when men could "quit" whenever they please. The word might be appropriate for a cow "out-fit" but not to a military company in the service of the State. If, as these rumors indicate, the belief exists among the members of your company that they can quit whenever they please, I wish you at once to disabuse their minds of that impression. The service cannot be made a convenience of whom

men who are out of employment can join and be fed and paid by the State until they can find something better to do and then "quit." Such a body of men would be [illegible word] and of no benefit to the State as they would devote the whole of their time and talent to hunting up something better to do instead of hunting Indians and fugitives from justice and attending to other duties as they [illegible word] enlisted.[63]

Roberts was somewhat defensive, feeling that even receiving an authorized discharge was considered by the men to be "quitting." He read the letter from Jones to his entire company, although he suggested that quitting was a worthwhile alternative to being considered "worthless." "My company being particularized will serve as my part of the reprimand, which shall not occur in the future, if I can help it." As an aside, Roberts advised Jones that he was selling "every dollar's worth of property I own outside of my necessary outfit for this service. Reduce & trim my baggage to force march proportions, ready for any quarter."[64]

In response to the same problem, Lieutenant Nevill of Company E told Jones that a recently discharged Ranger from his company, W. T. Sheffield, had lied about the reason for the discharge, his true intent to "do better than rangering." Nevill observed that the "government" was "constantly employing men as packers and teamsters, and a great many other employments are available to good men in this section which pay better than rangering and as Rangers are rated good men, they have no trouble to get a job when a man is wanted if he can get a discharge."[65]

On January 20, 1881, Governor Roberts renominated Jones for the position of adjutant general.[66] This time the appointment was confirmed without controversy.[67] He took his oath on January 24 and posted a $10,000 bond.[68] He had barely begun his new term when a riotous affair in West Texas required Ranger attention. In the very early hours of Monday, January 31, a black soldier from the Tenth Cavalry at Fort Concho, William Watkins, was shot dead in front of Charley Wilson's saloon in San Angelo. A few weeks earlier, a gambler had shot to death a white soldier. Two men, Henry Bacon and Thomas I. McCarty, both of Tom Green County, were subsequently arrested for Watkins' murder. Bacon was later released, but McCarty, a sheep raiser, was held in jail without bail. Amid rumors of soldiers mobbing the prisoner, Benjamin Grierson, the fort's commanding general, kept the camp locked down during the day. However, on Friday evening, February 4, an armed body of soldiers, both white and black, left the fort and surrounded the calaboose at San Angelo. Some of the white soldiers had blackened their faces. Not finding the prisoner where he was supposed to be (he was being held in jail at Ben Ficklin), they took the sheriff, J. D. Spears, into custody and threatened him if he didn't produce McCarty. They marched up and down the street, threatening to level the town if the prisoner wasn't produced. That same evening, Marsh and his twenty-one Rangers were in the saddle headed for Fort Concho, followed by Jim Werner, the company's African-American cook and teamster, carrying beds and rations.[69]

Some forty or fifty soldiers had poured a volley of shots into the Nimitz Hotel and surrounding stores and buildings, but fortunately no one was hurt. A number of families fled their homes into the cold blustery night. When an army guard approached, the rioters fled.[70] On February 7, the district judge and other officials sent a plea for help to Governor Roberts, who immediately called on General C. C. Augur, commander of the Department of Texas, to take steps to prevent further disturbances.[71] Captain Marsh and his company arrived in San Angelo on the evening of the 5th and found everything quiet. Guards were posted around town and five Rangers were sent to guard the jail at Ben Ficklin. Reportedly, Marsh met with General Grierson and threatened to shoot any soldier who came into town without a pass, and the conversation quickly deteriorated.[72] Jones ordered Marsh to remain at San Angelo until further notice, or as long as the local officials thought necessary.[73] McCarty was taken to Austin by Sergeant J. N. Hoffar for safekeeping to await further legal action, and he was subsequently released on bail.[74] For all practical purposes, the matter settled down.

The state's militia units met in convention in Austin beginning on Wednesday, February 16. On hand to greet them were Governor Roberts and Adjutant General Jones, among other state dignitaries.[75] The coming of March would begin the longest ordeal for John B. Jones.

18

PANGS OF SORROW

JONES ALWAYS HAD a fragile constitution. His health problems were a periodic problem, and he suffered frequent attacks of what was termed "derangement of the liver." In January and February of 1881, he felt rather good and even put on a few pounds. However, on March 6, his family doctor, W. A. Morris, was called to the Jones' Austin residence. The general was in severe pain and suffering from nausea, having been ill for about a week. The doctor diagnosed him with acute hepatitis involving the stomach. The next morning Jones was resting easier, but at noon was seized with "severe rigor," experiencing vomiting and pain across his stomach and liver area. By evening, those symptoms had abated, although they returned again on March 8, then abated again that same evening.[1] Over the next week and a half, Jones' gastric distress continued, and he was unable to eat, experiencing periodic "nervous shock."[2]

Despite Jones' absence from the office, the work of the Frontier Battalion continued, and Jones' clerk, Henry Orsay, stepped in until Jones could return. Captain Baylor reported he had "discharged nearly all my men," stating some wanted to go to the mines in Colorado and "some got on a drunk."[3] In Arrington's Company C, at least eight men were suffering from mumps, while in Nevill's camp "my men are all sick with severe colds and bilious fever."[4] Oglesby's area in South Texas was plagued by stock thieves and stage robbers.[5]

More ominous was the report the state legislature had authorized only $80,000 for the year ending February 28, 1882, and $60,000 for the following year, indicating that there would be another round of reductions of the Battalion.[6] Accordingly, on March 30, Governor Roberts issued an order reducing the Battalion to five captains, two lieutenants, seven sergeants, nine corporals, ninety-four privates, and five teamsters. At the same time, Oglesby's Special Troops were designated as Company F in the Battalion.[7] Coldwell came to Austin to fill in during Jones' absence.[8] An infuriated Charles Nevill sarcastically telegraphed the governor: "Your order takes all Company E. What shall I do with state property?" although he later claimed that he "misread" the order.[9] After complying with the governor's order and reducing his company, Nevill submitted his resignation, effective immediately, although he did not follow through and continued as a captain in the Battalion.[10]

Jones remained confined to bed, his recovery very slight up to March 19.[11] By the 23rd there really had been no improvement, and he was unable to take food or medicine by mouth. Doctor Morris oversaw that he was "nourished and medicated per rectum."[12] By Thursday the 24th, his condition was considered serious enough to send to Navarro County for his father, sisters, and brother-in-law Roger Q. Mills.[13] In the first week in April, news reports stated that Jones was in exceedingly critical condition and "his recovery is despaired of."[14]

On April 5, Morris called for the assistance of Dr. James W. McLaughlin, an Ohio-born Confederate veteran who also practiced medicine in Austin.[15] Jones continued to decline, with swelling over his liver and stomach.[16] Reports declared he was hardly expected to recover and had only five hours of sleep in the last twenty-four.[17] It was finally determined that Jones was suffering from an abscess of the liver, recognized in modern times as a bacterial malady, but recovery from which, given the advances of medicine of the time, was considered extremely doubtful.[18] Dr. E. G. Nicholson, former Battalion surgeon, came to assist in the treatment of his old friend, along with Dr. Richard M. Swearingen, a 43-year-old

Mississippi native and also a Confederate veteran.[19] By the 11th of April Jones was feeling much better and the physicians grew more optimistic, ruling his recovery would be "slow and tedious."[20] By the 18th, however, the doctors did not really note any improvement, Jones being further weakened by diarrhea.[21]

The world did not stop for Jones' illness. In far West Texas George W. Campbell (not to be confused with the former commander of Company B in Shackelford County) had been appointed El Paso city marshal on December 1, 1880.[22] On the plea of El Paso officials in January for Ranger assistance, Jones had directed Company B to move its headquarters after the city promised to supply quarters for the company, and Baylor moved his men onto the vacant Marsh Ranch some four-and-a-half miles south of town.[23]

When Marshal Campbell was refused additional salary, he abruptly resigned and allegedly entered into a deal with the shadier elements of the citizenry, with whom he had already been exceedingly friendly. Although there is no evidence that a conspiracy was in place, it has been claimed the intent was to create a major disturbance in the town, forcing city fathers to hire him back to keep the peace and at a more suitable salary. Accordingly, early one morning the town toughs fired promiscuously throughout the main street. Baylor was called on to help, and he sent Sergeant Jim Gillett and five Rangers to restore peace.[24] Instead of turning again to Campbell, however, the city council appointed Dallas Stoudenmire, a former Ranger who served in Company A for seven months in 1874, as its new marshal. Charges against Campbell for an attempt to assault the town's mayor and shooting up the town were dismissed. Two Rangers in Gillett's squad, Weldon and Johnson, refused to arrest the former marshal, claiming a personal friendship, their refusal leading immediately to their discharge from the service.[25]

On April 14, 1881, some ten days after Stoudenmire's appointment, it was reported to him that two Mexican boys out hunting cattle on the Texas side of the river had been murdered. Accompanied by Gus Krempkau, a former member of Baylor's command, the new marshal found the bodies, arresting two men for the killings and bringing them back to El Paso. The subsequent inquest dragged on with Krempkau acting

Dallas Stoudenmire (*James B. Gillett, Six Years With the Texas Rangers, Austin, Texas: Von Boeckmann-Jones, 1921.*)

as interpreter until a break was taken for lunch. Campbell had harassed Krempkau for helping the Mexicans in the case, and when Krempkau left the hearing, he was confronted by Campbell and John W. Hale, who pulled a pistol and shot him down.[26]

Stoudenmire, who was in a restaurant across the street, came out with pistol blazing. Unfortunately, his first shot went astray and killed an innocent Mexican bystander, but his second shot killed Hale. Unnerved, Campbell pulled his pistol, backed into the street, and proclaimed, "Gentlemen, this is not my fight." The mortally wounded Krempkau managed to get off a few shots, the first hitting Campbell in the hand and breaking his wrist, and another shot hitting the ex-marshal in the foot. Stoudenmire turned his attention to Campbell and shot him through the stomach. Campbell fell dying and, lying in the street, hissed at Stoudenmire: "You big son-of-a-bitch; you've murdered me!"[27]

With four men lying dead in the space of less than a minute, Stoudenmire's reputation as a deadly gunfighter was cemented, but the event also engendered hard feelings among the bad element in the town. Three days later Stoudenmire was forced to defend himself when he killed a former city official who drunkenly fired at him, others across the street also taking potshots at the marshal.[28] The harsh feelings among the El Paso underworld against the new marshal brought about by these killings subsequently resulted in Stoudenmire's death a year later. In the interim, there was friction between the Rangers and the marshal. Baylor commiserated with Coldwell about the efforts of his "small force" in El Paso to "keep down rowdyism & shooting, but they managed to lay out 7 men in a few days, but I trust there will be no more of it for some time."[29]

Baylor also had an international incident on his hands about this same time. Sergeant Gillett received information that a murderer wanted in New Mexico, Onofrio Baca, was a clerk in a store at Saragosa, Mexico, across the Rio Grande about four miles southwest of Ysleta. Gillett was well aware that an attempt to formally arrest Baca in Mexico would likely result in his immediate release by Mexican authorities. Early in May 1881, not telling Baylor of his plan, the Ranger and Corporal George Lloyd crossed into Mexico. Baca was taken from the store at gunpoint, thrust up behind Lloyd, and they hightailed it back across the river with their prisoner. When Baylor learned what his son-in-law sergeant had done, he was clearly irked, but eventually calmed down and took no action.[30] Baca was returned to New Mexico, but a mob took the prisoner from the officers and hanged him.[31] Governor Roberts asked Baylor for an explanation,[32] but there were no repercussions against Gillett or the company.

W. P. Patterson was a hard-drinking cattleman in Mitchell County, used to frequenting the saloons at Colorado City. When under the influence, he was considered a dangerous man, frequently firing off his pistol, for which he had recently been arrested three times in a few days. It was also reported that he had previously had a physical altercation with the equally hard-drinking Bryan Marsh. On the evening of May 16, 1881, in the company of a man named Adair, either Patterson or Adair popped off a shot during their spree. In a nearby house were Rangers J. M. Sedberry, L. B. Wells, and Jeff Milton. Upon hearing the shot, they ran into the street and confronted the two men, asking who fired the shot. One of the men answered that they didn't know. Sedberry insisted on examining Patterson's pistol and the cowman exploded: "Damn you, you must go and examine somebody else's pistol!" Sedberry and Wells took hold of Patterson's arms in order to grab his pistol, but he jerked loose from their grasp and pulled his pistol, getting off a round that barely missed Sedberry. The Rangers returned the fire, hitting Patterson three times. It was later said that Wells put a bullet into the cowman after he had fallen.[33]

Dr. Richard M. Swearingen (*Frank W. Johnson & Eugene C. Barker,* A History of Texas and Texans, *Chicago: American Historical Society, 1914.*)

A crowd began to gather, muttering threats against the Rangers. The lawmen surrendered to Sheriff and ex-Ranger Dick Ware, and on the 18th were arraigned in a tension-filled courtroom, closely guarded by fellow Rangers. Their bond was set at $1,500 each, and they returned to the Ranger camp.[34] Adjutant General Clerk Henry Orsay wired Sergeant John Hoffar at Colorado City to "act very cautiously and only under instruction of sheriff."[35] Dan Roberts of Company D was directed, probably by the governor, to go to Colorado City and "take command of men there and do what [he could] to quiet the troubles" on allegations that "Captain Marsh [was] unfit for duty." [36] The reference to Marsh was likely included because there was concern that the impulsive captain might do something in knee-jerk fashion that would further fan resentment of the Rangers and add to the tension already existing.[37]

Roberts went to Colorado City and gathered the facts, but did so without telling Captain Marsh that he was there or what he was about. After he had completed his investigation, he told Marsh, who actually was relieved he was there. Roberts concluded that he could "see nothing ominous of any further serious trouble here, the town being perfectly quiet at present." Roberts was directed to stay at Colorado City until he was finally authorized to leave on May 31.[38] Roberts concluded most folks at Colorado City conceded that the killing could not have been avoided unless the Rangers made a "complete backdown" from doing their duty.[39] Shortly thereafter, Marsh's company was moved to Big Springs in Howard County, instructed by Governor Roberts to "regard themselves as peace officers," except when fighting Indians and when protecting Texas and Pacific Railroad employees from the attack of a band of 100 to 200 "roughs" that were plaguing them.[40]

The close working relationship between El Paso Marshal Dallas Stoudenmire and Baylor's Company B deteriorated. The reasons are not clear, although it may have been that Baylor's men, being under loose discipline, went on an occasional spree, crossing paths with Stoudenmire. Stoudenmire even wrote Jones' office complaining, and Clerk Orsay responded that Baylor was properly in El Paso to keep a guard and to assist civil authorities. "As captain commanding a company of the Frontier

Battalion, he is authorized to do as he pleases for the best interests of the State & must use his own judgment of the matter of details or guard, as being on the spot, he can better judge of your necessities."[41] Stoudenmire was likely upset by the friendship of some Rangers with the Manning brothers, who operated a variety theater in El Paso.[42] Ranger Ben Kemp recalled that Baylor, in response to reports his men were not welcome in El Paso saloons, marched his men one morning into one of the town's saloons. He ordered a round of drinks for his men, which was reluctantly served, then formed his men outside in the street. To the gathering crowd, he announced that the Rangers were there to enforce law and order, "and by granny, I'll do it if I have to shoot this place down to a man." There were no more problems.[43] Stoudenmire subsequently resigned his office on May 30, 1882, succeeded by James B. Gillett.[44]

In Austin, a weak John B. Jones was able to visit his office on Thursday, June 2, for the first time in two months. He was there again the following Tuesday, but he was still far too feeble to resume a full workday.[45] In an order dated June 8, Jones, in response to Gillett's foray into Mexico, and likely at the urging of Governor Roberts, instructed the Battalion that they had no right to cross the border of another state in pursuit of fugitives from justice unless provided with a requisition from the governor, nor could they arrest parties in Texas who were fugitives from another state except "upon proper authority under the law."[46] At the same time, Governor Roberts issued a proclamation asking extradition officers in each of the judicial districts bordering the Rio Grande to closely follow the requirements of treaties with Mexico.[47]

Jones also directed Neal Coldwell to investigate charges concerning the fitness of Bryan Marsh:

> Reports have reached me of many instances of bad conduct on the part of Capt. Marsh. It is said that he was drunk all the time he was in San Angelo with his Company. That he gets drunk every time he goes to Colorado City or Big Springs and that he frequently has big sprees in camp, on all of which occasions he talks & acts in a very undignified, unofficer-like and offensive manner with & about the men of his

Company. That he had many personal difficulties and quarrels with them, and has acted toward them in such a manner as to cause them to lose all respect for and confidence in him. This has caused many of the best men of his Company to apply for discharges which he has granted, seeming to be anxious to get rid of them.[48]

Coldwell made a strict inquiry as ordered. He concluded the greater part of the allegations made by Jones were true, except that Marsh had never been drunk in camp and had never had any personal difficulties with his men:

> There is no doubt that he frequently drinks to excess. He was intoxicated at the time of the examining trial of his men and was not able to attend. He subsequently used very intemperate language concerning the "cowmen." He said publicly that he hoped the "cowmen" would do something as the Rangers were there for the purpose of fighting them.

Coldwell noted that discipline in the company was extremely lax, "the men doing pretty much as they pleased." His Rangers, as many as six at one time, frequented dance houses while on duty, and they were often drunk and disorderly in town. "The company has acted in such a manner as to lose the confidence of the good people of the town, and altogether the company is below par." For the most part, he opined, there were few good men in the company, the best Rangers having already been discharged by Marsh.[49]

In Austin, the doctors continued to treat Jones, and their discussions centered on aspirating or drawing infectious pus from his abscessed liver. In the meantime he had slowly improved to the point that he could walk about the house, take morning and evening drives, and briefly visit his office.[50] They authorized him and his wife to leave Austin on June 16 for a visit to Wootan Wells west of Bremond in northwest Robertson County. The high mineral content of the water there had led to the establishment of a health resort. Water from the well was bottled for sale and four hotels were built there to capitalize on the growing reputation. A mule-drawn train on a one-and-a-half-mile track transported visitors between the resort and the depot in Bremond.[51] Examined by the doctors before he left, Jones weighed only ninety pounds.[52]

Accompanied by Doctor Nicholson, Jones and his wife stayed at Wootan Wells for two weeks, and Jones gained a little in weight and strength, although every ten days or so he experienced "a sensation about the stomach of something breaking loose, as though attended with escape of fluid, from which he felt marked relief."[53] Jones and his wife returned to Austin on July 3, Jones now weighing ninety-eight pounds, and with an improved appetite. However, he had a continuous discharge of bile and complained of sharp pains in his liver.[54] It was decided that Jones needed to be examined in San Antonio by Doctor Ferdinand Herff, a German-born physician who was noted for abdominal and pelvic surgery.[55]

Mr. and Mrs. Jones, accompanied by a stepdaughter and Doctor Nicholson, left for San Antonio on the evening of July 5, staying at the Menger Hotel.[56] The next day Herff examined Jones and scheduled him for an aspiration of his liver the next day.[57] Using a large needle, Herff penetrated his patient's liver, creating a vacuum with a pump several times, but drew no infectious material. When the needle was withdrawn, Jones suffered agonizing discomfort, with paroxysms of pain every five minutes or so. "Although Gen. Jones was a man of strong nerve and unyielding fortitude, it threw his entire body, which was bathed in cold sweat, into violent tremor." Pain relievers and injections of morphine administered by the physicians gave only partial relief. That evening, Jones could only lie on his back with legs flexed; any other position caused him agony.[58] Being very weak, Jones was unable to return to Austin right away.[59]

While Jones was being attended to, the work of the Battalion went on. Lieutenant Charles Nevill of Company E reported that he was investigating information that the noted Billy the Kid and a gang of men were engaged in stock thefts and other lawlessness in the Pecos County area. In another incident, late on one evening, a man named James Venable unexpectedly fired into the Ranger camp, almost hitting Ranger E. J. Pounds. The Rangers in camp returned fire, actually shooting a pistol out of Venable's hand. They arrested their assailant and kept him overnight in camp, but because there was no local official in a nearby community to whom they could turn him over, they released him.[60]

Dr. Ferdinand Herff (*Frank W. Johnson & Eugene C. Barker,* A History of Texas and Texans, *Chicago: American Historical Society, 1914.*)

Jones returned to Austin from San Antonio on July 14 with a slight temperature and rapid pulse.[61] On Saturday, the 16th, Doctors Morris, Nicholson, McLaughlin, and Swearingen once more examined Jones, finding extensive swelling on Jones' right side. The possibility of another painful aspiration to relieve the swelling was discussed but postponed. Jones seemed to improve somewhat, even becoming more talkative and in better spirits.[62] The next day the physicians called in Doctor Thomas D. Wooten, a Kentucky-born physician who had been a surgeon for the Confederacy and had resided in Austin since 1876.[63] Wooten arrived at the Jones residence at about noon and was given the patient's history by the four doctors. He went into the general's bedroom and found Jones "entirely rational, but morose." Jones pointed to a very tender spot on his chest and asked the doctor not to touch it. After his examination, Wooten diagnosed the condition as "pleu-ritic effusion," with which the other doctors immediately disagreed. They diagnosed Jones with pneumonia and pulmonary edema. Wooten urged a reexamination, but because Jones was in a weakened condition, it was decided to postpone any further look until four that afternoon.[64]

Reassembling at the appointed hour, a further examination of Jones was made. It was decided another aspiration might be helpful and Morris inserted the needle. Pumping produced some three pints of pus from the pleural cavity.[65] The doctors left Jones to rest. At four the next morning, Monday, July 18, Doctor Morris was hastily summoned back to the Jones residence, finding his patient prostrated and in a great deal of pain. Because of the tremendous discomfort being experienced by Jones, it was determined to defer further examination until later that morning. At eleven o'clock, Morris met with Nicholson, Swearingen, and McLaughlin, and they once again examined their patient. The physicians felt the liver abscess had discharged into the pleural cavity, producing pleurisy. Mrs. Jones requested Doctor Wooten be called back in and he arrived at noon.

The doctors chose to aspirate Jones once more, and at four that afternoon, about forty ounces of infectious material were withdrawn. Morris left, but returned two hours later to find Jones rapidly failing.[66] Because the worst was now feared, Mrs. Jones wired her daughters at Wootan Wells to return home immediately.[67] At approximately 4:00 a.m., on Tuesday, July 19, 1881, John B. Jones, at the age of forty-six years, six months, and twenty-seven days, passed away. A stepdaughter later stated that, prior to his death, Jones was delirious and quoting from Shakespeare and other authors.[68] The saddened Jones family in Navarro County was devastated by the news. Jones' sister, Fanny Halbert, later observed:

> I don't think Pa [Henry Jones] will ever get over brother's [John B. Jones] and Annie's [her nine-year-old daughter] death—he will never be the same man again. He had always depended so much upon brother in all his business affairs and since his death he seems to be completely broken up.[69]

Clerk Henry Orsay sent a telegram to all of the Battalion commanders: "General Jones died this morning at four o'clock."[70] Funeral services were held on Wednesday morning at ten o'clock at the Baptist Church in Austin. The services were overseen with Masonic honors and an honor guard was made up of white-gloved members of the Austin Grays and Manning Rifles, local militia units that had been administered by the adjutant general's office.[71] The *Galveston Daily News* eulogized Jones:

> The announcement which THE NEWS makes this morning of the death of John B. Jones, Adjutant-General of the State of Texas, will be received with pangs of sorrow through the length and breadth of the State, for by his active, earnest work, by his upright, manly and consistent bearing, and his noble efforts to secure the reign of law and the supremacy of order, he has won a name and a fame that will be enduring, and has secured for himself a warm place in the affectionate regards of all the people of Texas.[72]

The Reverend G. W. Rogers delivered an eloquent and impressive funeral oration, and a large procession escorted Jones' body to Oakwood Cemetery. Among the cortege, in addition to family and friends and a band, were the governor and his staff, as well as the heads of state offices, all of the offices being closed.[73] One mishap occurred when the Austin Grays, miffed at the priority given to the Manning Rifles in the order of procession, left the cortege and returned to its armory.[74] Nevertheless, it was an impressive display of solemn respect for the late commander of Texas' Frontier Battalion. The mainstay of the Rangers since its original organization in 1874 was gone, leaving to speculation as to who would succeed him and what would be the Battalion's future.

The loss of Jones was felt throughout the state. At Carrizo Springs in Dimmit County, an assembly of citizens passed resolutions of respect: "That the frontier especially will ever revere his memory as one who possessed all the higher attributes of a true soldier and who was at all times prompt in extending to the weak through all their vicissitudes, that protection which only the sympathetic heart can feel for those unable to protect themselves."[75] Sergeant John Hoffar in Colorado City wrote, "I think the Frontier Battalion has lost its best friend."[76]

19

THE BEST OFFICERS AND MEN

ALMOST IMMEDIATELY the question arose as to Jones' successor. Speculation centered on Neal Coldwell, who had been acting adjutant general and Jones' pick to handle his inspection and quartermaster duties. General William P. Hardeman, a superintendent of the Texas Confederate Home and founder of Texas A&M University, was also mentioned as a candidate for the post.[1] But Governor Roberts did not waste any time. On Thursday, July 21, the day after Jones' funeral, he wired Wilburn H. King at Sulphur Springs, asking him to resign as a state representative and accept appointment as adjutant general.[2] Born in Georgia, King moved to Texas in 1857 and served in the Confederate Army from Cass County, rising to brigadier general. After the war, King practiced law at Jefferson, then moved to Hopkins County where he served as mayor of Sulphur Springs and from where he was elected to the state legislature.[3] In addition to serving during the Civil War with Governor Roberts, King was politically aligned with the Democrats, essentially a liberal populist.[4]

King accepted the appointment and promptly resigned from the state legislature.[5] But the quick appointment was not without controversy and was not met with favor in some quarters. It was asserted that King, as a legislator, had been critically opposed to the Frontier Battalion, repeatedly favoring reduction of the appropriation for frontier defense. Because the appointment was made quietly, without fanfare, it was anticipated the governor's agenda included soon disbanding the Battalion.[6] The *San Antonio Daily Express* was almost apoplectic:

> [W]e can scarcely believe that the governor, who must realize the importance of this frontier protection and the maintenance of a competent force in the field to insure that protection, would appoint to the position of adjutant-general a gentleman who knows nothing of the importance of the work to be performed in the west, or who, if he does understand the situation, would sacrifice the west to save to the people of the eastern portion of the state that proportion of the taxes collected from them to maintain the state troops. Gen. King, while in the legislature, was the most bitter opponent of the frontier protection bill, and would have voted to turn the frontier over to the roughs, thieves and desperadoes who would certainly take possession of a good portion of it with the withdrawal of state troops.[7]

Various frontier counties, apprehensive that Ranger troops were about to be yanked away, flooded Austin with requests for permission to organize local militia companies for frontier defense.[8] However, for all practical purposes, the Texas frontier was really disappearing; there were no longer any Indian raids, and local authorities were able to manage the lawlessness occurring in their communities. As one historian observed, although the Battalion consisted as such for another twenty years, it acted more in the capacity of "trouble-shooters," and it would likely have been far better to reorganize at this time to accommodate the changed state of affairs.[9]

In an interview before he left for Austin, King was adamant that there was no foundation for the claim he intended to disband the Frontier Battalion. He admitted supporting the retrenchment efforts that reduced funding to the Rangers, but said he felt demand from the frontier areas had exceeded the actual necessity for protection, and therefore "should yield to the demands of a prudent economy." He pledged to "labor, as my predecessor did, to make efficient and thorough the workings of the present frontier organizations, and I shall demand, in return, the exhibition

Wilburn H. King (*Dudley G. Wooten*, A Comprehensive History of Texas, 1685 to 1897, *Dallas, Texas: William G. Scarff, 1898.*)

and exercise of those qualities which go to make the good soldier and the good citizen."[10]

King reported for work on August 1 and took his oath of office, commenting that he thought he had been done an injustice by the comments in the press as to his intentions. He promised "to do as well, if not better, than Gen. Jones, towards protecting the frontier."[11] One of his first orders of business was to receive $1,238.28 from Jones' widow, being the "balance of indebtedness of said Jno. B. Jones to the State."[12] On August 4, King reorganized Oglesby's Company F, leaving it with one captain, one first sergeant, two corporals, fifteen privates, and one teamster. King also reminded company commanders that they should enlist "none but men of good moral character, sober, energetic, & unmarried."[13] Effective

August 31, Bryan Marsh's Company B was mustered out of service, due solely to Coldwell's findings as to Marsh's drunkenness.[14] The company was reactivated with S. A. McMurray at the reins as captain, Marsh having been "removed," and King pledged that the company would be "thoroughly reorganized and placed upon an efficient footing."[15]

As of September 1, the Frontier Battalion consisted of six companies, each composed approximately of one captain, one sergeant, two corporals, and a dozen or so privates, along with a teamster.[16] King also retained Jones' requirement that Rangers were not to carry arms into cities or towns unless "in discharge of some specific duty," nor to frequent saloons, circuses, or other places of amusement while armed.[17] In October and November, as Jones did early in his administration, King made a tour of the Ranger companies on the frontier.

King was in office barely one month when a recently-discharged Ranger was killed. On September 13, former private J. H. Williams, who had been discharged from the Battalion two days earlier,[18] was shot to death at Colorado City in Mitchell County. Captain McMurray had sent Williams and another Ranger, Grant, there on some business, and Sheriff Dick Ware wired McMurray to let them remain there a little longer to help him. The record is not clear and there are several conflicting accounts of the incident, but it is known that Williams was shot to death at Big Springs by a gambler named Jack McGhee. Although McGhee claimed that it was an accident, he was arrested, and a bond of $5,000 insured that he would stay jailed.[19] Other reports claimed there was a drunken brawl, while one report said that the shooting was the result of an old grudge.[20] McMurray, who described Williams as "a quiet, sober, and very brave man," was quoted as believing that McGhee would prevail, "as the roughs up there can prove anything they want."[21]

On February 28, 1882, Adjutant General King submitted to Governor Roberts a formal report on his office. He again denied that his intent had ever been to disband the Battalion. He dealt specifically with the charges of Bryan Marsh's drunkenness, as sustained by Coldwell's investigation, and explained how he responded to it by disbanding the company and then reorganizing it under McMurray. King expressed regret over the pending indictments of the three Rangers for the Colorado City shooting of W. P. Patterson, noting that Rangers are often faced with a significant dilemma arising from when to use deadly force. He concluded his report in glowing terms:

> I am glad to be able to say that the entire force, officers and men, in all the essentials of an active, energetic, gallant, orderly and law-abiding body, is meeting my approval, and that my efforts for improvement and increased efficiency in every direction have met the cordial support of the best officers and men, both among those I found in service and those who have since been enlisted.[22]

In Navarro County, probate matters ensued as a result of Jones' death. On January 10, 1882, his widow assumed the $2,255 in debt of his estate, but conveyed to Henry Jones all of her interest as surviving spouse in the "Jones Rancho," as well as Jones' one-half interest in the horses on the ranch.[23] Apparently she felt a marriage of less than two-and-a-half years did not entitle her to a share of the family's wealth. As it was, she was prosperous on her own.

Jones original treating physicians felt the care of Jones was of such interest that they made a presentation on his treatment to the Travis County Medical Society on September 1, 1881, not expecting the ensuing firestorm. Doctors Morris, Swearingen, and McLaughlin delivered their paper, expressing their opinion that Jones suffered from "supporative *[sic]* pleuritis," and a lively debate occurred.[24] The presentation and conclusions of the three doctors was published in the March 1882 edition of *The Texas Medical and Surgical Record*. Their paper included criticism by Doctor Morris of Doctor Thomas Wooten's claims and diagnosis to the contrary.[25]

Enraged at the criticism, Wooten was allowed to respond in the June issue of the *Record*. In discussing the March article, Wooten declared:

> There is so little of the "dry light" of science and truth, and so much of the flickering glare of vituperation and spite in their expressions, that one may well inquire the origin and motive of so remarkable a feature in a so-called scientific discussion.[26]

Wooten doggedly clung to his diagnosis of "empyemia *[sic]* resulting from suppurative pleuritis with effusion of pus in the pleural cavity."[27] When the *Medical and Surgical Record* refused to allow the original doctors to respond in yet another issue, they published their own forty-four-page booklet in which they defended themselves and lambasted Wooten.[28]

Ann Jones remained a widow for a little under two years. On April 26, 1883, she married Alexander Watkins Terrell, a former district judge, Confederate officer, and current state senator. One of his legislative successes had been the establishment of the University of Texas. He subsequently served four terms as a state senator and two terms as a state representative. In 1893 President Grover Cleveland appointed him minister plenipotentiary to the Ottoman Empire (Turkey), which post he held until 1897. His wife accompanied him to Turkey and the "charm and graciousness which had made [her] successful as one of Austin's distinguished hostesses brought her equal success in foreign lands."[29] Terrell subsequently served as a regent of the University of Texas.[30] Ann Holliday Anderson Jones Terrell died in Austin on November 25, 1908.[31] She was buried close to Jones while Judge Terrell, who died in 1912, was buried in the Texas State Cemetery, also in Austin.

Henry Jones, father of the late adjutant general, once again ran for the state legislature in 1884, this time unsuccessfully.[32] He died in Navarro County on December 26, 1888, his estate consisting of 3,204 acres in Navarro County worth $31,713. He also owned 1,550 acres in Bastrop County valued at $2,288, as well as 280 horses and mules, fifty head of cattle, one jack, as well as farm implements, proceeds from the sale of cotton and steers, and other cash, all totaling $5,290.30. All of this was bequeathed to his daughter Fannie Halbert and his grandson, Henry Jones Robbins.[33]

Wilburn H. King's tenure as adjutant general was longer than that of Jones, and he retired on January 23, 1891.[34] During his tenure, the Battalion continued to be reduced, ultimately shrunk to three small companies by the time he left office. During that ten-year period the Rangers accelerated their efforts to track down criminals. Expansion of railroads and the growth of settlement in the former frontier counties necessitated frequent relocation of Ranger detachments. Neal Coldwell continued as quartermaster, and for all practical purposes ran the Battalion under King's supervision until Coldwell retired in 1883, replaced by John O. Johnson.[35]

During King's tenure, in addition to violent railroad labor strikes, sheep killing and fence cutting became significant problems in Texas, largely brought on by conflict with cattlemen and by the introduction of barbed wire across what had previously been free range. The efforts of the Rangers to counter this was "vexing and frustrating," the average Texan being in sympathy with the fence cutters against large landholders.[36] In addition to J. H. Williams, several other Rangers were killed in the line of duty during King's tenure: Charles S. Smith,[37] Ben Warren,[38] Frank Sieker,[39] Thomas Nigh,[40] Jim Moore,[41] and Charley Fusselman.[42]

King was succeeded as adjutant general by W. H. Mabry in January 1891, who served until May 1898. Perhaps Mabry's most lasting legacy was to cut back on the paperwork required to be submitted by companies, unfortunately making it more difficult to delve into the details of Ranger operations.[43] It was during his administration that Governor James Hogg appointed to the Battalion a man who would be destined to be one of the more memorable Ranger captains, Bill McDonald.[44] Mabry's administration was marked by continuing conflict with Mexican bandits coming across the Rio Grande, as well as a revolutionary army led by Catarino Garza. Ranger Robert E. E. Doaty was killed in March of 1892 in a run-in with the Garza army.[45] Captain Frank Jones of Company D was shot and killed on June 30, 1893, while trying to arrest members of the Olguin clan on Pirate Island in the middle of the Rio Grande.[46]

Among the Ranger deaths that occurred in the line of duty during Mabry's tenure was the disappearance and presumed murder of J. W. Woods in November 1893.[47] Ranger Joe McKidrict was shot to death in El Paso on April 5, 1894, by former Ranger Baz Outlaw, who was then himself shot down by the notorious John Selman. Selman killed John Wesley Hardin in an El Paso saloon in August 1895, and was then himself shot to death in 1896.[48] Mabry incurred major press coverage in his attempt to use the Frontier Battalion to prevent a prize fight between Bob

Fitzsimmons and Peter Maher. However, Mabry and his Rangers could only watch from a surrounding bluff when the fight finally took place on a sandbar, a "no man's land" in the middle of the Rio Grande.[49]

A. P. Wozencraft succeeded Mabry as adjutant general in May 1898, formerly the city attorney in Dallas and active in local militia units.[50] In August of that year, Ranger Ernest "Diamond Dick" St. Leon was shot to death along with a deputized dentist, Oscar J. Breaux, at Socorro, Texas.[51] Wozencraft reinstated the requirement of detailed reports from company commanders, but he only served as adjutant general for nine months, being replaced by Dallas real estate man and Spanish-American War veteran Thomas Scurry on January 17, 1899.[52]

Grave Marker of John B. Jones, Oakwood Cemetery, Austin, Texas
(Courtesy of Doug Dukes, Austin, Texas)

The Frontier Battalion, as it had initially been organized by John B. Jones, came to an end during Scurry's tenure as adjutant general. Beginning with inquiries into the actions of the three Rangers who killed W. P. Patterson back in 1881, lawyers persistently questioned whether a Ranger other than an "officer" in the Frontier Battalion was authorized by law to make a legal arrest, even though the clear intent of the 1874 statute was to have each member of the Battalion to function as a peace officer in every nuance of that term. In May of 1900, Texas Attorney General Thomas Smith issued a formal opinion that because the language of the statute was specific as to what constituted an "officer," Ranger privates were not authorized to make arrests. In essence, most of the arrests made by the Frontier Battalion had been illegal. Until the legislature could act to correct the mistake, Scurry ordered that Rangers could do no more than support local law enforcement officials. He reorganized the Battalion to six companies with an average strength of four men, with only eighteen designated "officers" authorized to make arrests.[53]

When Rangers reported to Galveston in 1900 to assist in the aftermath of the disastrous storm that decimated the island, an active political campaign was under way to do away with the Frontier Battalion. The argument was made that the frontier had passed: there were no more Indians to fight, any remaining gunfighters and bad men were getting long in the tooth, and local law enforcement officers were more effective than before and did not want the Rangers poking their noses into their business. The only advantage the Rangers had was their statewide jurisdiction.[54] On July 8, 1901, the Texas legislature formally did away with the Frontier Battalion and created a statewide Ranger force consisting of four companies, each made up of a captain and no more than twenty men. These men were given the authority of peace officers and could make arrests. However, nothing had really changed except the name, now the "Force," and the ability to formally nab criminals.[55] The Texas Rangers went on in the Twentieth Century to experience several different organizational formats, ultimately becoming incorporated within the Texas Department of Public Safety. Equipped with high-powered automobiles, computer technology, and all of the sophisticated trappings of a modern law enforcement agency, today's Ranger force would not be recognized by John B. Jones as the entity for which he could take the greatest credit. But even today, its military infrastructure can be traced directly to the 1874 organizational structure developed and overseen by Jones.

On October 25, 1968, a tall monument was erected at Jones' gravesite in Section 1, Lot 337, of Austin's Oakwood Cemetery. The dedicatory ceremony was overseen by the Most Worshipful Grand Lodge of Texas. It was a befitting monument to a true Texas hero. Perhaps the most appropriate comments summing up John B. Jones' contribution to the Frontier Battalion and its successes were articulated by Frederick Wilkins in his seminal work, *The Law Comes to Texas*:

> It would be difficult to overstate Jones' importance in the development of the Rangers. He organized the Frontier Battalion after the long, lawless years of the Civil War and Reconstruction, and as battalion commander he occupied a position no other Ranger had filled in peacetime. Jones put his brand on the form and style of discipline, morale and conduct. He set the standard for administration, something no earlier Ranger command had been much required to consider. Jones developed a business-like fighting force which he personally supervised, riding up and down the frontier each year. When necessary, the slight major led them in battle or on major scouts.
>
> As adjutant general, Jones was forced to spend most of his time in Austin, but he never lost his love for his men and continued to visit the companies from time to time; he knew each officer and noncommissioned officer and many of the privates. In recurring times of financial crisis, he kept the battalion together, reduced perhaps but still viable. Without him the Rangers would probably have been dissolved, and it is a tribute to him that in his day he was known, admired and respected as *the* Texas ranger. Only with the passing of years and the emergence of more colorful captains has his fame diminished.[56]

The advent of the Frontier Battalion, led by John B. Jones, resulted in the disappearance of the chaotic law and order anarchy that characterized the post-Civil War and Reconstruction era. No longer did the raiding Indians freely plunder the Texas frontier (helped also a great deal by the army's efforts in the Red River War of 1874), nor did the John Wesley Hardins and Bill Longleys dispense their lead violence without recrimination. The law-abiding citizen could now look to local authorities, as well as to the Rangers, for protection from the senseless violence of the past. The rule of law and order was firmly established in the state, and, as much as anyone else, this legacy belongs to John B. Jones.[57]

NOTES

Preface

1. *Results of Operations of State Troops Since August 1, 1876, to December 31, 1881*, 109, Texas State Library.

Chapter 1: Irresistible on Horseback

1. Dr. Will D. Jones (brother of Henry Jones) to Mrs. Carrie Mills Woods (sister of John B. Jones), 3 April 1892, Genealogical File, Fairfield Archives and History, Winnsboro, South Carolina; Helen Francis Bonner, *Major John B. Jones: The Defender of the Texas Frontier* (master's thesis, University of Texas, Austin, 1950), 1–2.
2. William S. Speer and John Henry Brown, *Encyclopedia of the New West* (Marshall, Texas: United States Biographical Publishing, 1881), 388.
3. Bonner, *Major John B. Jones*, 1–2.
4. Will of Benoni Robertson, 6 October 1851, Genealogical File, Fairfield Archives and History.
5. Fitz Hugh McMaster, *History of Fairfield County, South Carolina* (Columbia, South Carolina: State Commercial Printing, 1946), 27.
6. Ibid.; Nancy T. Samuels and Barbara R. Knox, *Old Northwest Texas, vol. 1–B (Navarro County, 1846–1860)* (Fort Worth, Texas: Fort Worth Genealogical Society, 1980), 477–478.
7. Genesis 35:18.
8. *A Legislative Manual for the State of Texas, 1879–1880* (Austin, Texas: E. W. Swindells, 1879), 237; Bonner, *Major John B. Jones*, 2–3; Thomas W. Cutrer, "Joseph William Robertson," *The New Handbook of Texas*, vol. 5 (Austin, Texas: Texas State Historical Association, 1996), 618.
9. Bonner, *Major John B. Jones*, 2–3.
10. Donaly E. Brice, *The Great Comanche Raid* (Austin, Texas: Eakin Press, 1987), 69; *Texas Centennial*, 13 June 1840, as cited in Bonner, *Major John B. Jones*, 4–5.
11. Bonner, *Major John B. Jones*, 1–2.
12. Gifford White, ed., *First Settlers of Matagorda County, Texas* (St. Louis: Ingmire Publications, 1986), 36.
13. Bill Young, "Henry Jones Family," txgenweb (Internet).

14. Homer S. Thrall, *A Pictorial History of Texas* (St. Louis: N. D. Thompson, 1879), 322–326; Claudia Hazlewood, "Archive War," *The New Handbook of Texas*, vol. 1, 234.

15. Bonner, *Major John B. Jones*, 5; Speer and Brown, *Encyclopedia of the New West*, 388; *Biographical Souvenir of the State of Texas* (Chicago: F. A. Battey, 1889), 469.

16. *Navarro Express*, 27 March 1861.

17. Bonner, *Major John B. Jones*, 5.

18. Jones Family, Genealogical File, Fairfield Archives and History.

19. *Members of the Texas Legislature, 1846–1962* (Austin, Texas: Texas State Legislature, 1962), 4.

20. *House Journal of the First Legislature of the State of Texas*, 34, as cited in Bonner, *Major John B. Jones*, 5–6.

21. Sara Mason Bolick, *John Robertson, 1710–1811, of Fairfield County, South Carolina, and His Descendants* (Blair, South Carolina: Sara Mason Bolick, n.d.); 1850 United States Census (Matagorda County, Texas); Bonner, *Major John B. Jones*, 11.

22. Bonner, *Major John B. Jones*, 6.

23. Matagorda Historical Commission, *Historic Matagorda County*, vol. 1 (Houston: D. Armstrong, 1986), 141–142, 356.

24. Walter Prescott Webb, *The Texas Rangers: A Century of Frontier Defense* (Boston: Houghton Mifflin, 1935), 311; *Legislative Manual*, 237–238; Sid S. Johnson, *Texans Who Wore the Gray*, vol. 1 (Austin, Texas: Texas State Library, 1907), 161; Speer and Brown, *Encyclopedia of the New West*, 388.

25. Bonner, *Major John B. Jones*, 6, 7–9; Judson S. Custer, "Rutersville College," *New Handbook of Texas*, vol. 5, 733.

26. *Telegraph and Texas Register*, 11 November 1847, as cited in Bonner, *Major John B. Jones*, 8.

27. Dudley G. Wooten, ed., *A Comprehensive History of Texas, 1685 to 1897*, vol. 1 (Austin, Texas: Texas State Historical Association, 1986), 656.

28. Custer, "Rutersville College," *New Handbook of Texas*, vol. 5, 733.

29. Julian Stevenson Bolick, *A Fairfield Sketchbook* (Clinton, South Carolina: Jacobs Brothers, 1963), 7; McMaster, *History of Fairfield County*, 59–60.

30. McMaster, *History of Fairfield County*, 61.

31. *A Brief History of the Mount Zion Society* (Winnsboro, South Carolina: Winnsboro News and Herald, 1949), 2, as cited in Bonner, *Major John B. Jones*, 10.

32. Bonner, *Major John B. Jones*, 11; Bolick, *John Robertson*, 39; *Corsicana Semi-Weekly Light*, 23 January 1920.

33. *Henry Jones v. John Jones et al*, Cause No. 334, Civil Minutes, Navarro County, Texas, vol. B, 222; Deed Records, Navarro County, Texas, vol. G, 413–14, 416.

34. Deed Records, Navarro County, Texas, vol. M, 162–166.

35. Bill Young, "Henry Jones Family."

36. As quoted in Webb, *Texas Rangers*, 309; James B. Gillett, *Six Years With the Texas Rangers* (Austin, Texas: Von Boeckmann-Jones, 1921), 93.

37. Helen Groce, as quoted in Webb, *Texas Rangers*, 309.

38. Ibid., 310.

39. Ibid., 311.

40. Frederick Wilkins, *The Law Comes to Texas: The Texas Rangers, 1870–1901* (Austin, Texas: State House Press, 1999), 43.

41. *Galveston Weekly News*, 13 June 1857; *Galveston Daily News*, 4 August 1857.

42. Masonic Record (John B. Jones), Masonic Grand Lodge Library and Museum of Texas, Waco, Texas.

43. Bonner, *Major John B. Jones*, 15; *Navarro Express*, 30 June 1860.

44. Deed Records, Navarro County, Texas, vol. M, 279.

45. Deed Records, Navarro County, Texas, vol. M, 434.

46. Deed Records, Navarro County, Texas, vol. M, 600.

47. *Navarro Express*, 19 November 1859.

48. Ibid., 14 January 1860.

49. Ibid., 3 March 1860; Marriage Records, Navarro County, Texas, vol. 1, 51; Samuels and Knox, *Old Northwest Texas*, vol. 1-B, 439.

50. Deed Records, Navarro County, Texas, vol. A, 511–513.

51. James M. Smallwood, "The Impending Crisis: A Texas Perspective on the Causes of the Civil War," in *The Seventh Star of the Confederacy*, ed. Kenneth W. Howell (Denton, Texas: University of North Texas Press, 2009), 41; Linda S. Hudson, "The Knights of the Golden Circle in Texas, 1858–1861: An Analysis of the First (Military) Degree Knights," in *The Seventh Star of the Confederacy*, 52–62. See also Roy Sylvan Dunn, "The KGC in Texas, 1860–1861," *Southwestern Historical Quarterly* 70, no. 6 (April 1967), 543–573; Jimmie Hicks, "Some Letters Concerning the Knights of the Golden Circle in Texas, 1860–1861," *Southwestern Historical Quarterly* 65 (July 1961), 80–86; and C. A. Bridges, "The Knights of the Golden Circle: A Filibustering Fantasy," *Southwestern Historical Quarterly*, 44, no. 3 (January 1941).

52. *Navarro Express*, 17 March 1860.

53. Ibid., 21 April 1860.

54. Ibid., 26 May 1860.

55. Ibid., 9 June 1860.

56. Hudson, "Knights of the Golden Circle," 52–62.

57. Annie Carpenter Love, *History of Navarro County* (Dallas: Southwest Press, 1933), 104–105; *Navarro Express*, 2 June 1860.

58. *Navarro Express*, 7 July 1860.

59. Ibid., 25 August 1860.

60. 1860 United States Census (Dresden Post Office, Navarro County, Texas); *Navarro Express*, 5 October 1860.

61. *Navarro Express*, 16 November 1860.

62. Ibid., 23 November 1860.

63. Ibid., 30 November 1860.

64. Deed Records, Navarro County, Texas, vol. N, 375.

65. Deed Records, Navarro County, Texas, vol. N, 459.

66. *Navarro Express*, 16 January and 13 February, 1861; C. Alwyn Barr, "The Making of a Secessionist: The Antebellum Career of Roger Q. Mills," *Southwestern Historical Quarterly* 79 (1975), 143; Roger Quarles Mills was born in Kentucky on March 30, 1832, and moved to Jefferson, Texas, in 1849. He became a lawyer in 1852, and was a state representative from Navarro County from 1859–1860, a staunch states rightist. After the Civil War, in which he was wounded, he served in the United States Congress, and later as a senator, retiring in 1899. He died in Corsicana on September 2, 1911. Alwyn Barr, "Roger Quarles Mills," *New Handbook of Texas*, vol. 4, 751.

67. "Acts of the Eighth Legislature, Special Session, 1861," Articles 2899 and 2910, in *Early Laws of Texas*, vol. 2 (St. Louis: The Gilbert Book Co., 1891), 493, 495; James L. Haley, *Sam Houston* (Norman, Oklahoma: University of Oklahoma Press, 2002), 383–387.

68. Smallwood, "The Impending Crisis," 48.

69. *Galveston Daily News* as quoted in *Navarro Express*, 20 March 1861.

70. *Navarro Express*, 20 March 1861.

71. Ibid., 27 March 1861.

72. Ibid.

Chapter 2: Daring Gallantry

1. *Navarro Express*, 8 May 1861.

2. Ibid., 12 June 1861.

3. Ibid., 26 June 1861.

4. Ibid., 17 and 24 October, 1861.

5. Speer and Brown, *Encyclopedia of the New West*, 388; Johnson, *Texans Who Wore the Gray*, vol. 1, 161; *Biographical Encyclopedia of Texas* (New York: Southern Publishing, 1880), 99; *A Legislative Manual for the State of Texas*, 238.

6. Muster-In Roll (John B. Jones), Compiled Service Records of Confederate Soldiers, M323, Roll 377, National Archives, Washington, D.C.; Stewart Sifakis, *Compendium of the Confederate Armies: Texas* (New York: Facts on File, 1995), 126–127.

7. Requisition for Forage and Company Muster-In Roll (John B. Jones), Compiled Service Records.

8. Alwyn Barr, *Polignac's Texas Brigade* (College Station, Texas: Texas A&M University Press, 1998), 11.

9. Ibid., 12–13.

10. Receipt (John B. Jones), Compiled Service Records.

11. Bonner, *Major John B. Jones*, 23.

12. Regimental Return (John B. Jones), Compiled Service Records; Barr, *Polignac's Texas Brigade*, 13.

13. Barr, *Polignac's Texas Brigade*, 13; Ralph A. Wooster, *Lone Star Regiments in Gray* (Austin, Texas: Eakin Press, 2002), 251.

14. Barr, *Polignac's Texas Brigade*, 14–15.

15. Ibid., 18.

16. Register and Field and Staff Muster Roll (John B. Jones), Compiled Service Records.

17. Barr, *Polignac's Texas Brigade*, 18–22.

18. Ibid., 21–22; Jeff Kinard, *Lafayette of the South* (College Station, Texas: Texas A&M University Press, 2001), 113.

19. Barr, *Polignac's Texas Brigade*, 22–27.

20. U.S. War Department, *The War of the Rebellion: A Compilation of the Official Record of the Union and Confederate Armies*, series 1, vol. 26, part 1 (Washington D.C.: Government Printing Office, 1881), 331; *Austin Daily Statesman*, 1 April 1881.

21. Lt. Col. James E. Harrison to Col. S. S. Anderson, 23 October 1863 (John B. Jones), Compiled Service Records.

22. Ibid.

23. Barr, *Polignac's Texas Brigade*, 30–33.

24. Kinard, *Lafayette of the South*, 116.

25. Ibid., 116–118.

26. Field and Muster Roll (John B. Jones), Compiled Service Records.

27. Kinard, *Lafayette of the South*, 123.

28. Barr, *Polignac's Texas Brigade*, 38.

29. Kinard, *Lafayette of the South*, 127.

30. Ibid., 133–157; Barr, *Polignac's Texas Brigade*, 38–41.

31. Kinard, *Lafayette of the South*, 157.

32. Bonner, *Major John B. Jones*, 23.

33. Kinard, *Lafayette of the South*, 163.

34. Ibid., 164–168; Barr, *Polignac's Texas Brigade*, 44–46.

35. Kinard, *Lafayette of the South*, 169.

36. Ibid., 173–174.

37. Fannie Halbert to Capt. J. L. Halbert, 10 August 1864, as quoted in Bonner, *Major John B. Jones*, 24.

38. Barr, *Polignac's Texas Brigade*, 49–50.

39. Kinard, *Lafayette of the South*, 175–176.

40. Ibid., 180; Barr, *Polignac's Texas Brigade*, 51–52.

41. Oran M. Roberts, *Confederate Military History of Texas* (Gulf Breeze, Florida: eBooksOnDisk, 2003), 85; Muster Roll (John B. Jones), Compiled Service Records.

42. John B. Jones, Compiled Service Records; Bonner, *Major John B. Jones*, 25.

43. Carl H. Moneyhan, *Texas After the Civil War: The Struggle of Reconstruction* (College Station, Texas: Texas A&M University Press, 2004), 6.

44. Speer and Brown, *Encyclopedia of the New West*, 388; Johnson, *Texans Who Wore the Gray*, vol. 1, 161; *Biographical Encyclopedia of Texas*, 100; *Biographical Souvenir of the State of Texas*, 469; Webb, *Texas Rangers*, 310; *A Legislative Manual for the State of Texas*, 238.

45. Moneyhan, *Texas After the Civil War*, 7.

46. Barry A. Crouch, *The Freedmen's Bureau and Black Texans* (Austin, Texas: University of Texas Press, 1992), 12.

47. Charles William Ramsdell, *Reconstruction in Texas* (Austin, Texas: University of Texas Press, 1970), 39.

48. W. C. Nunn, *Escape From Reconstruction* (Fort Worth, Texas: Texas Christian University, 1956), 28–32.

49. Deed Records, Navarro County, Texas, vol. Q, 150.

50. Bonner, *Major John B. Jones*, 25–26; "Texas Frontier Troubles," *Report of Committee on Foreign Affairs of the U.S. With Mexico* (Washington D.C.: Government Printing Office, 1878), 58.

51. Deed Records, Navarro County, Texas, vol. S, 206.

52. Bonner, *Major John B. Jones*, 26; *A Legislative Manual for the State of Texas*, 238; Speer and Brown, *Encyclopedia of the New West*, 388.

53. Nunn, *Escape From Reconstruction*, 74.

54. Bonner, *Major John B. Jones*, 26; *Biographical Encyclopedia of Texas*, 100; *A Legislative Manual for the State of Texas*, 238; Speer and Brown, *Encyclopedia of the New West*, 388.

55. Bonner, *Major John B. Jones*, 27.

56. Ibid.; *A Legislative Manual for the State of Texas*, 238.

57. Lawrence F. Hill, *Diplomatic Relations Between the United States and Brazil* (Durham, North Carolina: Duke University Press, 1932), 239–244. See also William Clark Griggs, *The Elusive Eden: Frank McMullen's Confederate Colony in Brazil* (Austin, Texas: University of Texas Press, 1987) for a thorough account of an unsuccessful effort at colonization in Brazil.

58. *A Legislative Manual for the State of Texas*, 238; *Biographical Encyclopedia of Texas*, 100; Speer and Brown, *Encyclopedia of the New West*, 388.

59. Webb, *Texas Rangers*, 310–311.

60. Ibid., 311.

61. Bonner, *Major John B. Jones*, 29.

62. *Dallas Daily Herald*, 4 July 1868.

63. *A Legislative Manual for the State of Texas*, 238.

64. *Biographical Encyclopedia of Texas*, 100; Speer and Brown, *Encyclopedia of the New West*, 389.

65. *Members of the Texas Legislature*, 57–68.

66. Love, *History of Navarro County*, 216.

67. Wyvonne Putman, *Navarro County History*, vol. 1 (Quanah, Texas: Nortex Press, 1975), 200.

68. Deed Records, Navarro County, Texas, vol. 7, 732.
69. 1870 United States Census (Navarro County, Texas).
70. Love, *History of Navarro County*, 135.
71. *Corsicana Observer*, 25 March 1871.
72. Ibid., 8 April 1871.
73. Ibid., 27 May 1871.
74. Ibid., 9 September 1871.
75. Ibid., 12 November 1871.
76. Deed Records, Navarro County, Texas, vol. W, 451.
77. Marriage Records, Navarro County, Texas, vol. 2, 51.
78. *Austin Daily Democratic Statesman*, 9 August 1873, 4 and 5 September 1873.
79. Deed Records, Navarro County, Texas, vol. Y, 185.
80. Deed Records, Navarro County, Texas, vol. Y, 249.
81. *Y. W. H. McKissack v. John B. Jones & Co.*, Cause No. 1322, Civil Minutes, Navarro County, Texas, vol. F, 35.

Chapter 3: The Right Man

1. *Corsicana Observer*, 7 January 1874.
2. *John B. Jones & Co. v. S. J. T. Johnson, Sheriff*, Cause No. 1326, Civil Minutes, Navarro County, Texas, vol. F, 409, 473.
3. *Governors' Messages, Coke to Ross* (Austin, Texas: Texas State Library, 1916), 6–7.
4. *Brownsville Sentinel*, as quoted in the *Galveston Daily News*, 3 January 1874.
5. *Sherman Register* as quoted in the *Dallas Daily Herald*, 4 February 1874.
6. M. M. Morales to Governor Coke, 6 February 1874, Records of Gov. Coke, Texas State Library, Austin, Texas [hereafter "TSL"].
7. Coke to Steele, 16 January 1874, Executive Record Book 1874–1879, 21, TSL.
8. *Galveston Daily News*, 6 November 1879; "William Steele," *New Handbook of Texas*, vol. 6, 79.
9. Steele to Coke, 23 January 1874, Records of Gov. Coke, TSL.
10. *Governors' Messages*, 14–16; Governor's Address, Records of Gov. Coke, TSL; *Galveston Daily News*, 27 January 1874.
11. Ernest Wallace, *Texas Turmoil: The Saga of Texas, 1849–1873* (Austin, Texas: Steck-Vaughn, 1965), 234–263.
12. "An Act to Provide for the Protection of the Frontier," December 15, 1863, *The Laws of Texas, 1822–1897* (Austin, Texas: Gammel Book, 1898), 23–25.
13. *Galveston Daily News*, 29 January 1874.
14. Ibid., 6 February 1874.
15. Ibid., 12 February 1874.
16. Order, 2 February 1874, Executive Record Book 1874–1879, 75, TSL.

17. *Corsicana Observer*, 11 February 1874.

18. Petition circa February 1874, Adjutant General's Correspondence [hereafter "AGC"], TSL; Charles A. Crosby to Steele, 11 February 1874, AGC, TSL. See also Coke to P. C. Jackson, Fayette County, 13 February 1874, Records of Gov. Coke, TSL.

19. *Austin Daily Democratic Statesman*, 14 February 1874.

20. Steele to Coke, 5 March 1874, Letterpress Book, following p. 70, AGC, TSL.

21. *Corsicana Observer*, 18 March 1874.

22. Ibid.

23. Ibid., 8 April 1874.

24. Ibid., 1 April 1874.

25. *Galveston Daily News*, 2 April 1874.

26. *General Laws of the State of Texas (14th Legislature)*, vol. 8 (Austin, Texas: Gammel Book, 1898), 85–89; *Galveston Daily News*, 2 May 1874.

27. *General Laws of the State of Texas*, vol. 8, 85–89.

28. Bob Alexander, *Winchester Warriors: Texas Rangers of Company D, 1874–1901* (Denton, Texas: University of North Texas Press, 2009), 21.

29. *General Laws of the State of Texas*, vol. 8, 85–89; *Galveston Daily News*, 2 May 1874.

30. Robert M. Utley, *Lone Star Justice: The First Century of the Texas Rangers* (New York: Oxford University Press, 2002), 146.

31. *Galveston Daily News*, 18 April 1874.

32. Steele to Gen. C. C. Augur, 20 April 1874, Letterpress Book, 124, AGC, TSL.

33. Secretary of War W. W. Belknap to Steele, 29 April 1874, AGC, TSL.

34. For the best account, see Barry A. Crouch and Donaly E. Brice, *The Governor's Hounds: The State Police, 1870–1873* (Austin, Texas: University of Texas Press, 2011). Ann Patton Baenziger, "The Texas State Police During Reconstruction: A Reexamination," *Southwestern Historical Quarterly* 72, no. 4 (1969), 470–488; Ramsdell, *Reconstruction in Texas*, 301–302; Gen. W. H. King, "The Texas Ranger Service and History of the Rangers, With Observation on Their Value as a Police Protection," in *A Comprehensive History of Texas*, ed. Dudley G. Wooten (Dallas, Texas: William G. Scarff, 1898), 347–348; William T. Field Jr., "The Texas State Police, 1870–1873," *Texas Military History* 5, no. 3 (Fall 1965), 131–141.

35. Wilkins, *The Law Comes to Texas*, 25.

36. Message of the Governor, 12 January 1875, Executive Record Book, 1874–1879, 192, TSL.

37. A. J. Nicholson and L. M. Rogers to Coke, undated, AGC, TSL.

38. Representatives to Coke, 26 April 1874, AGC, TSL.

39. Citizens to Coke, undated, Records of Gov. Coke, TSL; Mike Cox, *The Texas Rangers: Wearing the Cinco Peso, 1821–1900* (New York: Tom Doherty Associates, 2008), 215.

40. Texas Ranger Service Records, TSL; Dorman H. Winfrey and James M. Day, eds., *The Indian Papers of Texas and the Southwest, 1825–1916*, vol. 5 (Austin, Texas: Texas State Historical Assn, 1995), 308–310.

41. Rick Miller, *Sam Bass & Gang* (Austin, Texas: State House Press, 1999), 368–369.

42. *Austin Daily Democratic Statesman,* 9 May 1874.

43. Kenneth Kesselus, ed., *Memoir of Capt'n C. R. Perry of Johnson City, Texas: A Texas Veteran* (Austin, Texas: Jenkins Publishing, 1990), 3–5; Thomas W. Cutrer, "Cicero Rufus Perry," *New Handbook of Texas,* vol. 5, 157.

44. W. J. Maltby, *Captain Jeff or Frontier Life in Texas with the Texas Rangers* (Colorado, Texas: Whipkey Printing, 1906); Lou Rodenberger, "William Jeff Maltby," *New Handbook of Texas,* vol. 4, 477; N. V. Gibbs, "Jeff Maltby Family," in *I Remember Callahan: History of Callahan County, Texas,* ed. Hicks A. Turner (Dallas: Taylor Publishing, 1986), 75–76.

45. Don H. Biggers, *Shackelford County Sketches* (Albany, Texas: Clear Fork Press, 1974), 16.

46. A. J. Sowell, *Early Settlers and Indian Fighters of Southwest Texas* (Austin, Texas: State House Press, 1986), 720–734.

47. Maltby, *Captain Jeff,* 66.

48. Ibid., 67–68.

49. Elkins to Coke, 24 May 1874; Steele to Elkins, 25 May 1874; Petition to Coke from Coleman County, 24 May 1874; Steele to Best, 30 May 1874, Letterpress Book, 217, AGC, TSL.

50. Captain John M. Elkins, *My Life on the Texas Frontier,* ed. Norman W. Brown (n.p.: Norman Wayne Brown and Don Merle Jay, 2010), 52.

51. Maltby to Steele, 3 July 1874, AGC, TSL.

52. *Austin Daily Democratic Statesman,* 25 August 1875; Robert W. Stephens, *Texas Ranger Captain Dan Roberts: The Untold Story* (Dallas: Robert W. Stephens, 2009), 6–8.

53. Dan W. Roberts, *Rangers and Sovereignty* (San Antonio: Wood Printing & Engraving, 1914), 33–34; Alexander, *Winchester Warriors,* 23.

54. Ed Carnal, "Reminiscences of a Texas Ranger," *Frontier Times* 1, no. 3 (December 1923), 20; *Austin Daily Democratic Statesman,* 29 May 1874; Recollections of James B. Hawkins, October 1923, Walter Prescott Webb Collection, Briscoe Center for American History, University of Texas, Austin [hereafter "Webb Collection"].

55. Roberts, *Rangers and Sovereignty,* 16; Wilkins, *The Law Comes to Texas,* 28–29.

56. *Corsicana Observer,* 13 May 1874.

57. *San Antonio Daily Express,* 10 May 1874.

58. *Dallas Daily Herald,* 14 May 1874.

59. *Houston Telegraph* as quoted in the *Corsicana Observer,* 12 August 1874. Clinton McKamy Winkler, a resident of Navarro County since 1847, was a member of the state legislature and a lawyer. He served as an officer in Hood's Texas Brigade during the Civil War, was Grand Master of the state Masonic Lodge in 1870, and served as an associate judge of the Texas Court of Criminal Appeals until his death in 1882. "Winkler," txgenweb (Internet).

60. *Austin Daily Democratic Statesman,* 30 May 1874.

61. General Order No. 2 (Steele), 6 May 1874, AGC, and Frontier Battalion Correspondence, 4 May 1874 [hereafter "FBC"], TSL.

62. Special Order No. 1 (Jones), 7 May 1874, AGC, TSL.

63. General Order No. 1 (Jones), 7 May 1874, AGC, TSL.

64. Jones to Steele, 1 December 1874, AGC, TSL.

65. General Order No. 1 (Jones), 7 May 1874; Coldwell to Jones, 22 May 1874, AGC, TSL; *Dallas Daily Herald*, 23 May 1874.

66. Telegram, Coke to Jones, 11 May 1874; telegram, Blocker to Jones, 12 May 1874; Steele to Jones, 12 May 1874, Letterpress Book, 161, AGC, TSL; *Austin Daily Democratic Statesman*, 12 May 1874.

67. Telegram, J. S. Giddings to Coke, 15 May 1874; Kenney to Jones, 17 May 1874, AGC, TSL.

68. Jones to Kenney, 20 May 1874; Special Order No. 3 (Jones), 21 May 1874, AGC, TSL. Five of the men were B. M. C. Patterson, N. B. DeJarnette, F. A. McIver, H. F. Damon, and Z. T. Wattles.

69. Carnal, "Reminiscences," 20.

70. *Corsicana Observer*, 27 May 1874.

71. Ibid., 10 June 1874.

72. Steele to Capt. J. H. Wells, 25, 27, and 30 May 1874; 5 June 1874, AGC, TSL.

73. United States Congress, "Texas Frontier Troubles," 58.

74. Curley Hatcher, "Got Fifty Dollars for an Indian's Scalp," *Frontier Times* 1, no. 10 (July 1924), 7.

75. Log, May–November 1874, FBC, TSL. The dates given in this log are questionable given that Maltby's company was not formally organized until May 30, 1874.

76. *Austin Daily Democratic Statesman*, 28 May 1874.

77. Ikard to Jones, 29 May 1874, AGC, TSL.

78. Steele to County Officials, 4 June 1874, Letterpress Book, 228, AGC, TSL.

79. Steele to Jones, 5 June 1874, Letterpress Book, 228, AGC, TSL.

80. Steele to Jones, 16 June 1874, Letterpress Book, 250, AGC, TSL.

81. Petition to Gov. Coke, 28 May 1874, AGC, TSL; *Dallas Daily Herald*, 5 June 1874.

82. Special Order No. 6 (Jones), 3 June 1874; Waller to Jones, 30 May 1874; Waller to Coke, 6 June 1874, AGC, TSL. On June 1, 1874, some of Waller's men accompanied a posse led by Comanche County Sheriff John Carnes that traded gunfire with and killed Hardin henchmen Alec Barekman and Alexander Hamilton "Ham" Anderson. Leon Metz, *John Wesley Hardin: Dark Angel of Texas* (El Paso: Mangan Books, 1996), 144–145; Walter Clay Dixson, "The Barekman-Anderson Prelude to Comanche," *Quarterly of the National Association and Center for Outlaw and Lawman History* 18, no. 2 (April–June 1994), 5–16; Robert K. DeArment, *Deadly Dozen: Forgotten Gunfighters of the Old West,* vol. 2 (Norman, Oklahoma: University of Oklahoma Press, 2007), 54–55.

83. Steele to Sheriff, DeWitt County, 15 June 1874; Coke to Sheriff, Calhoun County, 15 June 1874; Steele to Sgt. Atkinson, Co. A, 16 June 1874, Letterpress Book, 248,

249, AGC, TSL; *Austin Daily Democratic Statesman*, 16 June 1874; *Galveston Daily News*, 17 June 1874; *San Antonio Daily Express*, 19 June 1874.

84. John Wesley Hardin, *The Life of John Wesley Hardin* (Seguin, Texas: Smith & Moore, 1896), 95.

85. Maltby to Jones, 7 June 1874, AGC, TSL.

86. Log, May–August 1874, FBC, TSL.

87. Richard C. Marohn, *The Last Gunfighter: John Wesley Hardin* (College Station, Texas: Creative Publishing, 1995), 88.

88. *Dallas Daily Herald*, 21 June 1874.

89. Proclamation, 3 July 1874, Gov. Coke's Executive Record Book, 1873–1874, 291, TSL.

90. Montes to Steele, 31 May 1874, AGC, TSL. Telesforo Montes was born in San Elizario, Texas, in 1820. Two of his sons served under him in his Ranger company. He died in 1888, after having served as mayor of San Elizario. Conrado Montes, "Life History of Telesforo Montes and His Family", *Montes Family Website*, Internet.

91. *Galveston Daily News*, 17 June 1874.

92. Steele to Wallace, 29 June 1874, AGC, TSL.

93. Wallace to Steele, 7 July 1874, AGC, TSL.

94. Ibid., 14 July 1874. For a personal account of activities of this force by a member of Wallace's command, see J. B. (Red) John Dunn, *Perilous Trails of Texas* (Dallas: Southwest Press, 1932), 68–84.

95. Steele to Benevides, 12 June 1874, Letterpress Book, 242; Benevides to Steele, 13 June 1874, AGC; Coke to Wm. H. Russell, Brownsville, 13 June 1874, Records of Gov. Coke, Letterpress Book, 633, TSL.

96. Charles D. Williams, U.S. Department of Justice, to Steele, 23 July 1874, Records of Gov. Coke, TSL.

97. *Galveston Daily News*, 9 October 1874.

98. L. M. Rogers to Steele, 14 June 1874, AGC, TSL.

99. Gillett, *Six Years With the Texas Rangers*, 94; Steele to Nicholson, 19 June 1874, Letterpress Book, 255, AGC, TSL.

100. Nicholson to Steele, 2 July 1874, AGC, TSL.

101. Wilkins, *Law Comes to Texas*, 42–43.

102. Gillett, *Six Years With the Texas Rangers*, 95–96.

103. Recollections of George F. Steinbeck, Webb Collection.

104. Gillett, *Six Years With the Texas Rangers*, 94–95.

105. Jones to Steele, 13 June 1874, AGC, TSL; *Corsicana Observer*, 23 September 1874.

106. Jones to Waller, 14 June 1874; *Corsicana Observer*, 29 June 1874.

107. Maltby to Steele, 22 June 1874, AGC, TSL.

108. Steele to Jones, 23 June 1874; 26 June 1874, Letterpress Book, 269, AGC, TSL.

109. Steele to Maltby, 27 June 1874, Letterpress Book, 275–277, AGC, TSL.

110. Maltby to Steele, 3 July 1874, AGC, TSL.

111. Jones to Steele, 22 June 1874; Special Order No. 9 (Jones), 22 June 1874, AGC, TSL.

112. Wilson Hey to Coke, 25 June 1874, AGC, TSL.

113. Special Order No. 10, 30 June 1874; Jones to Perry, 27 June 1874, AGC, TSL; *Corsicana Observer*, 23 September 1874.

Chapter 4: No Carpet-Knight

1. Jones to Steele, 1 July 1874, AGC, TSL; *Corsicana Observer*, 23 September 1874.

2. Jones to Waller, 7 July 1874; Jones to Steele, 7 July 1874, AGC, TSL.

3. Steele to Coke, 10 July 1874, Letterpress Book, 297–1/2, AGC, TSL; *San Antonio Daily Express*, 15 July 1874; Chuck Parsons, *The Sutton-Taylor Feud: The Deadliest Blood Feud in Texas* (Denton, Texas: University of North Texas Press, 2009), 98–99.

4. Parsons, *Sutton-Taylor Feud*, 153; Steele to Coke, 10 July 1874, Letterpress Book, 297–1/2, AGC, TSL.

5. Special Order No. 2, 14 July 1874, Special Orders; Memorandum by Steele, 14 July 1874, Letterpress Book, 303–305, AGC, TSL; *Galveston Daily News*, 14 July 1874.

6. For the best account of McNelly and his men, see Chuck Parsons and Marianna E. Hall-Little, *Captain L. H. McNelly, Texas Ranger: The Life and Times of a Fighting Man* (Austin, Texas: State House Press, 2001).

7. William Callicott to Walter Prescott Webb, "The Lost Valley Fight as Told by William Callicott," Spring 1921, Webb Collection.

8. Jones to Steele, 14 July 1874, AGC, TSL; *Corsicana Observer*, 23 September 1874; "The Loss [*sic*] Valley Fight," *Frontier Times* 7, no. 3 (December 1929), 101.

9. Log, May–August 1874, FBC, TSL; *Corsicana Observer*, 29 July 1874.

10. *Corsicana Observer*, 22 and 29 July 1874; *Houston Daily Telegraph*, 18 July 1874, as quoted in *Corsicana Observer*, 22 July 1874; *Galveston Daily News*, 18 July 1874; W. S. Nye, *Carbine & Lance: The Story of Old Fort Sill* (Norman, Oklahoma: University of Oklahoma Press, 1942), 196; Thomas F. Horton, *History of Jack County* (Jacksboro, Texas: Gazette Print, 1932), 52–53; J. W. Wilbarger, *Indian Depredations in Texas* (Austin, Texas: Eakin Press/State House Press, 1985), 543; R. S. Purdy, "The Fight at Loving's Ranch in 1874," *Frontier Times* 16, no. 3 (December 1938), 96–98. See also John M. Turner, "Indian Fight in Loving [*sic*] County in 1874," *Frontier Times* 30, no. 2 (April–June 1953), 234–236, and R. S. Purdy, "Fight With Indians at Loving's Ranch," *Frontier Times* 2, no. 9 (June 1925), 1–2.

11. "The Loss Valley Fight," 101; Nye, *Carbine & Lance*, 196; James L. Haley, *The Buffalo War* (Austin, Texas: State House Press, 1998), 87; Jim McIntire, *Early Days in Texas*, ed. Robert K. DeArment (Norman, Oklahoma: University of Oklahoma Press, 1992), 49, 127.

12. Jones to Steele, 14 July 1874, AGC, TSL; Nye, *Carbine & Lance*, 196; Carnal, "Reminiscences of a Texas Ranger," 20. For other accounts of the Lost Valley fight, see Alexander, *Winchester Warriors*, 39–52, and Chuck Parsons and Donaly E. Brice,

Texas Ranger N. O. Reynolds, The Intrepid (Honolulu, Hawaii: Talei Publishers, 2005), 30–32.

13. Nye, *Carbine & Lance*, 182–183; Allen Lee Hamilton, *Sentinel of the Southern Plains: Fort Richardson and the Northwest Texas Frontier, 1866–1878* (Fort Worth, Texas: Texas Christian University Press, 1988), 147.

14. Jones to Steele, 14 and 13 July 1874, AGC, TSL; Sowell, *Early Settlers and Indian Fighters*, 798.

15. See Alexander, *Winchester Warriors*, 42–43; Nye, *Carbine & Lance*, 196; Haley, *The Buffalo War*, 87.

16. Haley, *The Buffalo War*, 87.

17. Nye, *Carbine & Lance*, 196. One Ranger later recalled seeing two Indians with red blankets walking toward them as a ruse to draw the Rangers in McIntire, *Early Days in Texas*, 49.

18. J. P. Holmes, *Austin Daily Democratic Statesman*, 19 July 1874.

19. Carnal, "Reminiscences of a Texas Ranger," 21.

20. Jones to Steele, 14 July 1874, AGC, TSL.

21. Nye, *Carbine & Lance*, 196; Sowell, *Early Settlers and Indian Fighters*, 799.

22. Carnal, "Reminiscences of a Texas Ranger," 21.

23. Jones to Steele, 14 July 1874, AGC, TSL; Sowell, *Early Settlers and Indian Fighters*, 799.

24. Sowell, *Early Settlers and Indian Fighters*, 801; Callicott, "The Lost Valley Fight."

25. Carnal, "Reminiscences of a Texas Ranger," 21.

26. Ibid., 22; Nye, *Carbine & Lance*, 197.

27. Mrs. Edgar T. Neal, "Runtiest Ranger is Hero of '74 Fight With Indians," *Frontier Times* 9, no. 2 (November 1931), 60. Another account says that Wattles was hit five times, none seriously, and also lost a boot heel. Sowell, *Early Settlers and Indian Fighters*, 800. Other accounts state that three men were sent to Glass' assistance and brought him back to the ravine. Carnal, "Reminiscences of a Texas Ranger," 22; Callicott, "The Lost Valley Fight." Jim McIntire indicated that he was one of the three men sent after Glass. McIntire, *Early Days in Texas*, 51.

28. "The Loss Valley Fight," 102.

29. Carnal, "Reminiscences of a Texas Ranger," 22.

30. Sowell, *Early Settlers and Indian Fighters*, 801.

31. Callicott, "The Lost Valley Fight."

32. Ibid.; Nye, *Carbine & Lance*, 197–198; Carnal, "Reminiscences of a Texas Ranger," 22; Sowell, *Early Settlers and Indian Fighters*, 802.

33. Callicott, "The Lost Valley Fight."

34. McIntire, *Early Days in Texas*, 52–53.

35. Nye, *Carbine & Lance, 200.*

36. *Corsicana Observer*, 2 September 1874.

37. Jones to Steele, 14 July 1874, AGC, TSL.

38. Hamilton, *Sentinel of the Southern Plains*, 151.

39. Steele to Jones, 14 July 1874, AGC, TSL; *Austin Daily Democratic Statesman*, 19 July 1874; Callicott, "The Lost Valley Fight."
40. *Galveston Daily News,* 18 July 1874.
41. Carnal, "Reminiscences of a Texas Ranger," 23; *Corsicana Observer*, 2 September 1874.
42. Carnal, "Reminiscences of a Texas Ranger," 23. Dave Bailey was remembered as "a fine looking man, had good clothes, and was refined." H. H. Halsell, "Cowboys and Cattleland," *Old West* 8, no. 1 (Fall 1971), 29.
43. Jones to Steele, 14 and 16 July 1874, AGC, TSL; *Corsicana Observer*, 2 September 1874.
44. *Houston Daily Telegraph*, 18 July 1874, as quoted in *Corsicana Observer*, 22 July 1874.
45. *Corsicana Observer*, 2 September 1874.
46. *Austin Weekly State Gazette*, 8 August 1874.
47. Jones to Steele, 14 July 1874, AGC, TSL.
48. Jones to Steele, 23 July 1874, AGC, TSL; *Austin Weekly State Gazette*, 8 August 1874.
49. Cox, *Texas Rangers*, 229; Allen G. Hatley, *Bringing the Law to Texas: Crime and Violence in Nineteenth Century Texas* (LaGrange, Texas: Centex Press, 2002), 69.
50. General Order No. 2 (Jones), 15 July 1874, AGC, TSL.
51. Probate Abstract Book, vol. 1, 200, Navarro County, Texas; Probate Record, vol. R, 673, Navarro County, Texas; *Estate of J. L. Halbert, Deceased*, Cause No. 192, Probate Papers, Navarro County, Texas; *Austin Daily Democratic Statesman*, 26 July 1874.
52. Jones to Steele, 23 July 1874, AGC, TSL.
53. Special Order No. 11 (Jones), 23 July 1874, AGC, TSL.
54. *Comanche Chief*, 8 August 1874, as quoted in *Dallas Daily Herald*, 13 August 1874; *Galveston Daily News*, 13 August 1874; *Corsicana Observer*, 26 August 1874; *San Antonio Daily Express*, 13 August 1874; *Dallas Daily Commercial*, 13 August 1874.
55. Maltby to Jones, 27 July 1874, AGC, TSL; *Austin Daily Democratic Statesman*, 11 August 1874.
56. Elkins, *Life on the Texas Frontier*, 94–95; Beatrice Grady Gay, *Into the Setting Sun: A History of Coleman County* (Santa Anna, Texas: n.p., 1936), 121.
57. Special Order No. 12 (Jones), 30 July 1874, AGC, TSL.
58. General Order No. 3 (Steele), 3 August 1874, AG General Orders, AGC, TSL.

Chapter 5: A Heavy Task

1. Steele to Nelson, 3 August 1874, AGC, TSL.
2. Jones to Steele, 9 August 1874, AGC, TSL.
3. *Austin Daily Democratic Statesman*, 9 August 1874; *Galveston Daily News*, 11 August 1874. A letter from Major Jones indicates that this fight may have occurred on July 25, 1874. Jones to Steele, 9 August 1874, AGC, TSL.
4. Nelson to Coldwell, 7 August 1874, AGC, TSL.

5. Coldwell to Jones, 8 August 1874, AGC, TSL.

6. Special Order No. 13 (Jones), 8 September 1874, AGC, TSL; Candace DuCoin, *Lawmen on the Texas Frontier: Rangers and Sheriffs* (Round Rock, Texas: Riata Books, 2007), 74.

7. Nelson to Jones, 27 August 1874, AGC, TSL.

8. Jones to Nelson, 8 September 1874, AGC, TSL.

9. Jones to Steele, 14 September 1874, AGC, TSL.

10. Coldwell to Jones, 1 October 1874, AGC; Texas Ranger Service Records, TSL.

11. Jones to Steele, 9 August 1874, AGC, TSL.

12. Ibid.

13. Jones to Maltby, 15 August 1874, AGC, TSL.

14. Steele to Jones, 21 August 1874, AGC, TSL.

15. Connell to Steele, 25 August 1874, AGC, TSL.

16. Jones to Perry, 17 August 1874, AGC, TSL.

17. David Johnson, *The Mason County "Hoo Doo" War, 1874–1902* (Denton, Texas: University of North Texas Press, 2006), 37–38; Miles Barler, *Early Days in Llano* (n.p., n.d.), 31.

18. *Fredericksburg Sentinel* as quoted in *San Antonio Daily Express*, 29 August 1874. An exception is taken to this account by Johnson, *Mason County War*, 42–46, contending that Doole's letter was unnecessarily inflammatory, and that other sources indicate that no threatening actions were made by Baird or Roberts. Roberts defended himself in the *Burnet Bulletin* on 5 September 1874 as an ordinary cowman, painting Doole as a lying villain. Johnson, *Mason County War*, 45–48.

19. Ibid.

20. Log, May–November 1874, FBC, TSL. The log appears to be a summary written some time after the fact by an unknown person, so it may not be accurate.

21. *Corsicana Observer*, 23 September 1874.

22. S. P. Elkins, "Served as a Texas Ranger," *Frontier Times* 5, no. 11 (August 1928), 447.

23. Jones to Doole, 25 August 1874; Doole to Jones, 4 September 1874, AGC, TSL.

24. Webb, *Texas Rangers*, 316.

25. *Corsicana Observer*, 23 September 1874.

26. Ibid.

27. G. B. Pickett to Steele, 26 August 1874, AGC, TSL.

28. Jones to Steele, 14 September 1874, AGC, TSL.

29. Maltby to Jones, 26 August 1874, AGC, TSL.

30. Jones to Steele, 14 September 1874, AGC, TSL.

31. General Order No. 4 (Jones), 15 September 1874, AGC, TSL.

32. Special Order No. 15 (Jones), 15 September 1874, AGC, TSL.

33. Undated petition to Jones from Company D; Special Order No. 16, 16 September 1874, AGC, TSL; Parsons and Brice, *N. O. Reynolds*, 37.

34. Jones to Waller, Stevens, Ikard, and Maltby, 15 September 1874, AGC, TSL.

35. Jones to Editor, *San Saba News*, 19 September 1874, AGC, TSL.

36. Special Order No. 17 (Jones), 20 September 1874, AGC, TSL.

37. Jones to Steele, 30 September 1874, AGC, TSL.

38. Maltby to Jones, 30 September 1874, AGC, TSL; *Dallas Daily Herald*, 10 October 1874; *Galveston Daily News*, 8 October 1874; Curley Hatcher, "A Waterspout in Coleman County in 1874," *Frontier Times* 4, no. 9 (June 1927), 47; Elkins, *Life on the Texas Frontier*, 98.

39. Special Order No. 28 (Jones), 13 November 1874, AGC, TSL; Elkins, *Life on the Texas Frontier*, 98.

40. Jones to Steele, 30 September 1874, AGC, TSL.

41. Special Order No. 22 (Jones), 8 October 1874; Jones to Kenney, 8 October 1874, AGC, TSL.

42. Jones to Steele, 4 October 1874, AGC, TSL.

43. *Comanche Chief* as quoted in *Austin Daily Democratic Statesman*, 6 November 1874.

44. Lt. J. W. Millican to Jones, 3 October 1874, AGC, TSL.

45. Sgt. G. M. Doolittle to Jones, 15 October 1874, AGC, TSL.

46. G. B. Morphis, Texas Ranger Service Records, TSL.

47. Jones to Steele, 24 October 1874, AGC, TSL.

48. General Order No. 5 (Jones), 27 October 1874, AGC, TSL.

49. Stevens to Jones, 27 October 1874, AGC, TSL; Wallace, *Turmoil in Texas*, 256–273.

50. Ibid.; Special Order No. 26 (Jones), 29 October 1874; Jones to Steele, 29 October 1874, AGC, TSL.

51. *Charges and Specifications Preferred Against Captain George W. Stevens*, unknown date in November 1874, AGC, TSL.

52. Jones to Stevens, 7 November 1874, AGC, TSL.

53. Stevens to Jones, 14 November 1874; Dr. John T. Robinson to Jones, 14 November 1874, AGC, TSL.

54. Affidavits of D. Manning, J. S. Hartman, J. J. Boyd, F. A. Lichlyter, and J. W. Newman, 14 November 1874, AGC, TSL.

55. Sgt. N. H. Murray to Jones, 28 October 1874, AGC, TSL; Parsons and Brice, *N. O. Reynolds*, 38.

56. Jones to Steele, 28 October 1874, AGC, TSL.

57. Steele to Jones, 6 November 1874, Letterpress Book, 544; telegram, Steele to Jones, 16 November 1874; Steele to Jones, 17 November 1874, AGC, TSL.

58. Steele to Jones, 17 November 1874, AGC, TSL.

59. Steele to Coldwell, 17 November 1874, Letterpress Book, 563; Steele to Jones, 17 November 1874, Letterpress Book, 561, AGC, TSL.

60. *Austin Daily Democratic Statesman*, 18 November 1874.

61. Steele to Jones, 17 November 1874, Letterpress Book, 561; Steele to Coldwell, 18 November 1874, Letterpress Book, 563, AGC, TSL.

62. Maltby to Jones, 30 November 1874, AGC, TSL; *Austin Daily Democratic States-man*, 28 November and 2 December 1874; *Dallas Daily Herald*, 1 December 1874; *Galveston Daily News*, 26 November 1874; Elkins, *Life on the Texas Frontier*, 96–97.
63. *Galveston Daily News*, 21 November 1874.
64. *Austin Daily Democratic Statesman*, 3 December 1874.
65. Sgt. N. H. Murray to Steele, 21 November 1874; Beavert to Jones, 25 [?] November 1874; Jones to Steele, 25 November and 2 December 1874, AGC, TSL; *Austin Daily Democratic Statesman*, 28 November 1874, 16 and 29 December 1874; Roberts, *Rangers and Sovereignty*, 45–51. In his recollections, Roberts confused Lieutenant Beavert with Lieutenant B. F. Best.
66. Sowell, *Early Settlers and Indian Fighters*, 644.
67. Kesselus, *Capt'n C. R. Perry*, 30.
68. *Galveston Daily News*, 28 November 1874; *Austin Daily Democratic Statesman*, 28 November 1874; S. P. Elkins, "Captured an Indian," *Frontier Times* 6, no. 6 (March 1929), 245–246.
69. *Austin Daily Democratic Statesman*, 1 December 1874. Little Bull was subsequently incarcerated in the state penitentiary at Huntsville where he died of consumption about 1876. Parsons and Brice, *N. O. Reynolds*, 40.

Chapter 6: The Abominable Legislature

1. General Order No. 8 (Steele), 25 November 1874, AGC, TSL; *Austin Daily Democratic Statesman*, 28 November 1874.
2. General Order No. 6 (Jones), 25 November 1874, AGC, TSL.
3. *Austin Daily Democratic Statesman*, 28 November 1874.
4. Jones to Steele, 1 December 1874, AGC, TSL; William Steele, *Supplemental Report of the Adjutant General of the State of Texas For the Year 1874* (Houston, Texas: A. C. Gray, State Printer, 1874), 8–10.
5. Ibid.
6. *Dallas Daily Herald*, 30 December 1874.
7. General Order No. 7 (Jones), 9 December 1874, AGC, TSL.
8. J. Evetts Haley, *Jeff Milton: A Good Man With a Gun* (Norman, Oklahoma: University of Oklahoma Press, 1948), 31.
9. Steele to Jones, 11 December 1874, Letterpress Book, 599, AGC, TSL.
10. Reminiscences of James B. Hawkins, Webb Collection; Roberts, *Rangers and Sovereignty*, 57–60; *Austin Daily Democratic Statesman*, 27 December 1874.
11. Roberts to Jones, 18 December 1874, AGC, TSL.
12. Coke to Gen. Sheridan, 22 December 1874, Letterpress Book No. 310, 404–405, Records of Gov. Coke, TSL.
13. Jones to Steele, 23 December 1874; Kenney to Steele, 24 December 1874, AGC, TSL.
14. Nicholson to Steele, 29 December 1874, AGC, TSL.

15. Jones to Steele, 31 December 1874, AGC, TSL.

16. Jones to Steele, 3 January 1875, FBC, TSL.

17. *Austin Daily Democratic Statesman*, 12 January 1875.

18. Message of the Governor, 12 January 1875, Executive Record Book, 1874–1879, 210.

19. Ibid.

20. *Dallas Daily Herald*, 23 January 1875.

21. Special Order No. 12 (Steele), 4 February 1875, FBC; 14 February 1875, AGC, TSL.

22. Wilkins, *Law Comes to Texas*, 56.

23. Coldwell to Jones, 20 January 1875, AGC, TSL.

24. Steele to Coldwell, 25 January 1875, Letterpress Book, 29, AGC, TSL.

25. Jones to Coldwell, 27 January 1875, AGC, TSL.

26. Coldwell to Jones, 28 February 1875, AGC, TSL.

27. Sgt. G. M. Doolittle to Jones, 15 October 1874, AGC, TSL.

28. Special Order No. 1 (Wilson), 1 February 1875, FBC, TSL.

29. Special Orders Nos. 2 and 4 (Wilson), 8 February 1875, FBC, TSL.

30. Special Order No. 3 (Wilson), 11 February 1875, FBC, TSL.

31. Wilson to Jones, 15 February 1875, AGC, TSL.

32. Special Order No. 5 (Wilson), 22 February 1875, FBC, TSL.

33. Special Order No. 6 (Wilson), 8 March 1875, FBC, TSL.

34. Steele to Jones, 16 February 1875, Letterpress Book, 47–48, AGC, TSL.

35. Long to Kenney, 16 February 1875, AGC, TSL.

36. Johnson, *Mason County War*, 7–17; Alexander, *Winchester Warriors*, 62–66; Stella Gipson Polk, *Mason and Mason County: A History* (Austin, Texas: The Pemberton Press, 1966), 48; Peter R. Rose, "Setting the Stage for the Hoo Doo War: Land, People, and History of Settlement," in *The Hoo Doo War: Portraits of a Lawless Time* (Ozark, Missouri: Dogwood Printing, 2003), 20.

37. Johnson, *Mason County War*, 52–56.

38. Ibid., 58–63; Roberts, *Rangers and Sovereignty*, 88–89.

39. Roberts, *Rangers and Sovereignty*, 88–89; Dave Johnson, ed., Mason County Historical Society, *The Life of Thomas W. Gamel* (Ozark, Missouri: Dogwood Printing, 1994), 17, 54–55.

40. Johnson, *Mason County War*, 64; Alexander, *Winchester Warriors*, 86; Chuck Parsons, "Captain Daniel Webster Roberts," *Mason County Hoo Doo War Anthology* (Mason, Texas: Mason County Historical Commission, 2006), 163–164.

41. Roberts, *Rangers and Sovereignty*, 90.

42. Roberts to Jones, 1 March 1875, FBC, TSL.

43. Telegram, Steele to Roberts, undated, Letterpress Book, 78, AGC, TSL.

44. Murray to Jones, 15 March 1875, AGC, TSL.

45. Jones to Roberts, 16 March 1875, AGC, TSL.

46. Roberts to Jones, 1 April 1875, FBC, TSL.

47. Roberts to Jones, 15 April 1875, FBC, TSL.

48. Jones to Steele, 20 February 1875, AGC, TSL.

49. Ibid., 22 February 1875.

50. *John B. Jones & Co. v. John Finch*, Cause No. 1496, vol. F, 308, Civil Minutes, Navarro County, Texas.

51. Alexander Lea to Coke, 4 March 1875; Lea to W. H. Russell, 4 March 1875, Records of Gov. Coke, TSL.

52. Coldwell to Jones, 11 March 1875, AGC, TSL.

53. Jones to Wilson, 13 March 1875, AGC, TSL.

54. Wilson to Jones, 23 March 1875, FBC, TSL.

55. Jones to Lts. Beavert and Long, 15 March 1875, AGC, TSL.

56. Jones to Beavert, 17 March 1875; Special Order No. 34 (Jones), 17 March 1875; Steele to Jones, 17 March 1875; Steele to Jones, 17 March 1875, Letterpress Book, 103, AGC, TSL.

57. Special Order No. 13 (Steele), 17 March 1875, AGC, FBC, TSL.

58. Jones to Sen. Charles Stewart, 22 January 1879, AGC, TSL.

59. Special Order No. 14 (Steele), 17 March 1875, AGC, FBC, TSL.

60. Steele to McNelly, 17 March 1875, Letterpress Book, 102, AGC, TSL.

61. *Galveston Daily News*, 18 March 1875.

62. Coldwell to Jones, 19 March 1875, AGC, TSL.

63. Jones to McIver, 25 March 1875, AGC, TSL.

64. *Dallas Daily Herald*, 30 March 1875.

65. Steele to Coke, 30 March 1875, Records of Gov. Coke, Letterpress Book, 135–136, AGC, TSL.

66. *Dallas Daily Herald*, 3 April 1875; *Galveston Daily News*, 1 April 1875.

67. Coldwell to Jones, 31 March 1875, AGC, TSL.

68. Steele to Coldwell, 2 April 1875, Letterpress Book, 142–143, AGC, TSL.

69. Parsons and Hall-Little, *Captain L. H. McNelly*, 160–163.

70. Steele to McNelly, undated, Letterpress Book, 149, AGC, TSL; *Galveston Daily News*, 13 April 1875.

71. Steele to Wm. Belknap, 9 April 1875, Letterpress Book, 152–153, AGC, TSL.

72. *Galveston Daily News*, 1 and 4 May 1875.

73. *Austin Daily Democratic Statesman*, 9 April 1875.

74. Jones to Coldwell, 9 April 1875, AGC, TSL.

75. Telegram, Sheriff John McClure to Steele, 18 April 1875, AGC, TSL.

76. *San Antonio Daily Herald*, 6 May 1875.

77. Jones to Steele, 20 April 1875, AGC, TSL; *Dallas Daily Herald*, 16 April 1875.

78. Special Order No. 16 (Steele), 26 April 1875, AGC, FBC, TSL.

79. Jones to Steele, 20 April 1875, AGC, FBC, TSL; Wilkins, *The Law Comes to Texas*, 64.

80. Citizens of Carrizo to Gov. Coke, 24 April 1875, Records of Gov. Coke, TSL.

81. Coke to Gen. E. O. C. Ord, 24 April 1875, Letterpress Book No. 311, 33–37, Records of Gov. Coke, TSL.

82. Gen. W. T. Sherman to Gen. E. O. C. Ord, 1 May 1875, Records of Gov. Coke, TSL.

83. *San Antonio Daily Herald*, 29 April 1875; *Galveston Daily News*, 29 April and 9 May 1875.

84. Jones to Steele, 30 April 1875; Special Order No. 39 (Jones), 30 April 1875, AGC, TSL.

85. Coldwell to Jones, 30 April 1875, AGC, TSL.

86. Telegram, Steele to Coldwell, 5 May 1875, Letterpress Book, 184, AGC, TSL.

87. Letter from Steele, 5 May 1875, Letterpress Book, 198–199, AGC, TSL.

88. Jones to Steele, 9 May 1875, AGC, TSL.

89. McIntire, *Early Days in Texas*, 56.

90. Jones to Steele, 9 May 1875, AGC, TSL; *Austin Daily Democratic Statesman*, 12 May 1875; *Galveston Daily News*, 11 May 1875; *Dallas Daily Herald*, 21 May 1875; McIntire, *Early Days in Texas*, 54–56; Cora Melton Cross, "Ira Long, Cowboy and Texas Ranger," *Frontier Times* 8, no. 1 (October 1930), 27–29.

91. Duval Beall to Long, 17 May 1875, Letterpress Book, 216, AGC, TSL.

92. Letter from Long, 11 May 1875; Jones to Steele, 10 May 1875; Special Order No. 18 (Steele), 18 May 1875, AGC; Special Order No. 40 (Jones), 10 May 1875, FBC, TSL.

93. Foster to Jones, 16 May 1875, AGC, TSL.

Chapter 7: Kill All the Dutch

1. Letter from Steele, 18 May 1875, AGC, TSL.

2. *Galveston Daily News*, 20 May 1875.

3. Coke to President Grant, 29 May 1875, Letterpress Book No. 311, 167–169, Records of Gov. Coke, TSL.

4. *San Antonio Daily Herald*, 14 June 1875.

5. Coldwell to Jones, 3 June 1875; telegram and letter, Duvall Beall to Coldwell, 8 June 1875, AGC, TSL.

6. Jones to Roberts, 23 May 1875, FBC, TSL.

7. *Galveston Daily News*, 1 June 1875; *Austin Daily Democratic Statesman*, 29 May 1875.

8. *San Antonio Daily Express*, 17 and 21 June 1875.

9. Jones to Stevens, 21 June 1875, AGC, TSL.

10. Jones to Foster, 23 June 1875, AGC; Jones to Roberts, 23 June 1875, FBC, TSL.

11. Coldwell to Jones, 28 June 1875, AGC, TSL.

12. Jones to Steele, 9 July 1875, AGC, TSL.

13. William Steele, *Report of the Adjutant General of the State of Texas for the Year 1875* (Houston, Texas: A. C. Gray, State Printer, 1875), 6–13.

14. Jones to Steele, 9 July 1875, AGC, TSL.

15. Jones to Coldwell, 9 July 1875, AGC, TSL.
16. Ibid.
17. Beall to Jones, 17 July 1875, Letterpress Book, 308, AGC, TSL.
18. Special Order No. 41 (Jones), 10 July 1875, AGC, TSL.
19. Johnson, *Mason County War*, 67–70.
20. Ibid., 72–73; Alexander, *Winchester Warriors*, 92; *Austin Daily Democratic Statesman*, 17 October 1875.
21. Johnson, *Mason County War*, 76.
22. Reminiscences of James B. Hawkins, Webb Collection.
23. Johnson, *Mason County War*, 82–83.
24. *Austin Daily Democratic Statesman*, 17 October 1875; Gillett, *Six Years With the Texas Rangers*, 74.
25. Johnson, *Mason County War*, 83.
26. Jones to Steele, 27 July 1875, AGC, TSL; *Frontier Echo* (Jacksboro, Texas), 28 July 1875.
27. *Dallas Daily Herald*, 20 August 1875.
28. General Order No. 5 (Jones), 5 August 1875, FBC, TSL.
29. Jones to Steele, 5 August 1875, AGC; Special Order No. 22 (Steele), 14 August 1875, FBC; Special Order No. 43 (Jones), 25 August 1875, AGC, TSL.
30. General Order No. 10 (Steele), 12 August 1875, General Orders Book, 47–49, AGC, FBC, TSL.
31. Johnson, *Mason County War*, 84–86.
32. *Fredericksburg Sentinel* as quoted in *San Antonio Daily Express*, 5 August 1875.
33. Roberts to Jones, 1 August 1875, FBC, TSL; Johnson, *Mason County War*, 88–89.
34. *Dallas Daily Herald*, 24 August 1875; Long to Roberts, 11 August 1875, AGC, TSL.
35. General Order No. 11 (Steele), 12 August 1875, General Orders Book, 49, AGC, FBC, TSL.
36. *Dallas Daily Herald*, 21 September 1875.
37. *San Antonio Daily Herald*, 18 August 1875, as quoted in Johnson, *Mason County War*, 92–93; *Austin Daily Democratic Statesman*, 22 August 1875; Gillett, *Six Years With the Texas Rangers*, 75.
38. Gillett, *Six Years With the Texas Rangers*, 75; Johnson, *Mason County War*, 95–96.
39. *Austin Daily Democratic Statesman*, 4 September 1875; *Galveston Daily News*, 4 and 7 September 1875; Record of Scouts for Company D, 31 August 1875, Webb Collection; Roberts, *Rangers and Sovereignty*, 67–75; Herman Lehmann, *Nine Years Among the Indians, 1870–1879* (Austin, Texas: Von Boeckmann-Jones, 1927), 98–104; Thomas P. Gillespie, "Fight on the Concho Plains," *True West* 10, no. 5 (May–June 1963), 32 *et seq.* Roberts refers to the red-haired Indian as Fisher, but was mistaken.
40. *San Antonio Daily Herald*, 6 September 1875.
41. Special Order No. 43 (Jones), 25 August 1875; Jones to Long, 25 August 1875, AGC, TSL.

42. Jones to Roberts, 27 August 1875, FBC, TSL.

43. Roberts, *Rangers and Sovereignty*, 81–82; Alexander, *Winchester Warriors*, 94–95; Mrs. D. W. Roberts, *A Woman's Reminiscences of Six Years in Camp with the Texas Rangers* (Austin, Texas: Von Boeckmann-Jones, 1928), 5.

44. Roberts, *Rangers and Sovereignty*, 81–82.

45. Jones to Coldwell, 27 August 1875, AGC, TSL.

46. Jones to Roberts, 6 September 1875, FBC; Jones to Coldwell, 6 September 1875, AGC, TSL.

47. Proclamation, 6 September 1875, Executive Record Book, 56; Letterpress Book No. 311, p. 466, TSL.

48. Henry M. Holmes to Coke, 8 September 1875, AGC, TSL; *Austin Daily Democratic Statesman*, 17 October 1875; Johnson, *Mason County War*, 98–99.

49. Jones to Steele, 28 October 1875, AGC, TSL; David Johnson, *John Ringo, King of the Cowboys: His Life and Times From the Hoo Doo War to Tombstone*, 2nd ed. (Denton, Texas: University of North Texas Press, 2007), 87.

50. Allen G. Hatley, "The Role of the Frontier Battalion During the Mason County Troubles," in *The Hoo Doo War: Portraits of a Lawless Time* (Ozark, Missouri: Dogwood Printing, 2003), 91–97.

51. Jones to Stevens, 17 September 1875, AGC, TSL.

52. Steele to Jones, 23 September 1875, Letterpress Book, 394, AGC, TSL.

53. Letter from Steele, 23 September 1875, Letterpress Book, 395, AGC, TSL.

54. Steele to W. T. Griffin, 23 September 1875, Letterpress Book, 398, AGC, TSL.

55. Steele to Jones, 23 September 1875, AGC, TSL.

56. Jones to Steele, 30 September 1875, AGC, TSL; *San Antonio Daily Express*, 6 October 1875.

57. Jones to Steele, 28 September 1878, AGC, TSL.

58. Jones to Steele, 30 September 1875, 28 October 1875, AGC, TSL.

59. Ibid., 28 October 1875, AGC, TSL.

60. Roberts, *Rangers and Sovereignty*, 90–91; Johnson, *Mason County War*, 116.

61. Petition to Major Jones, 4 October 1875; Jones to Steele, 28 October 1875, AGC, TSL.

62. Steele to Jones, 6 October 1875, Letterpress Book, 419, AGC, TSL.

63. Special Order No. 46 (Jones), 6 October 1875, AGC, TSL.

64. Peter R. Rose, *Essays on the Mason County War (Hoo Doo War), 1874–1876* (Austin, Texas: Peter R. Rose, 2002), 13; Wilkins, *Law Comes to Texas*, 74–75.

65. Jones to Steele, 28 October 1875, AGC, TSL.

66. Gillett, *Six Years With the Texas Rangers*, 77–78.

67. Ibid., 78.

68. Special Order No. 47 (Jones), 7 October 1875, FBC, TSL. See also Parsons and Brice, *N. O. Reynolds*, 63–64.

69. Roberts to Jones, 11 October 1875; Special Order No. 48 (Jones), 11 October 1875, AGC, TSL.

70. Jones to Roberts, 11 October 1875, FBC, TSL.

71. Ibid.

72. Jones to Steele, 12 October 1875, AGC, TSL.

73. Steele to Jones, 14 October 1875, Letterpress Book, 429, AGC, TSL.

74. Jones to Roberts, 16 October 1875, FBC, TSL.

75. Roberts to Jones, 17 October 1875, FBC, TSL.

76. Jones to Roberts, 18 October 1875, FBC, TSL.

77. Ibid., 21 October 1875.

78. Jones to Steele, 28 October 1875, AGC, TSL.

79. Jones to Steele, 20 October 1875; Jones to Coldwell, 25 October 1875, AGC, TSL; Margaret Bierschwale, *A History of Mason County, Texas, Through 1964*, ed. Julius E. DeVos (Mason, Texas: Mason County Historical Commission, 1998), 142.

80. *Austin Daily Democratic Statesman*, 14 November 1875.

81. Jones to Steele, 28 October 1875, AGC, TSL.

82. Ibid., 25 October 1875, AGC; General Order No. 6 (Jones), 25 October 1875, FBC, TSL.

Chapter 8: Gallant and Untiring

1. Jones to Steele, undated letter in November 1875, AGC, TSL.

2. *Galveston Daily News*, 17 November 1875.

3. Special Order No. 50 (Jones), 12 November 1875, FBC; Stevens to Steele, 12 November 1875, AGC; Special Order No. 24 (Steele), 22 November 1875, AGC, FBC, TSL.

4. Jones to Steele, 12 November 1875, AGC, TSL.

5. Roberts to Jones, 15 November 1875, FBC, TSL.

6. McNelly to Steele, 20 and 21 November 1875, AGC, TSL; *Galveston Daily News*, 21 November and 12 December 1875; *San Antonio Daily Express*, 24 November 1875; Parsons and Hall-Little, *Leander McNelly*, 221–233.

7. *Galveston Daily News*, 25 January 1876; Parsons and Hall-Little, *Leander McNelly*, 254–256.

8. General Order No. 7 (Jones), 30 November 1875, FBC, TSL.

9. Jones to Long, 4 December 1875, AGC, TSL.

10. Coldwell to Jones, 5 December 1875, AGC, TSL.

11. Steele to Jones, 17 December 1875; Steele to Coldwell, 17 December 1875, Letterpress Book, 11–12, AGC, TSL.

12. Coldwell to Jones, 25 December 1875, AGC, TSL.

13. Special Order No. 24 (Steele), 9 December 1875, AGC, FBC, TSL.

14. Special Order No. 52 (Jones), 14 December 1875, AGC, TSL.

15. Jones to Long, 14 December 1875, AGC, TSL.

16. G. W. Todd, Mason, to Jones, 14 December 1875, AGC, TSL.

17. *Corsicana Observer*, 25 December 1875.

18. Steele to Jones, 20 December 1875; Steele to Long, 20 December 1875, Letterpress Book, 18, AGC, TSL.

19. Long to Jones, 20 December 1875, AGC, TSL.

20. *Austin Daily Democratic Statesman*, 2 and 4 January 1876; Johnson, *Mason County War*, 143–144.

21. Steele to Long, 18 January 1876, Letterpress Book, 54–55, AGC, TSL.

22. Long to Steele, 28 January 1876, AGC, TSL.

23. Richard Coke, *Message From the Governor of Texas to the Fifteenth Legislature* (Houston: A. C. Gray, State Printer, 1876), 56.

24. Steele to Jones, 5 January 1876, AGC, TSL; *San Antonio Daily Express*, 4 January 1876.

25. Coldwell to Jones, 5 January 1876, AGC, TSL.

26. Steele to Coldwell, 5 January 1876, Letterpress Book, 33, AGC, TSL; *San Antonio Daily Express*, 7 January 1876.

27. *Galveston Daily News*, 5 January 1876.

28. Jones to Steele, 7 and 8 January 1876; Long to Jones, 26 December 1875 and 15 January 1876; Long to Steele, 30 January 1876; Special Order No. 27 (Steele), 2 February 1876, Letterpress Book, 87, AGC, TSL.

29. Steele to Coldwell, 7 January 1876, Letterpress Book, 36–37, AGC, TSL.

30. *Kerr County Frontiersman* as quoted in *Galveston Daily News*, 11 January 1876.

31. Coldwell to Jones, 11 January 1876, AGC, TSL.

32. Coldwell to Jones, 15 January 1876, AGC, TSL; *Galveston Daily News*, 29 January 1876.

33. *Galveston Daily News*, 10 February 1876.

34. *Corsicana Observer*, 22 January 1876.

35. Resolution of Mason County citizens, 27 January 1876, AGC, TSL; *San Antonio Daily Herald*, 31 January 1876; Johnson, *Mason County War*, 147.

36. Steele to Long, 28 January 1876, Letterpress Book, 62, AGC, TSL.

37. Long to Jones, 28 February 1876, AGC, TSL; *Frontier Echo*, 24 March 1876.

38. Johnson, *Mason County War*, 153. Cooley and John Ringo were transferred again to the Lampasas County jail, from which they escaped in April 1876. Cooley was reported to have subsequently died from "congestion of the brain," and Ringo left Texas and went on to notoriety at Tombstone, Arizona Territory. *Dallas Daily Herald*, 11 June 1876; Gillett, *Six Years With the Texas Rangers*, 80.

39. Jones to A. M. Hobby, 22 February 1876, Webb Collection.

40. Ibid.

41. John B. Jones, *Report of Maj. J. B. Jones, Commanding the Frontier Battalion, Texas State Troops, March 1876* (Houston: A. C. Gray, State Printer, 1876), 1–6.

42. General Order No. 9 (Jones), 1 March 1876, FBC, TSL.

43. Coke to Steele, 2 March 1876, Letterpress Book, 271, Records of Governor Coke, TSL.

44. Steele to Jones, 6 March 1876, Letterpress Book, 89, AGC, TSL.

45. Jones to Steele, 10 March 1876; Special Order No. 28 (Steele), 15 March 1876, Letterpress Book, 88, AGC, TSL.

46. *Corsicana Observer*, 25 March 1876.

47. Jones to Long, 26 March 1876, AGC, TSL.

48. Long to Jones, 3 April 1876; Jones to Steele, 13 April 1876, AGC, TSL.

49. Special Order No. 55 (Jones), 18 April 1876, AGC; Jones to Lt. C. H. Hamilton, 1 May 1876, FBC, TSL; *Dallas Daily Herald*, 23 April 1876; *Frontier Echo*, 28 April 1876.

50. *Galveston Daily News*, 2 May 1876; *Corsicana Observer*, 6 May 1876; *Austin Daily Democratic Statesman*, 16 June 1876.

51. Deed Records, Navarro County, Texas, vol. 26, p. 381.

52. Jones to Roberts, Coldwell, and Foster, 10 May 1876, AGC, TSL.

53. Jones to Coldwell, 26 May 1876, AGC, TSL.

54. *Corsicana Observer*, 27 May 1876.

55. Jones to Long and Coldwell, 13 June 1876; Jones to Hamilton and Foster, 16 June 1876, AGC, TSL; Gillett, *Six Years With the Texas Rangers*, 89.

56. Roberts to Jones, 18 June 1876, FBC, TSL.

57. Telegram, Jones to Steele, 28 June 1876, AGC, TSL.

58. Gillett, *Six Years With the Texas Rangers*, 89–91; *Corsicana Observer*, 12 August 1876; *San Antonio Daily Express*, 23 July 1876; *Galveston Daily News*, 17 August 1876.

59. Telegram, Jones to Steele, 14 July 1876, AGC, TSL.

60. Ibid., 15 July 1876.

61. Foster to Steele, 15 July 1876; telegram, Foster to Steele, 16 July 1876, AGC, TSL.

62. Telegram, Jones to Steele, 16 July 1876, AGC, TSL.

63. Ibid., 24 July 1876; *Galveston Daily News*, 25 August 1876.

64. Telegram, Jones to Steele, 7 August 1876, AGC, TSL; *Galveston Daily News*, 20 August 1876.

65. Telegram, Steele to Jones, 8 August 1876, Letterpress Book, 287, AGC, TSL.

66. Jones to Steele, 12 August 1876; Long to Steele, 12 August 1876; Special Order No. 33 (Steele), 23 August 1876, Letterpress Book, 91, AGC; Special Order No. 64 (Jones), 13 August 1876, FBC, TSL.

67. Roberts to Jones, 16 August 1876, AGC, TSL.

68. Maltby to Jones, 24 August 1876, AGC, TSL.

69. *General Laws of the State of Texas (15th Legislature)*, vol. 8, p. 250.

70. Telegram, Steele to Jones, 21 August 1876, Letterpress Book, 305, AGC, TSL.

71. Steele to Jones, 23 August 1876, Letterpress Book, 309–310, AGC, TSL.

72. William H. Steele, *Report of the Adjutant-General of the State of Texas for the Year Ending August 31st, 1876* (Galveston: Shaw & Blaylock, 1876), 4.

73. General Order No. 10 (Jones), 25 August 1876, AGC, FBC, TSL.

74. Jones to Steele, 26 August 1876; Coldwell to Coke, 28 August 1876, AGC, TSL.

75. Jones to Steele, 29 August 1876, AGC, TSL.

76. *Corsicana Observer*, 19 August 1876.
77. Special Order No. 67 (Jones), 29 August 1876, AGC; Special Order No. 68 (Jones), 1 September 1876, FBC, TSL; Alexander, *Winchester Warriors*, 114.
78. Special Order No. 67 (Jones), 29 August 1876, AGC, TSL.
79. Denton to Jones, 29 July 1876; Jones to Steele, 29 August 1876, AGC; Special Order No. 68 (Jones), 1 September 1876, FBC, TSL.
80. Jones to Steele, 31 August 1876, AGC, TSL.
81. Steele, *Adjutant-General Report*, 1876, 3–4.

Chapter 9: Terribly Tongue-Lashed

1. *San Antonio Daily Express*, 14 and 15 September 1876.
2. Ibid., 17 September 1876.
3. Ibid., 26 September 1876.
4. Ibid., 27 September 1876.
5. Ibid., 2 October 1876.
6. Steele to unknown officer, 12 September 1876, Letterpress Book, 339, AGC, TSL.
7. Steele to Hamilton, 14 September 1876, Letterpress Book, 343, AGC, TSL.
8. Wilkins, *The Law Comes to Texas*, 83.
9. Steele to "Comdg Officer, State Troops," 18 September 1876, Letterpress Book, 353, AGC, TSL.
10. *Austin Daily Democratic Statesman*, 20 September 1876.
11. Special Order No. 69 (Jones), 20 September 1876; Jones to Campbell, 20 September 1876; Jones to Hamilton, 20 September 1876, AGC, FBC, TSL.
12. *Corsicana Observer*, 23 September 1876.
13. Jones to Denton, 25 September 1876, AGC, TSL.
14. *Corsicana Observer*, 2 December 1876.
15. Special Order No. 70 (Jones), 25 September 1876; Jones to Denton, 25 and 26 September 1876; Jones to Dolan, 26 September 1876, AGC, TSL.
16. *Galveston Daily News*, 17 October 1876.
17. Ibid., 14 October 1876.
18. Jones to Moore, 21 October 1876, AGC, TSL; *San Antonio Daily Express*, 25 October 1876.
19. *Austin Daily Democratic Statesman* as quoted in *San Antonio Daily Express*, 24 October 1876.
20. Emerson Hough, *The Story of the Outlaw: A Study of the Western Desperado* (New York: Outing Publishing, 1907), 316.
21. *Results of Operations of State Troops Since August 1, 1876, to December 31, 1881*, 160, TSL; *San Antonio Daily Express*, 31 October 1876; *Austin Daily Democratic Statesman*, 28 October 1876; *Galveston Daily News*, 28 and 29 October 1876.

22. Steele to Charles Williams, 27 October 1876, Letterpress Book, 434; Steele to grand jury foreman of unknown county, 28 October 1876, Letterpress Book, 436, AGC, TSL.
23. *Austin Daily Democratic Statesman*, 29 October 1876.
24. Ibid., 1 November 1876.
25. *Austin Daily Democratic Statesman*, 7 November 1876; *Galveston Daily News*, 9 November 1876, which incorrectly credited the arrest to a detachment of the Battalion's Company C.
26. *Fanny J. Halbert v. John B. Jones*, Cause No. 1689, vol. G, p. 72, Civil Minutes, Navarro County, Texas; Deed Records, Navarro County, Texas, vol. W, p. 195.
27. Jones to citizens of Menard County, 6 November 1876, AGC, TSL.
28. Steele to Judge A. Blocker, 17 November 1876, Letterpress Book, 469; telegram, Jones to Steele, 17 November 1876, AGC, TSL; *Galveston Daily News*, 18 November 1876.
29. Jones to Steele, 17 and 20 November 1876, 6 December 1876, AGC, TSL; *Galveston Daily News*, 28 November 1876.
30. *Austin Daily Democratic Statesman*, 5 November 1876.
31. Ibid., 17 November 1876; *Galveston Daily News*, 17 November 1876; Steele to Ira E. Lloyd, 16 November 1876, Letterpress Book, 467, AGC, TSL.
32. *Results of Operations*, 161; *Dallas Daily Commercial* as quoted in *Galveston Daily News*, 24 November 1876.
33. *Ellsworth* (Kansas) *Reporter*, 30 November 1876; *Leavenworth* (Kansas) *Daily Times*, 5 December 1876; Monthly Report, Company C, 30 November 1876, AGC, TSL; *Corsicana Observer*, 2 December 1876.
34. *Austin Daily Democratic Statesman*, 13 and 21 December 1876.
35. Denton to Jones, 18 November 1876, AGC, TSL.
36. Jones to Steele, 24 November 1876; Special Order No. 80 (Jones), 5 December 1876; telegram and letter, Jones to Steele, 5 December 1876; Special Orders No. 35 and 36 (Steele), 8 December 1876, Letterpress Book, 92, AGC, TSL.
37. Special Order No. 78 (Jones), 30 November 1876, FBC; Nicholson to Steele, 30 November 1876; Jones to Steele, 30 November 1876; Special Order No. 37 (Steele), 8 December 1876, Letterpress Book, 93, AGC, TSL; *Galveston Daily News*, 22 December 1876.
38. Letter of resignation by Coke, 1 December 1876, Records of the Governor; undated petition to Hubbard, AGC, TSL.
39. Undated petition to Hubbard, AGC, TSL.
40. C. E. Poole to Jones, 28 February 1877, AGC, TSL.
41. Steele to Jones, 26 March 1877, AGC, TSL.
42. Jones to Steele, 27 May 1877, AGC, TSL.
43. Jones to Judge Hiram Lightner, 27 March 1877, AGC, TSL.
44. Petition to Hubbard, ca. April 1877; C. C. Poole to Jones, 9 April 1877, AGC, TSL.

45. Telegram, Jones to Steele, 13 December 1876, AGC, TSL; *Galveston Daily News*, 14 December 1876.

46. Gillett, *Six Years With the Texas Rangers*, 99–100.

47. Dolan to Jones, 15 December 1876 and 2 December 1877; Jones to Sparks, 16 December 1876, AGC, TSL.

48. Coldwell to Jones, 3 January 1877, AGC, TSL; *Report of Operations*, 101; *San Antonio Daily Express*, 4 January 1877.

49. *San Antonio Daily Express*, 20 and 21 December 1876; *Austin Daily Democratic Statesman*, 23 December 1876.

50. Telegram, Steele to Jones, 28 December 1876, Letterpress Book, 47, AGC, TSL.

51. Telegram, Jones to Steele, 31 December 1876 and 12 January 1877, AGC, TSL.

52. It may be noted that in 1880 David C. Paul was the sheriff of Rapides Parish in Louisiana. 1880 United States Census (Rapides Parish, Louisiana).

53. *Dallas Daily Herald*, 24 January 1877; Robert K. DeArment, *Bravo of the Brazos: John Larn of Fort Griffin, Texas* (Norman, Oklahoma: University of Oklahoma Press, 2003), 91–93.

54. Campbell to Jones, 31 January 1877, FBC, TSL.

55. General Order No. 14 (Steele), 18 January 1877, Letterpress Book, 52; Steele to railroad executives, 20 January 1877, Letterpress Book, 77–78, AGC, TSL; *San Antonio Daily Express*, 25 January 1877; *Galveston Daily News*, 23 January and 6 February 1877; Parsons and Hall-Little, *Captain L. H. McNelly*, 292.

56. Steele to Hubbard, 1 March 1877, Letterpress Book, 142–144, AGC, records of Gov. Hubbard, TSL.

57. *Galveston Daily News*, 30 January 1877; C. L. Douglas, *Famous Texas Feuds* (Dallas: Turner, 1936), 129–134; Bill O'Neal, *The Bloody Legacy of Pink Higgins* (Austin, Texas: Eakin Press, 1999), 37–38.

58. John W. Swindells to F. D. Walker, 29 January 1877, Letterpress Book No. 314, 96, Records of Gov. Hubbard; Sparks to Jones, 9 February 1877, AGC, TSL.

59. O'Neal, *Pink Higgins*, 41–42; Frederick Nolan, *Bad Blood: The Life and Times of the Horrell Brothers* (Stillwater, Oklahoma: Barbed Wire Press, 1994), 108.

60. *Report of Operations*, 163.

61. *Lampasas Dispatch* as quoted in *Galveston Daily News*, 6 March 1877.

62. *Results of Operations*, 163.

63. Dolan to Jones, 23 January 1877; petition to Dolan, 24 January 1877, AGC, TSL.

64. Special Order No. 85 (Jones), 8 February 1877, FBC; Dolan to Jones, 15 February 1877, AGC, TSL.

65. Jones to Coldwell, 8 and 10 February 1877, AGC, TSL.

66. Dolan to Jones, 15 February 1877, AGC; *Report of Operations*, 250–251, TSL.

67. Campbell to Jones, 17 February 1877, FBC, TSL; *Fort Worth Daily Democrat*, 22 February 1877.

68. Campbell to Jones, 28 February 1877, FBC, TSL.

69. Jones to Messrs. Martin and Clark, 28 February 1877, FBC, TSL.

70. Jones to Campbell, 28 February 1877, FBC, TSL.

71. Kisinger to Jones, 11 March 1877, FBC, TSL.

72. Special Order No. 87 (Jones), 20 March 1877; Jones to Campbell, 20 March 1877, FBC, TSL.

73. Norman Young to Jones, 4 June 1877; Young to Hubbard, 28 June 1877; Jones to Campbell, 28 June 1877; Campbell to Jones, 7 July 1877, FBC; Kisinger to Jones, 13 August 1877; Jones to Young, 20 September 1877, AGC, TSL.

74. Stevens to Jones, 1 March 1877, FBC, TSL.

75. Jones to Campbell, 20 March 1877, FBC, TSL.

76. Ibid.

77. Campbell to Jones, 29 March 1877, FBC, TSL.

78. *Galveston Daily News*, 3 March 1877.

79. Felix Burton to Jones, 22 February 1877, AGC, TSL.

80. *Galveston Daily News*, 28 February 1877.

81. Waddill to Jones, 27 February 1877, AGC, TSL; Parsons and Brice, *N. O. Reynolds*, 95–96.

82. Undated Statement of Arrests for March 1877, Company C, AGC, TSL; Wayne T. Walker, "Major John B. Jones: Ranger Who Tamed West Texas," *Real West* 24, no. 176 (April 1981), 10.

83. General Order No. 14 (Jones), 1 March 1877, AGC, TSL.

84. *Corsicana Observer*, 10 and 17 March 1877.

85. *Dallas Daily Herald*, 22 March 1877.

86. General Order No. 15 (Jones), 20 March 1877, AGC, TSL.

87. Newspaper advertisement, 5 March 1877, AGC, TSL.

88. Judge McFarland to Jones, 27 March 1877, AGC, TSL.

89. Petition to Gov. Hubbard, 8 April 1877, AGC, TSL.

90. *San Antonio Daily Express*, 13 April 1877; *Galveston Daily News*, 17 April 1877. There is no official report of this killing, and Ranger records show a James Quigley arrested for murder by Company A on January 20, 1878. *Report of Operations*, 108.

91. Jones to Col. H. C. King, 12 April 1877, AGC, TSL.

92. *San Antonio Daily Express*, 19 April 1877.

93. Sgt. M. F. Moore to Jones, 22 March 1877, AGC; *Report of Operations*, 192, TSL.

94. Jones to H. M. Holmes, 31 March 1877, AGC, TSL.

95. Jones to Judge W. A. Blackburn, 2 April 1877, AGC, TSL.

96. Sparks to Jones, 30 March 1877, AGC; *Report of Operations*, 163, TSL; *Galveston Daily News*, 5 April 1877; *Austin Daily Democratic Statesman,* 31 March 1877; Nolan, *Bad Blood*, 111–112.

97. Blackburn to Jones, 30 March 1877, AGC, TSL.

98. Jones to Sparks, 2 April 1877, AGC, TSL.

99. *Austin Daily Democratic Statesman*, 25 April 1877.

100. Blackburn to Jones, 6 April 1877, AGC, TSL.

101. *Report of Operations*, 192, TSL; *Galveston Daily News*, 11 April 1877; Sammy Tise, *Texas County Sheriffs* (Albuquerque, New Mexico: Oakwood Printing, 1989), 307.

102. Jones to Moore, 11 April 1877; Jones to Dolan, 11 April 1877. AGC, TSL.

103. Jones to Steele, 12 April 1877, AGC, TSL.

104. Jones to Frio County citizens, 13 April 1877, AGC, TSL; *Galveston Daily News*, 24 April and 1 May 1877.

105. Petition to Jones and response, 13 April 1877, AGC, TSL.

106. Letter from Hatch, McDonnell, and Romey, 18 April 1877, AGC, TSL.

107. Dolan to Jones, 19 April 1877, AGC, TSL.

108. Jones to Steele, 16 April 1877, AGC, TSL.

109. Telegram, Jones to Steele, 21 April 1877; Jones to Steele, 6 May 1877, AGC, TSL; *Galveston Daily News*, 15 May 1877; Wilkins, *Law Comes to Texas*, 126–129.

110. *San Antonio Daily Express*, 22 April 1877.

111. *Galveston Daily News*, 15 May 1877.

112. Richard Maxwell Brown, *Strain of Violence: Historical Studies of American Violence and Vigilantism* (New York: Oxford University Press, 1975), 247–248.

113. Jones to Blackburn, 23 April 1877, AGC, TSL.

114. Jones to Steele, 24 and 27 April 1877, AGC; *Report of Operations*, 102, TSL; Record of Scouts by Company A, April 1877, Webb Collection.

115. Steele to Sparks, 27 April 1877, Letterpress Book, 260, AGC, TSL.

116. Petition dated 25 April 1877, AGC, TSL.

117. Jones to Steele, 28 April 1877, AGC, TSL; *Galveston Daily News*, 29 April 1877; Parsons and Brice, *N. O. Reynolds*, 98–105.

118. *Galveston Daily News*, 8 May 1877.

119. Jones to Steele, 6 May 1877, AGC, TSL; *Galveston Daily News*, 15 May 1877; O. C. Fisher, *It Occurred in Kimble* (Houston: The Anson Jones Press, 1937), 207–212.

120. Utley, *Lone Star Justice*, 180.

Chapter 10: A Bedouin in the Saddle

1. Jones to Steele, 6 May 1877, AGC, TSL.

2. *Results of Operations*, 103; email from David Johnson, 7 June 2011.

3. Proclamation, 11 May 1877, Executive Record Book (Hubbard), 668, TSL.

4. Telegram, Sheriff Wilson to Jones, 11 May 1877; telegram, Jones to Steele, 15 May 1877, AGC, TSL.

5. *Galveston Daily News*, 20 May 1877.

6. Ibid., 19 May 1877; Steele to Sparks, 19 May 1877, Letterpress Book, 302; Hall to Steele, 31 May 1877, AGC; J. W. Swindells to Judge J. R. Fleming, 22 May 1877,

Letterpress Book, 137, Records of Gov. Hubbard; Mathis & Fulton to Hubbard, 28 May 1877, Records of Gov. Hubbard, TSL: Robert Ernst, *Deadly Affrays: The Violent Deaths of the U. S. Marshals* ([Avon: Indiana]: Scarlet Mask Enterprises, 2006), 127–128. The two brothers were finally arrested several years later. They were then taken from the Comanche jail by a mob on November 11, 1883, and lynched. *Gatesville Sun*, 23 November 1883.

7. Jones to Sparks, 16 May 1877, AGC, TSL.
8. Sparks to Jones, 5 July 1877, AGC, TSL; *Lampasas Dispatch*, 31 May 1877.
9. Fleming to Jones, 21 April 1877, AGC, TSL.
10. Telegram, Jones to Steele, 25 May 1877, AGC, TSL.
11. Jan Devereaux, *Pistols, Petticoats & Poker, The Real Lottie Deno: No Lies or Alibis.* (Silver City, New Mexico: High-Lonesome Books, 2008), 123.
12. Steele to Hubbard, 9 May 1877, Letterpress Book, 278, AGC, TSL.
13. *Galveston Daily News*, 1 June 1877.
14. Hubbard to Judge T. M. Paschal, 25 May 1877, Letterpress Book, 149–152, Records of Gov. Hubbard, TSL.
15. Petition, 26 May 1877; W. R. Friend to Steele, 27 May 1877, AGC, TSL.
16. H. Runge to Steele, 26 June 1877, AGC, TSL; *San Antonio Daily Express*, 23 June 1877; *Galveston Daily News*, 13 June 1877; *Austin Daily Democratic Statesman*, 23 June 1877; *Dallas Daily Herald*, 16 and 19 June 1877.
17. *Galveston Daily News*, 5 July and 5 September 1877.
18. *Lampasas Dispatch* as quoted in *Austin Daily Democratic Statesman*, 19 June 1877; Nolan, *Bad Blood*, 116–119; O'Neal, *Pink Higgins*, 45–49.
19. *San Antonio Daily Express*, 12 June 1877.
20. Foster to Steele, 7 June 1877; Jones to Steele, 7 and 15 June 1877; Special Order No. 92 (Jones), 7 June 1877, AGC, TSL.
21. Jones to Steele, 8 June 1877, AGC, TSL.
22. *Results of Operations*, 74, TSL.
23. Ibid., 14 June 1877.
24. Jones to Sparks, 15 June 1877; Jones to Steele, 15 June 1877, AGC, TSL.
25. Jones to Steele, 6 July 1877, AGC, TSL.
26. *Austin Daily Democratic Statesman*, 16 June 1877.
27. Jones to Coldwell, 25 June 1877; undated report of operations of Companies A and C during June 1877, AGC, TSL.
28. *Fort Worth Daily Democrat*, 1 July 1877; *Galveston Daily News*, 4 July 1877; *San Antonio Daily Express*, 7 July 1877.
29. Dolan to Jones, 18 July 1877, AGC, TSL; *San Antonio Daily Express*, 12, 17, and 29 July 1877; 8 July 1879; *Galveston Daily News*, 25 December 1878.
30. *San Antonio Daily Express*, 11 September 1877.
31. Dolan to Jones, 18 July 1877, AGC, TSL.
32. Dolan to Jones, 31 July 1877, AGC, TSL; *San Antonio Daily Express*, 29 July 1877.

33. *San Antonio Daily Express*, 25 July 1877, 8 July 1879; *Dallas Daily Herald*, 19 July 1877.

34. Jones to Steele, 11 July 1877, AGC, TSL.

35. Letter from Williams Ranch to Jones, 21 July 1877; Jones to citizens, 22 July 1877; Jones to Steele, 22 July 1877, AGC, TSL; *Galveston Daily News*, 25 and 26 July, 9 August 1877.

36. Jones to Steele, 22 July 1877, AGC, TSL.

37. Jones to Steele, 25 July 1877, AGC, TSL.

38. *Results of Operations*, 76, TSL.

39. *Lampasas Dispatch*, 9 August 1877; *San Antonio Daily Express*, 10 August 1877; Roberts, *Rangers and Sovereignty*, 167–170; Nolan, *Bad Blood*, 125–127; O'Neal, *Pink Higgins*, 50–54; Parsons and Brice, *N. O. Reynolds*, 124–126.

40. Jones to Steele, 28 July 1877; Report of N. O. Reynolds, 31 July 1877, AGC, TSL.

41. Jones to Steele, 31 July 1877, AGC, TSL.

42. Statement from Horrell Brothers to Pink Higgins et al., 30 July 1877, AGC, TSL; *Galveston Daily News*, 8 August 1877.

43. Higgins et al. to the Horrell Brothers, 2 August 1877, AGC, TSL; *Galveston Daily News*, 8 August 1877; *Austin Daily Democratic Statesman*, 10 August 1877; *Dallas Daily Herald*, 10 August 1877.

44. M. G. Northington, "I Saw Them Stack Their Guns," *Frontier Times* 36, No. 2 (Spring 1962), 18 et seq.

45. *Lampasas Dispatch*, 9 August 1877.

46. Ibid.

47. Telegram, J. W. Warren to Jones, 6 August 1877; undated report of operations for Reynolds' detachment, 1–24 August 1877, AGC, TSL; *Daily State Gazette* [Austin], 7 August 1877.

48. *Galveston Daily News*, 15 August 1877.

49. Ibid., 26 September 1877.

50. General Order No. 16 (Jones), 9 August 1877, AGC, TSL.

51. *Galveston Daily News*, 14 August 1877; *Austin Daily Democratic Statesman*, 15 August 1877.

52. Telegrams, Jones to Coldwell and Dolan, 15 August 187, AGC, TSL; *Galveston Daily News*, 17 August 1877.

53. Jones to Steele, 16 August 1877; Jones to Moore, Sparks, and Campbell, 20 August 1877, AGC, TSL; *Dallas Daily Herald*, 22 August 1877.

54. Jones to Steele, 20 August 1877, AGC, TSL; Parsons and Brice, *N. O. Reynolds*, 146–147.

55. Jones to Steele, 20 August 1877, AGC, TSL.

56. Coldwell to Jones, 22 August 1877, FBC; General Order No. 20 (Steele), 24 August 1877, AGC, FBC, TSL.

57. Coldwell to Jones, 9 September 1877; Jones to Coldwell, 20 September 1877, AGC, TSL.

58. See Rick Miller, *Bloody Bill Longley: The Mythology of a Gunfighter*, 2nd ed. (Denton, Texas: University of North Texas Press, 2011) for a full account of Longley and his criminal career.

59. Rick Miller, *Bounty Hunter* (College Station, Texas: Creative Publishing, 1988), 80–98. See also Chuck Parsons, *The Capture of John Wesley Hardin* (College Station, Texas: Creative Publishing, 1978), and Jesse Earle Bowden and William S. Cummins, *Texas Desperado in Florida* (Pensacola, Florida: Pensacola Historical Society, 2002).

60. *Galveston Daily News*, 11 September 1877.

61. Ibid., 7 October 1877; Leona Bruce, *Banister Was There* (Fort Worth, Texas: Branch-Smith, 1968), 15–16.

62. Steele to Jones, 27 August 1877, AGC; Hubbard to Gen. E. O. C. Ord, 27 August 1877, Letterpress Book, 418–420, Records of Gov. Hubbard, TSL.

63. Steele to Jones, 28 August 1877; General Order No. 17 (Jones), 7 September 1877, AGC, TSL.

64. Jones to Steele, 29 August 1877, AGC, TSL.

65. Steele to Jones, 31 August 1877, AGC, TSL.

66. Report of operations of Reynolds' detachment, 27–31 August 1877, AGC, TSL; *Galveston Daily News*, 4 September 1877; *Austin Daily Democratic Statesman*, 4 September 1877.

67. Gillett, *Six Years With the Texas Rangers*, 118–124.

68. Petition to Jones, 30 August 1877, AGC, TSL.

69. Worcester to Jones, 31 August 1877; citizens to Jones, 31 August 1877, AGC, TSL.

70. Moore to Jones, 6 September 1877, AGC; Special Order No. 45 (Steele), 19 September 1877, Letterpress Book, 95, AGC, FBC, TSL.

71. Petition to Jones, 5 September 1877; L. P. Sieker to Jones, 12 September 1877, AGC, TSL.

72. Roberts to Jones, 15 September 1877, AGC, TSL.

73. Jones to Coldwell, 20 September 1877, AGC, TSL.

74. Jones to Worcester, 20 September 1877, AGC, TSL.

75. Jones to Coldwell, 20 September 1877, AGC, TSL.

76. Michael Barr, *A Rumble in the Cedar Brakes: Central Texas in the 1870s* (Austin, Texas: Morgan Printing, 2010), 140–143; *Gatesville Sun* as quoted in *Dallas Daily Herald*, 16 September 1877.

77. W. A. Bridges to Steele, no date, Webb Collection; lessees of state penitentiary to Jones, 5 September 1877; W. B. Crawford to Jones, 10 September 1877; Thomas J. Goree to Steele, 21 September 1877; Goree to unknown person, 21 September 1877, AGC, TSL.

78. *Corsicana Observer*, 15 September 1877; *Dallas Daily Herald*, 20 September 1877.

79. *Comanche Chief* as quoted in *Austin Daily Democratic Statesman*, 27 September 1877; *Lampasas Dispatch*, 27 September 1877; *Fort Worth Daily Democrat*, 23 September 1877; Webb, *Texas Rangers*, 341.

80. Jones to Steele, 29 September 1877; General Order No. 21 (Steele), 29 September 1877, Letterpress Book, 56; Jones to Roberts, 29 September 1877, AGC, TSL; *Galveston Daily News*, 30 September 1877.

81. Paul Cool, *Salt Warriors: Insurgency on the Rio Grande* (College Station, Texas: Texas A&M University Press, 2008), 2.

82. *Austin Daily Democratic Statesman*, 25 June 1875.

83. For example, see laudatory praise of Cardis by Howard in *Austin Daily Democratic Statesman*, 21 November 1873.

84. *San Antonio Daily Herald*, 5 July 1877; *San Antonio Daily Express*, 7 October 1877; *Galveston Daily News*, 10 October 1877.

85. "El Paso Troubles in Texas," Letter From Secretary of War, Executive Document No. 93, 45th United States Congress, 106–197.

86. Ibid., 99–100; Cool, *Salt Warriors*, 116–117.

87. "El Paso Troubles in Texas," 140; *San Antonio Daily Express*, 4 October 1877.

88. "El Paso Troubles in Texas," 152; Hubbard to A. J. Fountain, 5 October 1877, Letterpress Book, 97, Records of Gov. Hubbard, TSL.

89. "El Paso Troubles in Texas," 142, 152; *Galveston Daily News*, 6 October 1877; *Mesilla Valley Independent*, 6 October 1877, as quoted in *Galveston Daily News*, 20 October 1870.

90. "El Paso Troubles in Texas," 141.

91. Ibid., 152–153; *San Antonio Daily Express*, 25 October 1877; Cool, *Salt Warriors*, 121.

92. "El Paso Troubles in Texas," 142.

93. Cardis to Hubbard, 9 October 1877, Webb Collection.

94. *Austin Daily Democratic Statesman*, 5 October 1877.

95. Jones to T. M. Sparks, 6 October 1877, AGC, TSL.

96. Miles to Jones, 15 October 1877, AGC, TSL.

97. Joseph Magoffin to Hubbard, 10 October 1877, Webb Collection; *Mesilla Valley Independent* as quoted in *San Antonio Daily Express*, 30 October 1877; "El Paso Troubles in Texas," 59–61, 63–64.

98. Joseph Magoffin to Hubbard, 12 October 1877, AGC, TSL.

99. *San Antonio Daily Express*, 31 October 1877.

100. *Galveston Daily News*, 16 October 1877; "El Paso Troubles in Texas," 153.

101. Hubbard to Judge Allen Blacker, 22 October 1877, Letterpress Book, 305, Records of Gov. Hubbard; Steele to Jones, 24 October 1877, AGC, TSL.

102. General Order No. 19 (Jones), 20 October 1877, AGC, TSL.

Chapter 11: Here Comes the Rangers!

1. *Austin Daily Democratic Statesman*, 24 October 1877; *Galveston Daily News*, 24 October 1877.

2. "El Paso Troubles in Texas," 154.

3. Ibid., 143; Steele to Jones, 12 November 1877, FBC, TSL.

4. "El Paso Troubles in Texas," 154. In an unsourced statement, Jones supposedly rode the train north to Topeka, Kansas, then southwest to Santa Fe, from where he took a stagecoach south to Mesilla. Cool, *Salt Warriors*, 138; C. L. Sonnichsen, *The El Paso Salt War of 1877* (El Paso, Texas: Texas Western Press, 1973), 36.

5. "El Paso Troubles in Texas," 155.

6. Kerber to Jones, 8 November 1877, AGC, TSL.

7. "El Paso Troubles in Texas," 99.

8. Ibid., 100; *San Antonio Daily Express*, 27 November 1877; C. L. Sonnichsen, *Pass of the North: Four Centuries on the Rio Grande* (El Paso, Texas: Texas Western Press, 1968), 201–202.

9. "Texas Frontier Troubles," *Report of Committee on Foreign Affairs on the Relations of the United States With Mexico* (Washington D. C.: Government Printing Office, 1878), 60–63; *Houston Telegram* as quoted in *Galveston Daily News*, 20 December 1877.

10. "El Paso Troubles in Texas," 155.

11. Ibid.

12. Ibid.

13. Utley, *Lone Star Justice*, 194; Cool, *Salt Warriors*, 140–141; *Austin Globe-Democrat* as quoted in *Denison Daily News*, 30 December 1877.

14. "El Paso Troubles in Texas," 79; Jones to Steele, 12 November 1877, AGC, TSL.

15. Howard to Jones, 13 November 1877, Webb Collection.

16. Cool, *Salt Warriors*, 143; Sonnichsen, *Pass of the North*, 202.

17. Special Order No. 109 (Jones), 12 November 1877, FBC, TSL.

18. *Houston Telegram* as quoted in *Galveston Daily News, 20 December 1877.*

19. Bob Alexander, "Tucker X Texas = Trouble!" *Journal,* Wild West History Association 1, no. 3 (June 2008), 9.

20. Paul Cool, "The Many Lives and Suggested Death of Jim McDaniels," *Revenge! And Other True Tales of the Old West*, ed. Sharon A. Cunningham and Mark Boardman ([Lafayette, Indiana]: Scarlet Mask, 2004), 21–36.

21. Special Order No. 110 (Jones), 15 November 1877, FBC, TSL.

22. Jones to Steele, 18 November 1877, FBC, TSL.

23. "El Paso Troubles in Texas," 80.

24. Ibid.

25. Telegram, Jones to Steele, 18 November 1877, FBC, TSL.

26. Steele to Jones, 19 November 1877, FBC, TSL; *Galveston Daily News*, 21 November 1877.

27. Telegram, Jones to Steele, 20 November 1877, FBC, TSL.

28. Alexander, "Tucker X Texas = Trouble!," 9.

29. *Mason News-Item* as quoted in *San Antonio Daily Express*, 8 December 1877; Gillett, *Six Years With the Texas Rangers*, 127–129; Parsons and Brice, *N. O. Reynolds,*

166–167. Dell Dublin was later acquitted of murder in Kimble County in November 1878, as was Lew Cathey. *Galveston Daily News*, 12 November 1878.

30. Hiram Lightner to Jones, 4 December 1877, AGC, TSL.

31. Sparks to Jones, 10 December 1877; Special Order No. 50 (Steele), 10 December 1877.

32. Special Order No. 51 (Steele), 19 December 1877; Special Order No. 52 (Steele), 22 December 1877, AGC, TSL.

33. Jones to Steele, 29 December 1877, AGC, TSL.

34. Special Order No. 54 (Steele), 29 December 1877, AGC, TSL.

35. Jones to Dolan, 31 December 1877, AGC, TSL.

36. Jerry Sinise, *George Washington Arrington: Civil War Spy, Texas Ranger, Sheriff and Rancher.* (Burnet, Texas: Eakin Press, 1979), 18–19; Allen G. Hatley, "Cap Arrington: Adventurer, Ranger and Sheriff," *Wild West* 14, no. 1 (June 2001).

37. Jones to Arrington, 8 January 1878, FBC, TSL; Walter Prescott Webb, *The Story of the Texas Rangers* (New York: Grossett & Dunlap, 1957), 70.

38. John B. Tays to Jones, 29 November 1877, AGC, TSL.

39. John B. Tays to Jones, 30 November 1877, Webb Collection.

40. Jones to Maj. A. M. Lea, 22 December 1877; affidavit, A. H. Arnett, 22 December 1877, AGC, TSL.

41. *Galveston Daily News*, 6 and 26 December 1877.

42. Ibid., 14 December 1877.

43. Ibid., 26 December 1877.

44. Jones to Maj. A. M. Lea, 22 December 1877, AGC, TSL. Hurlock was again arrested for land fraud in October 1879. *Galveston Daily News*, 9 October 1879.

45. "El Paso Troubles in Texas," 108–109.

46. *Dallas Daily Herald*, 16 December 1877; Cool, *Salt Warriors*, 164–165.

47. "El Paso Troubles in Texas," 145–146; *Dallas Daily Herald*, 16 December 1877; *San Antonio Daily Express*, 16 December 1877.

48. *San Antonio Daily Express*, 15 December 1877; *Galveston Daily News*, 19 December 1877.

49. Jones was not a lawyer.

50. *Houston Telegram* as quoted in *Dallas Daily Herald*, 22 December 1877.

51. Cool, *Salt Warriors*, 170–171.

52. "El Paso Troubles in Texas," 146.

53. Cool, *Salt Warriors*, 191–193.

54. Ibid., 193–195; "El Paso Troubles in Texas," 157–158; *Galveston Daily News*, 1 January 1878.

55. "El Paso Troubles in Texas," 96–98; *Mesilla Valley Independent* as quoted in *Galveston Daily News*, 8 February 1878; *Dallas Daily Herald*, 5 January 1878.

56. "El Paso Troubles in Texas," 158.

57. Tays to Jones, 30 December 1877, Webb Collection.

58. *Galveston Daily News*, 19 December 1877; *Denison Daily News*, 5 January 1878.

59. *St. Louis Globe-Democrat* as quoted in *Denison Daily News*, 30 December 1877.

60. *Galveston Daily News*, 11 January 1878.

61. Alexander, "Tucker X Texas = Trouble!," 12. For information about the Silver City militia group, see Bob Alexander, *Dangerous Dan Tucker: New Mexico's Deadly Lawman* (Silver City, New Mexico: High-Lonesome Books, 2001), 37–43.

62. Cool, "Jim McDaniels," 30–31.

63. Cool, *Salt Warriors*, 212–225; "El Paso Troubles in Texas," 85–86, 88–91, 93–94, 115–116.

64. Jones to Tays, 8 January 1878, AGC, TSL.

65. Utley, *Lone Star Justice*, 195.

66. Cool, *Salt Warriors*, 259.

67. *San Antonio Daily Herald*, 3 January 1878.

68. "El Paso Troubles in Texas," 5.

69. Telegram, John C. Thompson to Jones, 2 January 1878, AGC, TSL.

70. "El Paso Troubles in Texas," 86, 102–103, 112; *Galveston Daily News*, 19 February 1878. The victim's name has been spelled "Frazer," but Ranger records show it to be "Frazier."

71. Cool, *Salt Warriors*, 247–248.

72. "El Paso Troubles in Texas," 71.

73. Reynolds to Jones, 3 January 1878; telegram, Reynolds to Steele, 2 January 1878; telegram, Reynolds to Steele, 3 January 1878, AGC, TSL; *Austin Daily Democratic Statesman*, 12 January 1878; *Waco Examiner and Patron*, 11 January 1878; Gillett, *Six Years With the Texas Rangers*, 130–134.

74. *Austin Daily Democratic Statesman*, 17 February 1878.

75. Jones to Reynolds, 8 January 1878, AGC, TSL.

76. Ida Miller to Fritz Tegener, 21 March 1878, AGC, TSL; Parsons and Brice, *N. O. Reynolds*, 181–182.

77. Petition to Jones, 2 January 1878; Special Order No. 115 (Jones), 3 January 1878, AGC, TSL; *San Antonio Daily Herald*, 4 January 1878; *Dallas Daily Herald*, 6 January 1878.

78. *Austin Daily Democratic Statesman*, 9 January 1878.

79. Hubbard to Gen. E. O. C. Ord, 30 January 1878, Letterpress Book, 463, Records of Gov. Hubbard, TSL; *Fort Worth Daily Democrat*, 16 January 1878; *Galveston Daily News*, 5 February 1878.

80. See *Report of Committee on Foreign Affairs on the Relations of the U. S. with Mexico*, 53–62.

81. Gillett, *Six Years With the Texas Rangers*, 134–143.

82. Reynolds to Duvall Beale, 20 January 1878, AGC, TSL; *Lampasas Dispatch*, 7 February 1878.

83. Reynolds to Jones, 22 January 1878, AGC, TSL.

84. Telegram, Hubbard to Col. King, 23 January 1878, Letterpress Book, 418, Records of Gov. Hubbard, TSL; "El Paso Troubles in Texas," 6.

85. Jones to Dolan, 8 February 1878, AGC, TSL..

86. Steele to Jones, 8 February 1878, AGC, TSL; "El Paso Troubles in Texas," 48.

87. Telegram, Jones to Steele, 19 February 1878; telegram, Steele to Jones, 19 February 1878, AGC, TSL; "El Paso Troubles in Texas," 48–49.

88. *Galveston Daily News*, 22 February 1878.

Chapter 12: A Manly and Vigorous Effort

1. General Order No. 25 (Steele), 21 February 1878, Letterpress Book, 58, AGC, TSL.

2. *Galveston Daily News*, 22 February 1878; Gillett, *Six Years With the Texas Rangers*, 138–143; Parsons and Brice, *N. O. Reynolds*, 192.

3. *San Antonio Daily Express*, 23 February 1878.

4. Steele to Jones, 25 February 1878, AGC, TSL; "El Paso Troubles in Texas," 49.

5. Statement, 27 February 1878, AGC, TSL; "El Paso Troubles in Texas," 49.

6. Jones to Steele, 27 February 1878, AGC, TSL.

7. Miller, *Sam Bass & Gang*, 45–70.

8. Ibid., 107.

9. Proclamation, 23 February 1878, Executive Record Book (Gov. Hubbard), 470, TSL.

10. Miller, *Sam Bass & Gang*, 126–132; *Results of Operations of State Troops*, 15–16, TSL.

11. Undated testimony of Blacker, FBC, TSL; *Galveston Daily News*, 19 March 1878.

12. Steele to Jones, 5 March 1878, Letterpress Book, 2, AGC, TSL.

13. "El Paso Troubles in Texas," 13–18.

14. Ibid., 19; letter by Jones, 16 March 1878, AGC, TSL.

15. Miller, *Sam Bass & Gang*, 134–136.

16. Telegram, Jones to Steele, 19 March 1878, AGC, TSL.

17. Petition, 21 March 1878, AGC, TSL.

18. "El Paso Troubles in Texas," 19–33.

19. Jones to Steele, 25 March 1878; Special Order No. 123 (Jones), 25 March 1878; Special Order No. 59 (Steele), Letterpress Book, 101, AGC, TSL; Cool, *Salt Warriors*, 259.

20. *Galveston Daily News*, 29 March 1878.

21. Jones to James Tays, 7 May 1878, AGC, TSL.

22. Proclamation, 13 May 1878, Executive Record Book (Gov. Hubbard), 484; Thomas Martin to Kerber, 14 May 1878, Letterpress Book (Gov. Hubbard), 618; Steele to James Tays, 14 May 1878, AGC, TSL.

23. Lucy to Steele, 26 March 1878, AGC, TSL.

24. Parrott to J. L. Hall, 30 March 1878, Special State Troops Correspondence (hereafter "SSTC"), TSL.

25. *Galveston Daily News*, 10 April 1878.

26. Miller, *Sam Bass & Gang*, 150–152.
27. Proclamation, 6 April 1878, Executive Record Book (Gov. Hubbard), 473, TSL.
28. Miller, *Sam Bass & Gang*, 160–167.
29. Proclamation, 10 April 1878, Executive Record Book (Gov. Hubbard), 474, TSL; *Galveston Daily News*, 11 April 1878; *Dallas Daily Herald*, 13 April 1878.
30. Telegram, Steele to Jones, 10 April 1878; Steele to Jones, 11 April 1878, AGC, TSL.
31. Steele to D. J. Baldwin, 10 April 1878, Letterpress Book, 51, AGC, TSL.
32. Jones to Steele, 12 April 1878, AGC, TSL.
33. Steele to Jones, 12 April 1878, Letterpress Book, 55, AGC, FBC, TSL.
34. *Dallas Daily Herald*, 12 April 1878.
35. Ibid., 16 April 1878.
36. Telegram and letter, Jones to Steele, 16 April 1878; Special Order No. 126 (Jones), 16 April 1878; Special Order No. 60 (Steele), 17 April 1878, Letterpress Book, 102, AGC, TSL.
37. Jones to Steele, 16 April 1878, Webb Collection.
38. Ibid.; *Galveston Daily News*, 18 April 1878.
39. *Galveston Daily News*, 19 April 1878.
40. Miller, *Sam Bass & Gang*, 175–177, 185. William Scott would subsequently become a noted Ranger captain.
41. Telegram, Jones to S. H. Russell, 22 April 1878; Jones to Steele, 22 April 1878, FBC, TSL; *Galveston Daily News*, 23 April 1878; *Dallas Daily Herald*, 23 April 1878.
42. Telegram, Jones to Steele, 23 April 1878, FBC, TSL; *Dallas Daily Herald*, 23 April 1878.
43. *Galveston Daily News*, 27 April 1878; *Dallas Daily Herald*, 27 April 1878; Miller, *Sam Bass & Gang*, 180–183.
44. Jones to Egan, 28 April 1878, AGC, TSL.
45. Miller, *Sam Bass & Gang*, 188–191.
46. Telegram, Jones to Steele, 30 April 1878, Webb Collection.
47. *Dallas Daily Herald*, 1 May 1878.
48. Telegram, Steele to Jones, 1 May 1878, AGC, TSL.
49. Telegram, Jones to Steele, 1 May 1878, FBC, TSL.
50. DeArment, *Bravo of the Brazos*, 98.
51. Ibid., 100–101; Robert K. DeArment, "'Hurricane Bill' Martin, Horse Thief," *True West* 38, no. 6 (June 1991), 38 et seq.
52. DeArment, *Bravo of the Brazos*, 108–111. See also Leon Metz, *John Selman: Texas Gunfighter* (New York: Hastings House, 1966) for an account of Selman's life.
53. DeArment, *Bravo of the Brazos*, 110–112; Campbell to Jones, 26 and 28 February 1878, FBC, TSL; Charles M. Robinson III, *The Frontier World of Fort Griffin* (Spokane, Washington: Arthur H. Clarke, 1992), 124–125.
54. DeArment, *Bravo of the Brazos*, 112.
55. Campbell to Jones, 3 April 1878, FBC, TSL.

56. DeArment, *Bravo of the Brazos*, 114–115.

57. Fleming to Hubbard, 1 May 1878, AGC, TSL.

58. Jones to Reynolds, 3 and 7 May 1878, AGC, TSL.

59. Jones to Campbell, 7 May 1878, FBC, TSL.

60. Ty Cashion, *A Texas Frontier: The Clear Fork Country and Fort Griffin, 1849–1887* (Norman, Oklahoma: University of Oklahoma Press, 1996), 226–229.

61. Fleming to Jones, 16 May 1878, FBC, TSL.

62. Special Order No. 131 (Jones), 18 May 1878, FBC; Special Order No. 64 (Steele), 22 May 1878, Letterpress Book, 103, AGC, TSL.

63. Jones to Campbell, 18 May 1878, FBC, TSL.

64. Jones to Steele, 20 May 1878, AGC, TSL.

65. Petition, 26 May 1878, AGC, TSL.

66. Telegram, Drs. W. T. Baird and S. K. Smith to Jones, 31 May 1878, AGC, TSL.

67. Jones to J. S. Wright et al, 5 June 1878, FBC, TSL.

68. *Dallas Daily Herald*, 12 May 1878.

69. Jones to Arrington, 12 May 1878, AGC; Van Riper to Jones, 15 May 1878, FBC, TSL.

70. *Dallas Daily Herald*, 15 and 17 May 1878.

71. Telegram, Jones to Steele, 17 May 1878, FBC; Special Order No. 129 (Jones), 17 May 1878, AGC, TSL; *Dallas Daily Herald*, 18 May 1878.

72. Affidavit of J. W. Murphy, 23 July 1878; memorandum by Andrew J. Evans, 21 May 1878, Webb Collection; *Galveston Daily News*, 31 July 1878.

73. Miller, *Sam Bass & Gang*, 204.

74. *Galveston Daily News*, 25 May 1878.

75. Ibid., 26 May 1878.

76. Jones to Steele, 28 May 1878, AGC; Jones to Peak, 29 May 1878, FBC, TSL.

77. *San Saba News* as quoted in *Austin Daily Democratic Statesman*, 29 May 1878, and *San Antonio Daily Herald*, 31 May 1878; David M. Williams, *The Vicious Murder of S. S. Brooks* (San Saba, Texas: Edwards Plateau Historical Association, 2002), 6–7; Chuck Parsons, *James Madison Brown: Texas Sheriff, Texas Turfman* (Wolfe City, Texas: Henington Publishing, 1993), 65.

78. Letter from John T. Guinn, 23 May 1878, AGC, TSL.

79. Jones to Reynolds, 28 May 1878; Jones to Arrington, 28 May 1878, AGC, TSL.

80. Petition, 1 June 1878, AGC, TSL; *Galveston Daily News*, 10 July 1878.

81. Reynolds to Steele, 25 September 1878, AGC; Reynolds to Jones, 14 October 1878, FBC, TSL.

82. Gillett, *Six Years With the Texas Rangers*, 153–154. On September 16, 1878, San Saba County Attorney Brooks was assassinated and, in a dying declaration, identified Jim Brown as his assailant. An unsuccessful attempt was made on Kendall's life in Dallas in 1890, but the assailant was not recognized. Williams, *S. S. Brooks*, iii–v; Parsons, *James Madison Brown*, 68–70.

83. *Austin Daily Democratic Statesman*, 30 May 1878.

84. *Lampasas Daily Times*, 11 June 1878; *Austin Daily Democratic Statesman*, 4 June 1878.
85. Estill to Hubbard, 31 May 1878, AGC, TSL.
86. Embree to Hubbard, 31 May 1878, AGC, TSL.
87. Jones to Estill, 4 June 1878, AGC, TSL.
88. Jones to Estill, 7 June 1878, AGC, TSL; *Galveston Daily News*, 6 June 1878.
89. Estill to Jones, 9 June 1878, AGC, TSL.
90. Ibid., 10 June 1878, AGC, TSL.

Chapter 13: Agin' My Profession

1. Miller, *Sam Bass and Gang*, 205–210.
2. Ibid., 212–213.
3. Ibid., 220–221.
4. Ibid., 221–222; Peak to Jones, 14 June 1878, Webb Collection; Van Riper to Jones, 15 June 1878, FBC, TSL; H. Bryant Prather, *Come Listen to My Tale* (Talequah, Oklahoma: The Pan Press, 1964), 60–61.
5. Van Riper to Jones, 15 June 1878, Webb Collection.
6. Ibid.
7. Campbell to Jones, 16 June 1878, Webb Collection.
8. Telegram, James McIntire to Jones, 24 June 1878, Webb Collection; DeArment, *Bravo of the Brazos*, 133–135; Edgar Rye, *The Quirt and the Spur: Vanishing Shadows of the Texas Frontier* (Lubbock, Texas: Texas Tech University Press, 2000), 107–112.
9. W. R. Cruger to Jones, 30 June 1878, Webb Collection; Leon Clair Metz, *John Selman: Texas Gunfighter*, 90–91.
10. C. K. Stribling to Hubbard, 30 June 1878, AGC, TSL.
11. *Galveston Daily News*, 26 June 1878.
12. Cashion, *A Texas Frontier*, 230–231.
13. General Order No. 21 (Jones), 6 July 1878, FBC, TSL.
14. Jones to Van Riper, 6 July 1878, FBC, TSL.
15. Jones to Arrington, 13 July 1878, AGC, TSL.
16. Ibid., 1 August 1878, AGC, TSL.
17. *Austin Daily Democratic Statesman*, 12 July 1878.
18. Jones to James A. Tays, 12 July 1878, AGC, TSL.
19. Miller, *Sam Bass & Gang*, 227.
20. Ibid., 227–228.
21. *Galveston Daily News*, 31 July 178.
22. Ibid.; Miller, *Sam Bass & Gang*, 234–242.
23. Miller, *Sam Bass & Gang*, 242–243.
24. Ibid., 243–245; *Galveston Daily News*, 24 July 1878.

25. Telegrams from Jones, 18 July 1878, AGC, TSL.

26. Telegrams from Jones, 19 July 1878, AGC, FBC, TSL.

27. Miller, *Sam Bass & Gang*, 243–244

28. Ibid., 248.

29. Mike Cox, *Texas Ranger Tales: Stories That Need Telling* (Plano, Texas: Republic of Texas Press, 1997), 56–57.

30. *Galveston Daily News*, 20, 24, 25, and 31 July 1878; Miller, *Sam Bass & Gang*, 248–254.

31. Telegram, Steele to Jones, 20 July 1878, AGC, TSL; Miller, *Sam Bass & Gang*, 257–259.

32. Miller, *Sam Bass & Gang*, 258–262.

33. Murphy to Jones, 27 August 1878, FBC, TSL.

34. Letters by Jones, 23 and 25 July 1878, FBC, TSL; *Lampasas Daily Times*, 30 July 1878; Miller, *Sam Bass & Gang*, 238.

35. Jones to Peak, 1 August 1878, FBC, TSL.

36. Jones to Coldwell, 1 August 1878, AGC, TSL.

37. Affidavit of James W. Murphy, 26 July 1878, FBC, TSL.

38. Murphy to Jones, 2 and 9 August 1878, AGC, FBC, TSL.

39. Murphy to Jones, 6 September 1878, FBC, TSL. Murphy died in June 1879 when he accidentally swallowed a toxic medication.

40. W. P. Lane to O. M. Roberts, 24 July 1878; Frank B. Sexton to Roberts, 25 July 1878, Records of Gov. Roberts, TSL.

41. Thomas Devine to Roberts, 27 July 1878, Records of Gov. Roberts, TSL.

42. General Order No. 23 (Jones), 4 August 1878, FBC, TSL.

43. Jones to Tays, 4 August 1878, AGC, TSL.

44. Jones to Roberts, Dolan, and Peak, 19 August 1878, AGC, FBC, TSL.

45. Jones to Steele, 5 August 1878, AGC, TSL; *Galveston Daily News*, 9 August 1878.

46. Coldwell to Jones, 9 August 1878, AGC, TSL.

47. Jones to Coldwell, 22 August 1878, AGC, TSL.

48. Coldwell to Jones, 12 September 1878; Coldwell to Hubbard, 12 September 1878, AGC, TSL.

49. Ibid., 8 October 1878; Special Order No. 68 (Steele), 8 October 1878, Letterpress Book, 105, AGC, TSL.

50. Tays to Jones, 15 August 1878, AGC; Report of Frontier Battalion Operations, 1 March 1877–31 August 1878, File 401–1159(7), FBC, TSL; *Denison Daily News*, 1 September 1878; Gillett, *Six Years With the Texas Rangers*, 310.

51. Jones to Tays, 28 August 1878, AGC, TSL.

52. Tays to Jones, 2 September 1878; Wahl to Jones, 17 October 1878, AGC, TSL.

53. Jones to Wahl, 7 October 1878, AGC, TSL.

54. Jones to Tays, 7 October 1878, AGC, TSL.

55. *Galveston Daily News*, 9 August 1878.

56. Petition, 7 August 1878, AGC, TSL.

57. W. R. Wallace and J. D. Morrison to Jones, 16 August 1878, AGC, TSL.

58. D. M. Young to Jones, 17 August 1878, AGC, TSL.

59. Coldwell to Jones, 27 August 1878, AGC, TSL.

60. Young to Jones, 28 August 1878, AGC; Coldwell to Jones, 13 September 1878, FBC, TSL.

61. Coldwell to Jones, 31 August 1878; G. W. E. Clark to Steele, 30 October 1878, AGC, TSL; *Galveston Daily News*, 28 August 1878; *Luling Signal*, 12 September 1878. Varying accounts also spell his name as Bowman and Bauman. No record of him under any of these names could be located in Frontier Battalion records.

62. Chuck Parsons, *John B. Armstrong: Texas Ranger and Pioneer Ranchman* (College Station, Texas: Texas A&M University Press, 2007), 47–48.

63. Jones to Peak, 27 August 1879, AGC, TSL; *Austin Daily Democratic Statesman*, 29 September 1878.

64. Tays to Jones, 17 October 1878, AGC, TSL.

65. Guy Broadwater to Jones, 4 December 1878, AGC, TSL.

66. Jones to Reynolds, 5 September 1878, FBC, TSL; Parsons and Brice, *N. O. Reynolds*, 239–241.

67. *Austin Daily Democratic Statesman*, 18 September 1878.

68. Reynolds to Steele, 5 October 1878, AGC, TSL.

69. *Galveston Daily News*, 11 September 1878.

70. Ibid., 13 September 1878.

71. Telegram, Jones to Steele, 17 September 1878, AGC, TSL.

72. *Galveston Daily News*, 18 September 1878.

73. Jones to Steele, 23 September 1878, AGC, TSL; *Galveston Daily News*, 3 October 1878.

74. General Order No. 24 (Jones), 7 October 1878, AGC, TSL.

75. Jones to Arrington, 7 October 1878, FBC, TSL.

76. Jones to Roberts. 10 October 1878, AGC, TSL.

77. Telegram, Jones to Steele, 14 October 1878, AGC; Jones to Reynolds, 21 October 1878; General Order No. 142 (Jones), 21 October 1878, FBC, TSL; *Galveston Daily News*, 22 October 1878.

78. *Galveston Daily News*, 16 October 1878.

79. Reward offer by Steele, 4 November 1878, AGC, TSL; *San Antonio Daily Express*, 20 and 21 November 1878.

80. *San Antonio Daily Express*, 24 October 1878.

81. Jones to Reynolds, 24 October 1878, AGC, TSL; *San Antonio Daily Express*, 1 November 1878; *Galveston Daily News*, 3 November 1878.

82. *San Antonio Daily Express*, 31 October 1878.

83. Jones to Steele, 1 November 1878, AGC, TSL; *Galveston Daily News*, 9 November 1878.

84. Jones to Tays, 12 November 1878, AGC, TSL.

85. Telegram, Tays to Jones, 25 November 1878; Tays to Jones, 26 November 1878, AGC, TSL.

86. Tays to Jones, 16 December 1878, AGC, TSL; *Galveston Daily News*, 1 January 1879; *Mesilla Independent* as quoted in *Denison Daily News*, 27 December 1878.

87. Petition, 17 December 1878; telegram, Ludwick to Jones, 19 December 1878, AGC, TSL.

88. Nicholson to Steele, 28 November 1878; Special Order No. 71 (Steele), 6 December 1878, Letterpress Book, 106, AGC, TSL.

89. Steele to Gov. Roberts, 11 November 1878, Records of Gov. Roberts, TSL.

90. *San Antonio Daily Express*, 21 November 1878.

91. Telegram, Steele to Jones, 13 November 1878, Letterpress Book, 326; Steele to Jones, 14 November 1878, AGC, TSL; *San Antonio Daily Express*, 14 November 1878.

92. Jones to Steele, 14 November 1878, AGC, TSL.

93. William Steele, *Report of the Adjutant General of the State of Texas for the Fiscal Year Ending August 31, 1878* (Galveston, Texas: Galveston News, 1878), 5–8; *San Antonio Daily Express*, 18 December 1878; *Galveston Daily News*, 18 December 1878.

94. Steele, *Report 1878*, 2–31. Only four Rangers were killed or mortally wounded in 1878: Tim McCarty, A. A. Ruzin, Melvin E. Beauman, and Henry Crist.

95. Report of legislative committee, December 1878, AGC, TSL; *Austin Daily Democratic Statesman*, 21 December 1878.

96. Jones to Steele, 17 December 1878, AGC, TSL; *Kerrville Frontiersman* as quoted in *Galveston Daily News*, 5 December 1878.

97. General Order No. 25 (Jones), 10 December 1878, AGC, TSL.

98. Sparks to Jones, 12 December 1878, AGC, TSL. Sparks was subsequently involved in a stabbing incident in Waco in 1880, and was shot to death in Navarro County on April 7, 1883, by Bigman Fuller in a "cattle dispute." *Galveston Daily News*, 31 July 1880; *Fort Worth Daily Gazette*, 8 April 1883; *Waco Daily Examiner*, 10 April 1883.

99. Jones to Broadwater, 19 December 1879, FBC, TSL.

100. Special Order No. 72 (Steele), 21 December 1878, Letterpress Book, 196; *Galveston Daily News*, 24 December 1878.

101. Telegram, Steele to Peak, 14 December 1878, Letterpress Book, 353, AGC, TSL; *Galveston Daily News*, 15 December 1878.

102. John Mann to Peak, 12 November 1878, FBC, TSL.

103. McFarland to Jones, 28 December 1878, AGC, TSL.

Chapter 14: Stately as a Queen

1. Telegram, Arrington to Jones, 19 January 1879; Arrington to Jones, 20 January 1879, AGC, TSL; *San Antonio Daily Express*, 4 February 1879; *Galveston Daily News*, 21

January 1879; *Fort Griffin Echo*, 25 January 1879; Jerry Sinise, *George Washington Arrington*, 23–24; James M. Day and Dorman Winfrey, *Texas Indian Papers, 1860–1916* (Austin, Texas: Texas State Library, 1961), 409–419.

2. Wilcox to Steele, 17 January 1879, AGC, TSL.

3. Gov. Roberts to Gen. E. O. C. Ord, 10 February 1879, Letterpress Book, 29, Records of Gov. Roberts, TSL.

4. Gov. Roberts to state legislature, 10 February 1879, Executive Record Book, 63–65, TSL.

5. *San Antonio Daily Express*, 18 February 1879.

6. Jones to Gov. Roberts, 15 February 1879, Letterpress Book, 39–40, AGC, TSL.

7. Capt. S. H. Lincoln, Ft. Griffin, to Asst. Adj. Gen., U.S. Army, San Antonio, 17 February 1879, AGC, TSL.

8. Steele to Gov. Roberts, 2 January 1879, Records of Gov. Roberts, TSL.

9. Peak to Jones, 6 January 1879, AGC, TSL.

10. Jones to Peak, 14 January 1879, FBC, TSL.

11. Governors message, 14 January 1879, Executive Record Book, 1874–1879, 474, TSL.

12. *Galveston Daily News*, 18 January 1879.

13. Broadwater to Jones, 20 January 1879, FBC, TSL.

14. Jerry Thompson, "John Robert Baylor," *The New Handbook of Texas*, vol. 1, 423–424.

15. Jones to Broadwater, 25 January 1879, FBC, TSL.

16. Broadwater to Jones, 12 February 1879, AGC, TSL.

17. Day and Winfrey, *Texas Indian Papers*, 412–414.

18. Dolan to Jones, 22 January 1879; report of inquest, 20 January 1879; Report of Scout, Company F, January 1879, AGC, TSL.

19. Chuck Parsons, "Reese Gobles-Predator," *Quarterly of the National Association and Center for Outlaw and Lawman History* 14, no. 2 (Summer 1990), 23–24.

20. Jones to Stewart, 22 January 1879; Jones to Sen. Charles Grace, 25 January 1879, AGC, TSL; *Galveston Daily News*, 24 January 1879.

21. Steele to Sen. A. W. Terrill, 22 January 1879, Letterpress Book, 386–389, AGC, TSL.

22. Roberts to Texas Senate, 22 January 1879, Letterpress Book, 2; Executive Record Book (Gov. Roberts), 19, TSL; *Austin Daily Democratic Statesman*, 23 January 1879.

23. *Galveston Daily News*, 23 January 1879; Jimmy L. Bryan Jr., *More Zeal Than Discretion: The Westward Adventures of Walter P. Layne* (College Station, Texas: Texas A&M University Press, 2008), 158–159.

24. *Galveston Daily News*, 23 January 1879.

25. *Austin Daily Democratic Statesman*, 25 January 1879; *Galveston Daily News*, 25 January 1879.

26. *Austin State Gazette* as quoted in *Galveston Daily News*, 25 January 1879.

27. Senate to Gov. Roberts, 25 January 1879, records of Gov. Roberts; Executive Record Book (Gov. Roberts), 20, TSL; *Austin Daily Democratic Statesman*, 26 January 1879; *Fort Worth Daily Democrat*, 26 January 1879; *Denison Daily News*, 26 January 1879.

28. As quoted in *Galveston Daily News*, 15 February 1879.

29. Oath of office, 27 January 1879, unknown file, TSL.

30. As quoted in *Galveston Daily News*, 8 February 1879.

31. *San Antonio Daily Express*, 2 March 1879.

32. Ibid., 9 February 1879, 2 March 1879.

33. Jones to Gov. Roberts, 5 February 1879, Letterpress Book, 19–22, AGC, TSL.

34. Jones to Martinez, 1 February 1879, Letterpress Book, 8, AGC, TSL.

35. Proclamation, 1 February 1879, Executive Record Book (Gov. Roberts), 46–47, TSL; *Fort Worth Daily Democrat*, 12 February 1879.

36. Jones to Gov. Roberts, 5 February 1879, Letterpress Book, 19–22, AGC, TSL.

37. Jones to J. C. Douglass, 5 and 15 February 1879, Letterpress Book, 17–18, 41, AGC, TSL.

38. *San Antonio Daily Express*, 16 February 1879.

39. Reynolds to Jones, 14 February 1879; Special Order No. 3, 19 February 1879, Adjutant General Special Orders, 108; Jones to Reynolds, 19 February 1879, Letterpress Book, 51, AGC, TSL.

40. Petition, 28 February 1879, AGC, TSL.

41. Resolution, 6 March 1879, AGC, TSL; *Galveston Daily News*, 14 March 1879.

42. *Galveston Daily News*, 20 February 1879.

43. *San Antonio Daily Express*, 23 February 1879.

44. Marriage Records, Travis County, Texas, vol. 5, p.155; *Galveston Daily News*, 26 February 1879.

45. *Biographical Souvenir*, 470. Her birthplace has been variously described as Tennessee; Aberdeen, Mississippi; and Millican in Brazos County. Bonner, *Major John B. Jones*, 131; *Austin Statesman*, 26 November 1908.

46. *Biographical Souvenir*, 470; Speer and Brown, *Encyclopedia of the New West*, 389.

47. J. W. Baker, *A History of Robertson County, Texas* (Waco, Texas: Texian Press, 1970), 482; Richard Denny Parker, *Historical Recollections of Robertson County, Texas* (Salado, Texas: Anson Jones, 1955), 95.

48. Interview with Mrs. Walter Bremond, 10 July 1949, as quoted in Bonner, *Major John B. Jones*, 132.

49. Bonner, *Major John B. Jones*, 132.

50. Interview with Mrs. Walter Bremond, 10 July 1949, as quoted in Bonner, *Major John B. Jones*, 132–133.

51. Jones to Roberts, 10 October 1878; Special Order No. 150 (Jones), 25 January 1878, AGC, TSL. See also Stephens, *Dan Roberts*, 121.

52. *General Laws of the State of Texas (16th Legislature)*, vol. 8 (Austin, Texas: Gammel Book, 1898), 19; circular by Jones, 3 March 1879, AGC, TSL.

53. Gov. Roberts to legislature, 3 March 1879, Executive Record Book, 98–103.

54. *Sherman Register* as quoted in *Fort Worth Daily Democrat*, 2 March 1879.

55. Special Order No. 7, 25 March 1879, Special Orders, 110, AGC, TSL.

56. Jones to Coldwell, 3 April 1879, Letterpress Book, 146, AGC, TSL.

57. Jones to Gov. Roberts, 7 April 1879, Letterpress Book, 163–164, AGC, TSL.

58. Jones to Falhin & Schreiner, Kerrville, 11 April 1879, Letterpress Book, 173, AGC, TSL.

59. Jones to Mills, 29 March 1879, Letterpress Book, 133–134; Jones to Rep. Olin Wellborn, 15 April 1879, Letterpress Book, AGC, TSL.

60. Statute, 7 April 1879, *General Laws of the State of Texas (16th Legislature)*, vol. 8, 82–83.

61. Jones to F. W. James, 19 June 1879, Letterpress Book, 391–394, AGC, TSL.

62. Special Order No. 9, 24 April 1879, Special Orders, 111; Jones to Dolan, Sgt. R. Jones, and Broadwater, 24 April 1879, Letterpress Book, 204–206, AGC, TSL.

63. Jones to Arrington, 7 May 1879, Letterpress Book, 250; Special Orders, 9 May 1879, 112, AGC, TSL; *Galveston Daily News*, 31 May 1879.

64. *Galveston Daily News*, 2 April 1880; Jack Duane Redman, "General John B. Jones: Twenty Years of Service to Texas," (master's thesis, University of Texas at El Paso, 1983), 93.

65. Jones to Ludwick, 14 May 1879, Letterpress Book, 272, AGC, TSL.

66. Special Order No. 13, 19 May 1879, Special Orders, 113–114, AGC, TSL.

67. Jones to Blacker, 17 May 1879, Letterpress Book, 281–283, AGC, TSL.

68. Jones to R. C. Ware, 15 May 1879; open letter by Jones, 20 May 1879, Letterpress Book, 279 and 295, AGC, TSL.

69. Jones to Arrington, 23 May 1879, Letterpress Book, 298–300, AGC, TSL; *Galveston Daily News*, 25 May 1879.

70. Insp. J. W. Smith to Jones, 24 May 1879, AGC, TSL.

71. Jackson to Jones, 29 May 1879, AGC, RSL.

72. Jones to Jackson, 6 June 1879, Letterpress Book, 341–342, AGC, TSL.

73. Open letter, 10 June 1879, Letterpress Book, 353, AGC, TSL.

74. Open letter, 21 June 1879, Letterpress Book, 398, AGC, TSL.

75. *Fort Griffin Echo*, 31 May 1879; *Denison Daily News*, 28 May 1879; *Galveston Daily News*, 27 May 1879; *San Antonio Daily Express*, 27 May 1879.

76. *Austin Daily Democratic Statesman*, 8 June 1879.

77. Ibid., 25 June 1879; *Proceedings in the Forty-Fourth Annual Communication of the M.W. Lodge of Texas* (Houston: W. H. Coyle, 1879), 23.

78. *Forty-Fourth Annual Communication*, 23.

79. Arrington to Lt. C. D. Davidson, 18 June 1879; Arrington to Jones, 21 June 1879, AGC, TSL; Arrington to Jones as quoted in *Galveston Daily News*, 6 July 1879.

Chapter 15: Scared on Our Arrival

1. Jimmy M. Skaggs, "Pegleg Crossing," *The New Handbook of Texas*, vol. 5, p. 129.

2. Robert S. Weddle, "Pegleg Station on the San Saba," *The Edwards Plateau Historian* 3 (1967), (Ozark, Missouri: Dogwood Printing, 2004), 31.

3. *Galveston Daily News,* 16 and 18 December 1877; Lt. Harry Kirby, "Stage Hold-Up at Pegleg in 1877," *Frontier Times* 4, no. 5 (February 1927), 49–52.

4. *Galveston Daily News,* 7 July 1878.

5. Roberts to Jones, 1 October 1878, AGC, TSL; Alexander, *Winchester Warriors,* 142–143.

6. Roberts to Jones, 24 November 1878, AGC, TSL.

7. Ibid., 28 February 1879, AGC, TSL.

8. Roberts, *Rangers and Sovereignty,* 125.

9. Gillett, *Six Years With the Texas Rangers,* 147–148.

10. Jones to Walter Acker, 27 June 1879, AGC, TSL.

11. Peak to Jones, 5 July 1879, FBC, TSL. See also C. W. Grandy, "More About W. B. Anglin," *Frontier Times* 6, no. 6 (March 1929), 224.

12. *Fort Worth Daily Democrat,* 22 July 1879. Tom McConnell subsequently died of smallpox on September 3, 1879. Nevill to Jones, 4 September 1879, AGC, TSL.

13. Peak to Jones, 5 July 1879, FBC, TSL.

14. General Order No. 3, 3 July 1879, AGC, TSL.

15. Special Order No. 19, 3 July 1879, Special Orders, 117, AGC, TSL. Birdwell later served as sheriff of Howard County. For an account of his life see Capt. B. B. Paddock, *A History of Central and Western Texas,* vol. 1(Chicago: Lewis Publishing, 1911), 374–375.

16. Jones to Arrington, 3 July 1879, Letterpress Book, 437–438, AGC, TSL.

17. Ibid., 437–439.

18. Jones to Arrington, 13 August 1879, Letterpress Book, 93, AGC, TSL.

19. Petition, 4 July 1879, AGC, TSL.

20. Arrington to Jones, 8 July 1879, as quoted in *Galveston Daily News,* 9 July 1879.

21. Coldwell to Jones, 17 July 1879, AGC, TSL. The following is crossed out in Coldwell's letter: "The material of this company is not as good as it might be. There are a few men in the company who are in a chronic state of dissatisfaction, who seem to do the duties required of them, under protest at all times. The women and [illegible] of Fort Griffin have had a rather bad effect on the moral tone of the company, although Capt. Arrington is very strict with the company in that respect. Any man who is allowed to go to town is required to return to camp at the 'evening gun.' Capt. Arrington expects to get rid of the discordant element on the reorganization of the company."

22. *Galveston Daily News,* 31 July 1879.

23. Jones to Baylor, 5 July 1879, Letterpress Book, 444–445, AGC, TSL.

24. Thomas W. Cutrer, "George Wythe Baylor," *The New Handbook of Texas,* vol. 1, 422–423; Gillett, *Six Years With the Texas Rangers,* 200–201.

25. Jones to Baylor, 17 July 1879, Letterpress Book, 5; Special Order No. 24, 26 July 1879, Letterpress Book, 119, AGC, TSL; *San Antonio Daily Express,* 23 July 1879;

George Wythe Baylor, *Into the Far, Wild Country*, ed. Jerry D. Thompson (El Paso, Texas: Texas Western Press, 1996), 273.

26. Jones to Baylor, 26 July 1879, Letterpress Book, 22–24; 29 Jones to Baylor, 29 July 1879, Letterpress Book, 31, AGC, TSL.

27. Gillett, *Six Years With the Texas Rangers*, 198–210; Baylor, *Into the Far, Wild Country*, 1.

28. *General Laws of the State of Texas, Special Session, 16th Legislature*, vol. 9 (Austin, Texas: Gammel Book, 1898), 11; Special Order No. 22, 11 July 1879, Special Orders, 118–119, AGC, TSL.

29. Telegram, Jones to A. J. Evans, 14 July 1879, Letterpress Book, 465, AGC, TSL.

30. *Austin Daily Democratic Statesman*, 24 July 1879.

31. Roberts to Jones, 1 August 1879, FBC; 1 September 1879, AGC, TSL; *San Antonio Daily Express*, 7 August 1879.

32. Roberts to Jones, 1 August 1879, FBC, TSL.

33. Ibid., 10 August and 1 September 1879, AGC, TSL. Roberts identified Garland as sheriff, but he did not become sheriff of Kimble County until November 1880. Tise, *Texas County Sheriffs*, 307.

34. *Austin Daily Democratic Statesman*, 19 August 1879.

35. Ibid., 20 and 21 August 1879; *Galveston Daily News*, 20 August 1879. Bill Allison burned to death in 1885 while he was a prisoner in the Gillespie County Jail. Bob Alexander, *Rawhide Ranger, Ira Aten: Enforcing Law on the Texas Frontier.* (Denton, Texas: University of North Texas Press, 2011), 67.

36. *Austin Daily Democratic Statesman*, 22 August 1879.

37. *Griffin Echo*, 9 August 1879; *San Antonio Daily Express*, 5 August 1879.

38. Special Order No. 25, 1 August 1879, Special Orders, 120, AGC, TSL; *San Antonio Daily* Express, 3 August 1879; Dora Neill Raymond, *Captain Lee Hall of Texas* (Norman, Oklahoma: University of Oklahoma Press, 1940), 176–177.

39. Special Order No. 26, 5 August 1879, Special Orders, 120; Jones to Oglesby, 5 August 1879, Letterpress Book, 54–55, AGC, TSL.

40. Oglesby to Jones, 14 August 1879, AGC, TSL.

41. *Galveston Daily News*, 13 August 1879.

42. Monthly Report, Special Force, 30 September 1879; Hall to Jones, 20 September 1879, AGC, TSL.

43. Jones to Hall, 3 October 1879, Letterpress Book, 238–240, AGC, TSL.

44. Jones to Arrington, 13 August 1879, Letterpress Book, 90–91, AGC, TSL.

45. *Fort Griffin Echo*, 6 September 1879. This article also lists each man in the company and his original place of residence.

46. Special Order No. 27, 25 August 1879, Special Orders, 121, AGC, TSL.

47. Special Order No. 1 (Nevill), 14 September 1879, AGC, TSL.

48. *Galveston Daily News*, 19 August 1879.

49. *Galveston Daily News*, 18 September 1879.

50. Baylor to Jones, 10 October 1879, as quoted in *San Antonio Daily Express*, 24 October 1879, and *Galveston Daily News*, 23 October 1879; Gillett, *Six Years With the Texas Rangers,* 216–223.

51. *San Antonio Daily Express*, 29 October 1879.

52. Jones to Baylor, 6 November 1879, AGC, TSL.

53. Ibid., 30 December 1879, AGC, TSL.

54. Roberts to Jones, 24 August 1879; Jones to Roberts, 9 October 1879, AGC, TSL.

55. Jones to Roberts, 12 October 1879, Letterpress Book, 268–269, AGC, TSL.

56. Roberts to Jones, 16 October 1878, AGC, TSL.

57. Ibid., 18 and 31 October 1879, AGC, TSL; Alexander, *Winchester Warriors*, 144–145. Alexander suggests that a second search warrant was obtained to seize the items.

58. Jones to Roberts, 8 and 22 December 1879, AGC, TSL.

59. Petition, 15 October 1879, AGC, TSL; *Galveston Daily News*, 17 October 1879.

60. Jones to Hall, 16 October 1879, AGC, TSL.

61. *San Antonio Daily Express*, 1 and 18 November 1879.

62. Sgt. W. L. Rudd to Hall, 12 November 1879, AGC, TSL.

63. Ord to Gov. Roberts, 13 December 1879, Webb Collection.

64. Gov. Roberts to Ord, 29 December 1879, Letterpress Book No. 2 (Gov. Roberts), 634–637.

65. Hall to Jones, 5 November 1879, Webb Collection; *Galveston Daily News*, 8 November 1879; *San Antonio Daily Express*, 7 and 8 November 1879; Raymond, *Captain Lee Hall*, 182–183.

66. Hall to Jones, report of unknown date in November 1879, AGC, TSL.

67. Arrington to Jones, 23 October 1879, AGC; telegram, Gov. Roberts to Walter Johnson, 5 November 1879, Letterpress Book No. 2 (Gov. Roberts), 453, TSL; *Austin Daily Democratic Statesman*, 7 November 1879.

68. *Galveston Daily News*, 4 December 1879.

69. *San Antonio Daily Express*, 8 and 9 November 1879; *Galveston Daily News*, 8, 22, and 25 November 1879.

70. *Galveston Daily News,* 30 November, 2 and 4 December 1879.

71. Ibid., 25 November and 21 December 1879.

72. *San Antonio Daily Express*, 25 November 1879; *Austin Daily Democratic Statesman*, 25 November 1879.

73. Bob Alexander, *Sheriff Harvey Whitehill: Silver City Stalwart* (Silver City, New Mexico: High-Lonesome Books, 2005), 101.

74. Kathleen P. Chamberlain, *Victorio: Apache Warrior and Chief* (Norman, Oklahoma: University of Oklahoma Press, 2007), 161–162.

75. Ibid., 178; Baylor to Jones, 3 December 1879, AGC, TSL.

76. *San Antonio Daily Express*, 12 December 1879; *Galveston Daily News*, 12 December 1879.

77. *Proceedings in the Forty-Fourth Communication of the M.W. Grand Lodge of Texas*, 7.

78. Ibid.
79. Ibid., 9.
80. Ibid., 26.
81. *San Antonio Daily Express*, 16 December 1879.
82. *Galveston Daily News*, 17 December 1879; *Austin Daily Democratic Statesman*, 21 December 1879.

Chapter 16: Promptness and Fidelity

1. Statements by William Scott and W. R. Wallace, 9 February 1880, AGC, TSL.
2. Special Order No. 38, 29 November 1879, Special Orders, 125, AGC, TSL.
3. Van Riper to Arrington, 1 January 1880, AGC, TSL.
4. Jones to Arrington, 6 December 1879, Letterpress Book, 379, AGC, TSL.
5. Scott to Jones, 10 February 1880, AGC; Hagerman to Scott, unknown date in January 1880, FBC, TSL.
6. Hagerman to Scott, unknown date in January 1880, FBC, TSL.
7. Jones to Arrington, 6 January 1880, Letterpress Book, 428–431, AGC, TSL.
8. Jones to Peak, 8 January 1880, Letterpress Book, 432–435, AGC, TSL.
9. Scott to Jones, 10 February 1880, AGC, TSL.
10. Arrington to Jones, 9 February 1880, AGC, TSL.
11. Arrington to Peak, 9 February 1880, AGC, TSL.
12. Special Order No. 7 (Arrington), 29 February 1880; Special Order No. 48 (Jones), 31 March 1880, Special Orders, 129–130; Jones to Hall, 31 March 1880, Letterpress Book, 117–118; Arrington to Jones, 29 February 1880, AGC, TSL.
13. *Austin Daily Democratic Statesman*, 30 January 1880.
14. Ibid., 6 January 1880; *Galveston Daily News*, 6 January 1880.
15. Coldwell to Jones, 6 May 1880, AGC, TSL; *Galveston Daily News*, 21 March 1880.
16. Roberts to Jones, 15 January and 1 February 1880, AGC, TSL; *Galveston Daily News*, 18 August 1881.
17. Jones to Gov. Roberts, 12 January 1880, Letterpress Book, 442–451, AGC, TSL; Day and Winfrey, *Texas Indian Papers*, 436–439; *Galveston Daily News*, 17 January 1880.
18. Gov. Roberts to Sen. Coke, 13 January 1880, Letterpress Book No. 2 (Gov. Roberts), 702–703, TSL.
19. Jones to Baylor, 13 January 1880, Letterpress Book, 456, AGC, TSL.
20. Andrews to Jones, 26 January 1880, AGC, TSL.
21. G. W. Wahl to Jones, 5 February 1880, AGC, TSL.
22. *Dallas Daily Herald*, 24 February and 28 March 1880.
23. *Galveston Daily News*, 5 March 1880; *Austin Daily Democratic Statesman*, 7 March 1880.

24. *Galveston Daily News*, 7 March 1880.
25. Ibid., 11 March 1880; *Dallas Daily Herald*, 9 March 1880.
26. *Dallas Daily Herald*, 25 April 1880.
27. Telegram, Jones to Long, 6 and 24 March 1880, Letterpress Book, 72 and 103; Peak to Jones, 15 March 1880; Special Order No. 46 (Jones), 23 March 1880, Special Orders, 128–129, AGC, TSL.
28. Long to Jones, 12 March 1880, AGC; telegram, Long to Jones, 20 March 1880, FBC, TSL.
29. Resolution, 10 April 1880, FBC, TSL; *Galveston Daily News*, 24 April 1880.
30. *Dallas Daily Herald*, 25 April 1880.
31. Slaughter to Jones, unknown date in June 1880; telegram, Slaughter to Jones, 3 June 1880, AGC, TSL.
32. Peak to Coldwell, 9 June 1880, AGC, TSL.
33. Long to Jones, 17 April 1880, AGC, TSL.
34. *Dallas Daily Herald*, 25 April 1880.
35. Jones to N. L. Norton, 10 March 1880; Jones to Arrington, 12 March 1880, Letterpress Book, 84–88, AGC; Gov. Roberts to N. L. Norton and J. T. Munson, 23 March 1880, Letterpress Book No. 3 (Gov. Roberts), 23 and 24, TSL; *Galveston Daily News*, 9 March 1880.
36. Judge E. R. Morris to Jones, 2 March 1880; Jones to Judge Morris, 11 March 1880, Letterpress Book, 79; Jones to Arrington, 12 March 1880, Letterpress Book, 84–88; Arrington to Jones, 9 April 1880, AGC, TSL; *Galveston Daily News*, 7 April 1880.
37. Judge E. R. Morris to Jones, 7 April 1880, AGC, TSL.
38. Arrington to Jones, 8 May 1880, AGC, TSL.
39. Hall to Jones, 31 March 1880; McKinney to Hall, unknown date in March 1880; Oglesby to Jones, 3 April 1880, AGC, TSL; *Austin Daily Democratic Statesman*, 3 and 8 April 1880; Chuck Parsons and Gary P. Fitterer, *Captain C. B. McKinney: The Law in South Texas* (Wolfe City, Texas: Henington Publishing, 1993), 27–28.
40. *Galveston Daily News*, 2 April 1880.
41. *Dallas Daily Herald*, 3 April 1880.
42. *Galveston Daily News*, 17 April 1880.
43. *Dallas Daily Herald*, 9 May 1880.
44. F. W. James to Jones, 7 May 1880, AGC, TSL.
45. *Austin Daily Democratic Statesman*, 9 May 1880; *Galveston Daily News*, 9 and 12 May 1880; *Denison Daily News*, 12 May 1880.
46. *Austin Daily Democratic Statesman*, 20 May 1880.
47. Sheriff A. J. Leo to Gov. Roberts, 19 May 1880, AGC, TSL; *Galveston Daily News*, 18 May 1880.
48. Thaddeus Rhodes to Gov. Roberts, 17 May 1880, AGC, TSL; *Galveston Daily News*, 19 and 20 May 1880.
49. Telegram, Jones to Hall, 18 May 1880, AGC, TSL.

50. Telegrams, Rudd to Jones, Jones to Rudd, 29 May 1880, AGC, TSL.
51. Rudd to Jones, 18 June 1880, AGC, TSL.
52. Hall to Jones, 24 May 1880, AGC, TSL.
53. Raymond, *Captain Lee Hall*, 189.
54. Special Order No. 58, 26 May 1880, Special Orders, 135; Jones to Oglesby, 29 May 1880, AGC, TSL; *Austin Daily Democratic Statesman*, 27 May 1880.
55. Jones to Hall, 26 May 1880, AGC, TSL.
56. Dr. L. B. Wright to Jones, 30 June 1880, AGC, TSL.
57. Telegram, Baylor to Jones, 21 May 1880, AGC, TSL; *Austin Daily Democratic Statesman*, 2 June 1880.
58. Coldwell to Jones, 10 July 1880, AGC, TSL.
59. Telegram, Judge G. M. Frazer to Gov. Roberts, 24 May 1880, AGC, TSL.
60. Telegrams, Jones to Roberts and Frazer, 25 May 1880, AGC, TSL.
61. Jones to Caruthers, 31 May 1880; Jones to J. M. Dean, 31 May 1880, AGC, TSL.
62. Telegram, Frazer to Jones, 3 June 1880, AGC, TSL.
63. Telegram, Caruthers to Jones, 7 June 1880; Caruthers to Nevill, 8 June 1880, FBC, TSL.
64. Caruthers to Jones, 14 June 1880, AGC, TSL; Metz, *John Selman*, 113–117.
65. E. A. Sieker to Jones, 15 June 1880, AGC, TSL.
66. Telegram, Caruthers to Jones, 22 June 1880, FBC; Caruthers to Jones, 28 June 1880, AGC, TSL.
67. Telegram, Cruger to Jones, 30 June 1880; Cruger to Jones, 2 July 1880, AGC, TSL. Metz reports that the arrest took place on June 28 because Selman had been married on June 26 to Niconora Zarate. Metz, *John Selman*, 118.
68. Nevill to Jones, 2 March 1881, AGC, TSL.
69. Coldwell to Jones, 7 July 1880, FBC; Coldwell to Jones, 10 July 1880; Roberts to Jones, 12 July 1880, AGC, TSL; E. A. Sieker to Roberts, 8 July 1880, as quoted in "Texas Rangers Battle With Outlaws in 1880," *Frontier Times* 4, no. 11 (August 1927), 1–2; *Austin Daily Democratic Statesman*, 16 July 1880; Roberts, *Rangers and Sovereignty*, 111–115; Ed Bartholomew, *Jesse Evans: A Texas Hide-Burner* (Houston: Frontier Press of Texas, 1955), 52–53.
70. Jones to Nevill, 12 July 1880, AGC, TSL.
71. Jones to Ed Sieker, 12 July 1880, AGC, TSL. Selman was returned to Shackelford County where he somehow acquired a pistol and escaped on November 2, 1880. Metz states that Selman was actually allowed to escape. *Fort Griffin Echo*, 6 November 1880; Metz, *John Selman*, 123–124.
72. "Texas Rangers on the Border," *San Antonio Light*, 9 August 1914, as reprinted in *Frontier Times* 1, no. 7 (April 1924), 16.
73. Roberts to Jones, 12 July 1880, AGC, TSL.
74. Jones to Roberts, 14 July 1880, Letterpress Book, 314–315, AGC, TSL.
75. Jones to Caruthers, 15 July 1880, Letterpress Book, 321–322, AGC, TSL.

76. 1880 United States Census (Travis County, Texas), 67/79.
77. *Austin Daily Democratic Statesman*, 2 July 1880.
78. *Galveston Daily News*, 9 June 1880.
79. Roberts to Jones, 10 July 1880, AGC, TSL.
80. Jones to Roberts, 15 July 1880, Letterpress Book, 318, AGC, TSL.
81. Long to Jones, 15 July 1880, AGC, TSL.
82. Ibid., 16 July 1880, AGC, TSL.
83. Special Order No. 66 (Jones), 24 July 1880, FBC; Jones to Long, 29 July 1880, AGC, TSL.
84. Roberts to Jones, 1 August 1880, AGC, TSL.

Chapter 17: Sober, Steady, and Respectable Man

1. *Galveston Daily News*, 5 August 1880; *Dallas Daily Herald*, 5 August 1880.
2. Coldwell to Jones, 1 August 1880, AGC, TSL.
3. Telegram, Coldwell to Jones, 4 August 1880, FBC, TSL.
4. *San Antonio Daily Express*, 12 August 1880.
5. Ibid., 15 August 1880.
6. Nevill to Jones, 26 August 1880, Webb Collection; Baylor to Jones, 26 August 1880, AGC, TSL.
7. Nevill to Jones, 26 August 1880, Webb Collection; Nevill to Jones, 5 September 1880, AGC, TSL.
8. Nevill to Jones, 1 September 1880, Webb Collection.
9. Nevill to Jones, 16 October 1880, AGC, TSL; *San Antonio Daily Express*, 19 October 1880; Bartholomew, *Jesse Evans*, 72; Grady E. McCright and James H. Powell, *Jesse Evans: Lincoln County Badman* (College Station, Texas: Creative Publishing, 1983), 195–204.
10. Jones to Oglesby, 4 August 1880, Records of Gov. Roberts; Letterpress Book, 388, AGC, TSL.
11. Oglesby to Jones, 31 August 1880; Judge W. R. Hages to Jones, 3 September 1880, AGC, TSL; *Galveston Daily News*, 11 September 1880.
12. Letter to Gov. Roberts, 17 September 1880, Records of Gov. Roberts; Gov. Roberts to William M. Evarts, 28 September 1880, Records of Gov. Roberts, Letterpress Book, 862–866, TSL.
13. *Austin Daily Statesman*, 6 August 1880.
14. Ibid., 10 August and 7 September 1880.
15. Ibid., 24 and 26 August 1880; *Galveston Daily News*, 25 August 1880; *Dallas Daily Herald*, 27 August 1880.
16. Jones to Reynolds, 23 August 1880, Letterpress Book, 432; telegram, Reynolds to Jones, 28 August 1880, AGC, TSL.

17. Parsons and Brice, *N. O. Reynolds*, 277–279.

18. Special Order No. 71 (Jones), Letterpress Book, 142; Jones to Baylor, 8 September 1880, AGC, TSL.

19. Jones to Baylor, 9 September 1880, Letterpress Book, 469, AGC, TSL.

20. *San Antonio Daily Express*, 18 September 1880.

21. Oglesby to Jones, 30 May 1880, AGC, TSL.

22. Jones to T. J. Goree, 17 September 1880, Letterpress Book, 496; Jones to J. H. Martin, 24 September and 3 October 1880, Letterpress Book, 10 and 20, AGC, TSL.

23. Jones to McNelly, 14 October 1880, AGC, TSL.

24. Jones to Walker, 14 October 1880, Letterpress Book, 54, AGC, TSL.

25. McNelly to Jones, 20 November 1880, AGC, TSL.

26. Jones to McNelly, 1 December 1880, Letterpress Book, 95–96, AGC, TSL.

27. W. W. Walker to Jones, 13 December 1880, AGC, TSL.

28. Roberts to Jones, 9 October 1880; telegram, Roberts to Jones, 13 October 1880; Nevill to Jones, 23 October 1880, AGC, TSL; *Galveston Daily News*, 12 October and 5 November 1880; *San Antonio Daily Express*, 12 October 1880; Roberts, *Rangers and Sovereignty*, 117–120; Wilkins, *The Law Comes to Texas*, 206–209.

29. Roberts to Jones, 13 October 1880, AGC, TSL.

30. *Dallas Daily Herald*, 27 October 1880.

31. Ibid., 14 October 1880.

32. Jones to N. O. Reynolds, 15 October 1880, Letterpress Book, 56, AGC, TSL; *San Antonio Daily Express*, 19 October 1880; *Galveston Daily News*, 19 October 1880; *Dallas Daily Herald*, 20 October 1880; *Austin Daily Statesman*, 19 November 1880.

33. *Fort Griffin Echo*, 13 November 1880.

34. *Austin Daily Statesman*, 17 and 19 November 1880; *Galveston Daily News*, 17 November 1880.

35. Long to Jones, 30 November 1880; telegram, Jones to Marsh, 17 November 1880, Letterpress Book, 61, AGC, TSL.

36. Telegram, Marsh to Jones, 17 November 1880, AGC, TSL; Tise, *Texas County Sheriffs*, 468; John Hoffer, "Captain Marsh and His Rangers," *Frontier Times* 6, no. 7 (April 1929), 300–301.

37. Franklin Reynolds, "Who Was This Man?," *Frontier Times* 40, no. 4 (June–July 1966), 69.

38. Haley, *Jeff Milton*, 35.

39. Special Order No. 81 (Jones), 24 November 1880, Letterpress Book, 145, AGC, TSL.

40. Gillett to Jones, 17 October 1880, AGC, TSL.

41. Jones to Gillett, 24 November 1880, Letterpress Book, 79, AGC, TSL. The marriage later ended in divorce.

42. Jones to Baylor, 27 November 1880, Letterpress Book, 82, AGC, TSL.

43. Gov. Roberts to William M. Evarts, 29 November 1880, Letterpress Book 4-2/35 (Gov. Roberts Records), 94–97, TSL; Chamberlain, *Victorio*, 206.

44. *San Antonio Daily Express*, 5 December 1880; *Austin Daily Statesman*, 5 December 1880; *Galveston Daily News*, 5 December 1880.

45. John R. Baylor to Jones, 5 December 1880, AGC, TSL; *San Antonio Daily Express*, 8 December 1880; *Galveston Daily News*, 8 December 1880.

46. Jones to S. H. Darden, 16 December 1880, Letterpress Book, 122–123, AGC, TSL.

47. Jones to "John Henry," 17 December 1880, Letterpress Book, 127, AGC, TSL.

48. Special Order No. 90 (Jones), 15 March 1881, Letterpress Book, 148, AGC, TSL.

49. *Texas Land and Railway Journal*, as quoted in *Fort Griffin Echo*, 25 December 1880.

50. Official of El Paso to Jones, 23 December 1880, AGC, TSL; John B. Jones, *Report of the Adjutant General of the State of Texas, 1880* (Galveston, Texas: News Book and Job Office, 1881), 25; *Galveston Daily News*, 9 January 1881.

51. Jones to Baylor, 6 January 1881, Letterpress Book, 149, AGC, TSL.

52. Nevill to Coldwell, 31 December 1880, AGC, TSL; Gillett, *Six Years With the Texas Rangers*, 264–273.

53. Telegram, Jones to Baylor, 12 January 1881, Letterpress Book, 153, AGC, TSL.

54. Jones, *Report of the Adjutant General, 1880*, 3–34.

55. *Fort Worth Daily Democrat*, 16 January 1881; *Dallas Daily Herald*, 5 February 1881; *Austin Daily Statesman*, 14 January 1881.

56. *Fort Concho Times*, as quoted in *Galveston Daily News*, 21 January 1881.

57. Ben W. Kemp with J. C. Dykes, *Cow Dust and Saddle Leather* (Norman, Oklahoma: University of Oklahoma Press, 1968), 26.

58. Ibid., 27–28.

59. Baylor to Jones, 16 January 1881; telegram, Baylor to Jones, 31 January 1881; Baylor to Jones, 9 February 1881; Nevill to Jones, 6 February 1881; Nevill to Jones, 7 February 1881, AGC, TSL; *Galveston Daily News*, 24 February 1881; *Austin Daily Statesman*, 20 February 1881; W. C. Jameson, "Last Stand of the Mescalero Apaches in Texas," *True West* 38, no. 12 (December 1991), 14–19.

60. Charles M. Robinson III, *The Men Who Wear the Star* (New York: Random House, 2000), 243–244.

61. Nevill to Jones, 8 February 1881, AGC; Nevill to Coldwell, 9 February 1881, FBC, TSL.

62. Nevill to Coldwell, 2 March 1881, AGC, TSL.

63. Jones to Roberts, 15 February 1881, Letterpress Book, 214–216, AGC, TSL.

64. Roberts to Jones, 19 February 1881, AGC, TSL.

65. Nevill to Jones, 2 March 1881, AGC, TSL.

66. Gov. Roberts to Texas Senate, 20 January 1881, Letterpress No. Book 4–2/35 (Gov. Roberts), 268, TSL.

67. H. L. Spain to Jones, 21 January 1881, AGC; Letterpress Book No. 4–2/35 (Gov. Roberts), 276, TSL.

68. Oath of Office (John B. Jones), 24 January 1881, TSL.

69. J. Evetts Haley, *Fort Concho and the Texas Frontier* (San Angelo, Tex: San Angelo Standard-Times, 1952), 276–280.
70. *Fort Concho Times*, 5 February 1881, as quoted in *San Antonio Daily Express*, 11 February 1881; *Galveston Daily News*, 2 and 3 February 1881; *Austin Daily Statesman*, 8 February 1881; Haley, *Jeff Milton*, 36–37.
71. Gov. Roberts to Gen. C. C. Augur, 7 February 1881, Letterpress Book (Gov. Roberts), 197–199, TSL.
72. Telegram, Marsh to Jones, 7 February 1881, FBC; Marsh to Jones, 11 February 1881, AGC, TSL; Haley, *Jeff Milton*, 38; Haley, *Fort Concho*, 282.
73. Telegram, Jones to Marsh, 7 February 1881, Letterpress Book, 200; telegram, Jones to Marsh, 18 February 1881, Letterpress Book, 218, AGC, TSL.
74. *Galveston Daily News*, 17 February 1881; *Austin Daily Statesman*, 16 February 1881; *Dallas Daily Herald*, 26 February 1881.
75. *Austin Daily Statesman*, 18 February 1881.

Chapter 18: Pangs of Sorrow

1. Dr. R. H. L. Bibb, "Discussion of the Causes Which Led to the Death of Adjutant-General Jones," *The Texas Medical and Surgical Record* 2, no. 3 (March 1882), 82, 90; *Austin Daily Statesman*, 12 March 1881.
2. Bibb, "Discussion of the Causes," 83.
3. Baylor to Coldwell, 11 March 1881, AGC, TSL.
4. Arrington to Jones, 15 March 1881; Nevill to Coldwell, 22 March 1881, AGC, TSL.
5. *Galveston Daily News*, 23 and 26 March 1881; *San Antonio Daily Express*, 26 March 1881.
6. Orsay to Oglesby, 29 March 1881, Letterpress Book, 273, AGC, TSL; *General Laws of the State of Texas*, vol. 9 *(17th Legislature)* (Austin, Texas: Gammel Book, 1898), 89.
7. General Order No. 10 (Gov. Roberts), 30 March 1881, Letterpress Book, 676, AGC, TSL.
8. *Austin Daily Statesman*, 6 April 1881.
9. Telegram, Nevill to Gov. Roberts, 6 April 1881, FBC; Nevill to Coldwell, 13 April 1881, AGC, TSL.
10. Nevill to Gov. Roberts, 10 April 1881, AGC, TSL.
11. *Austin Daily Statesman*, 18 and 20 March 1881.
12. Bibb, "Discussion of the Causes," 83.
13. *Galveston Daily News*, 25 and 27 March 1881.
14. *San Antonio Daily Express*, 6 April 1881.
15. Inci A. Bowman, "James Wharton McLaughlin," *The New Handbook of Texas*, vol. 4, 425.

16. Bibb, "Discussion of the Causes," 83.

17. *Galveston Daily News*, 6 April 1881.

18. Ibid., 7 April 1881.

19. Frank W. Johnson and Eugene C. Barker, *A History of Texas and Texans*, vol. 5 (Chicago: American Historical Society, 1914), 2471–2474; *Galveston Daily News*, 9 April 1881.

20. *Austin Daily Statesman*, 12 and 14 April 1881.

21. Bibb, "Discussion of the Causes," 83.

22. Leon C. Metz, *Dallas Stoudenmire: El Paso Marshal* (Norman, Oklahoma: University of Oklahoma Press, 1969), 3; see also Fred Egloff, *El Paso Lawman: G. W. Campbell* (College Station, Texas: Creative Publishing, 1982), 53–92.

23. Ibid., 5; Baylor to Jones, 8 May 1881, AGC, TSL.

24. Metz, *Dallas Stoudenmire*, 6–8; Gillett, *Six Years With the Texas Rangers*, 324; James B. Gillett, "The Killing of Dallas Stoudenmire," *Frontier Times* 1, no. 10 (July 1924), 21; Owen White, *Out of the Desert: The Historical Romance of El Paso* (El Paso, Texas: McMath, 1923), 139–142.

25. Metz, *Dallas Stoudenmire*, 38; Egloff, *El Paso Lawman*, 58.

26. Metz, *Dallas Stoudenmire*, 42–43.

27. Ibid.; *San Antonio Daily Express*, 30 April 1881.

28. *San Antonio Daily Express*, 30 April 1881.

29. Baylor to Coldwell, 23 April 1881, AGC, TSL.

30. Gillett, *Six Years With the Texas Rangers*, 296–303; Wilkins, *The Law Comes to Texas*, 230–235.

31. Gillett, *Six Years With the Texas Rangers*, 304–307; Leon C. Metz, "An Incident at Christmas," *Quarterly of the National Association and Center for Outlaw and Lawman History* 14, no. 1 (1990), 1 *et seq.*

32. Telegram, Gov. Roberts to Baylor, 10 May 1881, Letterpress Book No. 4-2/35 (Gov. Roberts), 407; *Galveston Daily News*, 13 May 1881; Gillett, *Six Years With the Texas Rangers*, 293–308. See also Keith Milton, "Whistlin' Extradition," *True West* 39, no. 5 (May 1992).

33. Roberts to Jones, 27 May 1881, AGC, TSL; *Dallas Daily Herald*, 18 May 1881; *Galveston Daily News*, 27 May 1881; Haley, *Jeff Milton*, 49–50.

34. Haley, *Jeff Milton*, 51–52.

35. Orsay to Hoffar, 18 May 1881, Letterpress Book, 346, AGC, TSL.

36. "Jones" to Roberts, 21 May 1881, Letterpress Book, 351, AGC, TSL.

37. Haley, *Jeff Milton*, 52.

38. Roberts to Jones, 27 May 1881; telegram, "Jones" to Roberts, 30 May 1881, Letterpress Book, 358; telegram, "Jones" to Roberts, 31 May 1881, Letterpress Book, 360, AGC, TSL; Roberts, *Rangers and Sovereignty*, 63–65.

39. Roberts to Jones, 1 June 1881, AGC, TSL.

40. "Jones" to John C. Brown, 13 June 1881, Letterpress Book, 378; "Jones" to Marsh, 13 June 1881, Letterpress Book, 379, AGC, TSL; *Dallas Daily Herald*, 9 June 1881; *Austin Daily Statesman*, 9 June 1881; *Galveston Daily News*, 9 June 1881.

41. Orsay to Stoudenmire, 1 June 1881, Letterpress Book, 359, AGC, TSL.

42. Egloff, *El Paso Lawman*, 108.

43. Kemp, *Cow Dust*, 30–31.

44. *Dallas Daily Herald*, 31 May 1882; Gillett, *Six Years With the Texas Rangers*, 329.

45. *Galveston Daily News*, 3 June 1881; *Austin Daily Statesman*, 8 June 1881.

46. General Order No. 11 (Jones), 8 June 1881, Letterpress Book, 68, AGC, TSL.

47. Proclamation, 11 June 1881, Executive Record Book (Gov. Roberts), 17; Gov. Roberts to James Blaine, 13 June 1881, Letterpress Book No. 4–2/35 (Gov. Roberts), 474–478.

48. Jones to Coldwell, 10 June 1881, Records of Gov. Roberts, TSL.

49. Coldwell to Jones, 22 June 1881, AGC, TSL.

50. Bibb, "Discussion of the Causes," 83–84.

51. *Galveston Daily News*, 16 June 1881; Janet Mace Valenza, "Wootan Wells, Texas," *The New Handbook of Texas*, vol. 6, 1073.

52. Bibb, "Discussion of the Causes," 84.

53. Ibid.; *San Antonio Daily Express*, 30 June 1881.

54. Bibb, "Discussion of the Causes," 84–85.

55. Johnson and Barker, *A History of Texas and Texans*, vol. 5, 2282–2284.

56. *San Antonio Daily Express*, 6 July 1881.

57. Bibb, "Discussion of the Causes," 85–86.

58. Ibid., 86.

59. Ibid.; *San Antonio Daily Express*, 9 July 1881.

60. Nevill to Jones, 10 July 1881, Webb Collection.

61. Bibb, "Discussion of the Causes," 87; *San Antonio Daily Express*, 15 July 1881.

62. Bibb, "Discussion of the Causes," 87–88.

63. L. E. Daniell, *Texas: The Country and Its Men* (n.p., n.d.), 197–201; Johnson and Barker, *A History of Texas and Texans*, vol. 4, 1602–1603.

64. Bibb, "Discussion of the Causes," 98–99.

65. Ibid., 100.

66. Ibid., 88–89.

67. *Galveston Daily News*, 20 July 1881.

68. Bonner, *Major John B. Jones*, 135.

69. Fanny J. Halbert to Sarah Hightower Jones, 3 March 1883, as quoted in Bolick, *John Robertson*.

70. Orsay to Battalion commanders, 19 July 1881, Letterpress Book, 403, AGC, TSL.

71. *Austin Daily Statesman*, 20 July 1881.

368 TEXAS RANGER JOHN B. JONES AND THE FRONTIER BATTALION, 1874–1881

72. *Galveston Daily News*, 20 July 1881.
73. *Austin Daily Statesman*, 21 July 1881.
74. *Dallas Daily Herald*, 21 July 1881.
75. *San Antonio Daily Express*, 31 July 1881.
76. Hoffar to Coldwell, 29 July 1881, AGC, TSL.

Chapter 19: The Best Officers and Men

1. *Galveston Daily News*, 22 July 1881; Nicholas P. Hardeman, "William Polk Harde-man," *The New Handbook of Texas*, vol. 3, 450–451.
2. Telegram, Gov. Roberts to King, 21 July 1881, Letterpress Book No. 4–2/35 (Gov. Roberts), 567, TSL.
3. *Austin Daily Statesman*, 26 July 1881.
4. Wilburn Hill King, *With the 18th Texas Infantry: The Autobiography Of Wilburn Hill King*, ed. L. David Norris (Hillsboro, Texas: Hill College Press, 1996), 93.
5. King to Gov. Roberts, 22 July 1881, Records of Gov. Roberts, TSL; *Galveston Daily News*, 23 July 1881.
6. *Austin Daily Statesman*, 26 July 1881; *Galveston Daily News*, 24 July 1881; *Dallas Daily Herald*, 24 July 1881.
7. *San Antonio Daily Express*, 25 July 1881. See also *Texas Siftings*, 30 July 1881, for a similar sentiment.
8. *San Antonio Daily Express*, 11 August 1881.
9. Webb, *Texas Rangers*, 425.
10. *Galveston Daily News*, 11 August 1881.
11. *San Antonio Daily Express*, 2 and 3 August 1881; *Austin Daily Statesman*, 3 August 1881.
12. Receipt signed by King, 3 August 1881, AGC, TSL.
13. General Order No. 2 (King), 4 August 1881, FBC, TSL. King made an exception for Jim Gillett and George Lloyd, who were allowed to remain in the service while married. King to Baylor, 5 August 1881, Letterpress Book, 417, AGC, TSL.
14. King to Marsh, 4 August 1881, Letterpress Book, 415, AGC, TSL; William Hill King, *Report of the Adjutant General of the State of Texas* (Galveston, Texas: A. H. Belo, Printers, 1881), 23.
15. *Dallas Daily Herald*, 1 September 1881; *San Antonio Daily Express*, 7 September 1881.
16. *San Antonio Daily Express*, 6 August 1881.
17. General Order No. 3 (King), 25 August 1881, FBC, TSL.
18. Clifford R. Caldwell and Ron DeLord, *Texas Lawmen, 1835–1899: The Good and the Bad* (Charleston, South Carolina: The History Press, 2011), 338.
19. *San Antonio Daily Express*, 28 September 1881.

20. Ibid., 22 September 1881; *Dallas Daily Herald*, 17 September 1881.

21. *Austin Daily Statesman*, 28 September 1881.

22. King, *Report of the Adjutant General*, 23–27.

23. Deed Records, Navarro County, Texas, vol. 40, 327–2.

24. Thomas D. Wooten, "The Case of the Late Adjutant-General John B. Jones," *The Texas Medical and Surgical Record* 2, no. 6 (June 1882), 213–214.

25. Bibb, "Discussion of the Causes," 81–125.

26. Wooten, "John B. Jones," 209.

27. Ibid., 237.

28. W. A. Morris, J. W. McLaughlin, and R. M. Swearingen, *A Review of Dr. Wooten's Review of the Causes That Led to the Death of the Late Adjt. Gen. John B. Jones* (Austin, Texas: Eugene Von Boeckmann, Book and Job Printer, 1882), 4–44.

29. Bonner, *John B. Jones*, 136.

30. Marriage Records, Travis County, Texas, vol. 6, 8; Irby C. Nichols, "Alexander Watkins Terrell," *The New Handbook of Texas*, vol. 6, 258–259; Richard Denny Parker, *Robertson County, Texas*, 201–202.

31. *Galveston Daily News*, 26 November 1908.

32. *Galveston Daily News*, 5 April 1884.

33. Estate of Henry Jones, Deceased, Cause No. 893, vol. 11, pp. 40–42, 109–110, Probate Minutes, Navarro County, Texas.

34. Wilkins, *The Law Comes to Texas*, 295.

35. Ibid., 238.

36. Ibid., 242.

37. Caldwell and DeLord, *Texas Lawmen*, 340–341.

38. Ibid., 342; *Dallas Daily Herald*, 12 February 1885.

39. Caldwell and DeLord, *Texas Lawmen*, 343–344; Wilkins, *The Law Comes to Texas*, 254–256.

40. Caldwell and DeLord, *Texas Lawmen*, 343–344; *Dallas Daily Herald*, 20 And 23 August 1885.

41. Caldwell and DeLord, *Texas Lawmen*, 346.

42. Ibid., 347–348; Chuck Parsons, *Captain John R. Hughes: Lone Star Ranger* (Denton, Texas: University of North Texas Press, 2011), 59; Wilkins, *The Law Comes to Texas*, 291–292.

43. Wilkins, *The Law Comes to Texas*, 296.

44. Harold J. Weiss, Jr., *Yours to Command: The Life and Legend of Texas Ranger Captain Bill McDonald* (Denton, Texas: University of North Texas Press, 2009), 49–50.

45. Wilkins, *The Law Comes to Texas*, 306; Caldwell and DeLord, *Texas Lawmen*, 349.

46. Caldwell and DeLord, *Texas Lawmen*, 351–352; Parsons, *Captain John R. Hughes*, 81–85.

47. Caldwell and DeLord, *Texas Lawmen*, 352–353; Wilkins, *The Law Comes to Texas*, 314.

48. Parsons, *Captain John R. Hughes*, 102–104; Metz, *John Selman*, 148–150, 174–175, 198–200; Robert K. DeArment, *George Scarborough: The Life and Death of a Lawman on the Closing Frontier* (Norman, Oklahoma: University of Oklahoma Press, 1992), 145–147.

49. Parsons, *Captain John R. Hughes*, 132–133; Robinson, *The Men Who Wear the Star*, 253–263.

50. Joan Jenkins Perez, "Alfred Prior Wozencraft," *The New Handbook of Texas*, vol. 6, 1086–1087.

51. Caldwell and DeLord, *Texas Lawmen*, 354–355; Wilkins, *The Law Comes to Texas*, 334.

52. Claudia Hazlewood, "Thomas Scurry," *The New Handbook of Texas*, vol. 5, 945–946.

53. Wilkins, *The Law Comes to Texas*, 345–346.

54. Robinson, *The Men Who Wear the Star*, 244.

55. Ibid., 347–348; Utley, *Lone Star Justice*, 272–273; Parsons, *Captain John R. Hughes*, 172–173.

56. Wilkins, *The Law Comes to Texas*, 227.

57. T. R. Fehrenbach, *Lone Star: A History of Texas and the Texans* (New York: American Legacy Press, 1983), 588. See also Allen G. Hatley, "Keeping Score: A New Look at the Frontier Battalion," *Revenge! And Other True Tales of the Old West*, ed. Sharon A. Cunningham and Mark Boardman ([Lafayette, Indiana]: Scarlet Mask, 2004), 97–111, for a critique giving the Frontier Battalion its best marks for enforcing the law against desperadoes, but criticizing Jones and other incidents involving the Frontier Battalion.

BIBLIOGRAPHY

BOOKS

Alexander, Bob. *Dangerous Dan Tucker: New Mexico's Deadly Lawman*. Silver City, New Mexico: High-Lonesome Books, 2001.

_____. *Sheriff Harvey Whitehill: Silver City Stalwart*. Silver City, New Mexico: High-Lonesome Books, 2005.

_____. *Winchester Warriors: Texas Rangers of Company D, 1874–1901*. Denton, Texas: University of North Texas Press, 2009.

_____. *Rawhide Ranger, Ira Aten: Enforcing Law on the Texas Frontier*. Denton, Texas: University of North Texas Press, 2011.

Baker, J. W. *A History of Robertson County, Texas*. Waco, Texas: Texian Press, 1970.

Barler, Miles. *Early Days in Llano*, n.p., n.d.

Barr, Alwyn. *Polignac's Texas Brigade*. College Station, Texas: Texas A&M University Press, 1998.

Barr, Michael. *A Rumble in the Cedar Brakes: Central Texas in the 1870s*. Austin, Texas: Morgan Printing, 2010.

Bartholomew, Ed. *Jesse Evans: A Texas Hide-Burner*. Houston: Frontier Press of Texas, 1955.

Baylor, George Wythe. *Into the Far, Wild Country*. Edited by Jerry D. Thompson. El Paso, Texas: Texas Western Press, 1996.

Bierschwale, Margaret. *A History of Mason County, Texas, Through 1964*. Edited by Julius E. DeVos. Mason, Texas: Mason County Historical Commission, 1998.

Biggers, Don. *Shackelford County Sketches*. Albany, Texas: Clear Fork Press, 1974.

Biographical Encyclopedia of Texas. New York: Southern Publishing, 1880.

Biographical Souvenir of the State of Texas. Chicago: F. A. Battey, 1889.

Bolick, Julian Stevenson. *A Fairfield Sketchbook*. Clinton, South Carolina: Jacobs Brothers, 1963.

Bolick, Sara Mason. *John Robertson, 1710–1811, of Fairfield County, South Carolina, and His Descendants*. Blair, South Carolina: Sara Mason Bolick, n.d.

Bowden, Jesse Earle and William S. Cummins. *Texas Desperado in Florida*. Pensacola, Florida: Pensacola Historical Society, 2002.

Brice, Donaly E. *The Great Comanche Raid*. Austin, Texas: Eakin Press, 1987.

Brief History of the Mount Zion Society, A. Winnsboro, South Carolina: Winnsboro News and Herald, 1949.

Brown, Richard Maxwell. *Strain of Violence: Historical Studies of American Violence and Vigilantism*. New York: Oxford University Press, 1975.

Bruce, Leona. *Banister Was There*. Fort Worth, Texas: Branch-Smith, 1968.

Bryan, Jimmy L. Jr. *More Zeal Than Discretion: The Westward Adventures of Walter P. Layne*. College Station, Texas: Texas A&M University Press, 2008.

Caldwell, Clifford R. and Ron DeLord. *Texas Lawmen, 1835–1899: The Good and the Bad*. Charleston, South Carolina: History Press, 2011.

Cashion, Ty. *A Texas Frontier: The Clear Fork Country and Fort Griffin, 1849–1887*. Norman, Oklahoma: University of Oklahoma Press, 1996.

Chamberlain, Kathleen P. *Victorio: Apache Warrior and Chief*. Norman, Oklahoma: University of Oklahoma Press, 2007.

Coke, Richard. *Message From the Governor of Texas to the Fifteenth Legislature*. Houston: A. C. Gray, State Printer, 1876.

Cool, Paul. *Salt Warriors: Insurgency on the Rio Grande*. College Station, Texas: Texas A&M University Press, 2008.

Cox, Mike. *Texas Ranger Tales: Stories That Need Telling*. Plano, Texas: Republic of Texas Press, 1997.

_____. *The Texas Rangers: Wearing the Cinco Peso, 1821–1900*. New York: Tom Doherty Associates, 2008.

Crouch, Barry A. *The Freedman's Bureau and Black Texans*. Austin, Texas: University of Texas Press, 1992.

_____. A. and Donaly E. Brice. *The Governor's Hounds: The State Police, 1870–1873*. Austin, Texas: University of Texas Press, 2011.

Daniell, L. E. *Personnel of the Texas State Government*. Austin, Texas: Smith, Hines & Jones, State Printers, 1889.

Daniell, L. E. *Texas: The Country and Its Men*. N.p., n.d.

Day, James M. and Dorman Winfrey. *Texas Indian Papers, 1860–1916*. Austin, Texas: Texas State Library, 1961.

DeArment, Robert K. *Bravo of the Brazos: John Larn of Fort Griffin, Texas*. Norman, Oklahoma: University of Oklahoma Press, 2003.

_____. *Deadly Dozen: Forgotten Gunfighters of the Old West, Vol. 2*. Norman, Oklahoma: University of Oklahoma Press, 2007.

_____. *George Scarborough: The Life and Death of a Lawman on the Closing Frontier*. Norman, Oklahoma: University of Oklahoma Press, 1992.

Devereaux, Jan. *Pistols, Petticoats & Poker, The Real Lottie Deno: No Lies or Alibis*. Silver City, New Mexico: High-Lonesome Books, 2008.

Douglas, C. L. *Famous Texas Feuds*. Dallas: Turner, 1936.

DuCoin, Candace. *Lawmen on the Texas Frontier: Rangers and Sheriffs*. Round Rock, Texas: Riata Books, 2007.

Dunn, J. B. (Red). *Perilous Trails of Texas*. Dallas: Southwest Press, 1932.

Early Laws of Texas. St. Louis: Gilbert Book, 1891.

Egloff, Fred. *El Paso Lawman: G. W. Campbell.* College Station, Texas: Creative Publishing, 1982.

Elkins, Captain John M. *My Life on the Texas Frontier.* Edited by Norman W. Brown. N.p.: Norman Wayne Brown and Don Merle Jay, 2010.

Ernst, Robert. *Deadly Affrays: The Violent Deaths of the U.S. Marshals.* With the assistance of George R. Stumpf. [Avon, Indiana]: Scarlet Mask Enterprises, 2006.

Fehrenbach, T. R. *Lone Star: A History of Texas and the Texans.* New York: American Legacy Press, 1983.

Fisher, O. C. *It Occurred in Kimble.* Houston: Anson Jones Press, 1937.

Gay, Beatrice Grady. *Into the Setting Sun: A History of Coleman County.* Santa Anna, Texas: n.p., 1936.

General Laws of the State of Texas. Austin, Texas: Gammel Book, 1898.

Gillett, James B. *Six Years With the Texas Rangers.* Austin, Texas: Von Boeckmann-Jones, 1921.

Governors' Messages, Coke to Ross. Austin, Texas: Texas State Library, 1916.

Griggs, William Clark. *The Elusive Eden: Frank McMullen's Confederate Colony in Brazil.* Austin, Texas: University of Texas Press, 1987.

Haley, J. Evetts. *Jeff Milton: A Good Man With a Gun.* Norman, Oklahoma: University of Oklahoma Press, 1948.

_____. *Fort Concho and the Texas Frontier.* San Angelo, Texas: San Angelo Standard-Times, 1952.

Haley, James L. *The Buffalo War.* Austin, Texas: State House Press, 1998.

_____. *Sam Houston.* Norman, Oklahoma: University of Oklahoma Press, 2002.

Hamilton, Allen Lee. *Sentinel of the Southern Plains: Fort Richardson and the Northwest Texas Frontier, 1866–1878.* Fort Worth, Texas: Texas Christian University Press, 1988.

Hardin, John Wesley. *The Life of John Wesley Hardin.* Seguin, Texas: Smith & Moore, 1896.

Hatley, Allen G. *Bringing the Law to Texas: Crime and Violence in Nineteenth Century Texas.* LaGrange, Texas: Centex Press, 2002.

Hill, Lawrence F. *Diplomatic Relations Between the United States and Brazil.* Durham, North Carolina: Duke University Press, 1932.

Horton, Thomas F. *History of Jack County.* Jacksboro, Texas: Gazette Print, 1932.

Hough, Emerson. *The Story of the Outlaw: A Study of the Western Desperado.* New York: Outing Publishing, 1907.

Johnson, David. *The Mason County "Hoo Doo" War, 1874–1902.* Denton, Texas: University of North Texas Press, 2006.

_____. *John Ringo, King of the Cowboys: His Life and Times From the Hoo Doo War to Tombstone.* 2nd ed. Denton, Texas: University of North Texas Press, 2007.

_____, ed. Mason County Historical Society. *The Life of Thomas W. Gamel.* Ozark Missouri, Dogwood Printing, 1994.

Johnson, Frank W. and Eugene C. Barker. *A History of Texas and Texans.* Chicago: American Historical Society, 1914.

Johnson, Sid S. *Texans Who Wore the Gray*. Austin, Texas: Texas State Library, 1907.

Jones, John B. *Report of Maj. J. B. Jones, Commanding the Frontier Battalion, Texas State Troops, March 1876*. Houston: A. C. Gray, State Printer, 1876.

_____. *Report of the Adjutant General of the State of Texas, 1880*. Galveston, Texas: News Book and Job Office, 1881.

Kemp, Ben W. with J. C. Dykes. *Cow Dust and Saddle Leather*. Norman, Oklahoma: University of Oklahoma Press, 1968.

Kesselus, Kenneth, ed. *Memoir of Capt'n C. R. Perry of Johnson City, Texas: A Texas Veteran*. Austin, Texas: Jenkins Publishing, 1990.

Kinard, Jeff. *Lafayette of the South*. College Station, Texas: Texas A&M University Press, 2001.

King, Wilburn Hill. *Report of the Adjutant General of the State of Texas*. Galveston, Texas: A. H. Belo, Printers, 1881.

_____. *With the 18th Texas Infantry: The Autobiography of Wilburn Hill King*. Edited by L. David Norris. Hillsboro, Texas: Hill College Press, 1996.

Laws of Texas, 1822–1897. Austin, Texas: Gammel Book, 1898.

Legislative Manual for the State of Texas, A. Austin, Texas: E. W. Swindells, 1879.

Lehmann, Herman. *Nine Years Among the Indians, 1870–1879*. Austin, Texas: Von Boeckmann-Jones, 1927.

Love, Annie Carpenter. *History of Navarro County*. Dallas: Southwest Press, 1933.

Maltby, W. J. *Captain Jeff or Frontier Life in Texas with the Texas Rangers*. Colorado, Texas: Whipkey Printing, 1906.

Marohn, Richard C. *The Last Gunfighter: John Wesley Hardin*. College Station, Texas: Creative Publishing, 1995.

Matagorda Historical Commission. *Historic Matagorda County*. Houston: D. Armstrong, 1986.

McCright, Grady E. and James H. Powell. *Jesse Evans: Lincoln County Badman*. College Station, Texas: Creative Publishing, 1983.

McIntire, Jim. *Early Days in Texas*. Edited by Robert K. DeArment. Norman, Oklahoma: University of Oklahoma Press, 1992.

McMaster, Fitz Hugh. *History of Fairfield County, South Carolina*. Columbia, South Carolina: State Commercial Printing, 1946.

Members of the Texas Legislature, 1846–1962. Austin, Texas: Texas State Legislature, 1962.

Metz, Leon. *John Selman: Texas Gunfighter*. New York: Hastings House, 1966.

_____. *Dallas Stoudenmire: El Paso Marshal*. Norman, Oklahoma: University of Oklahoma Press, 1969.

_____. *John Wesley Hardin: Dark Angel of Texas*. El Paso, Texas: Mangan Books, 1996.

Miller, Rick. *Bounty Hunter*. College Station, Texas: Creative Publishing, 1988.

_____. *Sam Bass & Gang*. Austin, Texas: State House Press, 1999.

_____. *Bloody Bill Longley: The Mythology of a Gunfighter*. 2nd rev. ed. Denton, Texas: University of North Texas Press, 2011.

Moneyhan, Carl H. *Texas After the Civil War: The Struggle of Reconstruction.* College Station, Texas: Texas A&M University Press, 2004.

Morris, W. A., J. W. McLaughlin, and R. M. Swearingen. *A Review of Dr. Wooten's Review of the Causes That Led to the Death of the Late Adjt. Gen. John B. Jones.* Austin, Texas: Eugene Von Boeckmann, Book and Job Printer, 1882.

Nolan, Frederick. *Bad Blood: The Life and Times of the Horrell Brothers.* Stillwater, Oklahoma: Barbed Wire Press, 1994.

Nunn, W. C. *Escape From Reconstruction.* Fort Worth, Texas: Texas Christian University Press, 1956.

Nye, W. S. *Carbine & Lance: The Story of Old Fort Sill.* Norman, Oklahoma: University of Oklahoma Press, 1942.

O'Neal, Bill. *The Bloody Legacy of Pink Higgins.* Austin, Texas: Eakin Press, 1999.

Paddock, Capt. B. B. *A History of Central and Western Texas.* Chicago: Lewis Publishing, 1911.

Parker, Richard Denny. *Historical Recollections of Robertson County, Texas.* Salado, Texas: Anson Jones Press, 1955.

Parsons, Chuck. *The Capture of John Wesley Hardin.* College Station, Texas: Creative Publishing, 1978.

_____. *Captain John R. Hughes: Lone Star Ranger.* Denton, Texas: University of North Texas Press, 2011.

_____. *James Madison Brown: Texas Sheriff, Texas Turfman.* Wolfe City, Texas: Henington Publishing, 1993.

_____. *John B. Armstrong: Texas Ranger and Pioneer Ranchmen.* College Station, Texas: Texas A&M University Press, 2007.

_____. *The Sutton-Taylor Feud: The Deadliest Blood Feud in Texas.* Denton, Texas: University of North Texas Press, 2009.

_____ and Donaly E. Brice. *Texas Ranger N. O. Reynolds, The Intrepid.* Honolulu, Hawaii: Talei Publishers, 2005.

_____ and Gary P. Fitterer. *Captain C. B. McKinney: The Law in South Texas.* Wolfe City, Texas: Henington Publishing, 1993.

_____ and Marianna E. Hall-Little. *Captain L. H. McNelly, Texas Ranger: The Life and Times of a Fighting Man.* Austin, Texas: State House Press, 2001.

Polk, Stella Gipson. *Mason and Mason County: A History.* Austin, Texas: Pemberton Press, 1966.

Prather, H. Bryant. *Come Listen to My Tale.* Talequah, Oklahoma: Pan Press, 1964.

Proceedings in the Forty-Fourth Annual Communication of the M.W. Lodge of Texas. Houston: W. H. Coyle, 1879.

Putman, Wyvonne, *Navarro County History.* Quanah, Texas: Nortex Press, 1975.

Ramsdell, Charles William. *Reconstruction in Texas.* Austin, Texas: University of Texas Press, 1970.

Raymond, Dora Neill. *Captain Lee Hall of Texas.* Norman, Oklahoma: University of Oklahoma Press, 1940.

Roberts, Mrs. D. W. *A Woman's Reminiscences of Six Years in Camp With the Texas Rangers.* Austin, Texas: Von Boeckmann-Jones, 1928.

Roberts, Dan W. *Rangers and Sovereignty.* San Antonio: Wood Printing & Engraving, 1914.

Roberts, Oran M. *Confederate Military History of Texas.* Gulf Breeze, Florida: eBooks-OnDisk, 2003.

Robinson, Charles M. III. *The Frontier World of Fort Griffin.* Spokane, Washington: Arthur H. Clarke, 1992.

_____. *The Men Who Wear the Star.* New York: Random House, 2000.

Rose, Peter R. *Essays on the Mason County War (Hoo Doo War), 1874–1876.* Austin, Texas: Peter R. Rose, 2002.

Rye, Edgar. *The Quirt and the Spur: Vanishing Shadows of the Texas Frontier.* Lubbock, Texas: Texas Tech University Press, 2000.

Samuels, Nancy T. and Barbara R. Knox. *Old Northwest Texas, Vol. 1–B (Navarro County, Texas, 1846–1860).* Fort Worth, Texas: Fort Worth Genealogical Society, 1980.

Sifakis, Stewart. *Compendium of the Confederate Armies: Texas.* New York: Facts on File, 1995.

Sinise, Jerry. *George Washington Arrington: Civil War Spy, Texas Ranger, Sheriff and Rancher.* Burnet, Texas: Eakin Press, 1979.

Sonnichsen, C. L. *Pass of the North: Four Centuries on the Rio Grande.* El Paso, Texas: Texas Western Press, 1968.

_____. *The El Paso Salt War of 1877.* El Paso, Texas: Texas Western Press, 1973.

Sowell, A. J. *Early Settlers and Indian Fighters of Southwest Texas.* Austin, Texas: State House Press, 1986.

Speer, William S. and John Henry Brown. *Encyclopedia of the New West.* Marshall, Texas: United States Biographical Publishing, 1881.

Steele, William. *Supplemental Report of the Adjutant General of the State of Texas for the Year 1874.* Houston: A. C. Gray, State Printer, 1874.

_____. *Report of the Adjutant General of the State of Texas for the Year 1875.* Houston: A. C. Gray, State Printer, 1875.

_____. *Report of the Adjutant-General of the State of Texas for the Year Ending August 31st, 1876.* Galveston, Texas: Shaw & Blaylock, 1876.

_____. *Report of the Adjutant General of the State of Texas for the Fiscal Year Ending August 31, 1878.* Galveston, Texas: Galveston News, 1878.

Stephens, Robert W. *Texas Ranger Captain Dan Roberts: The Untold Story.* Dallas: Robert W. Stephens, 2009.

Thrall, Homer S. *A Pictorial History of Texas.* St. Louis: N. D. Thompson, 1879.

Tise, Sammy. *Texas County Sheriffs.* Albuquerque, New Mexico: Oakwood Printing, 1989.

Utley, Robert M. *Lone Star Justice: The First Century of the Texas Rangers.* New York: Oxford University Press, 2002.

Wallace, Ernest. *Texas in Turmoil: The Saga of Texas, 1849–1875.* Austin, Texas: Steck-Vaughn, 1965.

Webb, Walter Prescott. *The Texas Rangers: A Century of Frontier Defense.* Boston: Houghton Mifflin, 1935.

_____. *The Story of the Texas Rangers.* New York: Grossett & Dunlap, 1957.

Weiss, Harold Jr. *Yours to Command: The Life and Legend of Texas Ranger Captain Bill McDonald.* Denton, Texas: University of North Texas Press, 2009.

Wharton, Clarence R. *Texas Under Many Flags.* Chicago: American Historical Society, 1930.

White, Gifford, ed. *First Settlers of Matagorda County, Texas.* St. Louis: Ingmire Publications, 1986.

White, Owen. *Out of the Desert: The Historical Romance of El Paso.* El Paso, Texas: McMath, 1923.

Wilbarger, J. W. *Indian Depredations in Texas.* Austin, Texas: Eakin Press/State House Press, 1985.

Wilkins, Frederick. *The Law Comes to Texas: The Texas Rangers, 1870–1901.* Austin, Texas: State House Press, 1999.

Williams, David M. *The Vicious Murder of S. S. Brooks.* San Saba, Texas: Edwards Plateau Historical Association, 2002.

Winfrey, Dorman H. and James M. Day, eds. *The Indian Papers of Texas and the Southwest, 1825–1916.* Austin, Texas: State Historical Association, 1995.

Wooster, Ralph A. *Lone Star Regiments in Gray.* Austin, Texas: Eakin Press, 2002.

Wooten, Dudley G., ed. *A Comprehensive History of Texas, 1685 to 1897.* Dallas, Texas: William G. Scarff, 1898.

ARTICLES

Alexander, Bob. "Tucker X Texas = Trouble!" *Journal, Wild West History Association* 1, no. 3 (June 2008).

Baenziger, Ann Patton. "The Texas State Police During Reconstruction: A Reexamination," *Southwestern Historical Quarterly* 72, no. 4 (1969).

Barr, C. Alwyn. "The Making of a Secessionist: The Antebellum Career of Roger Q. Mills," *Southwestern Historical Quarterly* 79 (1975).

Bibb, R. H. L. "Discussion of the Causes Which Led to the Death of Adjutant-General Jones," *The Texas Medical and Surgical Record* 2, no. 3 (March 1882).

Bridges, C. A. "The Knights of the Golden Circle: A Filibustering Fantasy," *Southwestern Historical Quarterly* 44, no. 3 (January 1941).

Carnal, Ed. "Reminiscences of a Texas Ranger," *Frontier Times* 1, no. 3 (December 1923).

Cool, Paul. "The Many Lives and Suggested Death of Jim McDaniels." In *Revenge! And Other True Tales of the Old West*, edited by Sharon A. Cunningham and Mark Boardman. [Lafayette, Indiana]: Scarlet Mask, 2004.

Cross, Cora Melton. "Ira Long, Cowboy and Texas Ranger," *Frontier Times* 8, no. 1 (October 1930).

DeArment, Robert K. "'Hurricane Bill' Martin, Horse Thief," *True West* 38, no. 6 (June 1991).

Dixson, Walter Clay. "The Barekman-Anderson Prelude to Comanche," *Quarterly of the National Association and Center for Outlaw and Lawman History* 18, no. 2 (April–June 1994).

Dunn, Roy Sylvan. "The KGC in Texas, 1860–1861," *Southwestern Historical Quarterly* 70, no. 6 (April 1967).

Elkins, S. P. "Served as a Texas Ranger," *Frontier Times* 5, no. 11 (August 1928).

_____. "Captured an Indian," *Frontier Times* 6, no. 6 (March 1929).

Field, William T. Jr. "The Texas State Police, 1870–1873," *Texas Military History* 5, no. 3 (Fall 1965).

Gibbs, Mrs. N. V. "Jeff Maltby Family." In *I Remember Callahan: History of Callahan County, Texas*. Edited by Hicks A. Turner. Dallas: Taylor Publishing, 1986.

Gillespie, Thomas P. "Fight on the Concho Plains," *True West* 10, no. 5 (May–June 1963).

Gillett, James B. "The Killing of Dallas Stoudenmire," *Frontier Times* 1, no. 10 (July 1924).

Grandy, C. W. "More About W. B. Anglin," *Frontier Times* 6, no. 6 (March 1929).

Halsell, H. H. "Cowboys and Cattleland," *Old West* 8, no. 1 (Fall 1971).

Hatcher, Curley. "Got Fifty Dollars for an Indian's Scalp," *Frontier Times* 1, no. 10 (July 1924).

_____. "A Waterspout in Coleman County in 1874," *Frontier Times* 4, no. 9 (June 1927).

Hatley, Allen G. "Cap Arrington: Adventurer, Ranger and Sheriff," *Wild West* 14, no. 1 (June 2001).

_____. "The Role of the Frontier Battalion During the Mason County Troubles." In *The Hoo Doo War: Portraits of a Lawless Time*. Ozark, Missouri: Dogwood Printing, 2003.

_____. "Keeping Score: A New Look at the Frontier Battalion." In *Revenge! And Other True Tales of the Old West*. Edited by Sharon A. Cunningham and Mark Boardman. [Lafayette, Indiana]: Scarlet Mask, 2004.

Hicks, Jimmie. "Some Letters Concerning the Knights of the Golden Circle in Texas, 1860–1861," *Southwestern Historical Quarterly* 65 (July 1961).

Hoffer, John. "Captain Marsh and His Rangers," *Frontier Times* 6, no. 7 (April 1929).

Hudson, Linda S. "The Knights of the Golden Circle in Texas, 1858–1861: An Analysis of the First (Military) Degree Knights." In *The Seventh Star of the Confederacy*, edited by Kenneth W. Howell. Denton, Texas: University of North Texas Press, 2009.

Jameson, W. C. "Last Stand of the Mescalero Apaches in Texas," *True West* 38, no. 12 (December 1991).

King, Gen. W. H. "The Texas Ranger Service and History of the Rangers, With Observation on Their Value as a Police Protection," In *A Comprehensive History of Texas*, edited by Dudley G. Wooten. Dallas, Texas: William G. Scarff, 1898.

Kirby, Lt. Harry. "Stage Hold-Up at Pegleg in 1877," *Frontier Times* 4, no. 5 (February 1927)

"Loss [*sic*] Valley Fight," *Frontier Times* 7, no. 3 (December 1929).

Metz, Leon. "An Incident at Christmas," *Quarterly of the National Association and Center for Outlaw and Lawman History* 14, no. 1 (1990).

Milton, Keith. "Whistlin' Extradition," *True West* 39, no. 5 (May 1992).

Montes, Conrado. "Life History of Telesforo Montes and His Family." *Montes Family Website*. Internet (2011).

Neal, Mrs. Edgar T. "Runtiest Ranger is Hero of '74 Fight With Indians," *Frontier Times* 9, no. 2 (November 1931).

Northington, M. G. "I Saw Them Stack Their Guns," *Frontier Times* 36, no. 2 (Spring 1962).

Parsons, Chuck. "Reese Gobles—Predator," *Quarterly of the National Association and Center for Outlaw and Lawman History* 14, no. 2 (Summer 1990).

_____. "Captain Daniel Webster Roberts." In *Mason County Hoo Doo War Anthology.* Mason, Texas: Mason County Historical Commission, 2006.

Purdy, R. S. "Fight With Indians at Loving's Ranch," *Frontier Times* 2, no. 9 (June 1925).

_____. "The Fight at Loving's Ranch in 1874," *Frontier Times* 16, no. 3 (December 1938).

Reynolds, Franklin. "Who Was This Man?" *Frontier Times* 40, no. 4 (June–July 1966).

Rose, Peter R. "Setting the Stage for the Hoo Doo War: Land, People, and History of Settlement." In *The Hoo Doo War: Portraits of a Lawless Time.* Ozark, Missouri: Dogwood Printing, 2003.

Smallwood, James M. "The Impending Crisis: A Texas Perspective on the Causes of the Civil War." In *The Seventh Star of the Confederacy.* Edited by Kenneth W. Howell. Denton, Texas: University of North Texas Press, 2009.

"Texas Rangers Battle With Outlaws," *Frontier Times* 4, no. 11 (August 1927).

"Texas Rangers on the Border, *Frontier Times* 1, no. 7 (April 1924).

Turner, John M. "Indian Fight in Loving County in 1874," *Frontier Times* 30, no. 2 (April–June 1953).

Tyler, Ron, ed. *The New Handbook of Texas.* Austin, Texas: Texas State Historical Association, 1996:

Barr, Alwyn. "Roger Quarles Mills," vol. 4, 751.

Bowman, Inci A. "James Wharton McLaughlin," vol. 4, 425.

Custer, Judson S. "Rutersville College," vol. 5, 733.

Cutrer, Thomas W. "George Wythe Baylor," vol. 1, 422–423.

_____. "Cicero Rufus Perry," vol. 5, 157

_____. "Joseph William Robertson," vol. 5, 618.

Hardeman, Nicholas P. "William Polk Hardeman," vol. 3, 450–451.

Hazelwood, Claudia, "Archive War," vol. 1, 234.

Nichols, Irby C. "Alexander Watkins Terrell," vol. 6, 258–259.

Perez, Joan Jenkins. "Alfred Prior Wozencraft," vol. 6, 1086–1087.

Rodenberger, Lou. "William Jeff Maltby," vol. 4, 477.

Skaggs, Jimmy M. "Pegleg Crossing," vol. 5, 129.

Thompson, Jerry. "John Robert Baylor," vol. 1, 423–424.

Valenza, Janet Mace. "Wootan Wells, Texas," vol. 6, 1073.

"William Steele," vol. 6, 79.

Walker, Wayne T. "Major John B. Jones: Ranger Who Tamed West Texas," *Real West* 24, no. 176 (April 1981).

Weddle, Robert S. "Pegleg Station on the San Saba," *The Edwards Plateau Historian* 3 (1967).

Wooten, Thomas D. "The Case of the Late Adjutant-General John B. Jones," *The Texas Medical and Surgical Record* 2, no. 6 (June 1882).

PUBLIC RECORDS

National Archives:

Compiled Service Records of Confederate Soldiers (John B. Jones)

Navarro County, Texas:

CIVIL MINUTES:

Fanny J. Halbert v. John B. Jones, Cause No. 1689, Vol. W, 195

Henry Jones v. John Jones et al., Cause No. 334, Vol. B, 222

John B. Jones & Co. v. John Finch, Cause No. 1496, Vol. F, 308

John B. Jones & Co. v. S. J. T. Johnson, Sheriff, Cause No. 1326, Vol. F, 409

Y. W. H. McKissack v. John B. Jones & Co., Cause 1322, Vol. F, 135

DEED RECORDS:

Vol. A, 511–513

Vol. G, 413–1, 416

Vol. M, 162–166, 279, 434, 600

Vol. N, 375, 459

Vol. Q, 150

Vol. S, 206, 732

Vol. W, 451

Vol. Y, 185, 249

MARRIAGE RECORDS:

Vol. 1, 51

Vol. 2, 51

PROBATE RECORDS:

Estate of Henry Jones, Deceased, Cause No. 893, Vol. 11, 40–42, 109–110.
Estate of J. L. Halbert, Cause No. 192; Abstract Book Vol. 1, 200; Probate Record Vol. R, 673.

Texas State Library:
Adjutant General's Correspondence
Frontier Battalion Correspondence
Governors' Correspondence (Coke, Hubbard, Roberts)
Results of Operations of State Troops Since August 1, 1876, to December 31, 1881
Texas Ranger Service Records

Travis County, Texas:
MARRIAGE RECORDS:
Vol. 5, 155
Vol. 6, 8

United States Census:
Matagorda County, Texas (1850)
Navarro County, Texas (1860, 1870)
Rapides Parish, Louisiana (1880)
Travis County, Texas (1880)

Other:
United States Congress. "Texas Frontier Troubles," *Report of Committee on Foreign Affairs on the Relations of the United States With Mexico*. Washington D.C.: Government Printing Office, 1878.

United States Secretary of War. "El Paso Troubles in Texas," Executive Document No. 93, 45th United States Congress.

United States War Department. *The War of the Rebellion: A Compilation of the Official Record of the Union and Confederate Armies*. Washington D.C.: Government Printing Office, 1881.

THESES
Bonner, Helen Francis. *Major John B. Jones: The Defender of the Texas Frontier*. Master's Thesis, University of Texas, Austin, 1950.

Redman, Jack Duane. *General John B. Jones: Twenty Years of Service to Texas*. Master's Thesis, University of Texas at El Paso, 1983.

NEWSPAPERS

Austin (*Texas*) *Daily Statesman*
Austin (*Texas*) *Daily Democratic Statesman*
Austin (*Texas*) *Daily State Gazette*
Austin (*Texas*) *Globe-Democrat*
Austin (*Texas*) *Weekly State Gazette*
Brownsville (*Texas*) *Sentinel*
Comanche (*Texas*) *Chief*
Corsicana (*Texas*) *Observer*
Corsicana (*Texas*) *Semi-Weekly Light*
Dallas Daily Commercial
Dallas Daily Herald
Denison (*Texas*) *Daily News*
Ellsworth (*Kansas*) *Reporter*
Fort Concho (*Texas*) *Times*
Fort Griffin (*Texas*) *Echo*
Fort Worth (*Texas*) *Daily Democrat*
Fort Worth (*Texas*) *Daily Gazette*
Fredericksburg (*Texas*) *Sentinel*
Frontier Echo (Jacksboro, Texas)
Galveston (*Texas*) *Daily News*
Galveston (*Texas*) *Weekly News*
Gatesville (*Texas*) *Sun*
Houston Daily Telegraph

Houston Telegram
Houston Telegraph
Kerr County (*Texas*) *Frontiersman*
Lampasas (*Texas*) *Daily Times*
Lampasas (*Texas*) *Dispatch*
Luling (*Texas*) *Signal*
Leavenworth (*Kansas*) *Daily Times*
Mason (*Texas*) *News-Item*
Mesilla Valley (*New Mexico Territory*)
   Independent
Navarro Express (Corsicana, Texas)
San Antonio Daily Express
San Antonio Daily Herald
San Antonio Light
San Saba (*Texas*) *News*
Sherman (*Texas*) *Register*
St. Louis (*Missouri*) *Globe-Democrat*
Telegraph and Texas Register
Texas Centennial
Texas Land and Railway Journal
Texas Siftings
Waco (*Texas*) *Daily Examiner*
Waco (*Texas*) *Examiner and Patron*

ARCHIVES AND PRIVATE COLLECTIONS

Fairfield Archives and History, Winnsboro, South Carolina
Masonic Grand Lodge Library and Museum of Texas, Waco, Texas
Pioneer Village, Corsicana, Texas
Texas Ranger Hall of Fame, Waco, Texas
Walter Prescott Webb Collection, Center for American History, University of Texas, Austin
Young, Bill. "Henry Jones Family," txgenweb (Internet)

INDEX